Y0-CBQ-053

Discerning Characters

EARLY AMERICAN STUDIES

SERIES EDITORS: Daniel K. Richter, Kathleen M. Brown, Max Cavitch, and David Waldstreicher

Exploring neglected aspects of our colonial, revolutionary, and early national history and culture, Early American Studies reinterprets familiar themes and events in fresh ways. Interdisciplinary in character, and with a special emphasis on the period from about 1600 to 1850, the series is published in partnership with the McNeil Center for Early American Studies.

A complete list of books in the series is available from the publisher.

Discerning Characters

The Culture of Appearance in Early America

Christopher J. Lukasik

PENN

UNIVERSITY OF PENNSYLVANIA PRESS

PHILADELPHIA · OXFORD

Copyright © 2011 University of Pennsylvania Press

All rights reserved. Except for brief quotations used for
purposes of review or scholarly citation, none of this book
may be reproduced in any form by any means without
written permission from the publisher.

Published by
University of Pennsylvania Press
Philadelphia, Pennsylvania 19104-4112
www.upenn.edu/pennpress

Printed in the United States of America on acid-free paper
10 9 8 7 6 5 4 3 2 1

Library of Congress Cataloging-in-Publication Data
Lukasik, Christopher J.
    Discerning characters : the culture of appearance in
early America / Christopher J. Lukasik.
        p. cm. — (Early American studies)
    Includes bibliographical references and index.
    ISBN 978-0-8122-4287-4 (hardcover : alk. paper)
    1. Physiognomy—United States—History. 2. Social
perception—United States—History. 3. Literature and
society—United States—History. 4. United States—Social
life and customs—1775–1783. 5. United States—Social life
and customs—1783–1865. I. Title.
    BF859.L85 2011
    138.0973'09034—dc22
                                                2010022354

For my parents, and for Charlyne, Ainsley and Quincy

Contents

Introduction

O visage of man! Mirror more true, more expressive, than his gesture,
his speech, or even his accent, thou canst not extinguish the rapid
lightning emitted by the soul! She has an involuntary course; she even
shines in the eyes of the impostor.
　　—*Pennsylvania Herald and General Advertiser* (1787),
　　　　from Louis-Sébastien Mercier, *The Night Cap*

Who is not in fact to himself, a physiognomist by habit? Who does
not pass a mental verdict on the appearance of a stranger? We are all
such.
　　—*Analectic Magazine* (1818)

The Deity, in kindness to our race,
Hath set a stamp on every human face,
By which, together with the shape and air,
A shrewd observer may at once declare,
From characters of no ambiguous kind,
What are the leading lineaments of mind. (ll. 1–6)
　　—Thomas Green Fessenden, "Physiognomy" (1825)

IT IS DIFFICULT to imagine a more memorable and self-conscious description
of public visibility in early American culture than the one given by Benjamin
Franklin in his *Autobiography* (1771–88) when he enters Philadelphia for the
first time in 1723. It is, as one historian puts it, "one of the most familiar episodes in American history" (Wright 29). Seemingly oblivious to the image he
presents before the eyes of strangers, he struts down Market Street with his

pockets brimming with dirty laundry and his youthful body adorned with "three great Puffy Rolls," one under each arm and a third rapidly disappearing into his mouth.[1] The puffy rolls intensify the image of Franklin's poverty at this moment since their reference to his immediate hunger indicates a proximity to the urgent necessities of life that might have been satisfied with less vulgarity and visibility at some inn or private residence.[2] As this nineteenth-century illustration of the episode makes clear (Figure 1), Franklin's puffy rolls are imagined to offend the refined sensibilities of his future wife, Deborah Read, as much as they whet the appetite of a wandering stray dog. The point of the Puffy Roll spectacle, Franklin explains, is to enable the reader to mentally "compare such unlikely beginnings with the Figure I have since made" (*F* 27) so that the image of this ravenous runaway can be contrasted with the exemplary public gentleman that he would later become.

Even though at this narrative moment Franklin actually *is* an impoverished runaway, his description attributes his appearance as such to a variety of noncorporeal visual signifiers such as his "Working Dress," "dirty" hygiene, and, of course, those "three great Puffy Rolls" eaten on the street (*F* 27). Thus, the effect of Franklin's "most awkward ridiculous Appearance" is the result of impermanent causes whose signifiers he understands as socially defined, yet ultimately subject to his own volition, rational discipline, and, at times, healthy appetite. Like the misplaced letters of compositor's type, Franklin recognizes the errata of his public appearance, as he does elsewhere with the errata of his life, and he recomposes himself to communicate a message more consistent with both his intentions and social norms (Warner *Letters* 74). After establishing himself as a printer, for instance, Franklin returns home to display "a genteel new Suit from Head to foot" (*F* 33) and a new watch to his family, while those pockets that "were stuff'd out with Shirts and Stockings" (*F* 27) when he first entered Philadelphia are now "lin'd with near Five Pounds Sterling in Silver" (*F* 33).

Part of the great appeal of Franklin's *Autobiography* for his readers then and now is that he presents the relationship between the visibility of a person and the legibility of that person's public character in terms of performance. As such, that relationship is articulated as voluntary, revisable, and—as we can see from this early twentieth-century gathering of The Poor Richard's Club in Philadelphia (Figure 2)—seemingly universally available. By decorporealizing his person and explaining his success in the generalized terms of pure genteel performance, Franklin allows the acquisition of his social mobility to seem as available as the acquisition of his conduct. If one wants to obtain

FRANKLIN'S FIRST ENTRANCE INTO PHILADELPHIA.

Figure 1. "Franklin's First Entrance Into Philadelphia." From Benjamin Franklin, *Autobiography of Benjamin Franklin*, ed. John Bigelow. 4 vols., illustrated by Joseph M. P. and Emily Price (1868; Philadelphia: J. B. Lippincott and Co., 1887). Image courtesy of the Historical Society of Pennsylvania.

Figure 2. Photograph of The Poor Richard's Club. c. 1920. Image courtesy of The Library Company of Philadelphia.

"Credit and Character as a Tradesman," Franklin explains, then one should "not only . . . be in *Reality* Industrious & frugal, but . . . avoid all *Appearances* of the Contrary" (*F* 73). What makes Franklin appear industrious, he reasons, are the same things that make him appear ridiculous: his visible appearance on the street as communicated by his public performances and his attention or inattention to their appropriate social signifiers: clothes, manners, gestures, and conversational practice.

My point in stating this is only to emphasize that the social perception of character as described by Franklin bears little or no relationship to his particular corporeality. If there were many different Franklins in the *Autobiography*—the apprentice, the reader, the printer, the scientist, and the politician—none of them are described as having a permanent and exclusive relationship to the corporeal Franklin. It is not as though Franklin's *actual* body contains no social information—for it reveals his age, gender, and race among other things—but rather for Franklin those social identifications are not described as integral to the legibility of his character in public.[3] In fact, the seemingly unlimited social fluidity that Franklin's narrative promises—one in which he can appear genteel before his family and plain before his customers—depends on the corporeal body being unassigned to either of those distinctions. As the strange facelessness of this nineteenth-century image of a young Franklin at the press suggests (Figure 3), the particularity of Franklin's face is secondary to the industry of an obscure boy printing the pages that will later distinguish him. As Franklin repeatedly advises in the *Autobiography*, his social mobility was not a product of his particular body, but of his personal performances; he attributes the success of those personal performances to his familiarity with books.[4]

Through books, Franklin acquires not only knowledge, but access to the written performances of others in print (especially those of the *Spectator*). Books furnish Franklin with behavioral models of polite performance to imitate; the knowledge gained from such reading provides him with the cultural capital needed to gain access to the actual conversational spaces where those models of sociability can be practiced before members of an equal and, at times, superior social station (as he does when he is before governors and other benefactors in the *Autobiography*).[5] Access to such actual conversational spaces, in turn, advances Franklin's printing career, demonstrating how cultural capital can be converted into economic capital.[6] Yet, what is crucial about the body's relationship to such social mobility, Franklin insinuates, is recognizing that the revelation of one's character to the public is not simply a voluntary process of social performance, but one in which corporeal legibility is understood apart from the particular corporeality of the body—as a product of the construction and management of that body according to the normative codes and manners of the class to which you seek inclusion. Thus, for Franklin, the corporeal legibility of distinction in public does not appear prior to the agency of an individual, but subsequent to it.

More than thirty years after Franklin started composing his *Autobiography*, the publication of both volumes of the *Memoirs of Stephen Burroughs* (1811) reflects how the social perception of character was becoming increasingly an assessment made prior to the agency of an individual, while the corporeality of the body, particularly the face—as opposed to the performances of the self—was becoming increasingly more urgent in its determination. Similar to Franklin's attention to his own visibility as he loafs down Market Street,

FRANKLIN AS A PRINTER,
Showing the Press at which he worked in London.

Figure 3. "Franklin as a Printer." From Benjamin Franklin, *Autobiography of Benjamin Franklin*, ed. John Bigelow. 4 vols., illustrated by Joseph M. P. and Emily Price (1868; Philadelphia: J. B. Lippincott, 1887). Image courtesy of the Historical Society of Pennsylvania.

Stephen Burroughs relates a visual exchange he has with a country physician who knows him by name, but not by face. In the episode, the physician, who is unaware that he is speaking to the actual Stephen Burroughs, tells him of how Burroughs has "deceived many people" and how he would "continue to deceive them, notwithstanding all their precautions."[7] As if to distinguish himself from the undiscerning multitude, the doctor brags to Burroughs that he would be able to detect Burroughs should he ever encounter him face to face. For if "there ever was the appearance of deceit in his looks," the physician continues, "I should have known him to be a rogue, had I never heard of his character" since "I believe . . . that the countenance of a man is a strong index of his natural disposition" (*B* 224). To prove his point, the physician looks Burroughs in the eye before proclaiming, "I never saw a more striking contrast, than between the designing, deceitful countenance of Burroughs, and your open, frank, and candid countenance" (*B* 224).

The joke, of course, is that the physician's physiognomic reading fails to detect that the "open, frank, and candid countenance" of the man standing before him is actually the face of Burroughs himself. Even as this scene stages the failure of reading character from the face—and as an impostor Burroughs's motivations for doing so should be obvious—it also discloses how the social perception of his character was imagined as having more to do with his corporeality in general and his face in particular than his personal performance. Of course, this is not to say that Burroughs might not be performing in this scene, but rather that if he is, his performance is described in terms of conforming his face to the expectation of an "open, frank, and candid countenance" instead of changing his clothes, modifying his conduct, or suppressing his appetite. The irony in the physician's reading of Burroughs's face consists in the fact that he is not entirely wrong; for an "open, frank, and candid countenance" *is* the face of an impostor and in this sense, as Burroughs himself admits in the episode, the physician's ability to discern faces is quite accurate.[8] Yet, I am less interested in Burroughs's assessment of physiognomy's validity than I am in its mere presence in this scene and its absence in Franklin. If social mobility is understood in both the *Autobiography* and the *Memoirs* as the effect of the character generated by personal performance in public, then what distinguishes the two is that the functional, almost incidental relation of corporeality to social performance described in Franklin has been replaced in Burroughs by the conflation of social performance to corporeality. That Burroughs's social performance is reduced to his face reveals just how inseparable they were imagined to be.

As a narrative of failed social mobility, the *Memoirs* also dramatizes the limitations of the performative model of self so artfully championed in Franklin's classic narrative of successful (albeit gradual) social mobility, the *Autobiography*.[9] Despite his Franklinian rise from fugitive impostor and counterfeiter to small-town schoolteacher and library-founder, Burroughs never manages to escape the residual negative public character assigned to him by his criminal past. However successfully Burroughs may play the part of model citizen and dedicated educator, the community members of Long Island have him typecast as a villain and their criminal accusations of sexual assault eventually deplete his wealth, destroy his school and reputation, and drive him from the town. The social fluidity promised by Franklinian performances and enabled by the impersonality of the print public sphere harden into a character type that Burroughs can never quite shed in the *Memoirs*. Even worse, that formerly theatrical self, whose juvenile prankishness and personal performances were originally under Burroughs's sole direction, has evolved into the character of "Stephen Burroughs," a career criminal, whose persona is now being used by others to cheat, steal, and seduce. By the end of the narrative and undoubtedly in an effort to solicit sympathy from the reader, Burroughs attempts to represent himself as a victim to the very entity he had initially sought to exploit: that performative notion of selfhood.

Burroughs's face continued to attract the scrutiny of strangers well into the nineteenth century. In 1839, the famous New York phrenologist Lorenzo Fowler measured, examined, and cast a bust of Burroughs's head, the results of which were subsequently published in the *American Phrenological Journal and Miscellany* the following year (Figure 4). Unsurprisingly, Fowler's phrenological examination concluded that one of Burroughs's strongest traits was "an ability to assume any character he chooses, and conceal his own" (88). The *Journal* even enlisted Burroughs's *Memoirs* as proof of his "real character" (88), but not quite in the sense that he had intended. If in his *Memoirs* Burroughs depicted his face as fooling the country physiognomist in person, then phrenology had the last laugh as the *Journal* editors used Burroughs's skull not only as evidence of "the actual harmony between his life and cerebral organization" (88), but as proof of "the correctness of phrenology in the delineation of character" (88). In this way, the *American Phrenological Journal and Miscellany* offered the public a more quantitative, if equally arbitrary, system for discerning Burroughs's "real" character from his face as the country physician's physiognomic one had imagined. Despite the publication of his *Memoirs*, Burroughs's criminal reputation not only trumped his performances in life and in print, it eventually became identified with his face.

ARTICLE V.

PHRENOLOGICAL DEVELOPEMENTS AND CHARACTER OF STEPHEN BURROUGHS.

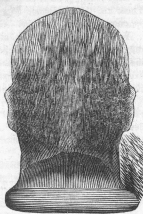

Measurements.

	Inches.
Circumference of the head around Philoprogenitiveness, Destructiveness, and Individuality, ...	23
From Occipital Spine to Individuality, ...	14 5
" Ear to Ear, over Firmness, ...	14 5
" Philoprogenitivenes to Individuality, . . .	6
" Destructiveness to Destructiveness, . . .	8
" Secretiveness to Secretiveness, . . .	6 3
" Cautiousness to Cautiousness, ...	6 2
" Ear to Individuality, ...	5 4
" " Philoprogenitiveness, ...	5 2
" " Firmness, ...	6
" " Benevolence, ...	5 9

Developements on a scale of 7.

Amativeness,	7	Combativeness,	3
Philoprogenitiveness,	6	Destructiveness,	6
Adhesiveness,	5	Alimentiveness,	6
Inhabitiveness,	6	Acquisitiveness,	6
Concentrativeness,	3	Secretiveness,	6

Figure 4. From "Phrenological Developments and Character of Stephen Burroughs." *American Phrenological Journal and Miscellany* 3:2 (1 Nov. 1840): 86–89. Image courtesy of the American Antiquarian Society.

In Franklin's rise and Burroughs's fall, we find both the great attraction of and the corporeal limitations to a performative understanding of selfhood in the social perception of character in early America. With its promise of individual agency and upward mobility, Franklin's *Autobiography* presents a viable model of the relationship between body and character in which the face becomes a malleable part of the more general performance of genteel distinction. The voluntary and instrumental nature of Franklin's social performances resonates with the liberal notion of a free and autonomous subject at the center of the nation's new democracy and its emergent market economy.[10] His image of the self-made man would be emulated by generations of aspiring nineteenth-century Americans and his narrative would be identified—for better or worse—with capitalism itself.[11] The case of Burroughs, however, demonstrates how that same performative notion of the self might be constrained by the face. As much as Burroughs's *Memoirs* celebrate his social performances, they also disclose how they can be inhibited by a sense of character that is not self-fashioned, but rather assigned to a person in advance.[12] In this sense, the Long Island community's character assassination of Burroughs as a criminal and Fowler's subsequent identification of that assessment with his skull confirms and converges with what the country physician imagined his physiognomic reading might do as a social practice (even if it proved erroneous): uncover a more permanent, essential, and involuntary sense of character from a person's face that no amount of individual performance could obscure.

•   •   •

As the examples of Franklin and Burroughs suggest, there is a face that you put on before the public, and there is a face that the public puts on you. The ways in which the latter were imagined to affect the former in early American culture is the subject of *Discerning Characters*. In general and more theoretical terms, this book is concerned with how a variety of cultural forms imagine the visibility of distinction and the dynamics of social space following the political and social transformations of the revolutionary era.[13] In particular and more historical terms, *Discerning Characters* explores the face's relationship to the social perception of character in early America and examines how transatlantic discourses for reading the face (such as civility and physiognomy) and cultural forms for representing the face (such as portraiture) shape the representation of distinction within postrevolutionary literature.[14] This book studies how late eighteenth-century physiognomy, particularly the widely distributed ideas of Johann Lavater, transformed the face's relationship to distinction in early American culture by privileging the permanent and unalterable features of the face in the social perception of character. Where Chesterfieldian civility stressed the strategic management of facial expression, including dissimulation, as an integral component in the signification of genteel distinction, Lavaterian physiognomy claimed to see through such polite performances by reading moral character from the involuntary features of the face. I argue that the ensuing struggle between the face as the pliable medium of civility on the one hand and the durable sign for moral character and social origin on the other was at the center of the postrevolutionary seduction narrative's imagination of social space and, as such, reflects a more general struggle over how distinction would be recognized in early America and, more broadly, how culture—specifically literature—would participate in that struggle (as an agent in the reproduction or transformation of the colonial social order of gentility).

Discerning Characters explores how the face mattered in the signification of subject positions and objective class conditions in the cultural and discursive practices of postrevolutionary America.[15] Recent work in the historiography of class in early America has called for a greater understanding of how relationships and other forms of capital (such as cultural or social capital) structure social space as much as material substances and economic capital do.[16] "The story of class in the Atlantic world," as Simon Newman puts it, "is as much about consciousness and perception as it is about material reality" (30). "Social standing may be indicated in terms lying outside, or beneath, the activities of a particular social grouping," Christopher Clark reasons, "or may be contingent upon criteria not generated by external material or political 'bases'" (558). The question of how symbolic systems might exist in a homologous or an analogous relation to the economic power they legitimate has challenged scholars to conceive of culture as more than the expression of the lived experience of material inequality. *Discerning Characters* hopes to contribute to our understanding of early American social relations by discussing the relationship between two of the more dominant discourses for the social perception of character (civility and physiognomy) and two of the more dominant cultural forms of the period (the novel and the portrait). The cultural representation of the face across a wide range of media was an important, though by no means exclusive, discursive site for the mediation of distinction in the wake of the revolution's political and social transformations. Although the physiognomic distinction of the face was not the only cultural logic from which the problem of imagining distinction following the revolution was articulated, it is, I argue, a salient one in the cultural history of early America.

Despite the fact that there are at least a half-dozen books examining physiognomy and European culture during the eighteenth and nineteenth centuries, there is little research devoted to its reception in the early republic and even less to its presence in early American literature.[17] Even as historians of American art continue to reveal the importance of physiognomy to postrevolutionary portraiture, there is no comprehensive discussion of its history in early American culture.[18] This omission is surprising considering physiognomy's enormous impact in its own time—one scholar claims that "Lavaterian physiognomy can be equated with modernity" itself (Percival 20)—and the critical attention paid to the history of modern forms of race in our own. *Discerning Characters* refines our understanding of physiognomy's role in the formation of more modern and essentialized notions of race in early America by showing how the face was used to register distinctions within races as much as it was used to discriminate between them. The physiognomic distinction of the face, as Part I demonstrates, contributed primarily to the social differentiation of white men in early America. With global political and economic forces circulating people beyond the local networks and technologies traditionally used to establish their identities and verify their status, the face served as an additional site from which individual character might be discerned and social capital established. Lavaterian physiognomy's emphasis on the involuntary and unalterable features of the face was particularly attractive, I argue, in the postrevolutionary American context in which status was often a matter of genteel performance and, as an emergent technology of surveillance, physiognomy was frequently discussed as a weapon against dissimulation. For those whose economic and social capital were most threatened by dissimulation— particularly the genteel elite—the logic, if not practice, of physiognomic distinction offered a means to establish moral character, embody social origin, and restrain the mobility enabled by the cultural capital of civility alone.[19] I say logic because when early American culture engaged physiognomy, its interest often had more to do with how the discourse transformed the social perception of character than with the validity of its specific practice. As the following pages will show, the accuracy of any particular reading of character from the face frequently mattered less than the more general relocation of discerning character from the voluntary performances of an individual to the involuntary features of the face.

This book examines how early American cultural forms, particularly the novel, renegotiated older forms of social status—what Stuart Blumin calls "the culture of rank" (64)—and participated in the transformation of the model of genteel social relations prevalent at the end of the eighteenth century to the emergent model of social relations based on racial difference that would be dominant at the end of the nineteenth century.[20] Part I offers a detailed historical account of the relationship between cultural and social forms in the years following the revolution when the primary determinants of the previous social order, particularly kinship, were being challenged by other forms of capital. As Christopher Clark explains, the American revolution and its aftermath left the new United States without a single social order and "the debate over 'aristocracy' in American society, which usually focused on questions of elite stability and access to inherited wealth, was shaped by this absence of a single-headed social order in which people could array themselves" (559).[21] "Self-making, self-shaping, and spontaneous claims to preeminence," Clark notes, "were responses to this fragmentation and multiplications of social orders" (559). The shift in the social perception of character from the voluntary performances of the self to the involuntary features of the face, I would add, was another kind of response to such social volatility. The physiognomic distinction of the face initially was thought to supply the means to confront the "the problem of establishing and recognizing social identity in a republic based theoretically on the boundless potential of each individual" (Haltunnen xvi) and, as Part I demonstrates, it was imagined as providing stability during a time of political uncertainty, cultural division, and social confusion.

Where recent scholarship has emphasized the centrality of performance and orality within early American culture and, in doing so, has remedied the prior critical dominance of a decorporealized model of communicative reason, *Discerning Characters* seeks to broaden our knowledge about the relationship between the visibility of the body and social relations during this period beyond the fleeting and inconstant terms of performance.[22] This book's study of the transformation in the social perception of character in early America—one that physiognomy facilitated and that postrevolutionary culture reproduced and elaborated across a wide range of forms—both confirms and complicates our understanding of the period's culture of performance. While the end of the eighteenth century saw a continuing and even heightened potential for "identity play" in North America, as Dror Wahrman and others suggest, fixed, essential notions of identity were not only circulating, but were, in fact, central to how a number of seduction novels—arguably early America's most significant fictional form—imagined social space. This is not to deny that "mutability gained rather than diminished in significance" for Americans in the immediate postrevolutionary context (Wahrman 251), but rather to reconsider "the hold of the old regime on the imaginations of Americans" (Bushman xix). Where the spread of gentility has been read as affording "a convenient identity and a definition of position in the confusing fluidity of democratic society" (Bushman xix), the following pages consider how the democratization of gentility was also viewed as obfuscating the visibility of distinction. However much gentility made strangers more familiar by enabling them to fit into a vernacular or emulative form of gentility, its downward distribution, particularly its promotion of cultural over social capital, was represented as disrupting social relations as well. The first four chapters of this book explore how early American culture, particularly the seduction novel, sought to locate the absence of distinction in social aspirants on the one hand and its presence among the established gentry on the other on the permanent and involuntary features of the face. I argue that the kind of social space imagined within these novels, largely predicated on immobility, relocated the visibility of distinction from the genteel, yet voluntary performances of the body to the permanent, involuntary, and unalterable features of the face. It did so in ways resonant with and informed by the cultural practices of physiognomic distinction.

I should make it clear from the onset that *Discerning Characters* does not intend to be a work of social or political history. While it is my hope that many of the arguments contained within the following pages—particularly those found in Chapters 1 and 4—might be of interest to social and political historians, this book is ultimately a work of cultural (primarily literary) history.[23] It examines how the processes of social differentiation were imagined culturally, with particular attention paid to how physiognomy operated as a social category of perception in early America and analyzes how the face was imagined to mediate social space within early American fiction.[24] In doing so, it hopes to follow the important work of Amy Lang, Wai-Chee Dimock, Michael Gilmore, and others in bringing concepts of class to bear on the formal consideration of late eighteenth- and early nineteenth-century American literature.[25] The centrality of looking at faces and portraits to the imagination of social space found within postrevolutionary seduction narratives, I argue, reflects how discourses such as physiognomy operated as a cognitive structure that social agents implemented in their practical knowledge of the social world (as it was symbolically registered within fiction and as it may have been enacted by those whose actions were shaped by reading such fiction).[26]

Discerning Characters thus seeks to join a growing body of interdisciplinary scholarship dedicated to revising and broadening our conceptions of Anglo-American literacy during the colonial and early national period.[27] This impressive body of work in the fields of media, book, and reading history has "challenged the primacy of 'word' as the dominant building block out of which Anglo-Americans simultaneously invented and transmitted ideas of individual and communal identity" (Brückner 13). The practices and forms of visibility studied in the work of Patricia Crain, Robert St. George, Martin Brückner, Eric Slauter, Wendy Bellion, Ellen Miles, Margaretta Lovell and others are at the core of *Discerning Characters*. My purpose here is to recover what Deidre Lynch refers to elsewhere as the "transmedia" context of the novel as it emerges in postrevolutionary and early national America.[28] The logic of physiognomic distinction under discussion here appears not only within the context of the material and visual culture of postrevolutionary America—ranging from full- and half-length portraiture, medals, sculpture busts, wax-work figures, and miniatures to engravings, profile portraits, silhouettes, book illustrations, mourning rings, and porcelain—but more specifically through that visual culture's intertextual appearances within the novel. As such, *Discerning Characters* identifies and argues for the fundamental intermediality of early American fiction.[29] By intermediality, I refer to what Peter Wagner calls the intertextual use of one medium (such as painting) within another (such as fiction). Intermediality differs from comparative approaches to the arts in that it urges "the reader not to give preference to one medium or the other but to consider both" (Wagner 18). "Acknowledging intermediality as a constitutive element in fiction," Janet Aikins explains, "enables us to perceive that the reader of any verbal narrative is also a spectator to narrated action, and most especially so when in the presence of an actual 'iconotext,' a verbal narrative that makes use of an image, either by reference or allusion (real or imaginary)" or explicitly, as in the case of an illustrated edition (471). "Spectatorship (the look, the gaze, the glance, the practices of observation, surveillance, and visual pleasure)," W. J. T. Mitchell suggests, "may be as deep a problem as various forms of reading" (*Picture Theory* 16). The iconotextual practices of early American fiction, I argue throughout *Discerning Characters*, provide us with singular opportunities to consider how the production and consumption of cultural forms (such as writing and reading novels as well as drawing and looking at portraits) were imagined as mediating postrevolutionary social space.

Although *Discerning Characters* traces the transposition in the social perception of character across and within a variety of early American cultural forms, it concentrates its analysis on how visual strategies for discerning character in the face were distributed through and, at times, identified with the novel. The significance of intermediality to the novels under discussion here should prompt us to expand our sense of what reading novels meant in America prior to the mid-nineteenth century. Too often, Deidre Lynch reminds us, we project notions of the "literary" and "novel" back onto the genre before the fact and those designations prevent us from apprehending the intermedial nature of much postrevolutionary fiction. The formal distinctions between the iconic and the narrative, the visual and the verbal, as Chapters 2 and 3 explore, were considered secondary to the social practices of reading and looking that they represented within their texts. Reading faces and reading novels were indistinguishable practices for discerning character during the period and the benefits as well as dangers derived from each were frequently discussed together. To know how writers and readers made character the center of their stories is "to understand how the period's discursive transformations went in hand with new protocols for organizing class relations" (Lynch 5).[30] While the importance of faces and character to the emergence of the novel in British print culture has been well documented, the critical conversation on the subject within early American studies has been comparatively quiet.[31]

By historicizing postrevolutionary novels into the contemporary discourses and cultural forms of the face that their iconotextual practices invoke, *Discerning Characters* also hopes to provide the framework for developing an alternative history of the early American novel. Although I have by no means accounted for each novel of seduction, let alone every early American novel, the centrality of the physiognomic logic of distinction to the postrevolutionary seduction novel—from its presence in *The Inquisitor* to its critique in *Ormond*, as well as its reproduction and transformation in later antebellum fiction—should invite us to reconsider the social and political aims of the genre. There has been longstanding association of the novel with individualism, the rise of the middle class, and the processes of democratization and market expansion in the American context. At the very least, the novels analyzed in this book complicate influential critical models that understand the rise of the novel in America either in terms of a critique of gentility or its democratization.[32] With the single exception of *Ormond*, all of the novels under discussion in Part I imagine social spaces in which the promise and possibility of individual acts of self-creation are circumscribed by the logic of physiognomic distinction. The social spaces imagined within these novels frequently fantasize about the durability of moral character and social origin, and decry the downward distribution of civility, its culture of performance, and its promotion of cultural over social capital in the signification of genteel distinction.

• • •

Discerning Characters is divided into two uneven parts. The first four chapters comprising Part I attend to the variety of textual and visual practices surrounding the literary representation of distinction and the face in the fifty years from the publication of Chesterfield's *Letters* and Lavater's *Essays on Physiognomy* during the last quarter of the eighteenth century to the emergence of phrenology and "scientific" racism and the development of literary nationalism in the United States during the first quarter of the nineteenth century. Chapter 1 offers the first comprehensive discussion of the reception of physiognomy in imprints, newspapers, and periodicals published in America between 1775 and 1825 in order to demonstrate how the discourse was used to register distinctions within races as much as it was used to discriminate between them. As Chapter 1 explains, Lavater's distinction between pathognomy (the study of man's passions and their visible, but impermanent expressions) and physiognomy (the study of the correspondence between man's moral character and his permanent and unalterable facial features) limited the power of persons to manipulate the reception of their image, in theory, since it disassociated gestural expression, and thus volition, from the legibility of moral character.

The physiognomic anecdotes and textual sketches analyzed in Chapter 1 disclose how physiognomy's transposition in the determination of character from the voluntary acts of the individual to the involuntary features of his or her face was particularly attractive in a social space in which both genteel distinction and dissimulation were a matter of polite performance. For those whose economic and social capital were most at risk in such a fluid social world—such as the established gentry—the logic, if not practice, of physiognomic distinction offered a means to establish moral character, embody social origin, and restrain the mobility enabled by the cultural capital of civility alone.

Chapter 2 considers the remarkable interest in the physiognomic distinction of the face, in part, as a response to the downward distribution of the codes of civility occasioned by the massive publication of texts such as Chesterfield's *Letters* during the last quarter of the eighteenth century. The discourse surrounding Chesterfield's *Letters*, I argue in Chapter 2, appears as a key element in the transformation and survival of genteel distinction in postrevolutionary America. The negative response to Chesterfield's *Letters* in the Anglo-American press—particularly to his equation of social power with the capacity to dissimulate one's permanent character—and the specificity of Chesterfieldianism in the postrevolutionary literary depiction of the seducer, I argue in Chapters 2 and 3, reflect a struggle over the distributive effects of print culture itself and its perceived threat to the residual social order of colonial gentility. I maintain that the discourse surrounding Chesterfieldianism in postrevolutionary America was part of a more general struggle over how distinction would operate within the social space of democracy and, more broadly, how culture—specifically literature—might participate in that struggle. Chesterfield was at the center of this conflict because his *Letters* were thought to offer those who either had lost or who never had superior status a way of escaping the limits of social condition. If books such as Chesterfield's *Letters* contributed to the transformation of distinction in early America by distributing a model of civility less dependent on economic or social capital and thus less subject to the institutions and networks traditionally responsible for reproducing such capital (such as family, state, and church), other cultural forms, such as Susanna Rowson's *The Inquisitor* and Hannah Foster's *The Coquette* (discussed in Chapter 3), imagined social spaces in which the individual performances and mobility of Chesterfieldian civility would be restrained by the apparent ineradicability of social origin on the face.

As Chapter 2 discusses, Anglo-American criticism of Chesterfield's *Letters*—whether in periodical, dramatic, or fictional form—often represented the struggle between the cultural capital of social aspirants and the social capital of established elites in terms of seduction. Chapter 3 examines how the postrevolutionary seduction novel—perhaps the postrevolutionary period's most significant literary genre—imagined the face as a location from which the absence of distinction would be made visible through physiognomy and did so in an effort to minimize the legitimacy of the cultural capital of Chesterfieldian civility in the signification of genteel distinction. I assert in Chapter 3 that the transposition in the determination of character that physiognomy promised was central to how the postrevolutionary novel of seduction imagined social space and the reading practices and ways of looking promoted by these novels positioned culture—especially dispositions to culture—as a means to restrict rather than facilitate social mobility. Chapter 3 explores how postrevolutionary seduction fiction frequently associated the dissembling male seducer with the cultural capital of Chesterfieldian civility and imagined his individual polite performances as unaffected by either the vigilance of parental surveillance or the reputation assigned by familial, moral, and social networks. The invocation of Chesterfieldianism by Rowson, Foster, Tabitha Tenney, and numerous other postrevolutionary novelists was an effort to distinguish and distance the social effects of reading their works (and of reading literature in general) from the negative social effects associated with reading books such as Chesterfield's *Letters* and romance novels. The immobile social space imagined within these postrevolutionary seduction novels relocated the visibility of distinction from the genteel yet voluntary performances of the body to the permanent, involuntary, and unalterable features of the face, doing so in ways resonant with and informed by the cultural practices of physiognomic distinction detailed in Chapter 1. The social spaces and trajectories symbolically imagined within these novels and the dispositions and ways of looking generated by reading them distinguished the postrevolutionary seduction novel from other forms of print culture and shielded the genre from its Anglo-American critics by enlisting culture to restrict rather than facilitate mobility.

If seduction novels such as *The Coquette* dramatized the social consequences of failing to discern character from the face, other postrevolutionary texts specifically addressed the political consequences of locating character in the face. Chapter 4 complements recent explanations of the body's relationship to the public in the postrevolutionary period by situating two texts—Philip Freneau's "The Picture Gallery" and Hugh Henry Brackenridge's *Modern Chivalry*—into the contemporary discourses of portraiture and physiognomy that they invoke. This chapter explores how the burgeoning visual culture of the early republic—its public portrait galleries, waxwork figures, prints, sculpture, profile portraits, silhouettes, and printed biographical portrait galleries—utilized the face to represent the abstract ideals of civic virtue and communicate exemplary character, thus participating in creating a visual national imaginary. Various episodes from *Modern Chivalry* reveal how on the one hand the facial features of subordinate groups might be used to exclude them from embodying exemplary public character, while on the other physiognomically informed portraits might be used to embody otherwise abstract political ideals in the faces of specific individuals. The asymmetries in *Modern Chivalry's* application of the logic of physiognomic distinction to the public—individual and politically inclusive for dominant groups, collective and politically exclusive for subordinate groups—provides us with a postrevolutionary precursor to the epistemology of race in America, one in which the representation of racial

difference consists in whether a person's face first identifies the essential features of his individual character or his collective identity.

Part II of *Discerning Characters* studies how the transposition in the social
perception of character imagined within postrevolutionary seduction fiction
would continue to shape not only the representation of distinction within the
novel but, more broadly, the practices of literary production and reception in
nineteenth-century America. I concentrate my analysis on the fiction of two
authors in particular, James Fenimore Cooper and Herman Melville, in order
to examine the ways in which the terms of literary value would remain coincident with the representation and reproduction of genteel distinction during
the second quarter of the nineteenth century even as the conditions for the social perception of character were changing in America. Chapters 5 and 6 consider how the emphasis on the social perception of character shifts within the
fiction of Cooper and Melville from discerning the visibility of its absence to
addressing the invisibility of its presence. The final two chapters of *Discerning
Characters* tell a different kind of literary history than the previous four. Where
the previous four chapters understood the presence of the physiognomic logic
of distinction inside the postrevolutionary novel of seduction within the larger
cultural history of the social perception of character in the early republic, the
final two chapters consider why the logic of physiognomic distinction would
continue to inform novel reading and writing in nineteenth-century America
even as the discourse of civility was being democratized and the discourse of
physiognomy was yielding to more modern conceptions of racial difference.
Chapter 5 argues that Cooper's early seduction fiction, *Precaution* and *Tales
for Fifteen*, appropriates and transforms the physiognomic logic of distinction found within the postrevolutionary novel of seduction so that the face
no longer serves as the site from which to discern the absence of distinction,
but confronts the problem of the invisible aristocrat—that is, the illegibility
of superior social status within the social space of democracy. Reading remains
central to the task of picturing men and discerning their character accurately,
but in Cooper's early fiction, those pictures no longer serve to expose the
wrong man—such as unmasking Chesterfieldian seducers—but to distinguish
the right one.

Discerning Characters concludes by reading Herman Melville's novel *Pierre*
as a critique of the structuring effect of the physiognomic fallacy on the genre
of the novel, its model of reading, and on the representation of distinction in
early America.[33] The trajectory of *Pierre* reproduces the visual cultural history
described within the first five chapters of *Discerning Characters* by moving

from the portraiture of the colonial aristocratic world to the physiognomic portraits of the postrevolutionary generation before closing with the daguerreotypes, frontispieces, and picture galleries of the urban and democratic antebellum present. Unlike Cooper's seduction fiction, which reproduced the structure and physiognomic logic of the postrevolutionary seduction novel only to modify its function, Melville's seduction novel inhabits the form to expose the fallacy of its physiognomic logic. In fact, *Pierre*, in astonishingly precise terms, inverts the tragedy of postrevolutionary seduction novels like *The Coquette*—which, as Chapter 3 demonstrated, ensues from not reading character from the face—by dramatizing the consequences of reading character from the face. By challenging both assumptions of the logic of physiognomic distinction (that a person has one essential character over time and that a face can express it) the final portrait gallery scene in *Pierre* exposes the physiognomic fallacy—the false opposition between a model of character read from performance and one read from the face—an opposition that, as I argue throughout *Discerning Characters*, was foundational to how early American culture imagined the structure of social relations.

PART I

Distinction and the Face

Chapter 1

Discerning Characters

The state of the purse impresses as striking a character upon
the face of the rich and the poor, as does vanity and abjection
upon the powerful and the weak.
— Richard Harlan, *American Medical Recorder* (1822)

OVER THE PAST fifteen years, there has been an increasing amount of scholarship in the humanities devoted to discussing the cultural and social implications of late eighteenth- and early nineteenth-century physiognomy in Europe.[1] Dror Wahrman, for example, has read the rise of the physiognomic mode across so many late eighteenth-century English cultural forms as signaling the arrival of a new modern regime of selfhood featuring more innate and fixed categories of identity. Physiognomy's role in the formation of more modern notions of race has been the subject of a number of studies. Work by Judith Weschler, Kay Flavell, and Richard Gray, for example, has shown how eighteenth-century physiognomy and its visual strategies for representing human variety developed into nineteenth-century European racism. Yet, as Miriam Meijer and David Bindman remind us, nineteenth-century racial science distorted eighteenth-century classification theories such as Petrus Camper's facial angle and Johann Lavater's physiognomy as much as it was derived from them.[2] As Bindman puts it, the most influential text on physiognomy in the eighteenth- and nineteenth-century Atlantic world, Lavater's popular *Physiognomische Fragmente* [*Essays on Physiognomy*] (1775–78) "does not deal methodically with questions of nationality or human variety, nor does it attempt a human or racial hierarchy based on physiognomy. In fact, the volumes contain relatively little reference to national or racial types, and Africans make very few appearances" (111). While the scholarship of Bindman and

Meijer—like that of Weschler, Flavell, Gray, and Roxann Wheeler—continues to refine our understanding of physiognomy and race, their work—like that of Wahrman, Françoise Delaporte, Martin Porter, Melissa Percival, and Lucy Hartley—concentrates almost exclusively on the European context. In contrast, the reception of physiognomy in North America is less well known.[3]

This chapter provides a better understanding of how physiognomy was received in early America and also reconsiders physiognomy's relationship to the formation of modern notions of racial difference. This is not to claim that physiognomy had nothing to do with race during this period, but rather it is to ask whether the production of modern forms of racial difference is adequate to account for physiognomy's initial diffusion in postrevolutionary American culture. The relationship of physiognomy to race following the revolution and before the emergence of phrenology and the "American" school of anthropology during the 1830s and 1840s, as scholars well know, is particularly complex.[4] Racial identity during this period was "complicated because of the way the categories themselves shifted over time" (Sweet 9).[5] This was an era when physiognomy was in the process of yielding to the allegedly more quantitative sciences of crainology and phrenology and when race, as Winthrop Jordan explains, "was characterized by the absence of precise meaning" and "was being brought into use by writers . . . who sought to avoid the customary dichotomy between species and varieties" (Jordan in Smith 1965 xxxix).[6] "Until the very end of the eighteenth century," Roxann Wheeler notes, "*variety*, not race, was the scientific term of choice to designate different groups of people" (*Complexion* 31). Even when the influential "scientific" racism arose in the United States during the middle decades of the nineteenth century, it "was neither unchallenged nor the only racial theory around" (Dain viii). Race, as the following pages will demonstrate, appeared infrequently in discussions of physiognomy in postrevolutionary America and when it did, its relationship to physiognomy was imprecise. If physiognomy was not distinguishing between the races in early America, then what was it distinguishing?

This chapter surveys the reception of physiognomy in imprints, newspapers, and periodicals published in America between 1775 and 1825 in order to examine how the face was used to register distinctions *within* races as much as it was used to discriminate *between* them. As both the pliable medium of polite performance and the durable marker of moral character and social origin, the face was an important site in the struggle for distinction in early America. The strategic management of the face, as the introduction suggested, facilitated individual acts of self-creation and legitimated spontaneous claims to distinction in a culture of genteel performance. Yet, the face also served to restrict such social performances. Physiognomy operated as a social category of perception in early America and provided people with a practice of visibility from which to discern permanent moral character from the face. Even though "women, children, and blacks could be assigned a fixed place in society, . . . because they were easily identified," Joyce Appleby observes, "the case became more complicated with white men" (40). After the revolution, the democratization of ambition "undermined a fixed system of status" and "fueled new forms of differentiation" (Appleby 34). Physiognomy, I would like to propose, contributed to the social differentiation of white men in postrevolutionary America.

• • •

Although the practice of reading character from the face dates back to antiquity, physiognomy underwent a series of important transformations over the course of the eighteenth century. From the middle of the eighteenth century forward, physiognomy in Europe and North America developed in parallel, but vertically stratified ways, as the emergent science of physiognomy gradually distinguished itself from a much older and more common occult practice for reading faces.[7] As Melissa Percival explains with respect to physiognomy in eighteenth-century France, "a split can be perceived in physiognomical thought between objective rational science and more divinatory practices which were linked with the astral world" (17). Prior to the eighteenth century, physiognomy was an occult practice that combined humoural physiognomy with astrology, chiromancy and other prognostic pursuits (Berland 254).[8] The astrological component of pre-Lavaterian physiognomy—in which stars were believed to influence the physiognomical disposition of the individual—proved troublesome for both church and state during the early modern period (Rivers 24). By the sixteenth century, "books on physiognomy had become the Bible and New Testament for English 'artsmen' and 'cunning men'" (Porter 37) who undoubtedly studied them in order to improve their social performances. Physiognomy was eventually prohibited during the Elizabethan era and "by Act of Parliament in 1743 . . . all persons even 'pretending to have skill in physiognomy were deemed rogues and vagabonds and were liable to be publicly whipped'" (Shortland, "Lavater," 380). In fact, statutes barring physiognomy in colonial America remained on the books in Massachusetts, New York, New Hampshire, Vermont, and New Jersey long

Figure 5. "Mépris and Haine. Scorn and Hatred." Engraving after LeBrun from *The Complete Drawing Book* (London: Robert Sayer, 1755). Image courtesy of the Library Company of Philadelphia.

after the revolution.[9] Yet, even as physiognomy was being outlawed on both sides of the Atlantic, a more rational form was being developed in Europe as texts such as Guillaume Bougeant and Jacques Pernetti's *Lettres Philosophiques sur les Physiognomies* (1746) and James Parson's *Human Physiognomy Explained* (1746–47) abandoned the astrological basis of physiognomy in favor of more empirical approaches (Percival 18). This "science" of physiognomy would receive its most influential articulation with the publication of Lavater's *Physiognomische Fragmente* [*Essays on Physiognomy*] during the last quarter of the eighteenth century.[10] "If prior to the end of the eighteenth century physiognomics was traditionally identified with such esoteric and 'irrational' pursuits as chiromancy and oneiromancy, and hence associated with occultist prophetic practices," Richard Gray remarks, "the physiognomic doctrines of Lavater . . . mark a notable turn toward codifying physiognomics as a strictly positivistic and empirical science in the Enlightenment sense" (xix).

•   •   •

While Lavaterian physiognomy was not the only theory of corporeal legibility at the end of the eighteenth century, it was one of the principal lexicons for understanding the cultural meaning of the face and its representations.[11] The extraordinary influence of physiognomy "was readily evident not only in directly related fields such as medical practice and physical anthropology . . . but also in other arenas of cultural production, such as the novel, the theater, and visual art high and low" (Wahrman 294). The rejuvenation of physiognomy during the last quarter of the eighteenth century, as Martin Porter and Dror Wahrman have shown, had much to do with its claims to discern involuntary and permanent moral character. Lavater's theoretical distinction between *pathognomy* (Figure 5) (the study of man's passions and his visible, but impermanent facial expressions) and *physiognomy* (Figure 6) (the study of the correspondence between man's moral character and his permanent and unalterable facial features) was central to his *Physiognomische Fragmente* [*Essays on Physiognomy*] and pivotal to understanding how people of the period thought about the relationship between faces and characters. As Michael Shortland explains, these "two discourses were . . . almost always . . . inadequately differentiated before Lavater, and his creation of physiognomy as a 'new science' is largely due to having separated it from pathognomy" ("Lavater" 389).[12] One effect of Lavater's distinction between physiognomy and pathognomy was that, in theory, it limited the power of persons to manipulate the reception of their image in public (as early modern English "cunning men" had done) since it

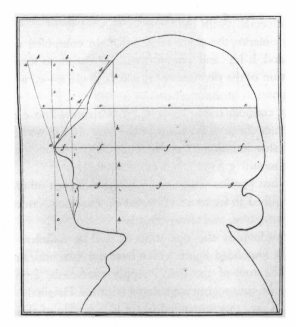

Figure 6. From Johann Caspar Lavater, *Essays on Physiognomy*, trans. Henry Hunter, 5 vols. (London: J. Murray, 1789–98), 2.1.226. Image courtesy of Special Collections, The Sheridan Libraries, The Johns Hopkins University.

disassociated gestural expression, and thus volition, from the legibility of moral character. Unlike Giambattista Della Porta's *De Humana Physiognomia* (1586) and Charles Le Brun's *Conférence sur l'impression des différents caractères des passions* (1668) (Figure 5)—which were the leading manuals for depicting the facial expression of emotional states during the eighteenth century—Lavaterian physiognomy read moral character from unalterable and involuntary facial features, creating a visual system for reading a person's permanent moral character despite their social masks (Figures 6 and 7).[13]

Lavater's subordination of pathognomy to physiognomy, however, depended upon an opposition between a model of character read from performance and one read from the permanent and involuntary physiognomic features of the face. This opposition—or what I will refer to throughout *Discerning Characters* as the physiognomic fallacy—distinguished physiognomy from pathognomy on the grounds that its assessment of character was neither temporary nor subject to the manipulation of the individual to be judged. The term "physiognomic fallacy," however, should not be taken to mean that

Take the outline from *a* above the bone of the eye to *c* on the hind-head—it will be fufficient alone to determine pofitively enough the principal character of the mind. An ordinary Phyfionomift will pronounce of what that head is capable or incapable, as foon as he has feen the very remarkable fection of the profile which is between *a* and *b;* a good Obferver will decide it by that which is between *e* and *d;* and finally, the real Connoiffeur will need no more, to fettle his judgement, than the fpace between *a* and *e.*

Figure 7. From Johann Caspar Lavater, *Essays on Physiognomy*, trans. Henry Hunter, 5 vols. (London: J. Murray, 1789–98), 1.1.251. Image courtesy of Special Collections, The Sheridan Libraries, The Johns Hopkins University.

the opposition between a model of character read from performance and one read from the physiognomic features of the face was somehow false in historical practice. It was, as the following pages document, widely distributed, reproduced, and debated in early America. Rather, my purpose in using the term "physiognomic fallacy" is to acknowledge that the theoretical opposition informing this historical practice was false.

It is important to keep in mind, however, that Lavaterian physiognomy created the very faces it claimed to interpret. Lavater maintained "that we judge the qualities of a person not by his actions, but by his face," François Delaporte notes, "but he did not perceive that with the description of portraits, he was giving in advance the qualities that he was claiming to deduce from representation" (40). Physiognomy's popular hermeneutics of the body was thus "instrumental in constructing the very archive [it] claimed to interpret" (Sekula 12). Instead of discerning character from the face, it merely collapsed the difference between the two: "The measure of the facial angle and the curve of a forehead are not signs, but they become so from the moment when character deposits—or rather, transposes—its qualities onto the face. In the eighteenth century, the mutation of the gaze was linked not to measurement but to the formation of the physiognomic method: a constitution of a domain of visibility where the gaze perceives signs right from the start" (Delaporte 39). The transposition that Delaporte identifies as the "physiognomic method" and the domain of visibility that it enables, this book argues, is particularly important to the representation of distinction in postrevolutionary America. As this and the following chapters will explore, when postrevolutionary American culture engaged physiognomy, its interest had more do with its transposition in the determination of character than the validity of its specific practice. What mattered most was not the accuracy of any particular reading of character from the face but rather the more general relocation of discerning character from the voluntary performances of an individual to the involuntary and immediately visible features of the face.

•   •   •

By the time Lavater died in 1801, New York's *Lady's Monitor* would summarize his impact by noting how "in Switzerland, in Germany, in France, in Britain, and in America, all the world became passionate admirers of the physiognomical science of Lavater" ("Lavater" 102). His books, the author pronounced, "were studied and admired" and "thought as necessary in every family, as even the Bible itself" ("Lavater" 102). If the eulogistic context of this last claim renders it suspicious, similar assessments of physiognomy's ubiquity in postrevolutionary America can be found elsewhere and, to a certain extent, they are supported by its impressive publication history.[14] At least twenty editions of Lavater's *Essays* were published in English, including two in America, before 1810 and American publishers later added numerous editions of *The Pocket Lavater* (1817), *The Juvenile Lavater* (1815), and *The Physiognomist's Own Book . . . Drawn from the Writings of Lavater* (1841), among others. Booksellers from Newburyport to North Carolina regularly advertised Lavater's *Essays* (Figure 8)—and a number of circulating libraries listed copies as part of their collections.[15] Lavater's *Essays* "was reprinted, abridged, summarized, pirated, parodied, imitated, and reviewed so often that it is difficult to imagine how a literate person at the time could have failed to have some general knowledge of the man and his theories" (Graham, "Lavater in England," 562).[16] A number of notable early American intellectuals—John Adams, Jedidiah Morse, Noah Webster, Lydia Sigourney, Sarah Wentworth Morgan, and Benjamin Rush among them—wrote on the subject. "Do we observe a certain size of the brain, and a peculiar cast of features, such as the prominent eye, and the aquiline nose, to be connected with extraordinary portions of genius?" Rush reasoned. "We observe a similar connection between the figure and temperament of the body and certain moral qualities" (183). By 1826, no fewer than 677 articles referring to physiognomy had been published in newspapers and periodicals from Maine to Florida, Massachusetts to Illinois. "Physiognomy is a subject so interesting, and so universal," the *Virginia Chronicle* declared in 1792, "that to imagine it a mere fashionable novelty, which it has lately on some occasions, been affirmed to be, is as strange as it is absurd" (4). It is "a subject in which all persons, more or less, become interested," the *Lancaster Hive* remarked in 1805, "whenever we behold a new face, we involuntarily form some conclusion respecting the one who wears it; that it is the index of a mind either honest, or dishonest; cultivated, or barren; generous and friendly, or inimical and covetous; with many other qualities the gazer is ready to attribute to it" ("Essays" 137). The prevalence of such physiognomic scrutiny in early America led Frances Wright to observe that "when the American stumbles upon a foreigner, he is wont, during a few moments, to take a quiet perusal of his physiognomy, and if opportunity permits, to remain the silent auditor of his remarks and comments, and thus to satisfy himself of the temper of the man, before he evinces any disposition to make him his companion" (370). The social perception of character from the face was common enough for another author to note "how very apt persons are to form an opinion of

The First AMERICAN EDITION,
[ILLUSTRATED WITH EIGHT HANDSOME EN-
GRAVINGS, BY S. HILL.]

just Published,

LAVATER's *Essays* on *Physiognomy ;*
for the promotion of the knowledge and the love of mankind : Abridged from Mr. HOLCROFT's translation.

"The Essay on Physiognomy of Mr. LAVATER, are now
so universally known and celebrated, that it is unnecessary to
attempt their eulogium ; even those who consider the science
they are written to support as visionary, cannot but admire
the lively force of imagination and animated argument, with
which the author has explained and defended his favourite
hypothesis." The following is a summary of the contents :
On Physiognomy as a science—on the Nature of Man, which
is the foundation of the science of physiognomy—Signs of Bodily strength and weakness, health and sickness ; of the con-
geniality of the human form and its excellence—of the forehead, eyes, eyebrows, nose, mouth, lips, teeth, chin, &c.—
Remarks on national physiognomy ; extracts from other writers on national physiognomy ; on the resemblance between
parents and children ; observations on the newborn, the dy-
ing and the dead ; of the influence of countenance on countenance, imagination on the countenance, and imagination
on the human form ; general remarks on women ; general
remarks on male and female ; on the physiognomy of youth ;
a word to travellers, governors, judges, magistrates and the
clergy, &c. &c.

Boston : Printed and sold by DAVID WEST, No. 36, and
WILLIAM SPOTSWOOD, No. 11, Marlborough-street—
Price neatly bound, eight shillings.   Sept. 3, 1794.

French Revolution.

Just Published, price *Two Dollars,* (the London edition sells
for *Four*) and may be had of BENJAMIN LARKIN,
JAMES WHITE, THOMAS and ANDREWS, DAVID

Figure 8. "Advertisement for the first American edition of Lavater." *Columbian Centinel* [Boston, Mass.] 13 September 1794. Image courtesy of the American Antiquarian Society.

other persons with whom accident or design makes them acquainted, . . . on the *very* wise principles of Lavater" ("Familiar Letters" 51).

The publication of Lavater's lavishly illustrated *Essays* during the 1780s and 1790s not only distributed this logic of physiognomy widely, it also trans-formed how faces were represented in portraiture (a subject discussed more fully in Chapter 4) by elevating traditionally low forms—such as the silhouette

and profile portrait—above oil portraiture as the preferred mediums for reading character. Lavater recommended the silhouette and profile portrait in particular because they emphasized the solid and presumably unalterable features
of the face. A profile portrait drawn by Charles B. F. Saint-Mémin, for example,
was sufficient to convince one author that "this is the kind of man, that, from
his countenance, I should choose to associate with" (Zophyrus 284). While
portrait painters used physiognomic theory to transform their individual sitters
into generalizable types, dozens of itinerant artists encouraged physiognomic
readings by producing thousands of silhouettes (Figure 9) and profile portraits
(Figure 10) that emphasized the particularity of the face.

To be sure, physiognomy had its critics in postrevolutionary America as
it did elsewhere, but the objections more often than not resembled those of
Thaddeus Harris in his 1803 *Minor Encyclopedia or Cabinet of General Knowledge* when he endorsed "the truth of physiognomy itself," but "not that of any
particular physiognomical observation" (68). Although the arbitrary nature of
some of Lavater's specific pronouncements made it "impossible to establish a
general and uniform system" (Coxe 21), few denied physiognomy's pervasive-
ness as a social practice or its general truth as an imperfect and still evolving science of moral character. The fact that "Lavater himself, the greatest of
Physiognomists, should pronounce a wrong judgment," one physiognomist
argued in 1806 in Baltimore's *Companion and Weekly Miscellany*, was no reason to assert that "there is . . . no truth in Physiognomy" for even "Lavater
admits that the science of Physiognomy is not more certain than other sciences" (Zophyrus 148). According to its proponents, inconsistent, contradictory, and erroneous readings were not the fault of physiognomy, but rather of
the physiognomist. "All are not alike skilled in faces, any more than in unrav-
elling characters; even the most penetrating eye may be mistaken," the 1797
*South Carolina Weekly Museum and Complete Magazine of Entertainment and
Intelligence* admitted, yet "the face is seldom a false glass; and when it proves
so, is generally the fault of the beholder" ("Of Physiognomy" 590). According
to Lavater, the discriminating physiognomist needed to possess a number of
traits—beauty, education, leisure, and, by extension, capital among them—in
order to read faces accurately.[17] Part of the attraction of physiognomic expression for Lavater (as it would be for the Scottish philosophers and postrevolutionary America) was its simultaneous claim to universality—its claim to be
like a common sense or a natural language—and its exclusionary force, where
the capacity for physiognomic discernment varied with the attention, experience, education, and wealth of the observer.

R. Letton,

TAKER OF PROFILE LIKENESSES,

RESPECTFULLY informs the Ladies and Gentlemen of   that he has taken a retired and convenient room, at

where he will continue if meeting with liberal encouragement. The superiority of his Machine, to those in common use, and his extensive practice, enable him to give correct Profiles. He has selected a few specimens that may be examined at his room. He takes the Profile on a beautiful wove paper, and three minutes sitting. He respectfully assures those Ladies and Gentlemen who will favor him with a call, that his whole endeavours will be to please; and that for the small sum of 25 cents, they may depend on receiving two correct Profiles, or no pay will be required.

R. Letton engraves them in gold, or paints them black on glass. He constantly keeps a handsome assortment of Profile Frames for sale, oval or square, black or gilt. Families may be attended at their own houses, at the same expence.

N. B. Hours of attendance, from 8 o'clock in the morning, till 9 in the evening.

Figure 9. Broadside for Ralph Letton, c. 1808. Image courtesy of the American Antiquarian Society.

Figure 10. Charles B. F. Saint-Mémin. Folio 10 from the Collection of Saint-Mémin Engravings at the National Portrait Gallery. Gift of Mr. and Mrs. Paul Mellon. Image courtesy of The National Portrait Gallery, Smithsonian Institution.

Despite the racial, ethnic, and national diversity of the colonial and post-revolutionary American populations (whose displacement from their native continents complicated environmental theories of racial and national difference), the initial reception of Lavaterian physiognomy in America suggests it was used to visualize differences within races as much as it did between them. Unquestionably, physiognomy contributed to the equation of superior moral character with the image of a white European face and thus played a significant role in the "diffusion and legitimation of European racism" (Flavell 9), but the comparatively small number of non-European faces in the initial print archive on physiognomy as well as their virtual absence in the visual archive of the same period suggest that, in early America at least, the discourse also defined the category European negatively. Of the 787 references to physiognomy published in American imprints, newspapers, and periodicals between 1775 and 1825, for example, only fifty-nine (7.5 percent) discuss people of specifically non-European descent.[18]

One of the more ardent defenders of physiognomy in early America, for instance, wondered why the celebrated Lavater "says nothing of complexion." Writing under the pseudonym of Zophyrus in 1806, the author asked the readers of Baltimore's *Companion and Weekly Miscellany*: "Is it possible to conceive that physiognomy has nothing to do with colour" (283)? If Lavater's failure to address this question specifically suggested that his answer might be "yes," Zophyrus's response was an unequivocal "no." Yet, the "colour" Zophyrus imagined for an ideal face was not white, but a "complexion the lightest of brown, animated with a mixture of red with deeper brown" (283). "A florid complexion," the 1809 Richmond *Visitor* explained in its "Familiar Letters on Physiognomy," "expresses a better temper than a pale and livid hue" (148). This "scientific lecture" informed its audience that in "the complexion of the Africans . . . the attentive and constant observer will discover as much real difference between their black, as between the white of the Europeans. But we are more used to behold men of our own colour and seldom find ourselves in company with several negroes, to be able to descry distinctly their every shade" ("Familiar" 148). For these two articles, at least, complexion, while invoking skin color, was not limited to delineating black and white, but recalled an older humoural model of temperament.[19] While it is clear from the *Visitor* article that race operates as a category of difference, it is also evident that a physiognomic consideration of skin color would distinguish "real differences" within those groups as well as between them. These two articles, however, are the exceptions rather than the rule when it comes to the complicated conversation surrounding physiognomy in early America. The articles are exceptional because they feature "complexion" as an element of physiognomic distinction, whereas Lavaterian physiognomy tended to emphasize more permanent and unalterable facial features such as the shape and length of the nose. What makes these articles unusual is that they are two of only eleven periodical articles to even mention "complexion" or "skin colour" out of the nearly 370 discussing physiognomy in America in the fifty years from 1775 to 1825.[20]

Similarly, of the fifty engravings included in the 1801 *Physiognomical Sketches by Lavater*, the twenty in the 1815 New York edition of *The Juvenile Lavater*, the thirty-two in the various Hartford, New York, New Haven, and Philadelphia editions of *The Pocket Lavater*, and the thirty-one "physiognomical sketches" included in the 1831 Boston edition of *The Characters of Theophrastus*, not a single African or Native American face can be seen. Most depict profiles of white Euro-American males, such as this one from the 1817 *Pocket Lavater* (Figure 11). The text accompanying the image concludes that: "The bony formation of the head shows that this person possesses a constancy of mind not easy to be shaken. . . . This physiognomy is peculiarly appropriate to a lawyer or a magistrate" (Lavater *The Pocket Lavater* 54–55). From such physiognomic interpretations, readers learned how to look at the faces of various white males in order to distinguish "the physiognomy of . . . a man of business" (63) or "a lawyer" (66) from that of a "scoundrel" (85) or "a rogue" (89) (Figure 12). In general, the images contained within Anglo-American imprints on physiognomy indicate that the practice was equally, if not more, committed to the identification of criminals and men of genius as it was to the production of a coherent racial taxonomy.

The minimal presence of non-European faces in the initial visual and print archive surrounding physiognomy in early America might also have been influenced by the belief that uncivilized men could not dissemble their permanent moral character behind a social mask. For those theorists who asserted the state of society as a causal agent in human variety (such as Samuel Stanhope Smith and Richard Harlan in America and James Beattie, Henri Grégoire, and Alexander von Humboldt abroad), dissimulation could only be the product of a civilized society. "People in civilized life . . . are at pains to curb, or least to hide, their more violent emotions," James Beattie observed in his *Elements of Science* (1790–93), "whereas among savages, and persons little acquainted with decorum, there is hardly any restraint of this sort" (Beattie 12). Even those skeptical of physiognomy, such as Jean-Henri-Samuel Formey, admitted in his "Les Physiognomies Appréciées" (1775) that "no face is entirely

Figure 11. Engraving No. 16 from *The Pocket Lavater* (New York: Van Winkle & Wiley, 1817). Image courtesy of the American Antiquarian Society.

Figure 12. Engraving No. 28 from *The Pocket Lavater* (New York: Van Winkle &
Wiley, 1817). Image courtesy of the American Antiquarian Society.

pure and unadulterated, unless it is the face of a savage. The savage's face, unlike that of the civilized man, reveals 'les vraies empreintes de la nature'" (quoted in Percival 179). The Princeton divine, Samuel Stanhope Smith, argued that "the differences in physiognomy, between the Anglo-American, and the Indian depend principally on the state of society" (*Essay* 172). The state of society, some argued, was what diversified the facial features. "Intellectual cultivation is what contributes the most to diversify the features," Humboldt reasoned, "In barbarous nations there is rather a physiognomy peculiar to the tribe or horde than to any individual" (Humboldt 278).[21] The asymmetries inherent in the state of society explanation of human variety—that civilization produces distinct individuals (as well as dissimulation), whereas savagery produces tribal or group ones—are consistent with the asymmetries accompanying the cultural reception of physiognomy in postrevolutionary America in which the face generally distinguished and included individuals belonging to (or having the potential to belong to) civil society on the one hand and collectively discriminated and excluded those at its margins on the other.

Of course, this is not to suggest that there were no physiognomically detailed images of non-Europeans from the period. The profile portraitist Charles B. F. Saint-Mémin, for example, made nine physiognomically detailed chalk drawings and six watercolors of Native Americans between 1804 and 1807 (Figure 13). Although Ellen Miles has determined that "there is no evidence to indicate why Saint-Mémin made the Indians' portraits" (*Saint-Mémin* 148)—in fact, his Indian profiles represent only fifteen of the almost nine hundred he drew—their faces might have been worth depicting because they were as physiognomically transparent and thus as exemplary as those of Washington and Jefferson (see Figure 18). This 1804 profile of the Osage Indian, *Payouska*, for instance, seems equally invested in asserting his potential humanity as a still uncivilized product of the North American climate as it is in differentiating him as a non-European. Payouska's wig and Western clothes seem designed to complement what one contemporary writer identified as his "large Roman nose" (quoted in Miles "Saint-Mémin's Portraits" 14). Payouska's face prompted another writer to remark in 1806 that "These Osages were noble specimens of the human race and would have afforded fine studies for the painter or sculptor" (Miles "Saint-Mémin's Portraits" 9). The idea that the character of Native Americans and Africans might be both legible on their face and incapable of being concealed not only might account for their virtual absence from the initial Anglo-American physiognomical archive, but it also might explain why the more virulent images of nineteenth-century American

Figure 13. Charles B. F. Saint-Mémin. *Payouska*. ca. 1806. [1860.92] Image
courtesy of the New-York Historical Society.

racism would only develop after those presumed continental differences between African, North American, and European began to be obscured by an
increasingly heterogeneous, mixed-race population in America.[22]

Similar to the images found within physiognomical imprints, the pages
of many early American books, magazines, and newspapers were filled with
"physiognomical anecdotes" or textual "sketches" testifying to the science's capacity to make intraracial discriminations. While the social contexts in which
physiognomy is described within these anecdotes varied according to the age,
gender, and status of the observer and the observed, these scenes of looking—
like those found in novels from the period (a subject addressed most fully in
Chapters 3, 5, and 6)—almost always involved scrutinizing an unknown or a
dissembling person's face in order to discern his or her permanent moral character; and they, like the engravings found within the imprints, rarely involved
discerning the physiognomy of a non-European face. Typically, these anecdotes acknowledged physiognomy's universality, explained how it read moral
character from the face, and debated whether it could be made into a coherent
scientific system. The 1806 *Literary Magazine and American Register*, for instance, proclaimed the by-then familiar observation that "every one is in some
degree a master of that art which is generally distinguished by the name of
physiognomy; and naturally forms to himself the character . . . of a stranger,
from the features and lineaments of his face. We are no sooner presented to
any one we never saw before, than we are immediately struck with the image
of a proud, a reserved, an affable, or a good-natured man" ("The Gleaner"
379). As the source of immediate sympathy or antipathy, the face provided the
location for the social perception of character in early America.

In general, the people being inspected in these textual "physiognomic anecdotes" were unnamed strangers in public, but at other times they were being
considered as potential business partners, marital prospects, servants, or politicians (Figure 14). "Whenever any one entered my shop, whose countenance
did not betoken a man of business," one shopkeeper wrote in 1802, "the goods
were offered to him at less than prime cost. If another one appeared of a more
penetrating physiognomy, the profit I put upon the goods was so small, that
it would not pay the shop rent" (Truepenny 2). The ability to read the faces
of customers and potential commercial partners was thought to be invaluable
for merchants in an emerging market economy in which credit and commercial paper were often a matter of familiarity and trust.[23] Henry Laurens,
one of early America's more celebrated businessmen, for example, was lauded
for having "an exact knowledge of human nature, and in his own mercantile

Figure 14. Engraving No. 15 from *The Pocket Lavater* (New York: Van Winkle & Wiley, 1817). Image courtesy of the American Antiquarian Society.

language, soon found out the par of exchange of every man with whom he transacted business. His eye was uncommonly penetrating, and the correct opinions he frequently formed of the real characters of men from their looks would, if known to Lavater, have confirmed that philosopher in his theory of physiognomy. Such diligence and knowledge of men and of business could not fail of success" (Ramsay 483).[24] For this reason, Thomas Branagan reproduced "extracts from the works of the celebrated Lavater" in order to guide "young people, while choosing matrimonial and mercantile partners, and travelling companions" (n.p.). "A servant would . . . scarcely be hired," the *Lady's Magazine and Musical Repository* noticed in 1801 "till the descriptions and engravings of Lavater had been consulted, in careful comparison, with the lines and features of the young man's or woman's countenance" ("Sketches" 290) (Figures 15 and 16).[25] Noah Webster boasted in his popular *The Prompter* that he "would as soon employ a man, with Lavater's straight Nose, to make laws for the state, as a man or woman with a monstrous Under Lip, to labour for me. Nature has been kind enough to hang out, upon every man's face, the sign of the commodities for market within. Then look at the sign before make a bargain" (16).[26] Webster's description of the face as "the sign of the commodities for market within" affirms the utility of physiognomy as an actual practice for selecting servants and politicians and discloses how the face itself was understood as the supposedly natural sign of social value, an embodied form of capital itself. Reading faces in early America not only facilitated commerce, it was another form of it.

Since physiognomy was a rapid and informal means for measuring trust, it was often imagined within these anecdotes and sketches as the foundation for affiliation in the absence of social and familial networks or as the basis of familial resemblance in the presence of them.[27] The truth of physiognomy," the *Philadelphia Medical Museum* stated in 1807, "constitutes the basis of all sudden attachments between the sexes, as well as of many friendships between individuals of the same sex" (cvii). In 1817, for example, the *Raleigh Register and North-Carolina Gazette*, told the story of a wealthy Philadelphia butcher who boarded a ship arriving from Amsterdam looking for help in his business. "After examining the physiognomy of several of the passengers, without being able to please himself," the narrator describes how the butcher's "attention was arrested by the tranquil and composed countenance of a man rather advanced in years" (n.p.). The man's face convinces the butcher to hire him and his wife as indentured servants and "upon further enquiry, he ascertained them to be, in fact, his father and mother, the latter declaring, that if he was their son,

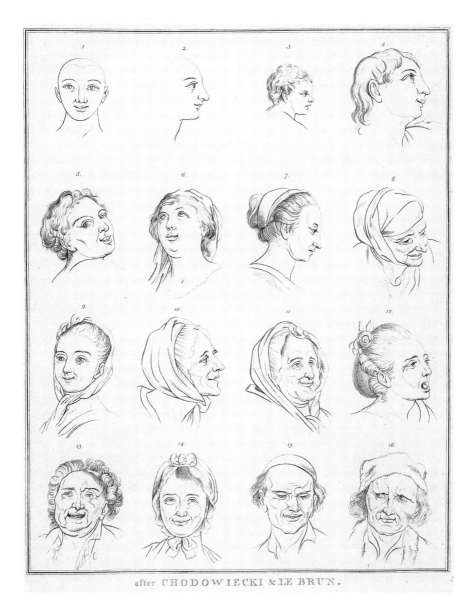

after CHODOWIECKI & LE BRUN.

Figure 15. Engraving from Johann Caspar Lavater, *Essays on Physiognomy*, trans. Henry Hunter, 5 vols. (London: J. Murray, 1789–89), 2: page opposite 64. Image courtesy of Special Collections, The Sheridan Libraries, The Johns Hopkins University.

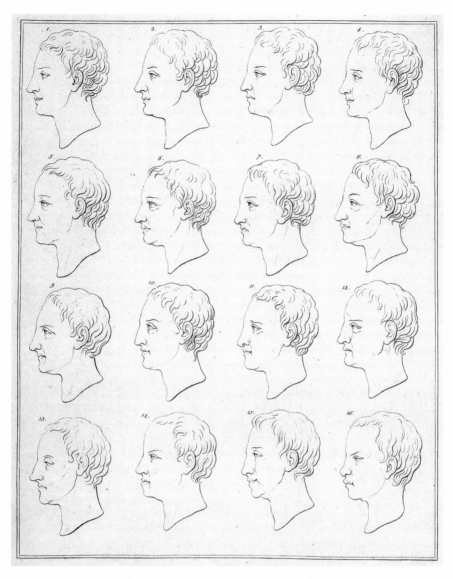

Figure 16. Engraving from Johann Caspar Lavater, *Essays on Physiognomy*, trans. Henry Hunter, 5 vols. (London: J. Murray, 1789–89), 2: page opposite 63. Image courtesy of Special Collections, The Sheridan Libraries, The Johns Hopkins University.

he had a remarkable mole upon his left arm—which proved to be the case!" (n.p.).[28] The butcher's mole corroborates what he had sensed in the old man's face all along—a familial relation—and in doing so the anecdote presents face and birthmark as equivalent involuntary corporeal signs of an otherwise dislocated familial identity.

As the butcher's tale suggests, physiognomy as a practice was understood at times as a surrogate for familial or social networks disrupted by mobility across the Atlantic or up and down its North American coast. With global political and economic forces circulating people beyond the local networks and technologies traditionally used to establish their identities and verify their status, the face served as an additional site from which individual character might be discerned and social capital established. The 1790 *Cumberland Gazette*, for instance, published a widely reprinted letter in which a doctor explains how the face of a displaced revolutionary war soldier solicited his sympathy and his capital.[29] While visiting a hospital, the doctor "perceived a soldier whose countenance struck me" (1). The soldier soon eyes the doctor, calls him over, and tells him that his father "possesses a considerable estate in Virginia" (1) before asking him for "an hundred dollars" (1). "Struck by the bold, but honest request," the doctor "examined the traits of his countenance very attentively," "consulted the secret impression which his physiognomy produced," and "granted the sum which he requested of me" (1). If the soldier's face secures him credit, then the doctor's discernment is repaid with ample interest. Five weeks later, the doctor receives letters from the soldier's family promising compensation.[30] The soldier's father informs the doctor that he is now "the adopted father" of his son and, as his "brother," he has been formally "incorporated into our family" (1). He sends the doctor "an authentic and legal contract of one half the plantation of—accompanied by a negro which I give you, a second coming from my son, a third from my wife's mother, and a servant from each of my brothers. This contract, as well as the bill of sale . . . are signed, sealed, and recorded according to law. This new property is irrevocably yours" (1). In his letter, the father also asks the doctor what caused him to choose his "son from among so many others who equally merited your attention? Blessed be the invisible hand which conducted you secretly towards his bed, and made you listen attentively to his proposal" (1). The "invisible hand" that led the doctor to his son was, of course, the physiognomic distinction of his son's face. It is interesting that what was initially a visual exchange between strangers is now described in terms of invisibility. The father's characterization of the doctor's discernment in terms of secrecy and invisibility as well as the absence of any physical description of the soldier's face in the anecdote reveals how the specific practice of physiognomic distinction matters less than what that practice was thought to accomplish (in this case, forming a homosocial affiliation equivalent to a familial relationship). The anecdote's fantasy of homosocial affiliations indistinguishable from familial bonds, however, depends upon the mediation of the face. The displaced soldier's face serves as a mobile, yet embodied, form of capital that is recognized by the doctor whose physiognomic discernment is rewarded in turn with economic (property) and social capital ("we are brothers"). Physiognomy thus serves as the basis through which familial relationships are transformed into homosocial affiliations grounded in white male privilege.

Besides serving as the source for affiliation, the physiognomic distinction of the face also supplied the grounds for intraracial discrimination. If virtue could be read from the face so, too, could its absence. Although physiognomy's prejudicial function was occasionally criticized in print, it appeared more often as an extra-juridical instrument for discerning a wide range of vices and crimes from slander and adultery to theft and murder.[31] The *New Haven Gazette*, for instance, printed a rather gruesome tale in 1784 recounting the story of a count who first suspects and then catches a thief from his countenance.[32] Similarly, The *Ladies Port Folio* informed its readers in 1820 of how a woman who was traveling "with a considerable amount of money about her" was able to detect and deter her theft and murder from the "physiognomy of her hosts" ("Horrible Crime" 171). As an emergent technology of surveillance, physiognomy was frequently described as combating dissimulation. The *Philadelphia Minerva*, for example, related an incident in 1796 in which a man saved his own life by looking past the "assumed tranquility" on his murderer's features and traced "in his countenance the formation of some shocking design."[33]

Physiognomy's potential to expose dissimulation was perhaps its most desirable and discussed feature during the period. Numerous articles, anecdotes, tales, and novels applauded physiognomy's ability to see through polite performances and uncover seducers, gamblers, idlers, fortune hunters, and impostors. In 1787, for instance, the *Pennsylvania Herald and General Advertiser* celebrated the involuntary revelation of the impostor by his face: "O visage of man! Mirror more true, more expressive, than his gesture, his speech, or even his accent, thou canst not extinguish the rapid lightning emitted by the soul! She has an involuntary course; she even shines in the eyes of the impostor" (4).[34] "People may form their language, their manners, their tone, their attitude, their style," the author claimed, "but the physiognomy, moulded, as one may say, by the interior character, is not to be destroyed" (4). Unlike words, manners, tone, or deportment—all of which could be acquired to erase the traces of moral character or social origin—the unalterable features of the face were thought to be incapable of being dissembled and thus served as the durable sign of individual character and, at times, social origin. Dissimulation was futile, one author concluded, because "the physiognomist can judge by the size and figure of the head, the dimensions of the eye, its colour, and its expression, and indeed by a thousand signs . . . the disposition and designs of every man that he sees, and, therefore, in all his dealings he is happily exempted from those various impositions which the ignorant and unobserving are daily compelled to endure" (Von Tromp 30).[35] "The moment I see the contour of a face, whether cut in paper, or modeled in plaster," another physiognomist proclaimed in the 1808 the *Literary Mirror*, "I can trace out the inward man, and follow him into the inmost recesses of his heart, what pains so ever he may take to conceal himself" (Musaeus 30).[36] The idea that physiognomy would expose "the word rake" in "black letters" on the faces of dissimulating seducers led another author to conclude that "Lavater's doctrine . . . has, to my own knowledge, arrested youth in an unreflecting career of licentiousness" (Y. 123).[37] For this author at least, physiognomy not only promised to detect dissimulation, but to deter it as well.

Yet, physiognomy's capacity to penetrate dissimulation, especially among the genteel, was also its most contested point. Although critics were willing to concede the general truth of physiognomy, a number expressed doubts about whether it could really unmask deception. "Even if we could suppose such progress in this science within the bounds of probability," Samuel Miller reasoned, "we must believe that the arts of concealment, deception, and every concomitant of artifice and false refinement will, at the same time, make equal progress, and thus leave us in the same relative situation as at present" (434). Miller's remarks disclose how physiognomy was positioned as part of a more general struggle in the determination of genteel refinement. Impostors "assume so many different shapes," Boston's *American Herald* observed in 1786, "that the sagacity of a Mentor, or the watchfulness of an Argus, would scarcely be sufficient security. Physiognomy . . . is of little avail" ("New York" 3).[38] This was particularly the case when the dissembler was or pretended to be genteel. The polished manners of civility, which advocated dissimulation, upset "the rules of physiognomy" and made it difficult to see past "the advantage of figure, education, and of all the agreeable accomplishments of a Gentleman" ("The Man of the World" n.p.). "It is indeed extremely difficult to discover the true sentiments and character of a man of the world," the *New York Weekly Museum* added in 1813, with "the lines of his face, blended and moulded to every circumstance and occasion" ("The Man of the World" n.p.).[39] Misreading the character of gentlemen at such moments could prove to be costly. In 1801, the *Philadelphia Repository and Weekly Register* warned its readers "of the extensive evil effects a person with a handsome exterior may cause" by telling them a familiar seduction tale in which a man "who had the impudence to assume the character of a person of respectability, and the art to support it . . . married several wives in succession, within a short space of time and after having spent their estates, left them bankrupts in happiness, to curse those arts to which they had become victims" (J. 4).[40] While physiognomy was not to be considered "an infallible index," the author reasoned, faces were nonetheless more reliable than "insinuating manners" (J. 4) when it came to discerning character and protecting fortunes. "If the features of the mind correspond with the exterior," the author concluded, "it is more difficult to deceive, than by assuming fascinating manners, which being the offspring of education alone, are made with more facility subservient to deception than the physiognomy" (J. 4). Whereas "fascinating manners" could be acquired through education and culture, the physiognomic features of the face were neither so easily obtained nor manipulated. "Even if we grant that many have deceived in the world," another critic added, "it does not necessarily follow that their faces have not been faithful indices of their hearts; the greatest reason why deception so much prevails is, that people are too much prejudiced against physiognomy to submit to its direction" (M., "Physiognomy," 20). The problem was not too much faith in physiognomy, but rather, too little.

•   •   •

The relationship of physiognomy to the scientific racism of the later discourses of nineteenth-century anthropology, ethnology, and phrenology—which Jared Gardner calls America's "first unique contributions to science" (20)—thus appears to be more complex than simply helping whites misrecognize their face as superior. If physiognomy was one of the Enlightenment visual strategies for imaging the unseen, as Barbara Stafford contends, then what it seeks to make visible in early America are the subtle differences in moral character that, at times, translate into the signs of social origin or rank. "Individuals are clearly distinguished . . . in the different combinations and expressions of their features; and the same general observation is true of class and communities of men," the *Christian Disciple and Theological Review* observed in 1820. "Occupations and professions give to those engaged in them a specific, moral, and intellectual physiognomy; rank, wealth, and power produce on the habits and feelings of those who possess them, an effect which marks them, as distinctly as their external relations, from the poor, humble, or the abject" (147). The face distinguished poor from rich as well as vicious from virtuous. "The state of the purse impresses as striking a character upon the face of the rich and the poor," Richard Harlan argued, "as does vanity and abjection upon the powerful and the weak" (604). As John Wood Sweet notes, "white claims to racial preeminence became more urgent, rigid, and consistent in the 1820s and 30s, just as new democratic ideals were becoming established and new class divisions were becoming entrenched" (11). What we need to consider, then, is how the distinctions imagined by physiognomy participated in the shift from the model of genteel social relations dominant at the end of the eighteenth century in America to a model of social relations based upon modern conceptions of racial difference dominant at the end of the nineteenth century.[41]

The decades following the revolution, as scholars well know, were marked by volatile class dynamics in America as the distinction between elite and non-elite grew more tenuous.[42] The downward distribution of gentility, as the following chapter on Chesterfieldian civility will discuss, "confused rather than clarified the issue of class" (Bushman xv) as the legitimacy of distinction became more difficult to determine in a culture of genteel performance and social emulation.[43] In such a dynamic environment, the legibility of the face was crucial in mediating the social space of postrevolutionary America. The face served both as the pliable medium of polite performance and the durable marker of moral character and, as such, it was an important site in the struggle for distinction in postrevolutionary America. On the one hand, civility strategically managed the face in its genteel performances. The face was considered a social mask to be put on as the occasion demanded—even to the point of dissimulation—and its legibility was understood to be temporary and expedient. On the other hand, physiognomy claimed to see through such social masks. Its transposition in the determination of character from the voluntary performances of the individual to the involuntary features of his or her face was particularly attractive in a social space in which genteel distinction was often a matter of performance.[44] For those whose economic and social capital were most at risk in such a fluid social world—such as the established gentry— the logic, if not practice, of physiognomic distinction offered a means to establish moral character, embody social origin, and restrain the mobility enabled by the cultural capital of civility alone. The cultural representations of the face across a range of media—newspapers, periodicals, scientific lectures, conduct manuals, travel literature, moral criticism, plays, novels, portraits, sculpture, silhouettes, and engravings—as this and the following four chapters will explore—both reflected and shaped how distinction was imagined to operate in early America.

Chapter 2

Reading and Breeding

If judgment, wit and knowledge of mankind;
A polish'd style, and manners most refin'd,
Can make a letter, or a man complete,
All these in Chesterfield united meet;
But if an upright heart, religious truth,
Morals and honour, form the perfect youth,
From purer lights catch thou thy guiding ray,
And spurn the courtier, and his book away"
    —"On Chesterfield's Letters," *Massachusetts Magazine* (1789)

"When I read his [Chesterfield's] letters, I regret, a book so fatal
to the happiness of the community, so replete with poison to the
youthful mind, should ever have been published."
    —*The Hapless Orphan* (1793)

CIVILITY APPEARS AS an integral, yet complicated, feature of the political
and social transformations of the pre- and postrevolutionary periods in America.[1] As a social practice, civility was a prominent feature in the signification
of gentility, and its importance grew during the eighteenth century as the
traditional sources of gentility—wealth and birth—became increasingly "sur-
rounded and squeezed by other means of distinction, by cultivated, man-made
criteria having to do with manners, taste, and character" (Wood *Radicalism*
32).[2] With its models for personal behavior in public (such as politeness) and
its institutions for their practice and reproduction (such as face-to-face conversational spaces and print culture), civility regulated the body's movements
in its genteel performances and it structured the deferential nature of its social

relations. The discourse of politeness and its related vocabulary of breeding, refinement, sociability, and manners corresponded to a range of distinctive social and cultural practices in the eighteenth-century Atlantic world. Politeness was, Lawrence Klein explains, the "art or technique, governing the 'how' of social relations" (*Shaftesbury* 4).[3] Since politeness was often used as a rough equivalent to gentility, "it marked distinctions in the social order, signifying and congratulating an elite" (Klein "Politeness" 362). As Franklin's *Autobiography* demonstrates, the genteel body—the intense attention paid to the tone and cadence of the voice, the display of the countenance, the style of one's hair, the type of clothes one wore, the proper gestures, the appropriate conduct, and the grace of one's deportment—was a corporeal theater from which the drama of distinction was performed and observed in early America.

On the one hand, the discourse of politeness—with its structure of genteel deference, its historical association with the corrupt courts of Europe, and its emphasis on a politics of deceit and individual manipulation—has been identified as antithetical to the disinterestedness and egalitarianism of civic republicanism.[4] On the other, civility's culture of performance—its textually and visually reproducible codes of conduct, its capacity to bridge distinctions, and its ties to commercial self-interest—has been read as instrumental to the development of the role-playing self of postrevolutionary economic liberalism and its developing "bourgeois version of gentility" (Hemphill 80).[5] It has been suggested that civility's anti-republican values of sociability, formality, and exclusivity survived the Revolution's more radical impulses by retreating into private society (Shields), where their eventual diffusion as "vernacular gentility" (Bushman xiii) aided the formation of middle-class identity in antebellum America (Haltunnen).[6]

Perhaps no cultural form was more responsible for the downward distribution of civility in postrevolutionary America than Lord Chesterfield's *Letters* (1774). "If the Declaration of Independence in 1776 did not in itself cause much a stir in manners," C. Dallett Hemphill explains, "the nearly contemporaneous American publication (in 1775) of Lord Chesterfield's *Letters of Advice to His Son*, was quite important" (70). When the various authorized and unauthorized editions, adaptations, and abridgments are counted, the *Letters* went through no less than thirty editions in America between 1775 and 1800 (Gulick), prompting Richard Bushman to appoint Chesterfield as "the foremost teacher of fine manners in the eighteenth century" (30) and Karen Haltunnen to pronounce the *Letters* as "the most important influence on nineteenth-century American etiquette" (94). Between 1775 and 1790, Chesterfield's *Letters* was among "the most frequently reprinted titles in America" (Reilly and Hall 398).[7]

In what follows, the discourse surrounding Chesterfield's *Letters* in post-revolutionary America appears as a key element in the survival of genteel distinction. The initial cultural response to Chesterfield—particularly the specific reference to Chesterfield in the literary depiction of the seducer—may have helped civility re-imagine and retain its pre-revolutionary function in structuring social relations in two ways. First, civility's anti-republicanism becomes associated with immorality, dissimulation, and self-interest (especially rapid social and political mobility) rather than exclusivity; second, the visibility of distinction is relocated away from the genteel performances of the body and on to the permanent and unalterable features of the body, particularly the face.

The cultural response to Chesterfieldianism in postrevolutionary America, I want to suggest, reflects a struggle over how distinction would operate in the social space of early America and, more broadly, how culture—specifically literature—would participate in that struggle (as an agent in the reproduction or in the transformation of the social order). Chesterfield was at the center of this struggle because his *Letters* were thought to offer those who either had lost or never had superior social status a way of escaping the limits of social condition. The self-assurance and performance of Chesterfieldian civility plays on what Pierre Bourdieu calls "the relative autonomy of the symbolic (i.e., of the capacity to make and perceive representations) . . . to impose a self-representation normally associated with a higher condition and to win for it the acceptance and recognition which make it a legitimate, objective representation" (253). If books such as Chesterfield's *Letters* contributed to the transformation of distinction in early America—what Mercy Otis Warren would describe as a "revolution in manners" (quoted in Davies 225)—by distributing a model of civility less dependent on economic or social capital and thus less subject to the institutions and networks traditionally responsible for reproducing such capital (such as family, state, and church), other cultural forms, such as Royall Tyler's *The Contrast* and Hannah Foster's *The Coquette* (discussed in Chapter 3), imagined social spaces in which the individual performances and mobility of Chesterfieldian civility would be restrained by the apparent ineradicability of social origin on the face.

Chesterfield in America

The widespread publication of Chesterfield's *Letters* in America not only diffused the principles of politeness to an aspiring middling sort, it promoted the idea that dissimulation, particularly command of one's countenance, was integral to gentility itself. The chief lesson the *Letters* taught was "to cultivate appearances—even, when necessary—to dissimulate" (Hemphill 71). Throughout the *Letters*, Chesterfield reminds his son of the importance of dissembling his facial expressions.[8] In the most widely reprinted adaptation of Chesterfield's *Letters* in America, the *Principles of Politeness and of Knowing the World* (1778), he recommends mastering "that coolness of mind and evenness of countenance, which prevents a discovery of our sentiments, by our words, our actions, or our looks" (*Principles of Politeness* 48). "Care, with a little reflection," Chesterfield tells his son, "will soon give you this mastery of your temper and countenance" (*Principles of Politeness* 48). Chesterfield's calculating "advice to watch others' faces while keeping a guard on one's own was new" and it underscores "the role played by manipulation of the outward self in the developing bourgeois version of gentility" (Hemphill 80).[9] Manipulating one's face, however, like mastering one's manners, required knowing what kind of mask the situation demanded. A gentleman had to have "a countenance adapted to the occasion" (*Letters* 1775 3:206). "In the course of the world, a man must very often put on an easy, frank countenance, upon very disagreeable occasions," Chesterfield observed, and "he must seem well pleased, when he is very much otherwise; he must be able to accost and receive with smiles, those whom he would much rather meet with swords" (*Letters* 1775 3:169). "Few people have penetration to observe, or even concern enough to examine beyond the exterior," Chesterfield remarked, continuing, "they take their notions from the surface, and go no deeper, they commend, as the gentlest and best natured man in the world, that man who has the most engaging exterior manner, though they have been but once in his company. An air, a tone of voice, a composure of countenance to mildness and softness, which are all easily acquired, do the business" (*Letters* 1775 3:85). For Chesterfield, the "composure of countenance" required for dissimulation signified a superior form of gentility that was associated not merely with the court, but with bustling urban centers and the risky world of commerce.[10] "Dissimulation," he explains, "introduced that habit of politeness which distinguishes the courtier from the country gentleman" (*Letters* 1775 2:86) because any man "who cannot command his temper, his attention, and his countenance should not think of being a man of business" (*Letters* 1775 4:183). To be truly genteel in an era of burgeoning mercantile capitalism, Chesterfield suggests, is to know how to dissemble one's face.[11] Thus, at the core of the most influential model of genteel distinction for late eighteenth- and nineteenth-century America was the unequivocal promotion of an insincere relationship between character and the face.

Although the democratization of genteel culture propelled by the publication of Chesterfield's *Letters* undoubtedly threatened the exclusivity of polite society (at least fourteen editions of the *Principles of Politeness* were printed in America before 1800), it was Chesterfield's immorality—especially his equation of social power with the capacity to dissimulate one's permanent character—that Anglo-American critics immediately targeted for censure.[12] As early as June 1775, the *Pennsylvania Magazine* began reprinting Hester Chapone's anti-Chesterfieldian remarks as "a seasonable antidote to the poison diffused by" the *Letters*. The transatlantic publication of Samuel Pratt's anti-Chesterfieldian novel, *The Pupil of Pleasure* in London (1776; 1777), Philadelphia (1778), and Boston (1780), circulated the notion that "the general stigma upon these Letters has been, that they are calculated to recommend deceit, and to conceal the most destructive hypocrisy, under the smiling aspect, plausible exterior, fair-seeming sentiments, and a complacent flexibility" (Melmoth iv).[13] "Politeness . . . like lord Chesterfield's," the Reverend John Bennett explained to the 1792 readers of *American Museum*, was entirely "made up of dissimulation" ("Letter" 139).[14] Bennett wished that "the memory of his immoral graces, and his refined dissimulation" would "sleep for ever with him in his grave" (*Strictures* 5). No fewer than ten American editions of Bennett's *Letters* were published by 1818, each calling on readers "to burn" Chesterfield's books (*Letters* 2:50). Likewise, John Burton warned American readers in 1794 that Chesterfield's two "grand maxims are—to conceal his own opinions, but artfully discover those of the persons with whom he should have any concerns—and to disguise his own temper" (259). According to Burton, Chesterfield's *Letters* did little more than endorse "the practice of dissimulation for the purpose of promoting . . . worldly interest" (258). His immoral "creed" of "hypocrisy, fornication, and adultery," the 1786 *New Haven Gazette and Connecticut Magazine* protested, enlisted "the graces of civility" in the pursuit of self-interest ("New Office" 327).[15] In fact, "the malignant effects of Lord Chesterfield's scheme of education" were significant enough for Timothy Dwight to vituperate from the pulpit its "great doctrine" of self-gratification as "the basis of the most winning, most deceitful, and most ruinous system of evil, hitherto devised by the great adversary of men" (15). If gentility had been characterized formerly by pleasing others, now it was in danger of being epitomized by pleasing oneself. Whether those personal pleasures were defined in terms of political, commercial, or sexual interests, Chesterfield's model of genteel conduct opposed the republican ideal of civic virtue based on disinterest (Lewis "The Republican Wife" 690).

As elite postrevolutionary republicans such as Mercy Otis Warren lambasted Chesterfield's promotion of genteel dissimulation and immorality in the American press, others—such as an anonymous author from Easton, Maryland—urged the public to consider the effects Chesterfield might have on those who lacked the moral character necessary to discern "that under a theory of politeness would be introduced a system at professed variance with our morality" ("Remarks" 89). The author nervously predicted to his readership that, "The arts of printers will disseminate the work in places where its test, public opinion, cannot accompany it—it may be read in the country; and if there are colonies at a distance, where the vibrations and operations of public opinion can be but feebly felt, such a book will there find admission, and, if as artful as these letters, may be relished" ("Remarks" 90). As both people and print exceeded the reach of existing institutional sources of moral authority—such as family, school, and church—the spread of Chesterfieldianism exacerbated concerns over uninstructed individual reading practice.[16]

The widespread adoption of Chesterfield, our anonymous author from Easton concluded, should remind people in particular "to guard against deception" for "the same people who could be polite" might also be, at the same time, indecorous and dishonest ("Remarks" 91). Indeed, those who practiced dissimulation, John Burton noted, often "assume a deportment, contrary to their station; and step out of their own sphere in order to act a part for which they are not qualified, by genius, education, or fortune" (256). "To affect the manners of a station, superior to our own, is absurd," Burton declared. Those "who behave in a manner unbecoming their situation, and assume a part in the great drama of life, not adapted to their abilities or station," he continued, "must unavoidably incur the censure of affectation" (Burton 266). Burton's doctrine of social immobility advised inferiors to learn "contentment in whatever station they are placed" (265) rather than ape the manners of their superiors. "Were the influence of these Letters confined to those in the same rank of life with the person to whom they are addressed, perhaps the cause of virtue would be very little injured by them," William Crawford reasoned, "but the reader, let his station be ever so different, if he brings himself to approve of the licentious instructions they contain, though he does not consider them as either addressed or applicable to himself, will feel insensibly their pernicious effects on his own conduct" (97). What makes the *Letters* immoral,

Burton and Crawford suggest, is how their distribution disassociates the codes of superior "station" and "rank" from high social origin. The *Letters* were considered dangerous because the social origin of their actual reader was usually beneath that of their implied reader.

Although the *Letters'* imagined destabilization of the social order was registered on both sides of the Atlantic, Chesterfieldianism's effects were particularly pronounced in postrevolutionary America. The revolution fragmented a colonial social order based primarily on kinship and politics and left the new democracy without a single social structure in which people could array themselves. With the demise of legally enforced sumptuary distinction, primogeniture, and fee tail tenure, the rise in economic and cultural capital among the middling as well as their expanding access to consumer goods, increased immigration from Europe, the disruption of familial and social networks by the Atlantic, and the growth of a print culture that made the codes for civility more broadly accessible, the line demarcating elite from nonelite was fading in 1790s America.[17] During the revolutionary era "the gap between the middling sort and the elite so evident in the earlier period was narrowing" (Hemphill 74) so that "by the end of the eighteenth century, fears about dissimulation suffused American culture" (Bullock 254). It seemed as if almost any man, even the most vulgar and immoral, could pass himself off as a gentleman so long as he had a little wit and learning, a fashionable appearance, and a well-rehearsed genteel persona (Shields 276).[18] "Persons of every description, in town and country, cannot be too much on their guard against the company of strangers," the *American Herald* warned in 1786, for "the artifices, by which villains introduce themselves, are various" and "they assume so many different shapes, personating clergymen, gentlemen, men of business, seamen, [and] countrymen" ("New York" 3). The necessity of such vigilance was corroborated by the *Philadelphia Repository and Weekly Register* when it informed its readers of how a man assumed a character of a person of respectability, married several wives in succession, and, after having spent their estates, left them bankrupt.[19] If supporters reasoned that the publication of Chesterfield's *Letters* promised a republic of refined gentleman, critics responded by claiming that Chesterfieldianism was threatening to deliver a nation of duplicitous rakes, rogues, and seducers. The exemplary image of gradual social mobility contained within Franklin's polite performances of character—what Benjamin Vaughan referred to in the *Autobiography* as "the propriety of every man's waiting for his time for appearing upon the stage of the world" (*F* 82)—was being challenged by one of a more rapid mobility characterized by dissimulation and associated with the print culture of Chesterfieldianism.

"The Loss of All Distinction"

The anti-Chesterfieldian harangues of Anglophone moralists and ministers making their way into American newspapers, periodicals, and presses during the last quarter of the eighteenth century find their literary counterpart in postrevolutionary plays such as *The Gubernatocial Collection, a Farce . . . Which Point Out the Variety of Characters That Have Arisen in the Political Uproar, Since the Confusion of Distinctions* (1779); *Sans Souci, Alias Free and Easy: Or An Evening's Peep into a Polite Circle* (1785); and Royall Tyler's *The Contrast* (1787). Each of these plays imagines postrevolutionary America as a fluid, at times contentious, social space and specifically identify such instability with Chesterfield.[20] *The Gubernatocial Collection*, for instance, is an odd, fragmented farce in which old gentility and "new-fangled gentry" (6) struggle for distinction. The "upstart gentry" (7) in *The Gubernatocial Collection* are associated with the immorality, dissimulation, and self-interest of Chesterfieldian civility. Those who have "read Chesterfield" (9), such as the allegorically named seducers, Mr. Pomposity and Count Dipper Dapper, acquire a "fund of knowledge" (9) that teaches them primarily how and where to seduce women. Although characters such as Esquire Runt insist that these "new-fangled gentry" "have no breeding" (6), the opportunistic accumulation of economic capital during the revolution and the conspicuous display of the cultural capital of civility after it challenge the social capital of old gentility and blur the distinction between the established elite and their perceived inferiors. "In this town they don't make proper / distinction between gentlemen of family, fortune and education, / and the common ruff scruff," Mr. Calfs-Head complains, "I see many of these upstart gentry / here, that were not known before the war, by jubbing and trading / about they have got a little paper money, and set themselves up to / be great folks—Why here's tavern-keepers, taylors, shoemakers, / skippers of vessels, negro lawyers, and the devil does not know / what all—Never mind it, I hope to see the time when every one / will know their place" (7). The desire for a social order in which "every one / will know their place" in postrevolutionary America is precisely what *The Gubernatocial Collection* hopes to fulfill through its allegorical satire. As the preface informs spectators, the play intends: "To give Mankind a just idea of themselves" so that they might be prevented from looking upon "their superiors with indifference" (1). To have such a declaration in the play's preface demonstrates how *The Gubernatocial Collection* seeks to overcome the anti-theatrical conditions of early American dramatic production and justify its performance by promising to preserve social hierarchy through the display of flat, emblematic character types.

Like *The Gubernatocial Collection*, the satire *Sans Souci* also reflects the struggle for distinction in postrevolutionary America; it, too, singles out Chesterfield in its characterization of upstart gentry. Young Forward and Little Pert, for instance, open the play by celebrating the Sans Souci, that "free and easy" "essence of Chesterfield" (3).[21] Masters of "the school of politeness," Pert and Forward are characterized as social revolutionaries, immoral radicals who seek to overthrow the "rigid manners" of republicanism. "D—n the old musty rules of decency and decorum" (4), Pert declares, as he and Forward eye potential sexual conquests from within their female "circle of temptations" (5). "The independence I aim at," he asserts, is that "free and easy air which so distinguishes the man of fashion from the self-formal republican" (4). While the stuffy "republican heroine" complains how the Sans Souci has plunged America into "the utmost excesses of dissipation" (11), her prudishness is less the target of *Sans Souci's* satire than the rising fashionable set who flatter each other that they have "improved on Chesterfield" (10). Chesterfieldianism in *Sans Souci* is represented as extending the more radical impulses of democracy and transforming them into a social revolution of manners. Like *The Gubernatocial Collection*, *Sans Souci* imagines postrevolutionary America as a turbulent social space in which "all distinctions will be lost in the leveling spirit of republicanism" (9).

Yet, what makes the depiction of Chesterfieldianism in *The Gubernatocial Collection* and *Sans Souci* remarkable is the fact that America and Britain seem to matter more as the locations for alternative social spaces and practices than they do as models for imagined national affiliation.[22] America and Britain are contrasted for the social spaces they contain and for the ways in which discourses such as Chesterfieldianism are imagined to relate to the dominant social order. In *The Gubernatocial Collection* and *Sans Souci*, foppish characters embrace Britain for the cosmopolitan social space it supposedly houses and for the mobility that it allegedly affords. In Britain, manners can supposedly mask low social origin. Alternatively, these same Chesterfieldian characters reject America as a rigidly defined colonial social space that inhibits mobility. America is imagined as a space in which manners cannot possibly overcome social origin (which is precisely the social crisis these plays address).

The Gubernatocial Collection's seducing Chesterfieldian, Mr. Pomposity, for example, can only forget "that I was brought up to the external ornament of books" (8) while in London. Conversely, in America, Pomposity remains a lowly bookbinder. However "accomplished I may be," Pomposity says, "I can't forget / when I walk the Boston streets [illeg.] I was brought up a book-binder" (9). Pomposity resents "this wooden / country" (8) for insisting on the durability of his low social origin. Similarly, the fashionable set of *Sans Souci* imagines America as antithetical to a cosmopolitan social space identi-fied with Europe. The old republican insistence on "national manners" and "national debts" was pertinent during the revolution, but now, Jemmy Satirist contends, independence should be "high court independence—independence of every restraint" (19). Dr. Gallant agrees, adding that "all political distinc-tions should be buried" in favor of a modern republicanism based on "socia-bility" (20). *The Gubernatocial Collection* and *Sans Souci* disavow the threat of Chesterfieldian social climbers by fantasizing about social immobility in terms of the production of national difference. If both plays worry about the "loss of all distinction" to emerging cosmopolitan social spaces, the characters they imagine as most socially mobile (such as the Chesterfieldian Pomposity) turn out to be the ones who articulate distinction in terms of a less mobile, national space. Although it is unclear why or how America reminds Pomposity of his low social origin, it does. *The Gubernatocial Collection* and *Sans Souci* associ-ate the transformation of distinction with Chesterfieldianism, then disavow the threat of social equality it promises by defining its desired social spaces in terms of national difference. America becomes a nation, in other words, because it disavows the fluidity of its own social space.

The Contrast's "Unpolished American"

While allegorical farces such as *The Gubernatocial Collection* and *Sans Souci* understand Chesterfieldianism as a form of cultural capital deployed by social aspirants seeking to escape their low social origin, Royall Tyler's *The Contrast* addresses, in a much more substantial way, the problems associated with an alternative social trajectory associated with Chesterfieldianism.[23] *The Con-trast* reveals the problem when Chesterfieldianism is distributed to and by a dissembling white male who finds himself excluded from his former modes of distinction—wealth and the social capital of familial reputation. Having squandered his father's estate on gambling debts in Europe, the play's seducer,

Van Dumpling, returns to America literally transformed into a new man: the impoverished Chesterfieldian Billy Dimple. Dimple devotes his mornings to reading "Chesterfield's letters," his days to writing books on refinement, and his nights to chasing women (Tyler 11). While Dimple may fool the undiscerning father figure, Van Rough, his initial target, Maria Van Rough, is able to distinguish the virtuous Colonel Manlys of the world from the vicious Billy Dimples through her judicious reading. "The contrast" between "the good sense of her books" and "the flimsiness of her love letters" from Dimple (Tyler 11) enables Maria to detect his undissembled character as transparently and antithetically as his emblematic name would seem to suggest. Upon Dimple's return from England, Maria "watched his conduct and conversation" and found that he had "acquired the wickedness of Lovelace without his wit" (Tyler 11).

Maria's discernment of Dimple's character from her reading practice rather than from his Chesterfieldian performances allows her to avoid the nearly tragic fates of the coquettish Letitia and Charlotte, who barely escape moral and financial ruin. Maria's literary reading empowers her (much to the consternation of her money-driven father) to "metamorphose[d]" Billy Dimple from an eligible and seemingly desirable bachelor into "a flippant, pallid, polite beau" (Tyler 11).[24] Tyler's choice of the word "metamorphosed" reminds us that if books such as Chesterfield's *Letters* could facilitate the Protean shapeshifting of a male seducer like Dimple, they might also be able to pull off the mask and revert him back to his "natural" state. Just in case anybody misses this point, Dimple's final words at the play's close remind the audience that the Van Dumpling name was the real mask. Unsurprisingly, Van Dumpling prefers his newly acquired life as Billy Dimple and unapologetically exits the play in the same fashion as he entered it: "a gentleman who has read Chesterfield" (Tyler 56).

As I suggested above, Billy Dimple menaces more than Maria's sentimental wedding dreams and her father's ample real estate. He also reveals how Chesterfieldianism has as much to do with the distributive effects of print on distinction as it does with seduction and marriage. Dimple not only exploits the performative model of genteel distinction, but, as the author of a book of polite manners himself, he threatens to extend it downward to two servant characters.[25] In act five, scene one, for instance, Dimple's foppish servant Jessamy (who emulates his master by reading Chesterfield) tries to refine Colonel Manly's country-bumpkin servant Jonathan. He coaches the Yankee Jonathan in the "graces of person"—such as the Chesterfieldian directive to cut "off our nails at top, in small segments of circles" (Tyler 49)—in a lesson that culminates with his advice on the appropriate timing and quality of laughter at the theater. Using his master's book, which Dimple designed so that "the ignorant may know where to laugh" (50), Jessamy tries to instruct Jonathan on how to "regulate your laugh" (49). The implicit purpose of Dimple's book, according to Jessamy, is "to see the audience smile together" (50) so that the managed performances of artificial response would replace the cacophony of natural laughter.

Yet, it appears as if no amount of genteel instruction can overcome the "natural" difference of Jonathan's laugh. In fact, Tyler draws attention to this failure of individual volition by conflating the theological and social meanings of the word "grace" throughout the scene. After Jessamy informs Jonathan that he lacks "the Graces" necessary to romance a woman, for example, Jonathan wonders what his conversion has to do with his courtship (49). Tyler's joke suggests that for people like Jonathan attaining social grace might be more a matter of divine intervention than personal performance. Indeed, the scene demonstrates how books that seek to regulate the face of the subordinate—with its "directions [of] how to manage the muscles" and "purse the mouth into a smile" (51)—will inevitably fail just as Jonathan fails to laugh gracefully in the scene. "With a few years' close application," Jessamy remarks sarcastically to Jonathan at the end of the scene, "you may be able to smile gracefully" (51). Such mockery affirms that natural, corporeal differences (such as Jonathan's specifically inappropriate laugh and his inability to manage his face) are ineradicable, the central point that the rest of the play dramatizes. Gentility cannot be acquired from a book, Tyler suggests, because no amount of artificial performance can eliminate supposedly natural and durable differences in station, gender, or education.[26] The fact that a critique of print culture's distribution of the codes of distinction was being launched from Tyler's play discloses the extent to which *The Contrast* was aligned with an elite Federalist politics (which sought to reestablish and further entrench those social differences through its political policy).[27] It also demonstrates how dramatic form could literally embody those visible differences and perform them on stage in a way that print could only simulate technologically in its representation of dialect, employment of illustrations, and inclusion of portrait frontispieces.[28]

This last difference is vitally important because the play, at least as it was performed in 1787, probably extended beyond the literate community and may have included the illiterate as well.[29] The American viewer or reader who identified with the proper and stratified triumphs of the virtuous and Washingtonesque Colonel Manly and his patriotic servant Jonathan also accepted the rejection of European manners as artificial and the endorsement of "natural" appearance as a legitimate visible sign of distinction. So while the identification of spectators with the proto-Yankee Jonathan may have appeared to have been a home-spun American triumph over the falsity and artificiality of British aristocracy and its French-inspired manners, it was also a rejection of a powerful norm of distinction based on the performance of visible codes whose access was limited only by literacy or access to literacy (as Benjamin Franklin's *Autobiography* so wonderfully advocates and as Hugh Henry Brackenridge's *Modern Chivalry* so tirelessly satirizes). To identify with Jonathan's refusal of Jessamy on national terms was also to reject a performative model of upward social mobility facilitated by books on social terms.

Tyler's *The Contrast* not only identifies print's complicity in dissimulation by associating the unregulated diffusion of its books of politeness with the Chesterfieldian seducer, it demonstrates how dramatic literature might counter such genteel performances by emphasizing the body's "natural" forms of distinction instead (as we saw with Jonathan's failure to learn how to manage his laughter and his face). As Jeffrey Richards notes, "Tyler sought in *The Contrast* particularly to justify the ways of the theatre to his fellow Americans against religious prohibitions" (299) and in an early prologue to *The Contrast*, Tyler stresses "the moral dimension of drama" (Richards 298) in strikingly visual terms. Tyler hoped *The Contrast* would "shew the vile intentions of the mind" and "paint the real vices of mankind" through "black examples drawn with wondrous skill" (quoted in Richards 298, 299).

If the contrast of *The Contrast* is really between these two competing modes of accounting for distinction—the artificial and widely accessible codes of Billy Dimple's Chesterfieldian performances and the apparently natural distinction of Colonel Manly's virtuous gentility—then Peter Maverick's original 1790 frontispiece engraving after William Dunlap's drawing (Figure 17) displays just how instrumental Jonathan's body is toward the latter's triumph.[30] As Cathy Davidson notes, "the early theatrical success of *The Contrast* derived not from Manly but from Jonathan" and Maverick's engraving of the last scene of act five prominently features his character (214). In the image an angry— if diminutive—Jonathan stands comically, fists raised, midway between the raised sword of the overheated, yet still foppish Dimple and the lowered sword of the cool-headed Manly. The engraving, which places Jonathan at the center of the composition, stages the battle between Manly and Dimple as if the two were fighting over Jonathan as much as they were over Manly's sister, Charlotte.

Figure 17. Frontispiece for Royall Tyler, *The Contrast* (Philadelphia: Thomas Wignell, 1790). William Dunlap (designer) and Peter Maverick (engraver). Image courtesy of the Library Company of Philadelphia.

Manly's triumph in this contest is evident by Jonathan's emulative posture and by the reproduction of his loyal declaration in the caption below, and, perhaps more important, by how the engraving pictures Jonathan's final repudiation of Dimple. The engraving spotlights Jonathan standing directly in front of a closed door whose casement frames his face as if it were a profile painting. This effect is accentuated by the portrait bust attached to the top of the door's impediment that hovers directly above Jonathan's head. On the one hand, the portrait bust's wigged hair and its prominent display of forehead demonstrate how the heads of Manly, Van Rough, and Dimple might be confused visually; on the other, the portrait bust also offers a sharp contrast to the "naturally" wild hair and noticeably smaller forehead of Jonathan. Indeed, the engraving represents the contrast between Manly and Dimple as one between Jonathan and Dimple. Thus, the victory of "natural" corporeal differences over Chesterfieldianism is not embodied by Manly, as one might expect, but by Jonathan. His "dirty appearance, his bare-knuckles pose, and even his thick, dark, natural hair," Trish Loughran observes, stand out strikingly against the powdered wigs of the three other men portrayed here (192). By grounding distinction in the servant body's "natural" vocalic and physical differences, Jonathan's body in Tyler's *The Contrast*, as Dunlap and Maverick's illustration understands so well, unifies master and servant—without dissolving the distinction between them—in their patriotic fight against Chesterfieldianism's equation of genteel distinction and polite performance.

•   •   •

The same type of Chesterfieldian dissembler featured in Tyler's *The Contrast* and criticized by Anglo-American ministers and moralists also preoccupied many of the nation's dramatists and novelists at the end of the eighteenth century. Hannah Foster's *The Coquette* (1797), for example, specifically identifies its financially challenged seducer, Peter Sanford, as a "Chesterfieldian" (Foster 1996: 194) and William Hill Brown's *The Power of Sympathy* (1789) admonishes its readers to beware of men like Sanford who compose themselves "on the Chesterfieldian system" (Brown 1996: 53). The 1793 seduction novel, *The Hapless Orphan*, criticized "that celebrated courtier, Lord Chesterfield" (37) for "instructing his son in the arts of seduction and adultery" and producing the conditions under which "a character practiced in deception, and educated in intrigue, can be styled *accomplished*" (38). From Billy Dimple to Colonel Egerton in James Fenimore Cooper's *Precaution* (1820), the dissimulating

Chesterfieldian seducer became a stock literary character within early American seduction literature, one who, to use Amy Lang's formulation, "while rarely acknowledged as figures of class per se, . . . are nonetheless conventional literary representations" (88).[31] William Dunlap's Oxford-educated murderer in *The Father; Or American Shandyism* (1789) and the exceptionally well-read highway robber in Tabitha Tenney's *Female Quixotism* (1801) are but two examples of how the seducing male dissimulator deployed genteel manners and book smarts to conceal their low social origin and criminal behavior.

William Hill Brown's *The Power of Sympathy* (1789), for example, repeatedly criticizes Chesterfieldianism and associates it with a variety of smooth-talking seducers from the fashionable and polite "Squire Billy" (28) to "the flattery and dissimulation of Martin" (39) and "the gay Williams" (50). Chesterfield is pilloried in Brown's novel, just as he was in the postrevolutionary periodical press, for facilitating the social mobility of inferiors. "The ridiculous figure of some of our young gentleman," Mrs. Holmes complains in letter 29, "who affect to square their conduct by his Lordship's principles of politeness . . . arises, not so much from their putting on this foreign dress, as from their ignorance or vanity in pretending to imitate those rules which were designed for an English nobleman" (54). Similar to the postrevolutionary dramas discussed above, Mrs. Holmes identifies the threat of Chesterfieldianism in social more than national terms. What makes these "young gentlemen" absurd is not their pretensions to Chesterfield's Englishness—"not so much from their putting on this foreign dress"—but their claims to his nobility. The ridiculousness of their behavior consists in their attempts to pretend that the distinction of birth (that of "an English nobleman") might be acquired by mere polite performance. Social aspirants who strive for such distinction through Chesterfieldian civility, she concludes, would be better served by "minding their [own] business" (54). "This affectation of fine breeding," she adds, "is destructive to morals. Dissimulation and insincerity are connected with its tenets; and are mutually inculcated with the art of pleasing" (54). Similar to the complaints registered by many of the Anglo-American moral critics mentioned above, William Hill Brown condemns Chesterfield for his immorality, dissimulation, and encouragement of rapid social mobility.

The Power of Sympathy, however, also explores how Chesterfieldianism contributes to the alternative social trajectory of the downward mobility of established gentry. The Honourable Harrington's seduction of Maria Fawcett, for example, is attributed in part to Chesterfieldian "flattery" (68). The elder Harrington blames the affair on his adoption of the Chesterfieldian "maxim" to acquire "a knowledge of the world" (69). "It was my policy," he admits, "to flatter the world, and exhibit a fair outside—for I was in love with Amelia—My licentious amour with Maria was secret" (70). The elder Harrington's remarks are telling for they not only associate his past seduction and its present concealment to his adoption of Chesterfieldian dissimulation, but they disclose how he strategically uses a language of feeling (his feelings "burst" and tears are shed in the letter [71]) to generate pity and defend himself from public censure (71). Thus, even after the affair is exposed, Harrington remains what he always has been: a Chesterfieldian dissembler who will don the mask and say what he must in order to pursue his own self-interests. Whether or not the affair jeopardizes the social capital of the "Honorable" Mr. Harrington matters less to *The Power of Sympathy* than the fact that its eventual exposure annihilates his family. Consequently, whatever capital he may have left to spend will not be reproduced, as both of his children die before him. In the struggle for distinction, Brown suggests that those who legitimate cultural capital—such as Chesterfieldian civility in the pursuit of personal pleasure—will ultimately sacrifice their own social and economic capital. *The Power of Sympathy* thus addresses both of the primary social trajectories associated with Chesterfieldianism in postrevolutionary American culture: the rapid upward mobility of inferiors (who strive for distinction by trying to convert cultural capital into the economic or social capital they lack) and the rapid downward mobility of superiors (who have risked or already lost their economic or social capital).

•   •   •

The specific invocation of Chesterfield alongside the figure of the dissimulating seducer by Hill Brown and other postrevolutionary authors was part of a more general struggle over how distinction would be imagined to operate in the social space of early America. As Hill Brown's novel suggests, this struggle was understood at times as one between the genteel community and those aspirants outside it. Yet, at other times, the struggle was cast as one between elements within the genteel community. In either case, the Chesterfieldian seducer was presented as someone who signified or legitimated a false form of gentility in the eyes of established gentry because his individual, frequently dissembling, performances privileged the cultural capital of civility rather than social or economic capital in the signification of genteel distinction. The initial negative response to Chesterfield's *Letters* in the postrevolutionary press and the specificity of Chesterfieldianism in the postrevolutionary literary depiction of the seducer reflect a concern with how the distributive effects of print culture, when coupled with unregulated reading practices, were transforming the residual social order of colonial gentility. Yet, by attacking Chesterfieldianism for its immorality, dissimulation, and self-interest—particularly its encouragement of rapid social mobility through seduction—these texts shifted the anti-republican elements of civility away from its exclusivity. In short, they made Chesterfieldianism's democratization of genteel culture appear anti-democratic and at times anti-American.

The discourse surrounding Chesterfieldianism in the years following the revolution discloses how the struggle over distinction was also a struggle over the relationship of culture to distinction, particularly the relationship of cultural capital to mobility. The Chesterfieldian seducer found within so many postrevolutionary seduction narratives not only equated gentility with dissimulation, he embodied the perceived threat of rapid mobility generated by the cultural capital of civility alone. The individual polite performances of Chesterfieldianism thus offered a legitimate form of gentility in which cultural capital would work independent of, rather than alongside, prior institutions for genteel distinction (namely, the familial and social networks of established gentry). The following chapter explores how postrevolutionary literature, particularly the seduction novel, would respond to Chesterfieldianism and examines the ways in which these cultural forms would position themselves against the fluidity, social emulation, and individual possibility so characteristic of the era's more general culture of performance. As the next chapter's discussion of the postrevolutionary seduction novel will demonstrate, civility's formerly anti-republican value of exclusivity would be maintained, despite the diffusion of its manners, by trying to relocate the visibility of distinction from the genteel, yet voluntary, performances of the body to the more involuntary features of the face.

Chapter 3

The Face of Seduction

THE ANSWER. BY A YOUNG LADY.

Teach me, my Friend, to understand
A gen'rous, from designing, Man;
For I have heard wise people say,
"Most men are formed to betray."

Now these, I think, we must conclude,
Are not the vulgar, rough, nor rude,
From such, the modest Virgin flies,
And Rakes and Foplings all despise.

Deceivers must, I think, inherit
External grace, truth, judgment, merit—
Now tell me, SALLY, if you can,
A virtuous, from a cunning, Man.

Physiognomy is oft deceiving;
An art, in which I'm unbelieving:
You must some safer rule point out;
And, till you do, I still will doubt.

THE REPLY

There's truth, I own, in what you say;
   Where Delicacy rules,
A Lady, blushing turns away
   From Knaves, and Fops, and Fools.

Sometimes a Fool doth look sedate,
   A Coxcomb looks demure:
A knowing look and shallow pate
   Do sometimes meet, 'tis sure.

But gen'rally, I think, you'll find
   The face and heart agree:
The eye's window of the mind,
   Thro' which the soul we see.
      —Sarah Anderson Hasting, *Poems on Different Subjects,* 1808

IN THE PRECEDING chapter, I suggested that the discourse surrounding Chesterfieldianism during the postrevolutionary era was part of a more general struggle over how distinction would be imagined to operate within the social space of early America and more broadly how culture, specifically literature, might participate in that struggle. Chesterfield's *Letters* downwardly distributed a model of civility less dependent on economic or social capital, thus less subject to the institutions and networks traditionally responsible for reproducing such capital (such as those associated with family, church, and state). As texts such as *The Contrast* and *The Power of Sympathy* demonstrate, criticism of the *Letters*—whether in periodical, dramatic, or fictional form— often represented the struggle between the cultural capital of social aspirants and the social capital of established gentry in terms of seduction.

Seduction, of course, was a staple of postrevolutionary sentimental fiction. Most sentimental fiction in America and "more than half of the novels of the early national period" were stories of seduction (Tennenhouse *Importance* 45). Seduction spun many of these sentimental plots, Cathy Davidson argues, because it "set forth and summed up crucial aspects of the society" (106). The political import of the seduction novel has been the subject of a number of studies that consider how these narratives mediate notions of democratic citizenship and national belonging through the discourse of sentimentalism and its related vocabulary of sensibility, sympathy, and fellow feeling.[1] Leonard Tennenhouse, however, contends that the nation for whom the sentimental novel of seduction produces feeling should be understood not merely as a political entity, but as part of a diasporic English culture. One reason seduction fiction was so popular in the new republic, he claims, was because it "offered both British and American readerships experiments in imagining who could in fact marry whom" (Tennenhouse 45). "At stake in these experiments," Tennenhouse explains "was the basis of civil society—the rules for exchanging women—that constituted kinship relations between men" (45). While the postrevolutionary seduction novel certainly reflects how British rules governing kinship relationships were transformed in the American context, it also addresses a more fundamental problem related to the fragmentation of families that accompanied the British diaspora in America: how do you discern the character of an unknown or dissembling man in the absence of established forms of distinction? And, more broadly, would reading novels—a practice considered analogous to reading men during the period—illuminate or obscure knowledge of a person's moral character and social origin in the actual world? These questions, as the following pages will demonstrate, were particularly important to the seduction novel as it emerged in postrevolutionary America. Their significance to the genre should prompt us to consider not only how these novels explore the possibilities or limitations of the new democracy, but how they imagine the social space of that democracy.

Postrevolutionary seduction fiction frequently associated the dissembling male seducer with the cultural capital of Chesterfieldian civility, and his individual polite performances were imagined as unaffected by either the vigilance of parental surveillance or the reputation assigned by familial, moral, and social networks.[2] Although not every postrevolutionary seduction novel featured a Chesterfieldian seducer, those that did typically assigned him one of the two social trajectories identified in *The Power of Sympathy* in the previous chapter: the rapid upward mobility of inferiors (who strive for distinction by trying to convert their cultural capital into the economic or social capital they lack) and the rapid downward mobility of superiors (who seek to reclaim or preserve distinction by trying to secure economic capital that they have either jeopardized or have already lost).[3] Novels such as Hugh Henry Brackenridge's *Modern Chivalry* (1792–1815) and Tabitha Tenney's *Female Quixotism* (1801), for example, address how Chesterfieldianism provides seducing males of low social origin with the cultural capital necessary to mask their moral or financial poverty. Alternatively, other novels such as *The Hapless Orphan* (1793), Hannah Foster's *The Coquette* (1797), and P. D. Manvil's *Lucinda, The Mountain Mourner* (1807) consider how Chesterfieldianism enables a variety of insolvent gentlemen to conceal their social descent, immorality, and lack of economic capital. Still others, such as *The Power of Sympathy*, Susanna Rowson's *The Inquisitor; or Invisible Rambler* (1793) and *Rebecca; or The Fille de Chambre*

(1794), Charles Brockden Brown's *Ormond* (1799), and Caroline Warren's *The Gamesters* (1805) address both trajectories.

This chapter argues that the specific invocation of Chesterfield alongside the figure of the dissimulating seducer by these and other postrevolutionary novelists was part of an effort to distinguish and distance the social effects of reading their works (and of reading literature in general) from the negative social effects associated with reading books such as Chesterfield's *Letters* and romance novels. While texts like the *Letters*, countless conduct manuals, and courtesy books strove to refine the mostly male uncouth, they were also blamed for producing the polite performances of upwardly mobile dissimulators. In response, a number of postrevolutionary seduction novels turned to the principles of less voluntary and more corporeal discourses of moral character—particularly physiognomy—in order to counteract the dissimulation associated with books such as Chesterfield's *Letters* and to curb the rapid social and political mobility of the men who read such books.[4] The transposition in the determination of character that discourses such as physiognomy promised was presented within these novels as a means to combat Chesterfieldianism's promotion of cultural capital in the signification of genteel distinction.[5] The kind of social space imagined within these postrevolutionary seduction novels—I argue, one largely predicated on immobility—relocated the visibility of distinction from the genteel, yet voluntary, performances of the body to the permanent, involuntary, and unalterable features of the face and did so in ways resonant with and informed by the cultural practices of physiognomic distinction detailed in Chapter 1. The social spaces and trajectories symbolically imagined within these novels as well as the dispositions and ways of looking generated by reading them distinguished the postrevolutionary seduction novel from other forms of print culture and shielded the genre from its Anglo-American critics by enlisting culture to restrict rather than facilitate mobility.

"Calculated to Seduce": Reading and Seeing the Postrevolutionary Novel

The spread of Chesterfieldianism discussed in Chapter 2 further underscored the necessity and value of discerning the character of men and women in public (especially if they were to be considered as potential sexual or commercial partners); reading books, as the fate of Maria in *The Contrast* confirms, was considered vital to one's success in this endeavor. Reading books and reading men were understood as equivalent practices at the end of the eighteenth century. "Reading a face was the most basic sort of reading" for much of the eighteenth century (Lynch 33). "To know mankind well," as Chesterfield himself remarked, "requires . . . as much attention and application as to know books, and, it may be, more sagacity and discernment" (Chesterfield 1:99). As Patricia Crain has shown, learning to read during the period meant "first and foremost learning how to look" (7).[6] Such discernment was especially crucial for young women, whose education emphasized "the associative link between deciphering human and literary characters" (Barnes 59).[7] John Burton, whose *Lectures on Female Education* went through no fewer than five editions in America between 1794 and 1799, claimed that "the characters of virtue, of vice, and of folly, have been so strongly marked by the historian or moralist, that you will be less liable to deception, when you see the living portraits: whereas the errors of the female sex have often proceeded from an ignorance of the world at their first outset. But in books are exhibited *just pictures* of human nature" (128; my emphasis). "If you read fifty authors," Isaac Taylor informed teenagers in 1812, "you have the advantage of fifty times the observation which can possibly come under your own eye" (12). For young women, whose opportunities for observation were limited by their age and gender in a patriarchal society, reading books offered an alternative way to see the world and obtain a knowledge of man. Books were, the sixteen-year-old Caroline Chester wrote in her journal, the means by which 'we learn how to live'" (Kelley *Learning* 166).

Although reading books could never replace life experience, reading the wrong ones, especially novels, could confound it. One of the central questions raised in this period, Elizabeth Barnes notes, is "how are readers going to be affected by narratives without being misled by them" (8). For this reason, Erasmus Darwin urged governesses to carefully select novels so that their pupils could see "human nature in all the classes of life . . . as it really exists" (49).[8] Others, such as Burton, disagreed and advised educators and parents to avoid novels altogether. "Novels," he concluded, "are the last books which should be read" (132). Those who "wish to see the characters of individuals delineated more distinctly, and with more minuteness" (132), Burton argued, should read histories and biographies instead. Burton's demand that books create distinct, "just pictures" in the minds of inexperienced and impressionable young readers was echoed by countless other anonymous and pseudonymous essayists before 1825.[9] As we will see in the pages and chapters to follow, the pictures that literature, particularly novels, might bring before the mind's eye of its readers was one of the most significant criteria for determining the value of a literary text in postrevolutionary America.[10]

As Burton's and Darwin's remarks suggest, the only reading considered more dangerous than Chesterfield's *Letters* in early America was novel reading.[11] The popularity of the genre put the novel at the center of discussions concerning "the critically important project of moral formation" in the early republic (Kelley *Learning* 157).[12] If the *Letters* were criticized for producing a nation of immoral, dissembling, self-interested, and upwardly mobile men of low social origin (or downwardly mobile men of high social origin), then novels, particularly European romances, were condemned for preparing their readers to be seduced and impoverished by such men.[13] *The Juvenile Mirror and Teacher's Manual* (1812) of New York, for example, claimed that novels "are unhappily calculated to seduce the unsettled minds of young persons" and to "encourage false views of life" (69). For such critics, novels not only seduced readers—usually imagined as women and almost always imagined as feminine—with the illusory prospects found within the fictional world, they prepared readers to be seduced by others in the actual one.[14] "The most profligate villain that was bent on the infernal purpose of seducing a woman," Concord's *New Star* lamented, "could not wish a symptom more favorable to his purpose, than an imagination inflamed with the rhapsodies of novels" ("Novels" 3).[15] "Novels . . . are the powerful engines with which the seducer attacks the female heart," the *Port Folio* added in 1802, "and if we judge from every days experience, his plots are seldom laid in vain. Never was there an apter weapon for so black a purpose" ("An Essay" 106). "A girl with her intellectual powers enervated by such a course of reading," the *Athenaeum* cautioned in 1817, "falls an easy prey to the first boy who assumes the languishing lover" ("Novel-Reading" 718). In 1801, the moral critic, Nathan Fiske, went so far as to place novels in the same troubling class as Chesterfield's *Letters*, complaining that, "Chesterfield, with all his nobility, with all his brilliant powers, and all his external graces, betrays an ignoble mind, and an impure heart. There are herds of novelists whose representations of life and manners tend to mislead the unwary youth of both sexes. The writings of these, and many other authors, are too well calculated to add new encouragements to licentiousness, and new difficulties to virtue" (153). The recurrence of the language of calculation within this criticism, with its overtones of financial self-interest, also discloses how the words of novels, like those of dissimulating Chesterfieldians, were understood to be deliberately seductive.[16]

Like Chesterfield's *Letters*, novels intensified concerns about uninstructed

reading practice and the power of cultural forms to exceed the reach of existing institutional sources of social and moral authority—especially one's family
and church.[17] In terms similar to those used by our author from Easton in
discussing Chesterfield in Chapter 2, an anonymous author from *The Boston
Weekly Magazine* characterized the negative effects of novels as much by where
they went as by what they said. "Every arrival from Europe," the author protests, "brings an importation of folly, impertinence, vice, immorality, and im-
piety, into every metropolis throughout the union, under the specious name
of works of imagination, works of amusement, commonly called *Novels*; and
from our metropolis make their way into the country towns, and even into the
house of our farmers and labouring husbandmen" ("The Gossip" 53). Romantic fiction, wrote one critic in 1792, "naturally prepares the mind for the admittance of vicious ideas," especially when "the warm representation painted
in the novel" is "read in the privacy of retirement" ("Character" 225). "What
can be expected from men and women, who in early life imbibe such pernicious principles," the author asks, "How my heart aches when I see lovely girls
just emerged from childhood, nay sometimes not more ten or twelve years
of age, allowed to have free access to the circulating libraries, and suffered to
read whatever book change or fashion might have put in their hands" ("The
Gossip" 53). As a result of "free access" to circulating libraries, the vagaries of
"change or fashion" were now determining the books young women brought
back to their room to read rather than their parents or ministers.

Most novels, according to their postrevolutionary opponents, took advantage of the undiscerning or inattentive reader by offering a "misrepresen-
tation of human character and human life" ("The Reading" 332) or worse by
depicting "characters which never existed and never can exist" ("Character"
225).[18] Novels, especially romances, were routinely criticized for producing
the wrong kind of pictures in the minds' eyes of their impressionable readers. They "present to the mind pictures too exaggerated and over colored to
convey just ideas of any thing in real life," one author complained in 1806,
"the habits of thinking and estimating mankind, acquired from early reading
them, are consequently unjust, so that persons who read them much, can very
seldom judge of their fellow creatures correctly, till they have had their erroneous imaginations (generally, too late) checked and rectified by experience.
The novel reader stands a chance of being violently attracted to some new
fledged acquaintance" ("Literature and Criticism" 8).[19] Those who formed
their "habits of . . . estimating mankind" from the images found within novels, critics argued, would be unable to see and thus judge men—particularly

a "new fledged acquaintance"—correctly in actual life. Consequently, these novels were understood as encouraging their readers "to cherish expectations that can never be realized, and to form notions of each other, which painful experience will every day refute" (Cento 8). "By the magic wand of the genius of romance," one author remarked, "the daughter of a cottager is exalted into a countess, and the labourer at the anvil and the mine soon graces the court and the drawing room" (Cento 8). "This contagion" of novel reading "is the more to be dreaded, as it daily spreads through all ranks of people," the *Port Folio* fretted: "the taylor's daughter, talks now as familiarly to her confidant, Miss Polly Staytape, of swains and sentiments, as the accomplished dames of genteel life" ("An Essay on the Modern Novel" 106). The effects were so severe that the *Juvenile Mirror and Teacher's Manual* unrealistically wished that "young persons" would simply stop reading novels so that they "would be less liable to be seduced into views of life so dissimilar from their actual prospects, and become better qualified for the discharge of their allotted duties in the world" (71). As the above examples demonstrate, novels were castigated in particular because they were thought to disturb, just as Chesterfield did, "the distinctions of rank" (Cento 8).[20]

Besides misrepresenting the actual community by disregarding the limitations of station in their fictionalized one, novels were also denounced for debilitating the minds of their readers. Critics frequently described the effects of novel reading in terms of "contagion" or imbibing poison.[21] Reading romance novels, the theory went, enfeebled the mind with a kind of "literary opium" (Leander 663), making it more likely to accept the imaginative projection of an actual person's character (one often facilitated by polite performance) rather than the supposedly more "rational" assessment offered by one's community or family.[22] In identifying the effects of novel reading in terms of contagion and poison, these critics disavowed the capacity of the novel and individual readers to imagine alternate social spaces (and thus alternative social trajectories) by associating the genre with the incapacitation of individual volition rather than its possible actualization. The novel's "potential for sparking a reader's imagination and transforming her sense of possibility," Mary Kelley explains, was part of fiction's power and the letters, commonplace books, journals, and diaries left by early American women readers "registered this power and potential, confirming that all who deplored the reading of fiction had taken the correct measure of the novel's appeal" (*Learning* 182).

Novels were also blamed for supplying the imagination with ways of seeing and models of behaving that departed from communal norms. "It is in the continual feeding of the imagination in which the great danger of Novels consists," *The Minerviad* reasoned, "the imagination, once deceived, becomes itself the deceiver" ("Opinions" 45). The struggle over the novel's relationship to an anterior social reality—a struggle over how individual readers and novelists might represent the social codes and structures that regulate their behavior and, in representing, possibly transform them—was often expressed by critics in terms of an opposition between the overly imaginative vision of a single reader quixotically at odds with the rational vision of communal norms.[23] "A young girl enters into the world with her novel in her head," the *Weekly Visitor, or Ladies' Miscellany* complained in 1803, and "she sees in every thing that can happen to her, only one or two pages of an adventure which she has read" ("On Novels" 116). "The swarms of foolish and worthless novels, incessantly spawned by dull and dissolute scribblers, and with unwearied industry disseminated from our circulating library," *The Philadelphia Minerva* admonished readers in 1796, "is alone sufficient to swallow up, amongst the young and the gay, all sober reflection, every rational study, with every virtuous principle; and to introduce into their room impure, extravagant desires, and notions of happiness alike fantastic and false. By the influence of those productions on the unguarded readers the whole system of life seems converted into romance; and nothing is regarded worth a thought which does not promise to gratify inclination, to cherish vanity, or to lead that vile and restless adventurer, Juvenile Fancy, through a fairy land of astonishment and rapture" ("Extract" n.p.).

The stakes of reading novels were, as the *Philadelphia Minerva* defines them, nothing less than the conversion of "the whole system of life." As the above examples suggest, the negative effects of reading novels (especially romances) were twofold: they distributed false images of people within a fictional community and, in doing so, they weakened the reader's mind, rendering it more likely to receive such false views as true in his or her subsequent experiences in the actual one. According to their critics, novels seduced their readers and, worse yet, prepared those readers to be seduced by others. The effects were imagined to be so severe that "A young person habitually and indiscriminately devoted to novels," as the Reverend Samuel Miller remarked, "is in a fair way to dissipate his mind, to degrade his taste, and to bring on himself intellectual and moral ruin" (179).

There were, of course, exceptions to the rule. Although novels were largely criticized in postrevolutionary periodical discussions of the genre, there were those who believed that the genre might enlighten rather than mislead readers.

"Those who condemn novels, or fiction in the abstract" ("The Novelist" 5), the *Minerviad* reasoned, are inconsistent and miss the pedagogical value of novels. Yet, the novel was defended for the same reason it was denounced: for the kind of pictures it produced. The pictures that novels brought before the eyes of its readers, as discussed earlier, was perhaps the most significant factor in determining its value in postrevolutionary America. Enos Hitchcock, for example, praised those novels that "address the heart with simplicity and chasteness, in a variety of images, where the likeness is caught warm from the life, sentiment is united with character, and the beautiful portrait presented to their mind" (86). That intermediality appears in descriptions of useful novels (such as Hitchcock's "beautiful portrait" "caught warm from the life") as well as in descriptions of pernicious novels (such as Caroline Warren's "too highly colored portrait of life"; iv) reveals the extent to which novel reading was understood in terms of seeing and novels in terms of pictures. Charles Brockden Brown claimed that "the most solid and useful reading," produces "a just and *powerful picture* of human life . . . vividly portrayed" (403; my emphasis), while Hannah Foster argued that novels should "exhibit *striking pictures* of virtue rewarded; and of vice, folly, and indiscretion punished" (*Boarding* 23).[24] Novelists such as Hitchcock, Brown, and Foster—and they were far from alone—located the novel's moral and social utility in the rationality, life-likeness, and vividness of its images as opposed to the irrationality, imagination, and exaggeration characteristic of romance. Novelists worth our attention, one critic wrote in 1803, "represent human nature as it is" and "paint men and manners, so as not to mislead the inexperienced heart, or vitiate the yet untutored judgment" ("The Gossip" 53).[25] "The principle object of those who make books," the *Monthly Review and Literary Miscellany of the United States* advised in 1806, should be "to lead their readers to the *study of man*, to lash vice, to expose the villainous frauds of hypocrisy and fanaticism, and to scourge the profligacy of the libertine" ("Literature and Criticism" 4). If, according to their postrevolutionary critics, novels were calculated to facilitate seduction, then according to their advocates they could just as easily prevent it by producing the right kind of pictures.

The idea that reading novels could adversely affect the imaginations of their readers, making them vulnerable to the same type of deception that dissembling seducers practiced, was not restricted to the pens of Anglo-American critics—it filled the pages of the novelists themselves, from William Hill Brown's *The Power of Sympathy* (1789) to James Fenimore Cooper's *Tales for Fifteen* (1823). Hannah Foster's didactic novel, *The Boarding School* (1798), for instance, regrets how the "romantic pictures" of novels "fill the imagination with ideas, . . . pervert the judgment, mislead the affections, and blind the understanding" (18). In fact, these same symptoms plague the minds of Fanny in *The Hapless Orphan* (1793), Dorcas in *Female Quixotism*, and the "well-read" Annie in Susanna Rowson's *The Inquisitor, or Invisible Rambler* (London, 1788; Philadelphia, 1793). Novels as a form of cultural capital were understood as challenging the social capital of established familial networks and its existing forms for recognizing distinction, just as Chesterfield's *Letters* had done, often at the expense of gentlemen with extensive economic capital (particularly property). Unsurprisingly, postrevolutionary seduction novels frequently imagined struggles that pitted socially rich but financially poor ministers and propertied but ineffectual patriarchs against culturally rich Chesterfieldian seducers.

The near-omnipresence of dissimulation within this period's fiction makes it hardly coincidental that the same type of Chesterfieldian dissembler criticized by Anglo-American ministers and moralists also preoccupied many novelists at the end of the eighteenth century.[26] Dissimulation was a central preoccupation of much postrevolutionary fiction not merely because it threatened the stability of domestic patriarchy by facilitating actual seductions, but also because it reflected an uneasiness with how books, such as Chesterfield's *Letters*, were affecting the way people represented themselves and read others in public.[27] As I mentioned above, the specific invocation of Chesterfield alongside the figure of the dissimulating seducer was an effort to distinguish and distance the social effects of reading their works (and of reading literature in general) from the negative social effects associated with reading books such as Chesterfield's *Letters* and romance novels. While texts like the *Letters*, countless conduct manuals, and courtesy books strove to refine the mostly male uncouth, they were also blamed for producing the polite performances of upwardly mobile dissimulators. In response, a variety of postrevolutionary novelists turned to the principles of less voluntary and more corporeal discourses of moral character—particularly physiognomy—in order to counteract the dissimulation associated with books such as Chesterfield's *Letters* and to curb the rapid social and political mobility of the men who read such books. Unlike European romances, which were said to facilitate dissimulation by adversely affecting the minds of their readers, postrevolutionary seduction novels like *The Coquette* and *Female Quixotism* promised pictures that would edify, not seduce, the imaginations of their readers; the physiognomic distinction of the face was a significant feature of that didacticism.

The Inquisitor and "The Eye of Justice"

The physiognomic distinction of the face, for example, is pivotal to the rather conservative imagination of social space found within Susanna Rowson's 1788 *The Inquisitor, or Invisible Rambler* (Philadelphia, 1793). The social and political aims of Rowson's fiction have undergone revision in recent years as critics widen their lens beyond her most famous novel *Charlotte Temple*. Rowson's reputation as a political progressive, for instance, has been tempered by both her "ardent Federalist sympathies and her antagonism to the ascendant Democratic-Republican administration" (Rust 3) and, more broadly, by the way her fiction addresses how gentility would be determined in a society presumably dedicated to the principle of equality (Rust 153).[28] The fiction of Rowson, as scholars have noted, rarely recommends "class equality and social mobility" (Weil 82), and *The Inquisitor* is certainly no exception.

　　The Inquisitor contains a number of interpolated seduction tales featuring dissimulating seducers on the one hand and physiognomic discernment as a means to unmask them on the other. The novel recounts the experiences of a wealthy gentleman who, after complaining about the amount of duplicity in the world, is mysteriously given a ring that can turn him invisible. With the power of invisibility, the gentleman boasts that now "I should find my real friends, and detect my enemies."[29] And that is more or less what happens. Over the next three volumes, the gentleman's morning rambles around London provide him with numerous occasions to use his invisibility for the benefit of mankind. He exposes rakes, protects the innocent, reunites families, and saves lives from ruin. Sometimes the gentleman intervenes after witnessing an immoral act while invisible, but far more often, he first suspects a person and then investigates his or her behavior invisibly. His ability to follow the duplicitous before they execute their designs is integral to the novel's imagination of social order and justice. Yet, if his invisibility is what enables him to spy on people unobserved, then how does he know whom to watch and whom to ignore?

　　He knows, we later learn, because he is a physiognomist. "I never cast my eye upon a stranger but I immediately form some idea of his or her dispositions by the turn of their eyes and cast of their features," he explains, "and though my skill in physiognomy is not infallible, I seldom find myself deceived" (*I* 150). Indeed, nearly all of the people the invisible rambler suspects eventually behave as their faces predicted. Throughout *The Inquisitor*, faces reveal seducers, gamblers, idlers, dissimulators, and a variety of crooks and fortune hunters. For Rowson, at least, fantasies of surveillance such as invisibility are predicated on prejudicial discourses such as physiognomy. A person's face, in other words, becomes the probable cause for the rambler's surveillance.

The idea that a person's face could belie his will and disclose his character, as we saw in Chapter 1, can be traced to Johann Lavater's enormously popular *Essays on Physiognomy*. By imagining physiognomy as a way to expose dissimulation, detect vice, and undermine social mobility, Rowson's novel, like so many others from the postrevolutionary period, reproduces the physiognomic fallacy (the false opposition between a model of character read from performance and one read from the permanent and involuntary physiognomic features of the face) at the center of Lavater's subordination of pathognomy to physiognomy. In contrast to the revisable, performed, and voluntary self of the fortune-hunting seducer Cogdie, for example, *The Inquisitor* posits the permanent, physiognomic, and involuntary one used by the rambler to unmask him.

Yet, not all of the episodes involving physiognomic discernment operate negatively in *The Inquisitor*. In tales like "The Mourner," for instance, the invisible rambler spies "something" in a woman's face "that engaged the affections and insensibly drew the heart towards her" (*I* 78). In another episode, he observes how a man's "eyes fixed such a dignity in his person, and yet such an apparent concern upon his countenance, that my affections were drawn towards him by an irresistible impulse—I longed to call him brother and friend—my heart was wrung with sensibility" (*I* 163).[30] If in its negative mode (which is its dominant mode in *The Inquisitor*) physiognomy is imagined as a discourse capable of discriminating among dissembling white males and deterring their mobility, in its positive mode physiognomy serves as a precondition for individual sympathy and charity as well as the potential foundation for urban homosociality.[31]

The Inquisitor's message of social justice through physiognomy and invisible surveillance, however, is accompanied by a more general advocacy of social immobility. The novel's imagination of social space, I would like to suggest, is largely based on how certain discourses that facilitate or restrict mobility (such as Chesterfieldianism and physiognomy) operate asymmetrically with respect to social origin. The narrative and social trajectories of two of the novel's more notorious seducers—the adulterous Chesterfieldian Lord Ernoff and the serial seducer Cogdie, for example—reflect how these asymmetries contribute to the imagination of a social space predicated on immobility. In the case of the aristocratic man of pleasure, Lord Ernoff, the didacticism of his tale functions as a means to prevent social descent, whereas in the case of social climbing inferiors like Cogdie, the didacticism of his tales function as means to discourage social ascent.

Lord Ernoff embodies the immoral gentility that Anglo-American moral critics excoriated in Chesterfield's *Letters*. He lounges "in an easy chair, dressed in a long *robe de chambre*" with "a dish of chocolate in one hand and the newspaper in the other" (*I* 81). His behavior is so appalling that the genteel rambler has trouble believing that he is "a peer of the realm" (*I* 83). Rowson's characterization of Lord Ernoff as a Chesterfieldian seducer in tales like "The Clergyman" and "The Courtier," however, departs from the prevailing depictions of Chesterfieldianism set in postrevolutionary America. The case of Ernoff, for example, identifies the threat of Chesterfieldianism with the social descent of the titled aristocracy ("peer of the realm") as opposed to the social ascent of either the fallen gentry or a rising middling sort. Aristocrats who participate in and, by participating, legitimate the cultural capital associated with Chesterfieldianism, are shown to risk their own economic and social capital. The aristocratic Chesterfieldian seducers who inhabit the imagined social space of *The Inquisitor*'s London (such as Ernoff and Winlove) are typically associated with social and economic capital (attributes typically missing from their American counterparts) and they are, at least in the case of Ernoff, capable of reform, whereas in the imagination of social space in American seduction fiction even those seducers who have some claim to a higher station—such as Sanford in *The Coquette* or even the "Honorable" Harrington in *The Power of Sympathy*—are imagined as incapable of reform. This last point is significant because even though the rambler's physiognomic discernment is imagined to detect the vicious and immoral regardless of their rank, Lord Ernoff is one of the few people in the novel who is able to rehabilitate his fallen character and reclaim his lost social capital. In contrast, those characters identified as socially inferior and physiognomically immoral are incapable of such change. The ruthless seducer, Cogdie, for instance, escapes justice twice only to seduce and steal again.[32] In fact, the worst of the social climbers, men like Cogdie and the swindling attorney Mr. Vellum, suffer fates in which not only they but virtually all of their family die, as if to suggest that the problem of self-interested and duplicitous social climbers can only be resolved by extinction.

Although *The Inquisitor* occasionally wags its finger at the artificial distinctions of aristocracy, it is clear that such criticism is motivated largely by a desire to preserve the integrity of its rank. The novel is dedicated to Rowson's aristocratic patron, Lady Cockburne, and its implied readers are those "sons and daughters of prosperity" (*I* 168) that the rambler addresses in the episode "Natural Reflection."[33] *The Inquisitor*'s didactic narratives about the dangers of social descent almost always involve members of the aristocracy, while its condemnation of social ascent invariably features those poor, middling, or ambitious residents of London who ape the manners of their superiors. Tales such as "The Happy Pair" and "The Village Wedding," for example, romanticize the pleasures of knowing your place, while others such as "The Morning Ramble," "The Arrest," and "The Study" dramatize the follies of social climbing. "Now you are again plain Jack Wouldbe, the Cabinet-maker," one man taunts near the end of the novel, continuing, "you must learn to bow, cringe, and mind your business—I am sorry it goes so hard with you; but depend upon it, this will always be the case with young men of trifling fortunes, who ape the manners, and launch into extravagancies, which are only becoming their superiors" (*I* 194–95). Wouldbe's demise not only dramatizes the failure of upward social mobility, it displays the absence of sympathy or charity for those ruined by such social ambition. Cabinet makers who try to rise above their social origin fail just as people who try to dissemble their character do in *The Inquisitor*, because the acquisition of gentility, like the physiognomic distinction of the face, is ultimately imagined as beyond the control of an individual's will.[34]

Jack Wouldbe's fate is consistent with *The Inquisitor*'s representations of the ineradicability of social origin. In "The Cottagers," for example, social origin proves durable despite upward social mobility. "Whatever circumstance a person is in," the rambler observes, "you may always discover by their behavior whether they have been inured to their situation from childhood—A person who has never known any thing but poverty, shews no other mark of chagrin at the entrance of a stranger than what proceeds from an aukwardness of manner which they ever betray when in the company of their superiors—and raise that person to the most exalted station, and you will still perceive the same disgusting aukwardness and rusticity—So, place a man of education in ever so obscure a situation, you will always discover the manners of a gentleman, though obscured by the garb of a beggar" (*I* 146). The habitus of the poor and rich endure, the rambler suggests, even if the former rises and the latter falls.[35] The habitus naturalizes and makes permanent social origin to such a degree that no amount of upward social mobility manufactured by the acquisition of capital can efface its features.

The durability of the habitus in "The Cottagers," however, is not conflated with the body itself (as it is in other tales, largely through the discourse of physiognomy). If social inferiors supposedly can never acquire the habitus of their superiors because social origin is ineradicable, then discourses such as physiognomy and novels like *The Inquisitor* should be unnecessary. Whether or not social origin is ineradicable belies the fact that the signs, practices, and dispositions by which social origin is recognized are fluid, heterogeneous, and generated by the dominant social order itself. It is precisely because social origin is read and, moreover, it is because culture and manners contribute to its legibility that the struggle over them ensues. "The Cottagers," in other words, discloses the struggle for domination over the very entity—culture and manners—it claims is ineffectual and, in doing so, reveals a contradiction at the heart of the novel's imagination of social space. *The Inquisitor* imagines an aristocratic social space which, if true, would render novels like *The Inquisitor* unnecessary.

It is significant that the episode in which physiognomy is most directly identified in *The Inquisitor* is also the moment in which the social space of the novel seems most contested and most "American." The moment occurs during the tale "The Steward" in which the rambler's chaise breaks down and he is forced to dine with some cottagers. As they are finishing dinner, a stranger enters the cottage and, from his face, the rambler immediately determines him to be haughty, coarse, and rude. The rambler exclaims that "I never cast my eye upon a stranger but I immediately form some idea of his or her dispositions by the turn of their eyes and cast of their features; and though my skill in physiognomy is not infallible, I seldom find myself deceived" (*I* 150). When the insolent stranger calls him a "young man," the rambler complains that "he addressed me, by this familiar epithet, on account of his supposed superiority" (*I* 151). The episode is striking because the moment in which physiognomy is most directly acknowledged in identifying the character of a stranger is simultaneously the only moment in *The Inquisitor* when the narrator is visible and yet *not* recognized as superior (*I* 151). With his carriage under repair and "dressed very plainly," the signifiers of the rambler's distinction are unavailable or insufficient for the steward to recognize. The rambler's condition at this moment resembles that of many elites in postrevolutionary America: he is visible, but his status is not. He is, even if temporarily, an invisible aristocrat.

The scene is singular because it is one of the few to actualize the legitimacy of the struggle that the novel otherwise works so hard to disavow as legitimate or even necessary.

Invisibility is important to *The Inquisitor*'s imagination of social space because it allows the rambler to indulge in a fantasy of pure observation, or what he calls "the eye of justice" (*I* 49). The stated necessity for such invisible surveillance, of course, is to prevent the duplicitous performances generated by those subversive to the social order and to the morality that sustains that order. Yet, the purpose of such invisibility is not exclusively disciplinary. Although the novel is interested in the relationship between surveillance and subjection, *The Inquisitor* seems equally invested in how invisibility allows the moral observer not to be seen seeing. Invisibility matters to *The Inquisitor*, I want to suggest, because it allows looking itself to be invisible at the moment when the act of social injustice occurs. Invisibility masks the aristocratic subject position from which criminal and immoral behavior is identified, justice determined, sympathy extended, and homosocial affiliation formed. We might consider invisibility in the novel as a trope for the privilege of the aristocratic white male subject position, but to do so would be to obscure how thoroughly that position is inhabited by the women who both write the novel and fund its publication. The rambler's invisibility is important because it eradicates his social origin in precisely the ways the novel otherwise suggests is impossible. With his ring, the rambler can look without consequence and observe without being seen. In other words, invisibility in *The Inquisitor* enacts a fantasy about the inconsequentiality of the rambler's looking. The novel tries to imagine a world with social justice and social stasis without having the social itself. The power of such invisibility is to avoid being subject to what Sartre called *le regard* (the look) or the social dimension of vision/visibility.[36] It is, in other words, an attempt to evade the inherent sociality of vision.

The social space of *The Inquisitor*, despite the fluidity and instability in its depiction of metropolitan London, remains strongly structured by the aristocracy. The "eye of justice" in the novel is almost exclusively practiced by a white male aristocrat and none of the novel's seduction tales directly involve or threaten members of his biological family (who remain safely at the margins of the inquisitor's rambles). Moreover, when seduction does occur in *The Inquisitor*, the Chesterfieldian seducer is the aristocrat Lord Ernoff, not the impoverished social climber Cogdie. The discourse of Chesterfieldianism in *The Inquisitor* matters for how it facilitates the social descent and possible illegibility of aristocracy more than the social ascent of inferiors. Physiognomy, in contrast, contributes to the naturalization of the habitus and to the imaginative identification of low social origin with the face.

"He Looks to Me Like a Chesterfieldian": *The Coquette* and the Face of Seduction

Like *The Inquisitor*, Hannah Foster's 1797 seduction novel, *The Coquette*, also imagines physiognomy as a deterrent to dissimulating seducers, but it is a young woman, not an aristocratic patriarch, who practices it. The aristocratic male subject position that occupies the "eye of justice" in *The Inquisitor* is precisely what is under duress in seduction novels set in postrevolutionary America such as *The Coquette* and *Female Quixotism*. The patriarchal surveillance practiced by the invisible rambler in Rowson's novel is either absent or ineffectual in these seduction novels. The value of physiognomy in *The Coquette,* however, has more to do with insisting on the permanence of moral character than it does with discerning it. Whereas fallen British seducers such as the aristocratic Lord Ernoff are shown to be capable of reform, *The Coquette*'s Peter Sanford is not.

Similar to *The Inquisitor*, *The Coquette* specifically identifies its seducer's dissimulation with Chesterfieldian performances on the one hand and the use of physiognomy as a potential counter-practice to them on the other. The episode takes place near the end of the novel, in letter 51, when the formerly coquettish, but now reclusive, Eliza Wharton sits alone in her bedroom fawning over a portrait of her beloved Peter Sanford. The miniature reflects Eliza's misplaced intimacy and Sanford's pictorial presence in her private "chamber" anticipates the ill-fated union that he and Eliza will share in person later. But for her more discerning friend Julia Granby, the painting possesses a quite different meaning. When Julia enters the room, Eliza asks her "You pretend to be a physiognomist, . . . what can you trace in that countenance?"[37] In response, Julia scrutinizes the portrait's face and instantly identifies what Eliza has been unable to see throughout the novel: that her beloved is "an artful, designing man" and that "he looks . . . like a Chesterfieldian" (*C* 194).

Of course, at this moment in the narrative, Julia's identification of Sanford as an "artful, designing man" is hardly a revelation. Virtually everyone in the novel, its readers included, is aware that Sanford is a man of "known libertinism" (*C* 168). They warn Eliza ad nauseam that Sanford is a "profligate man" (*C* 116), "a professed libertine" practiced in "the arts of seduction" (*C* 119), a "second Lovelace" (*C* 134), "an artful debauchee" (*C* 147), an "assassin of honor" (*C* 154), and "a deceiver" (*C* 171). Even Sanford himself joins the chorus when he admits to his confidant Deighton that Eliza's "sagacious friends have undoubtedly given her a detail of my vices" so that "she can blame none but herself, since she knows my character" (*C* 149). While Eliza's choice of intimacy with Sanford is notoriously difficult to understand, it does appear that one reason she chooses not to listen to her friends and family is that she believes that Sanford is capable of being reformed, whereas her community does not. What is emphasized in the community's failure to prevent Eliza's seduction is not its inability to communicate that Sanford is a rake, but rather its failure to communicate that he will *always* be a rake. Eliza can disregard Sanford's past "scenes of dissipation" because she believes that his moral character will be different in the future. Eliza embraces the Richardsonian adage that "*A reformed rake makes the best husband*" (*C* 146), whereas her foil, Julia, has "no charity for these reformed rakes" (*C* 202). After Sanford marries another woman for money, Julia begs Eliza to recognize that "marriage has not changed his disposition" (*C* 209), it has merely given him the means to indulge it. The eventual success of Sanford's seduction of Eliza therefore represents a more general failure in the communal norms of gentility to establish the permanency and visibility of immoral character in a person who, externally at least, appears like "a finished gentleman" (*C* 119) of virtue.

What makes Julia's physiognomic reading of Sanford's portrait so significant is not her assessment of his character—which everybody already knows—but rather her attempt to identify Sanford's seemingly innate immorality (and the durability of that immorality) with his face. Julia's physiognomic assessment of Sanford differs from the novel's chorus of ineffectual monitors, because she appears to derive her knowledge of Sanford's character not so much from his past conduct or present performances—which he, of course, can adapt to his own interests—but rather from his unalterable facial features. In fact, Julia is "astonished" that Eliza's "penetrating eye, has not long since read his vices in his very countenance" (*C* 202). When Eliza first solicits Julia's expert opinion regarding the miniature, she does so presumably in the hope that her physiognomic reading of the portrait's face will discover aspects of Sanford's moral character different from those being circulated by the community and more in line with her own romantic image of him (*C* 190). Instead, Julia's words confirm the community's image of Sanford, but beyond that, they also naturalize that image. Sanford's immorality now becomes more than a series of unwise decisions—it is essential to him.

While Julia is no more successful than the community in preventing Eliza's seduction, her late entrance into the novel and the fact that her physiognomic reading occurs after Sanford has already symbolically penetrated Eliza's chamber assures us that her remarks are meant more for readers than for Eliza. If Sanford's mastery of Chesterfieldian politeness helps him to satisfy his sexual urge for seduction and his economic need for marriage, Julia's physiognomic discernment informs the novel's readers of the value of seeing through such performative masks. As Foster reiterates throughout *The Coquette*, Sanford's cultural fluency, his mastery of the genteel codes of politeness, enables him to "assume any shape" (*C* 121) before Eliza, and his seduction depends largely on his ability to charm her eye (*C* 122) and cast "a deceptious mist over her imagination" (*C* 111). The cultural capital of Chesterfieldianism enables Sanford to conceal his moral and financial poverty. Eliza's "extensive reading" (*C* 140) prepares her to be "peculiarly entertaining" and "inexpressibly engaging" (*C* 140), but not discerning. Eventually, Eliza's "disturbed imagination" (*C* 191) deteriorates to the point that she is unable to describe the incidents of her life to her friends without evoking scenes from "a novel" or "romance" (*C* 190).[38] In contrast, "the powerful gaze of Julia Granby" (Waldstreicher 215) and her "inquisitorial eye" (*C* 211) are epitomized by a rational reflection sharpened by reading histories, not romances (*C* 117). Julia's reading practice exemplifies the course of reading that Burton and other Anglo-American moral critics were recommending at the time. The difference between reading novels and becoming the unfortunate victims of them, readers of *The Coquette* learn, is the difference between Julia's "reflecting and steady mind" (*C* 241) and Eliza's "enfeebled . . . mind" (*C* 222), the difference between Julia's model of reading moral character from Sanford's face and Eliza's model of reading it from his polite performances.

Julia's physiognomic reading of Sanford's portrait is odd, however, in that it lacks any detailed physical description.[39] Such an omission raises the possibility that Julia might have identified the portrait's character as a "Chesterfieldian" from her previous knowledge of his character rather than from his face. The manner in which the scene unfolds encourages this interpretation since Julia deduces that the portrait depicts Sanford—she says "I guessed whose it was" (*C* 194)—before she divulges what character she spies in his countenance. Although Foster does not disclose how Julia is able to guess that the image belonged to Sanford, it is probable that some account of his reputation would have been included in Julia's previous correspondence with others in the novel (see Letters 48 and 49). Whether or not Julia practices physiognomy—in the sense of producing an accurate reading of moral character from the details of Sanford's portrait—seems secondary here to the fact that she utilizes the logic of physiognomy to substantiate her desire to make his vice visible and ineradicable by associating the immorality of his known character to his face. In this sense, Julia's remarks confirm what was observed in Chapter 1: that physiognomy's hermeneutics of the body created the very faces it claimed to interpret. The portrait scene in *The Coquette* is less interested in the validity of specific physiognomic readings than it is in physiognomy's discursive potential as a counter-practice to Chesterfieldian dissimulation. The value of physiognomy in *The Coquette* resides in its transposition in the determination of character from the voluntary performances of the individual to the involuntary features of his or her face. Hardly a criticism of the patriarchy, as many critics have claimed, *The Coquette* instead recommends physiognomy's desire for a permanent, involuntary, and visible relationship between moral character and the face as a means to insulate the marital structures of patriarchal society from Chesterfieldians whose wealth was as false as their manners.[40] In doing so, *The Coquette* enlists culture in support of social capital as opposed to challenging it. Moreover, *The Coquette* establishes the seduction novel's value for its readership and defends the genre from those critics who sought to equate it with the romance by promoting a more rational and less imaginative reading practice.

Julia's exemplary reading practice (of portraits, letters, and men) also suggests that the kind of Protean image manipulation that Sanford practices so well as he seduces—that capacity to "cast a deceptious mist" over the imagination—is no longer exclusive to the world of masculine gentility. Julia becomes an exemplary female character for Foster since she has mastered both reading practices—reading books and men. Julia's epistolary reading enables her to identify Sanford as the portrait's original, while her physiognomic discernment allows her to assign a permanent moral character to his face. Even as such physiognomic discernment promises to protect the patriarchal social order from the threat of upwardly mobile, dissembling white males in *The Coquette*, it also elevates the social power of women within that system by attempting to make positive claims for their reading and their minds.[41] What is potentially, and somewhat pragmatically, attractive to established gentry about an exemplary female character like Julia is that her social power need not be defined in opposition to her subordinate status as a woman within the system of domestic patriarchy, but rather as a product of her ability to determine the character of men operating within it.[42]

Turning Heads in *Female Quixotism*

Although *Female Quixotism* has been read primarily in terms of the politics of the early republic, the novel appears to be less interested in discussing the possibilities of democratic politics than it is in shaping the social space of that democracy.[43] Tenney's novel is, as Gillian Brown puts it, "an aristocratic romance of arresting democratic movements" (*Consent* 167).[44] Similar to *The Coquette* and *The Inquisitor*, Tabitha Tenney's *Female Quixotism* (1801) imagines a social space in which Chesterfieldian civility provides seducing males with the cultural capital necessary to mask their moral or financial poverty; like those novels, it, too, considers physiognomy as a discourse capable of unmasking such seducers. The agency of seduction, however, shifts over the course of the two books of *Female Quixotism* from the polite performances of dissembling seducers to the reading practice of novel readers. The increasing passivity of the male seducer in Book 2 of the novel thus transfers the force of culture from funding the individual performances of Chesterfieldian males to shaping the reading practices of female quixotes.[45] Physiognomy remains an important feature of *Female Quixotism*'s didacticism, supplementing older, genteel social networks in preventing seductions and restricting mobility, but its significance diminishes as the struggle over culture shifts from restricting the kind of capital it provides to upwardly mobile men to contesting imagined social spaces and trajectories inconsistent with an anterior genteel community.

Part satire, part didactic tract, *Female Quixotism* is an anti-romance-novel novel that chronicles the life of the genteel Dorcas Sheldon whose "thousand pounds a year" estate and unregulated novel reading make her the target of a seemingly endless parade of dissembling seducers.[46] *Female Quixotism* dramatizes the postrevolutionary critical complaint, discussed earlier in this chapter, that novels seduced their readers and prepared them to be seduced by others. The language of poison and contagion, so frequently used by these critics to describe the debilitating effects of novels on the minds of their readers, also characterizes Dorcas's novel reading. Her father laments how "those pernicious books, from which she had evidently imbibed the fatal poison, . . . seemed to have, beyond cure, disordered every faculty of her mind" (*FQ* 50).[47] Her mind becomes "so warped by the false and romantic ideas" (*FQ* 71) contained within her novels that she soon contracts "novel-mania" (*FQ* 57) and changes her name to Dorcasina. The effects of Dorcasina's novel-mania also correspond with the postrevolutionary critical concern that novels disturbed "the distinctions of rank." Novels, for example, inspire Dorcasina to disguise herself as her servant in order to meet her first seducer, the duplicitous Patrick O'Connor, at a nearby inn. The idea "was one of the most extravagant that had ever entered the romantic imagination of the love-sick girl, and such as no lady, in her senses, would have attempted to execute, who was not blinded to all sense of propriety, and regard to reputation. She was, however, so far gone with novel-mania, that it appeared a proper attention to a lover" (*FQ* 57). The narrator's negative description of Dorcasina ("no lady"; no "propriety"; no "reputation") suggests that novel-mania has already cost Dorcasina her status before she has even left home. Unsurprisingly, her visit to the inn merely confirms the narrator's remarks. Upon executing her romantic plan, Dorcasina is mistaken for a prostitute, run out of the inn, chased through the streets, and has her clothes stripped off until she faints on the door of her genteel neighbor, Mrs. Stanly. The astonished Mrs. Stanly "knew, that Dorcasina had imbibed from the books she had perused, a most romantic turn; but she had no idea that she could have been led so widely astray from the path prescribed by reason and prudence" (*FQ* 61). Dorcasina's novel reading results not only in a loss of rational judgment, but in the literal, if temporary, loss of her distinction.

Throughout *Female Quixotism* the transformative power of a novel reader's imagination to eradicate distinction is contrasted specifically with the physiognomic transparency of the face to display it. Dorcasina judges and then refuses her first suitor, Lysander, for instance, after reading his letters as opposed to his face. Lysander, the son of "an old esteemed friend" of Mr. Sheldon (*FQ* 6), possesses sufficient social and economic capital to be considered as the preferred marital choice of her father. Moreover, Lysander's "ideas of domestic happiness," readers learn, "were just and rational," "his person noble and commanding," and "his countenance open and liberal" (*FQ* 7). Yet, before Dorcasina even sees Lysander, her imagination begins "forming ideas" of his appearance (*FQ* 10). When they finally do meet face to face, Dorcasina is disappointed that he did not display any of the qualities that her novels had led her to expect from a lover. After Lysander proposes to her in a letter, she refuses him because his missive was "so widely different in style and sentiment" from "her favourite authors" (*FQ* 13). Dorcasina's refusal of Lysander—arguably her only legitimate suitor in *Female Quixotism*—reflects a struggle between novels (which are held responsible for her choices) and the social capital of Mr. Sheldon, Lysander, and their genteel community. Although the distinction of Lysander is physiognomically transparent on his face, novels prevent Dorcasina from discerning it.

If Dorcasina fails to read the presence of distinction in Lysander's face, she is no better at discerning its absence in the countless men who attempt to seduce her after he departs. Over the course of the novel, a variety of smooth-talking criminals (Patrick O'Connor), mischievous schoolmasters (Philander), ambitious barbers (Puff), aspiring servants (James and John Brown), and dissipated rakes (the itinerant schoolmaster Wheaton/Mr. Seymore) all romance Dorcasina in an effort to acquire her substantial wealth. Despite their differences, these seducers all possess or are thought to possess the externals of civility (especially genteel manners and literary knowledge). Most are men of low social origin who seek to convert their cultural capital into the economic or social capital they lack, and each one takes advantage of Dorcasina's novel mania in order to conceal their moral character and social aspirations. O'Connor, for example, embodies the familiar Chesterfieldian seducer of low social origin and high social ambition. The conniving son of an Irish steward, O'Connor flees Europe after narrowly escaping the gallows for highway robbery. In America, however, he is able to pose as a fashionable "man of family and fortune" (*FQ* 142). "This smooth-tongued" Irishman (*FQ* 33) is a master of dissimulation who disguises "his pleasure, under the mask of hypocrisy" (*FQ* 44). His "genteel and engaging appearance" (*FQ* 17) masks the fact that he is a gambler, a thief, and now a fortune-hunting "impostor" (*FQ* 32). Similar to how Benjamin Franklin's reading facilitated his mobility, O'Connor's "taste for books" (*FQ* 71) gains him temporary admission into the genteel community that he seeks to join permanently. He begins his seduction of Dorcasina, for example, by discussing the "customs and manners of Europe; and of all the British authors" (*FQ* 26), dwelling particularly on "the writers of novels" (*FQ* 26). O'Connor cleverly adapts his performances to the romantic image Dorcasina projects onto him, and this enables him to overcome the suspicion of those closest to her—her father and her servant. Despite the fact that her father tells her that "O'Connor . . . is . . . a needy adventurer . . . who knowing you to be the only child of a man of some property, has addressed you in the clandestine manner, to gain possession of your heart, your person, and your father's estate" (*FQ* 48), she cannot distinguish the "actual" O'Connor—whom the genteel community describes as a "Hibernian fortune-hunter" (*FQ* 19)—from his Chesterfieldian performances.

The physiognomic transparency of O'Connor's moral character, like that of Lysander, magnifies the extent to which Dorcasina's novel-mania obscures her vision and it is an integral part of the novel's didacticism. O'Connor's face becomes the narrative focal point for locating the seemingly innate immorality that lurks beneath the polished surface of his polite performances. The narrator relates how his "fine black eyes, good features, and a florid complexion" (*FQ* 18) would have led "superficial observers" to call him handsome, but "those of more nice discernment would pretend to discover by the expression of his countenance, that he possessed neither a good heart, nor a good temper" (*FQ* 18). Mr. Sheldon, for instance, "viewed the man of his daughter's choice, with a scrutinizing eye," and instantly saw that "the expression of his [O'Connor's] countenance made him tremble for the happiness of his daughter" since "the bad qualities of [his] mind were written in such legible characters in the lineaments of his face" (*FQ* 66). Indeed, what even "an indifferent spectator would have there read" "instantly painted on his countenance" (*FQ* 71)—that O'Connor was, in the words of the genteel Mr. W, "a most worthless and abandoned profligate" (*FQ* 81)—Dorcasina cannot discern. Instead, she sees what her novel reading projects—"a perfect Sir Charles Grandison"—which makes her "certain of his being a gentleman, and a man of character" (*FQ* 28). Physiognomy's equation of moral character with the permanent and unalterable features of the face is imagined in *Female Quixotism*, as it was in *The Coquette*, as a discourse capable of seeing through Chesterfieldian performances and restricting the mobility facilitated by them. Moreover, the value of physiognomy in *Female Quixotism*, as it was in *The Inquisitor* and *The Coquette*, appears to matter less in terms of identifying O'Connor's moral character— which Dorcasina's father, her servant, and even "an indifferent spectator" all can do—than it does in assigning his apparently innate immorality (and the durability of that immorality) to his face. The physiognomic transparency of O'Connor's immorality, like that of Lysander's distinction, confirms and naturalizes the image of him that the discursive practices and social networks of the genteel community are otherwise unable to get Dorcasina to recognize.

Physiognomy in *Female Quixotism* appears alongside and, at times, serves as an extension of eroding residual social practices for legitimating genteel distinction such as letters of recommendation from members of the same social network. Mr. Sheldon, for example, attempts "to counteract the effects" of O'Connor's performances by confirming his character with those who belong to the same genteel community as himself (such as Lysander and later Mr. W.). When Lysander writes back, he informs Mr. Sheldon that O'Connor "is an impostor from Europe; too many of whom, I am sorry to say, are found in this country" (*FQ* 72). It is striking that Lysander's letter identifying O'Connor as a

European impostor arrives at precisely the narrative moment when O'Connor is on the verge of converting his cultural capital into the social and economic capital he does not possess. O'Connor's genteel performances—especially his taste and knowledge of literature in conversation (*FQ* 71) nearly succeed in revising Mr. Sheldon's original physiognomic discernment of his character. Lysander's letter, however, exposes O'Connor as an impostor and depicts his self-fashioning as a fraudulent practice. In doing so, these genteel letters of recommendation confirm what Mr. Sheldon had read from O'Connor's face.

Lysander's identification of O'Connor as "an impostor from Europe" also casts the struggle between the individual performances of upstarts and the social networks of established elites within America as one between European immigrants and natives of America. The struggle between the social capital of the genteel Sheldon/Lysander and the cultural capital of the aspirant O'Connor is displaced onto a discourse of nationalism. When Dorcasina believes O'Connor's account of Lysander's letter rather than Lysander's account of O'Connor, Mr. Sheldon reiterates the terms of this displacement. He exclaims, "Alas, my dear! I grieve to see you thus infatuated. Will you persist in giving less *credit* to one of your own *countrymen*, whose character for probity is well known and acknowledged, than to a *foreigner*, whom nobody knows, and who has nothing to recommend him but *his own bare assertions?*" (*FQ* 76; my emphasis). Sheldon's remarks disclose how the nationalist binary of native and immigrant is ultimately in the service of extending credit to those whose legitimacy is based on established social networks rather than embodied cultural capital alone. Similar to the dramatic invocation of America discussed in the previous chapter, America seems to matter more as the location for alternative social practices than it does as a model for imagined national affiliation.

Genteel letters of recommendation, like physiognomy, prove only partially effective in countering the effects of Dorcasina's novel-mania. *Female Quixotism* challenges the efficacy of such social networks by routinely having its letters of recommendations disregarded, forged, or delayed. O'Connor's literary performances, including forging a letter from a Philadelphia gentleman, enable him to elude the social networks for legitimating his character and status. He convinces Dorcasina, for example, to accept Lysander's damaging letter as an act of jealousy from a spurned lover. That Dorcasina disregards Lysander's letter as well as her father's assessment represents a more general failure of the communal norms of gentility to establish the visibility of immoral character in a man who had "so much the manners and appearance of a gentleman" (*FQ* 141). In fact, Dorcasina only relinquishes O'Connor's claims to gentility after witnessing the spectacle of his public whipping in Philadelphia. While physiognomy and genteel social networks are able to detect imposition and forestall the rapid social mobility of men of low social origin, they are also insufficient for recognizing and reproducing gentility in *Female Quixotism*. Although nobody actually succeeds in seducing Dorcasina and gaining her estate, nobody marries her either.

Female Quixotism is remarkable for its insistence on how the social and economic capital of gentility might be jeopardized as much by the participation of patriarchs who legitimate the cultural capital of novels as it is by the Chesterfieldian seducers who exploit it. Unlike *The Coquette*, which excuses the seduced's father with a premature death and an inconsequential patrimony, *Female Quixotism* characterizes the seduced's father as a wealthy man of discernment who should know better. Mr. Sheldon and the patriarchal authority he embodies are not missing in *Female Quixotism* so much as negligent. If Dorcasina's wealth continually attracts social climbing seducers and if her novel-mania facilitates their designs, at least part of the blame for her condition is assigned to her father.[48] By indulging his own "fondness for books" (particularly novels), Mr. Sheldon is shown to be as responsible as his daughter for putting his capital at risk. His large library had "every novel, good, bad, and indifferent, which the bookstore of Philadelphia afforded" (*FQ* 6), the narrator informs us, but he never considered "their dangerous tendency to a young inexperienced female mind; nor the false ideas and manners, with which they would inspire a fanciful girl, educated in retirement and totally unacquainted with the ways of the world" (*FQ* 6). It is only after throwing O'Connor out of his house that he "groaned, in bitterness of spirit, for having suffered her imagination to be so filled with descriptions of such scenes as those he had recently witnessed; and was upon the point of committing to the flames every novel within his daughter's reach" (*FQ* 89). Yet, he never burns them. Throughout the novel, Mr. Sheldon acknowledges his culpability and regrets that "he had injudiciously indulged her in making [novels] her chief amusement" (*FQ* 77). "Oh! those poisonous, those fatal novels!," he exclaims, "Would to heaven people could find some better employment than thus turning the heads of inexperienced females! Would to heaven I could have foreseen the fatal consequences of allowing you a free access to them!" (*FQ* 144).[49] Despite his protests, which resonate with the complaints made by Anglo-American critics of the novel, Mr. Sheldon appears helpless to stop the "free access" to culture.

Physiognomy appears far less frequently during the second half of *Female Quixotism*, in which the reading practices of the female quixote figure much more prominently in the seduction plots than the Chesterfieldian performances of male seducers. Whereas in Book 1, the Sheldon estate is repeatedly endangered by dissimulating Chesterfieldian seducers on the one hand and Dorcasina's novel-mania on the other, in Book 2 that threat is almost exclusively associated with her novel reading. The figure for cultural capital is transformed in Book 2 from the male seducer to the female quixote as Dorcasina projects gentility onto characters of low social origin who do not actively dissemble to seduce. As a result, the struggle over culture shifts from restricting the kind of capital it might provide to upwardly mobile men to contesting imagined social spaces and trajectories inconsistent with an anterior genteel community.

The shift in emphasis from the Chesterfieldian seducer to the female quixote is perhaps most strongly registered in the John Brown seduction plot. Smollett's *Roderick Random* convinces Dorcasina that one of her servants, John Brown, is "a gentleman in disguise" (*FQ* 227). Brown, however, is no gentleman. His manners are "awkward," his speech "boorish" (*FQ* 228). He does not aggressively seduce Dorcasina so much as let "her remain in her error" (*FQ* 232). Unlike earlier seducers in the novel (such as O'Connor), Brown is illiterate and "ignorant of polite language, and especially of that of novels" (*FQ* 238). Brown, in short, possesses no cultural capital in any form. Yet, novels still manage to facilitate his social and economic mobility by inspiring Dorcasina to recognize him as an equal, speak familiarly with him, increase his wages, and promote him to overseer of her estate. After Dorcasina's servant, Betty, reminds her that no one in town would think John genteel, Dorcasina replies, "I shall not trouble myself with the opinion of people of no penetration" (233). Novels are dangerous not merely because they facilitate seduction, but because they contest the norms constitutive of genteel social space. For Dorcasina, her copy of *Roderick Random* matters more than her genteel community in forming her categories of social perception.

Female Quixotism, like *The Coquette*, promotes a less imaginative, more "rational" model of reading by contrasting the reading practice and subsequent social trajectory of Dorcasina with another female from her same genteel social network. Harriot Stanly, like Julia Granby in *The Coquette*, is the younger, less imaginative, and more discerning neighbor of Dorcasina. Unlike Dorcasina, who reads her father's library full of novels indiscriminately, the boarding-school–educated Harriot has never read a novel without her mother's permission (*FQ* 221). Harriot, like Julia Granby, enters the novel late (Book 2) and her delayed appearance indicates that her exemplary reading practice is directed more toward readers than Dorcasina. As a type of implied reader of the novel, Harriot orients our understanding of the satire, and in this capacity she is far less sympathetic toward her foil than Julia Granby is toward Eliza. When Harriot first sees Dorcasina, for example, she can barely restrain her laughter and is later reprimanded by her mother for calling Dorcasina a ridiculous "old maid" (*FQ* 177).

Dorcasina and Harriot differ, however, not merely in the alternative reading practices they embody—unregulated and overly imaginative for the one, discriminating and rational for the other—but in the form of cultural capital that they believe novels possess.[50] For Dorcasina, novels matter mostly in reproducing cultural capital in its embodied state. They provide a form of knowledge that can be acquired and displayed conversationally in the metropolitan space of polite performance. Dorcasina informs Harriot, for instance, that if she had never read a novel, she would be considered "destitute of all taste and refinement" in Philadelphia (*FQ* 221). For Harriot, however, novels approximate cultural capital in its objectified state. Novels matter less for the "taste" they might signify in face-to-face conversation than for the social spaces and trajectories they might represent symbolically.[51] Harriot, like so many of the postrevolutionary moral critics discussed above, values novels for their power to impose a legitimate vision of the social world.[52] They are permissible to the extent that they imagine social spaces that conform to an anterior social reality recognized as legitimate by her genteel community (in this case, embodied by her mother). Dorcasina's novels, Harriot complains, "colour every thing much too highly, and represent characters and situations, which never have existed" (*FQ* 221). Tenney's novel suggests that the struggle between social and cultural capital is simultaneously a struggle over the form of symbolic cultural capital that novels will possess. The respective social trajectories of Dorcasina and Harriot in *Female Quixotism*, however, decide the contest in favor of reading novels with discretion and not as a form of embodied cultural capital. Harriot's less imaginative reading practice results in a marriage to the distinguished Captain Barry, whereas Dorcasina's lifetime of indiscriminate novel reading leaves her unmarried and depressed. Although Dorcasina narrowly escapes all of her seducers, she survives only to live alone with the "pleasing delusion which she had all her life fondly cherished, of experiencing the sweets of connubial love, . . . now entirely vanished, . . . she became pensive, silent, and melancholy" (*FQ* 322).

Dorcasina's melancholic fate—like Harriot's favorable one—symbolically promotes a less imaginative novel reading practice and helps *Female Quixotism* to distinguish itself from the genre it so tirelessly satirizes.[53] In fact, the novel concludes with Dorcasina's conversion to Harriot's position on novels. Her final letter to Harriot urges her to protect her daughters from the "false ideas of life" and "illusory expectations" (*FQ* 325) found within novels and to "describe life to them as it really is" (*FQ* 325). The didacticism of *Female Quixotism*, like so many postrevolutionary novels, is predicated on producing pictures that would edify, not seduce, its readers. Addressed to "To all Columbian Young Ladies, Who Read Novels and Romances," *Female Quixotism* promises to deliver the "true uncoloured history of a romantic country girl, whose head had been turned by the unrestrained perusal of Novels and Romances" (FQ 3). Dorcasina's conversion at the end of the novel brings the didacticism of *Female Quixotism* full circle as her demand to "describe life . . . as it really is" echoes the compiler's pledge at the beginning of the novel to provide "a true picture of real life" (*FQ* 1).

It is significant that Harriot's more discriminating reading practice occupies the same antithetical position to Dorcasina's overly imaginative reading practice in Book 2 as the physiognomic transparency of the face did in Book 1. This is not to suggest that the two are interchangeable, but rather to draw attention to how they, as social practices, are imagined to function in analogous ways in *Female Quixotism*. Just as physiognomy devalued the embodied cultural capital funding the performances of dissimulating seducers by identifying distinction (or its absence) with the face, the triumph of Harriot's less imaginative novel reading practice devalues the female quixote's conception of novels as a form of embodied cultural capital. Reading novels is like reading faces to the extent that both are practices that model categories of social perception and define the contours of social space. Physiognomy in *Female Quixotism* thus serves both as a discourse for discerning character *within* the novel and as an analogue for how and why novels should be read.

"A Sentinel In Their Bosoms": Physiognomy in *Lucinda*

The value of physiognomy to unmask dissimulating seducers is also expressed in P. D. Manvill's 1807 sentimental novel of seduction, *Lucinda, or, The Mountain Mourner*. The exemplary reader of men and novels, however, is no longer imagined through a character *within Lucinda*, but as the reader *of* it. The novel consists of twenty-one tear-filled letters that Mrs. Manvill writes to her sister Nancy over the course of her stepdaughter's seduction, pregnancy, and eventual death. Although published throughout the nineteenth century, *Lucinda* reproduces a number of features common to postrevolutionary seduction fiction: an orphaned female who is seduced, impregnated, and abandoned by an upwardly mobile, dissembling, and self-interested seducer; the failure of familial and social networks to prevent the seduction; a monitorial figure/narrator who laments the lack of a system for detecting the seducer and who proposes physiognomy as one; the death of the seduced; and a final "monumental inscription" (172) at the novel's close.[54] Yet, *Lucinda* departs from the seduction fiction previously discussed in at least two important ways. Unlike the largely metropolitan social spaces imagined in *The Inquisitor*'s London, *The Coquette*'s Boston, or *Female Quixotism*'s suburban Philadelphia, the social space of *Lucinda* is decidedly rural, set in the mountains of upstate New York. Moreover, the community affected by the cultural capital of Chesterfieldianism in *Lucinda* is no longer exclusively genteel. The problem of discerning the character of men, *Lucinda* suggests, is not necessarily restricted to the metropolitan world of the genteel.

The social trajectory of the dissimulating seducer in *Lucinda* initially demonstrates how cultural capital might be converted successfully into social and economic capital, but by the end of the novel that narrative is replaced by one of immobility and the apparent durability of social origin. The novel's seducer, Melvin Brown, is a combination of Franklinian ambition and Chesterfieldian duplicity. With no social or economic capital, Brown's only recommendation at first is his industry.[55] In the beginning, he treats Lucinda with "distinguished attention" (*L* 60) and gets her to accept his declarations of love as sincere. Yet, Lucinda fails to see that revenge, not love, fuels Brown's affection as his pride motivates him to seduce the woman who earlier rejected him. Although not specifically identified as a Chesterfieldian, Brown exhibits many of its attributes. He hides his vice and self-interest behind a "magnetic mantle of flattery" (*L* 65) and displays "all the pompous parade of disdainful arrogance" (*L* 109). "It was necessary that he should feign the most honorable and disinterested attachment," Mrs. Manvill writes to her sister, "To a heart wholly unacquainted with the deceit of man, it was morally impossible that his wretched victim should detect his complicated arts" (*L* 112). Yet, when his business falters, Brown eventually abandons her for a "young lady in Scipio, of some considerable prospects" (*L* 116). With his new friends and "studied improvement," Brown gains admission "into the society of gentlemen of respectability and figure" (*L* 114) and he declines marrying Lucinda in order to maintain his newly won reputation. Thus, Brown's mobility in the novel does not depend on his seduction, but on its concealment.

Lucinda is unusual in that the seducer appears to have a moment of transformation that would contradict the physiognomic logic the novel otherwise promotes. Upon learning of Lucinda's death, Brown declares her innocence and agrees to comply with the law that calls for him to support his daughter Julia (*L* 175). Brown's transformation from duplicitous seducer to penitent father, however, is short-lived as he soon devolves into drunkenness and insanity (*L* 178). By the novel's close, "a gentleman of veracity" reports how Brown has been "reduced to the most extreme poverty, and is now, literally speaking, a vagabond; supporting himself by the mean employment of a fiddler" (*L* 179). The denial of Brown's transformation and his failed mobility is emphasized in the closing passages when Mrs. Manvill reports that despite "his voluntary engagements, to become the father of the sweet babe, and his ready submission to the demand of public justice, by giving bail for its support; yet has he been totally regardless of former, and by some, to me inexplicable means, has hitherto avoided the latter" (*L* 180). Initially poor and with little education (*L* 144), Brown rises to mix with "people of distinction" (*L* 145) only to end the novel an impoverished itinerant.

If the denial of Brown's reformation and his mobility suggest the durability of both his moral character and his social origin, *Lucinda* advocates the face as the location for its detection. Upon reflecting on her daughter's seduction, Mrs. Manvill explains to her sister that Lucinda's death tragically demonstrates physiognomy's necessity:

> Would each one of our sex, my Nancy, instead of contemplating in their mirrors, real or imaginary beauties, devote a small proportion of the inestimable moments of time, to the general study of physiognomy, we should not, I presume, so often see the victims of perjury, sinking to their untimely graves. Little as the study of this science is recommended to the fair sex, yet believe me, I conceive it to be of the greatest importance. As those who have ever made any tolerable proficiency in the art, will seldom fail to discriminate, betwixt the electric glow of voluptiousness and the milder radiance of celestial love, which beams on the eyes of sacred affection. (*L* 68)

Lucinda, like *The Coquette*, proposes the physiognomic distinction of the face as a means to see past the polite performances of dissimulating seducers and to discern their permanent moral character and, moreover, specifically directs such discernment toward readers of the novel (imagined as "each one of our sex").[56] Similar to *The Coquette* and *Female Quixotism*, physiognomic discernment in *Lucinda* compensates for a parental surveillance that is either absent or ineffectual. Unlike Lucinda's father, who is unable to keep the promise he made to her birth mother to guard Lucinda "against the duplicity of the human heart, and those complicated arts of seduction concomitant of it" (*L* 48), Mrs. Manvill hopes that Lucinda's example "might prove an awful warning to all the youthful and innocent daughters of Adam" (*L* 68). She laments to her sister, "Oh! Nancy, how ardently could I wish, that every soul of unspotted innocence, might read and *mentally realize* the wrongs and sufferings of the unfortunate Lucinda," she tells her sister (*L* 155; my emphasis). The absence of any response to Mrs. Manvill's letters in *Lucinda*, as Mischelle Anthony notes, allows "readers to step into the role of Nancy, the watchful older sibling" (*L* 299). Nancy's silence collapses *Lucinda*'s implied and actual readers so that the exemplary reader of men, letters, and novels is no longer represented by an actual character in the novel (such as Julia Granby or Harriot Stanly), but is projected onto its recipient (Nancy Manvill and, by extension, the readers of *Lucinda*). "It is through the person of Manvill that social virtue will emanate," Anthony argues, "and through *Lucinda*'s readers that such practice will flourish" (299). *Lucinda* thus defends the novel from those critics who claim it facilitated seduction by claiming to provide its readers with a "sentinel in their bosoms—which will be ever watchful and ready to warn them of the approach of danger, under the mask of the most pure and disinterested attachment" (*L* 155) and, as Mrs. Manvill's remarks suggest, physiognomy was instrumental to its didacticism.

Like other seduction novels discussed in this chapter, *Lucinda* reflects the more general struggle over how distinction would operate in the social space of early America. On the one hand, Brown's initial upward mobility and Lucinda's seduction testify to the efficacy of cultural capital in overcoming poverty, low social origin, and immoral character on the basis of individual polite performance. On the other, Brown's eventual social and economic descent and Mrs. Manvill's recommendation of physiognomy imagine a social space in which the face might restrict the mobility generated by such cultural capital. Where parental surveillance and familial, moral, or social networks fail to prevent Lucinda's seduction by a smooth-talking seducer, *Lucinda* tells readers physiognomy will succeed.

Ormond and "The Vanity of Physiognomy"

I would like to conclude this chapter by examining how physiognomy's capacity to discern character in the face of dissimulating seducers and in the absence of parental surveillance is addressed in Charles Brockden Brown's seduction novel *Ormond* (1799). *Ormond*, provides one of the first sustained critiques of the physiognomic logic of distinction, its transposition in the determination of character, and the importance of both to the postrevolutionary seduction novel. Brown's novel questions how well the face might counter dissimulation by interrogating the same visual strategies that seduction novelists associated with the revelation of permanent moral character: portraiture and physiognomy.[57] The notoriously duplicitous nature of Ormond, the novel's villain and title character, has been identified as embodying 1790s conspiratorial anxieties, embracing a vision of ruthless necessity, questioning epistemological certainty, expressing America's self-interested brand of liberal individualism, unraveling the sympathetic bonds of social cohesion, and disclosing the performative nature of national and ethnic identity.[58] Although critics have demonstrated how Ormond's duplicity subverts contemporary models of psychological and political certainty, I believe that what is at stake in Ormond's unintelligibility is less a matter of determining who he is than a matter of determining how the characters and, by extension, the readers of the novel go about discerning his character. What is ultimately in question in Brown's novels, as Michael Davitt Bell puts it, is "not the sort of reality to be portrayed but the very act of portrayal" (159). *Ormond* is more than "a version of the standard eighteenth-century seduction tale" (89), as Steven Watts and others have recognized, it is a critique of how postrevolutionary seduction novels such as *The Coquette* proposed the face's legibility as a means for discerning character.[59] In contrast to the static, instantaneous, and permanent notion of character obtained by the physiognomic scrutiny of a face or portrait, *Ormond* proposes a more fluid, sequential, and revisable notion of character accumulated from multiple perspectives, times, and sources. In doing so, *Ormond* contends that the type of rational reflection produced by reading seduction novels—which was what distinguished those novels from the dangerous effects of romances and justified them in the eyes of its postrevolutionary moral critics—should be associated with the genre's temporal rather than its spatial features.

  Ormond revolves around the central problem of discerning the character of its eponymous villain. "Ormond will perhaps appear to you a contradictory or unintelligible being," writes Sophia Courtland at the start of *Ormond*, but, she assures us, he is "not a creature of fancy."[60] Despite Sophia's insistence on his actuality, she later confesses that "I know no task more arduous than a just delineation of the character of Ormond" (*O* 125) for "no one was more impenetrable than [he], though no one's character seemed more easily discerned" (*O*

131). The ability to penetrate Ormond's performances and discern his permanent character becomes one of the central, if more difficult, tasks in the novel. Reading him correctly confounds a number of characters, especially Thomas Craig, Helena Cleves, and the novel's heroine Constantia Dudley. Yet, as Sophia's remarks suggest, discerning Ormond's character is not just a problem for the persons within her story, it is a problem for her as the author of that story, and thus, for the readers of her narrative as well.

Since the intended reader of a novel "may reveal itself . . . through an individualization of the public [or] through apostrophes to the reader" (Iser 33), Sophia's allusion to the problem of discerning Ormond's character in her dedicatory epistle to I. E. Rosenberg testifies to its importance in the construction of the intended reader of *Ormond*. On the one hand, Rosenberg's familiarity with the "distinctions of birth" (*O* 38) and the artificiality of rank in his "native country" (*O* 38) of Germany recall the genteel distinction of colonial America's aristocratic past and its residual persistence into the postrevolutionary present.[61] On the other, Rosenberg's unfamiliarity with American "society and manners" (*O* 38) positions him as a reader who is curious to know what kind of social space might accompany the nation's new political order. In drawing our attention to the difficulty in discerning Ormond's character within the novel's opening address to Rosenberg, Brown aligns the daunting task Constantia and Sophia face in reading Ormond with the task readers face in reading *Ormond* itself. The question for each is the same: how might character be discerned in a postrevolutionary American society epitomized by both the absence of "distinctions" and "rank" (*O* 38) and the presence of deceivers like Ormond?

What is unusual and, I will contend, important about understanding Ormond's duplicity is that "to the vulgar eye" he "was equally inscrutable in his real and assumed characters" (*O* 131). Ormond can both dissimulate his character behind his own face—as he does when he asks Constantia if her "discernment [can] reach the bounds of [his] knowledge" and detect "the monsters that are starting into birth *here*" in "his forehead" (*O* 245)—and he can simulate another character and another face that is perceived to be separate from his own, as he does when he disguises himself as a "negro [. . .] chimney sweep" (*O* 145). In the former, Ormond dissembles his character without concealing his face. In the latter, he conceals both his character and his face. Ormond's capacity to disguise not only his character but his face across racial lines (just as his sister Martinette de Beauvais does across gender lines) confronts the physiognomic logic by which the face was believed to externalize permanent moral character during the postrevolutionary period, and it questions that logic's capacity to counter the performances of dissimulators like Ormond.

Ormond confronts the same problem that other postrevolutionary novels such as *The Coquette* and *Female Quixotism* do: how do you discern the character of an unknown or dissembling person in the absence of established forms of distinction? And, like those novels, *Ormond* didactically contrasts the educations, minds, and fates of two female characters—Constantia Dudley and Helena Cleves—as part of its response.[62] "The education of Constantia" Dudley, for instance, was carefully "regulated by the peculiar views of her father, who sought to make her not alluring and voluptuous, but eloquent and wise" (*O* 62). She reads Tacitus, Milton, Newton, and Hartley—authors frequently recommended by the moral critics discussed earlier in this chapter—instead of the "amorous effusions of Petrarch and Racine" (*O* 62) so that she can learn "the structure and power of the senses" and "the principles and progress of human society" (*O* 62). Vigilant and virtuous, Constantia is described as "ever busy in interpreting the language of features and looks" (*O* 97) and her physiognomic discernment is instrumental to how she navigates the treacherous and volatile urban world imagined in *Ormond*. In contrast, Helena Cleves's "intellectual deficiencies" (*O* 140) are explained in terms of her lack of regulated reading: "She was a proficient in the elements of no science. . . . She was ignorant of the past or present condition of mankind. History had not informed her of the one nor the narratives of voyages nor the deductions of geography of the other. The heights of eloquence and poetry were shut out from her view" (*O* 140). Unlike Constantia, Helena "had not reasoned on the principles of human action, nor examined the structure of society" (*O* 140). As a result, Helena lacks the "keener penetration" that "would have predicted" the characters and views of her seducer Ormond (*O* 135). Without a proper course of reading, Helena's education allows her "fancy" to be "occupied with the image of Ormond" (*O* 134); consequently, she is unable to see Ormond clearly and therefore fails to reflect on his character rationally.

Despite *Ormond*'s resemblance to the conventional postrevolutionary seduction novel, it departs from the genre in two important ways. First, *Ormond* separates the threat of seduction from social mobility by splitting the conventional dissembling seducer into two separate characters: one who seeks social mobility, but not seduction (Craig); the other who seeks seduction, but not social mobility (Ormond). In addition, the association of Chesterfieldianism with dissimulation is minimized in *Ormond* as it is associated with minor characters (such as Martynne or Sophia's mother). Neither of the two central dissemblers in the novel—Craig or Ormond—assume the mask of performed gentility to accomplish their goals. As a result, *Ormond*, unlike novels such as *The Coquette*, displays little interest in preserving the integrity of a genteel community whose distinction is otherwise threatened by the cultural capital of Chesterfieldianism. Second, *Ormond* repeatedly demonstrates how discourses such as physiognomy and cultural forms such as portraiture perpetuate rather than prevent dissimulation. Physiognomic distinction is an inadequate counter-practice for dissimulation in *Ormond* not so much because its claims are false, but because they are largely held to be true. Throughout the novel, characters and, by extension, readers of the narrative obtain information from the faces of other characters that is initially considered reliable, but is later shown to be erroneous.

No character is more strongly identified with physiognomy's limitations in *Ormond* than its heroine Constantia Dudley. If Julia Granby pretends to be a physiognomist in *The Coquette*, Constantia Dudley actively is one. Undoubtedly aided by her education into "the structure and power of the senses" (*O* 62), Constantia "delighted to investigate the human countenance and treasured up numberless conclusions as to the coincidence between mental and external qualities" (*O* 97). Yet, since she "judged, like the mass of mankind from the most obvious appearances," she was, like them, subject "to impulses which disdained the control of her reason" (*O* 70). Faces, it turns out, can be "heterogeneous" and thus perplexing to interpret (*O* 63). The dissembling swindler, Craig, for example, opens the novel by exploiting Constantia's physiognomically informed judgments and her father's profit-driven blindness. Craig's ability to meet the expectation of "an open and ingenuous aspect" allows him, as Stephen Burroughs did, to deceive and ruin the Dudleys. Their confidence in the transparency of Craig's character on his face, as opposed to its opacity, makes him "standing proof of the vanity of physiognomy" (*O* 116) as the novel discloses how physiognomy is not the instrument for rational reflection, but rather its antithesis.

Despite her disastrous experience in discerning Craig's character, Constantia is a slow learner when it comes to faces. In Chapter 8, her physiognomic discernment is again put to a test when the endlessly virtuous, yet hopelessly impoverished Constantia is left with little choice but to sell her prized lute in order to purchase fuel for the winter. As she enters a shop looking for a purchaser, "a face instantly arrested" her attention (*O* 97). Constantia's interest in the stranger's face is not surprising, the narrator explains, because, as a

physiognomist, "she had often been forcibly struck by forms that were acci-
dentally seen, and which abounded with this species of mute expression" and
which "conveyed at a single glance what could not be imparted by volumes"
(*O* 97). Although "the accuracy and vividness with which pictures of this kind
presented themselves" to Constantia's imagination "resembled the operations
of a sixth sense" (*O* 98), the narrator admits that these pictures may have been
the result of "the enthusiastic tenor" of Constantia's "own conceptions" (*O*
98) more than the face itself. Nonetheless, the narrator relates how the face of
the woman in the shop attests to the fact that "the genius conspicuous in her
aspect was heroic and contemplative" (*O* 98). As Constantia stands "absorbed"
(*O* 98), it is evident that she admires the woman's face and the character it
apparently so clearly expresses. Yet, the narrator, Sophia Courtland, is careful
to distance herself and her narration from the portrait she has just provided
for us as readers—saying that "such is the portrait of this stranger, delineated
by Constantia" (*O* 98)—so that we know that the face Constantia sees is the
result of her fancy as much as the stranger's countenance. "If we substitute
a nobler stature, and a complexion less uniform and delicate," Sophia adds,
the portrait "is suited, with the utmost accuracy to herself. She was probably
unconscious of this resemblance; but this circumstance may be supposed to
influence her in discovering such attractive properties in a form thus vaguely
seen. These impressions, permanent and cogent as they were, were gained at a
single glance" (*O* 98).

What Constantia is "unconscious" of in this scene is the influence of
countenance on countenance that was described by Lavater and reprinted in
periodicals like the *New York Magazine* in 1796 and in the Philadelphia *Literary
Museum* in 1797. The *New York Magazine*, for example, reprinted an excerpt
from Lavater's *Essays on Physiognomy* entitled "Of the Influence of Countenance on Countenance." The article asserts that "the fact is indubitable, that
countenances attract countenances, and also that countenances repel countenances; that similarity of features between two sympathetic and affectionate
men, increase with development and mutual communication of their peculiar
individual sensations" (251). The author contends that "this resemblance of
features, in consequence of mutual affection, is ever the result of internal nature and organization, and therefore, of the character of the persons. It ever
has its foundation in a preceding, perhaps, imperceptible resemblance" (252).
In short, the article suggests that people with similar faces might be attracted
to each other since they share similar characters. Moreover, it implies that

people might know the character of their facial duplicates without having met them since their duplicate's character is likely to be similar to their own.

Of course, the woman whom Constantia stares at so reverently and with whom she identifies so strongly at the shop is none other Martinette de Beauvais, the cross-dressing revolutionary assassin and sister of the novel's dissimulating villain, Ormond. When Constantia first meets Martinette, she fails to realize that although she and Martinette may resemble each other in terms of faces, they do not resemble each other in terms of moral character. Indeed, it is only after Constantia learns that Martinette has disregarded the "distinction of sex" (*O* 205), killed "thirteen officers" in the name of liberty (*O* 205), and was prepared to kill herself if an assassination attempt had materialized that she begins "to contemplate more deliberately the features of her guest" (*O* 207) than when she had first but "vaguely seen" her face at the shop. If "hitherto she had read in them nothing that bespoke the desperate courage of a martyr and the deep designing of an assassin" (*O* 207), now "the image which her mind had reflected from the deportment of this woman was changed" and "the likeness which she had feigned to herself was no longer seen" (*O* 207). The more Constantia hears about and reflects on Martinette's bloody and violent life, the less she sees their resemblance. That Constantia's de-identification with Martinette occurs at the moment they discuss "the love of liberty" (*O* 206) discloses the limitations of Constantia's desire for independence and situates her somewhere in between the sumptuous docility of Helena and the violent freedom of Martinette. Unwilling to go all the way like her two female counterparts, Constantia refuses to become the victim to her gender or the annihilator of it—a choice she reaffirms at the end of the novel when she decides to kill Ormond rather than submit to his rape or commit her own suicide. Yet, what is perhaps most striking about Constantia's recognition that she is not like Martinette is that her image of Martinette's face appears to have been modified by her knowledge of Martinette's story rather than further scrutiny of her face. Or, to put it more precisely, Martinette's story changes the way Constantia looks at her face. In doing so, *Ormond* directly challenges the physiognomic logic that its heroine Constantia so completely embraces at the start of the novel.

The idea that knowledge of a person's character or emotions might be more the product of the observer's fancy than the observed's face also figures prominently in Baxter's reading of Monrose/Martinette's visage earlier in *Ormond*. As Julia Stern and others have argued, Baxter's misrecognition of

Martinette says as much about the contamination of his vision by "the force of the imagination" (*O* 93) as it does about the unreliability of reading facial expressions.[63] "The rueful pictures of my distress and weakness which were given by Baxter," Martinette tells Constantia much later in the novel, "existed only in his own fancy" (*O* 208). Just as Constantia learns that her vision needs to be supplemented by what Martinette's narrative tells her about her character, the reader of *Ormond* eventually learns that what Baxter may have seen was his own "fancy" more than Martinette's face. Martinette's subsequent remarks, however, revise more than what kind of face Baxter actually saw, they also revise what has happened in the novel. As a result, it is impossible to understand *Ormond* in terms of a sequence of pictures because whatever images the reader may have had of characters or events in the novel turn out to be partial, incomplete, and revisable by information provided later.

If, as I discussed above, the portrait is represented in *The Coquette* as both a sign of genuine, but misplaced, sexual intimacy and as a cultural form specifically designated to discern moral character from the face, the inclusion of a pawned miniature portrait in *Ormond* inverts that logic.[64] Rather than imagine the portrait's physiognomic distinction as an instrument for countering dissimulation, Brown reveals how the portrait's legibility encourages it. A portrait of Constantia's friend and the novel's narrator, Sophia Courtland, for example, initially serves as a sign of genuine, if intense, intimacy between the two women. "Habit," Sophia confesses, "made this picture a source of a species of idolatry" (*O* 61). Economic circumstances, however, force Constantia to part with the portrait and eventually the picture is bought by a dissimulating émigré named Martynne. "A man of specious manners and loud pretensions" (*O* 218), Martynne's "supercilious and ceremonious" air (*O* 233) resembles that of the typical Chesterfieldian featured in much seduction fiction. He is, as one critic describes him, "a kind of Billy Dimple" (Grabo 53), embodying the threat of cultural capital frequently associated with Chesterfieldianism. Martynne comes to America "bringing with him forged recommendatory letters, and, after passing from one end of the country to the other, contracting debts which he never paid and making bargains which he never fulfilled, he suddenly disappeared" (*O* 218). With the traditional familial and social networks for legitimating genteel distinction disrupted by the Atlantic—Martynne had "no kindred, no friends, no companions" in America (*O* 218)—he purchases Sophia's portrait in order to elevate his own status by circulating rumors that the woman depicted in it is not only a person of "rank, fortune, and intellectual accomplishments," but also his mistress (*O* 234). Far from identifying the dissimulator, the legibility of Sophia's character within her portrait ends up corroborating his deceptions.

Whereas Eliza's imagination misplaces the intimacy associated with the portrait in *The Coquette*, the market dislocates and exploits the portrait's social connotation of intimacy in *Ormond*. After Constantia pawns the portrait to M'Crea, he sells it to a goldsmith "for as much as the gold was worth" (*O* 215). The goldsmith, in turn, sells it to Martynne on the basis that he must have been "acquainted with the original" (*O* 216). When Sophia finally offers Martynne "double the value as a mere article of traffic" (*O* 235) for the picture, her purchase suggests that a cultural form can only reproduce social relations legitimately when its value is determined by means other than the market. Or to put it another way, the market jeopardizes a system of social relations where faces externalize character in *Ormond* because it trades in faces as if they were commodities. Sophia's inflated purchase attempts to restrict the mobility of her portrait whose representation of elevated character (and virtue) the market had otherwise exploited and endangered. "This mode of multiplying faces," Sophia later reflects, is not only "extremely prevalent in this age," it enables her portrait to "be in the possession of one whom [she] had never before seen" (*O* 234). Thus, the problem with portraiture in *Ormond* lies not in the undiscerning eyes of the people who look at them—as was the case in *The Coquette*—but rather in the distribution and circulation of the form itself.

Constantia's idolatrous relationship to Sophia's portrait confirms what Walter Benjamin would call its ritual or "cult value" (225) as a unique and authentic representation of her friend. "The unique value of the 'authentic' work of art," Benjamin explains, "has its basis in ritual" (224) and what matters most in cult art objects is "their existence, not their being on view" (225). When Constantia is forced to sell Sophia's portrait, the miniature's value is discussed in similarly ritualistic terms as the power "of this inestimable relic" over Constantia is compared to "that possessed by a beautiful Madonna over the heart of a juvenile enthusiast" (*O* 96). On the other hand, the portability of Sophia's portrait allows it to be displayed in public—the goldsmith "hung it upon his shop" (*O* 216)—and to acquire what Benjamin describes as "exhibition value" (224). "Exhibition value," Benjamin argues, "begins to displace cult value" during the advent of mechanical reproduction. The "cult value" of a work of art, however, can resist its "exhibition value" by retiring "into an ultimate retrenchment: the human countenance" (Benjamin 225). "For the last time," Benjamin observes, "the aura emanates from the early photographs in the fleeting expression of a human face" (226).[65]

Yet, in *Ormond*, Martynne is not interested in the "cult value" of Sophia's portrait for how well it brings forth her unique existence (after all he does not even know who she is), but rather for how well it displays the type of person she is. Even as the cultural form of the portrait attempts to preserve the unique existence of Sophia (through the "cult value" that Constantia enthusiastically assigns to it), the legibility of Sophia's face enhances its "exhibition value" on the open market. In other words, Sophia's face does not resist the portrait's "exhibition value," as Benjamin suggests, so much as it facilitates it. *Ormond* demonstrates how the market enables Martynne to exploit the rapidly emerging visual culture of the face in early America—what Aaron Burr identified as "the rage for portraits" (Dickson 25)—and its evolving relationship to distinction. The market's reduction of portraiture to commodity grants Martynne access to a portrait he otherwise would have never possessed, and the "cult value" and physiognomic legibility of that portrait legitimate claims about his social status that otherwise would never have been credible. Portraits are shown to be dangerous in *Ormond* because, in a world of physiognomic distinction, their faces can establish false social relations just as easily as they can reflect legitimate ones.

In addition to establishing how physiognomy and portraiture might perpetuate rather than prevent dissimulation, *Ormond* proposes that the postrevolutionary seduction novel's identification of dissimulation with rapid mobility might be misplaced as well. If the postrevolutionary seduction novel typically combines the self-interest of sexual gratification with the desire for mobility in dissimulating Chesterfieldians, then this figure is divided into two separate characters in *Ormond*. As a result, *Ormond* resembles these seduction novels in characterization and plot, but diverges from them in that social mobility in *Ormond* is associated with the swindling impostor and forger, Craig, whereas only the wealthy and leisured Ormond, in Richardsonian fashion, aspires to the depraved sport of sexual conquest. Ormond conforms to neither of the two primary social trajectories identified with Chesterfieldianism in postrevolutionary American culture. He is not an inferior who attempts to convert cultural capital into the economic or social capital he lacks. Nor is he is superior who is trying to recuperate economic or social capital at risk or already lost.

Whether we consider Craig as he represents himself to be (a low-born, recently emigrated white male from England) or as what Sophia represents him to be (a low-born itinerant from New Hampshire), the fact remains that his combination of poverty, literacy, and low social origin is similar to that of the postrevolutionary Chesterfieldian seducer. Yet, unlike Patrick O'Connor,

Craig has no interest in using marriage to obtain wealth and so he does not, in Chesterfieldian fashion, pose as a gentleman to seduce Constantia and gain her fortune (although he will later invent just such a seduction tale in an attempt to mislead Ormond). *Ormond*'s modification of the seduction novel's structure realigns the threat of the cultural capital of Chesterfieldianism away from the mechanics of genteel distinction and exposes how the postrevolutionary seduction novel sustains the latter by regulating the former. In contrast to the libertine who masquerades as a gentleman, Craig pretends to be what many of those characters suppress: a poor and frequently itinerant man of low or fallen character. If the point of the postrevolutionary seduction novel is to expose the face of the rake lurking beneath the façade of gentility, or as the narrator of Susanna Rowson's *Charlotte Temple* (1794) puts it, to distinguish "a red coat and silver epaulet" from a "fine gentleman," then *Ormond* wonders whether there is a physiognomic foundation from which to discriminate (25). Craig does not conceal a criminal profile underneath a genteel appearance, he simply exchanges one kind of performance for another. If anything, the novel discloses how Craig's Franklinian rise from a low-born and poor itinerant to a prosperous partner in a drug shop is virtually identical to his fraudulent business relationship with Mr. Dudley. In *Ormond*, dissimulation seems less a threat to commerce than its very foundation.

Yet, as duplicitous and immoral as Craig is, he is nothing more than "a pliant and commodious tool" (*O* 266) in the hands of the novel's other dissembler: Ormond. By placing dissimulation's most sinister effects under the direction of Ormond rather than Craig, the novel questions whether the threat of dissimulation identified by the seduction novel—social mobility—might lie elsewhere as well. Ormond's dissimulation proves to be unsettling precisely because he seeks neither status nor wealth. Ormond's seduction is instead motivated by self-interested pleasure, be it sexual or intellectual. His chief social end, as Norman Grabo asserts, "is to know the intentions, plans, and motivations of others so that he can control them for his own sake" (33). As Sophia explains, "Ormond aspired to nothing more ardently than to hold the reins of opinion—to exercise absolute power over the conduct of others, not by constraining their limbs or by exacting obedience to his authority, but in a way of which his subjects should be scarcely conscious. He desired that his guidance should control their steps, but that his agency, when most effectual, should be least suspected" (*O* 180). What bothers Sophia about Ormond is not so much his duplicity, but its invisibility.

Ormond is more insidious than Craig not merely because his homicidal behavior nearly matches the carnage of the yellow fever in the novel—Ormond kills his first person at the age of eighteen and countless others thereafter (including five in one bloody day)—but because he can disperse his will into the agency of others, thus can deceive through agents other than himself. Even though Craig forges letters and invents second identities, he alone is the agent of his deception. Craig's duplicity depends on getting people to believe that acts committed by him are actually committed by others; as *Ormond* makes clear, he exploits the logic of physiognomic distinction to accomplish his deceptions. In contrast, Ormond sidesteps the epistemological questions of disguising or confusing his own agency by simply getting others to act on his behalf. Whereas the success of Craig's imposture depends on the Dudleys acting as they normally would, the success of Ormond's machinations depends on manipulating or coercing others to act differently. Helena is manipulated into seduction, Craig is blackmailed into murder. Ormond can elude the postrevolutionary seduction novel's logic of physiognomic distinction not only by manufacturing and inhabiting second body images, but by manipulating and coercing second bodies. Ormond is disturbing because he does not have to do what moral critics and didactic novelists claimed he must do in order to deceive: confuse imagined and actual communities. Since his is an "absolute power" whose agency is invisible, he evades the visual strategies for discerning character promoted by the postrevolutionary seduction novel and those associated with reading them.

Having revealed the inadequacy of physiognomy as a counter-practice to dissimulation and as a possible model for distinction, *Ormond* struggles to identify a didactic alternative that would retain the connection between discerning character and the novel but reject the face as the foundation for such distinction. Craig's "skill in chirographical imitation" (*O* 116), for example, exploits the autographic integrity of writing—where a person's handwriting reveals aspects of character and signifies his or her unique identity—in order to further his schemes. What eventually undoes Craig's deceptions is not his mother's signatory, which merely hastens his exit, but Constantia's declaration to Ormond that Craig's letters are forged because her "modes of thinking and expression were beyond the reach of his mimicry" (*O* 158). Constantia proves Craig's forgery to Ormond not by distinguishing her *hand* from his, but by distinguishing her *mind* from his. By doing so, she exposes how the epistolary fiction of Craig—no less than those penned by seduction novelists—depend on the body's, particularly the face's, transparency. Instead, Constantia insists that her mind is not reducible to the shape of her hand. When she finally kills Ormond with a penknife, her act symbolically asserts the capacity of the materiality of writing to vanquish dissimulation, but, unlike the seduction novel, that writing can only do so at the expense of its relationship to corporeality. *Ormond* proposes that the autographic integrity of print be identified with the inimitable connection between the conscious mind and the flow of words across the page. As Brown would write in "The Man at Home," "In the selection of subjects of useful history, the chief point is not the virtue of a character. The prime regard is to be paid to the genius and force of mind that is displayed" (71–72).[66] According to Brown, what constitutes "a very useful spectacle" for the reader is precisely what cannot be pictured "at a single glance" (*O* 97) nor forged: "the force of the mind." Indeed, in the final moments before her penultimate decision to kill Ormond, the knowledge gained from Constantia's scrutiny of "those lineaments of Ormond" (*O* 268) yields to "a new series of reflections" (*O* 268).

If, as I have argued earlier in this chapter, contemporary moral criticism had distinguished the novel from the romance by virtue of the kind of "striking pictures" it depicted and the type of rational reflection those pictures encouraged in the minds of its readers, *Ormond* challenges that model of reading as seeing in favor of one that aligns reflection not with the static visual arts (such as portraiture) and the kinds of discourses used to interpret them (physiognomy), but with the temporality, sequentiality, and multiple perspectives of the literary arts. Sophia, for example, specifically recognizes and disavows the kind of pictures produced by the seduction novel when she discusses the letters from Constantia that serve as the basis for *Ormond*. Constantia's letters, like those found within an epistolary novel like *The Coquette*, are powerful enough to dry Sophia's eyes of tears and vivid enough to produce a "picture" of "the many-coloured scenes of human life" (*O* 57). "It is not impossible but these letters may be communicated to the world at some future period" (*O* 57), she says. Yet, she chooses not to publish them. By editing and arranging rather than simply reproducing Constantia's letters, Sophia attempts to retain the novel's didactic force—she hopes that "the perusal of this tale may afford you as much instruction as the contemplation of the sufferings and vicissitudes of Constantia Dudley has afforded to me" (*O* 276)—without reducing novel reading to picture viewing.

By denying us access to the vivid pictures generated by Constantia's correspondence and by exposing the flaws in her friend's physiognomic judgments, Sophia's narrative offers an alternative image of Ormond's character that is more fluid than stable, more provisional than complete, and more cumulative than instantaneous. Unlike her rival for Constantia's hand, Ormond, who boldly pronounces that "my knowledge [. . .] is infallible" (*O* 265), Sophia insists that hers is limited. She withholds "all the means" by which she "gained a knowledge of [Ormond's] actions" (*O* 37) and she admits that these means may not be "unerring and complete" (*O* 37). Although Sophia confesses to the circumstantial and possibly erroneous nature of her narrative, she defends her tale's didactic value by saying that "The circumstances in which I was placed were, perhaps, wholly singular. Hence, the knowledge I obtained was more comprehensive and authentic than was possessed by any one, even of the immediate actors of sufferers" (*O* 237). "This knowledge," she insists, "will not be useless to myself or to the world" (*O* 237) and for this reason she refuses to relinquish "the pen" (*O* 237) to that which we are not allowed to see: the pictures produced by reading Constantia's letters.

Ormond defends the novel against the romance by asserting that the temporal and sequential features of Sophia's tale will provide a "more comprehensive and authentic" knowledge than that produced by the spatial and instantaneous ones (portraiture and physiognomy) associated with the seduction novel. Despite their initial differences, Constantia and Sophia prove to be less adversarial than complementary by the time the novel draws to a close. No longer separate individual agents, Sophia and Constantia's letters and late-night conversations enable "the stream of [their] existence [. . .] to mix" so that henceforth they "were to act and to think in common" (*O* 242). Their survival and eventual departure together at the end of the novel champion a temporal, revisable, and fluid conception of discerning Ormond's character that is derived from multiple sources, times, and places over a visual, static, and physiognomically informed notion of character seen "at a single glance" by an individual observer. "To comprehend the whole truth with regard to the character and conduct of another, may be denied to any human being," Sophia reasons, "but different observers will have, in their pictures, a greater or less portion of this truth" (*O* 126). "Permanence of character," Sophia remarks, "can flow only from the progress of time and knowledge" (*O* 53). The temporal features of the novel, more than its spatial ones, *Ormond* suggests, can provide models for the discernment of permanent moral character in a world subject to the fluctuations of the market, accident, incident, circumstance, bias, and error.

The preceding remarks should cause us to reevaluate what has long been regarded by readers as one of the problems in *Ormond*: Sophia's unreliability as a narrator.[67] William Verhoeven is correct to suggest that "the relevant issue" in

Ormond "is not so much that Sophia is 'unreliable,'" but rather that "as readers *we rely entirely on her*" (213). While it is true that Sophia's narration "leads us nowhere—except [. . .] to the fictionality of the tale itself" (Verhoeven 213), this is not, as I have tried to demonstrate, a necessarily negative destination for the novel. The fictionality of Sophia's tale—the incomplete, partial, sequential, and therefore revisable nature of her narration—counters the era's didactic insistence that readerly visualization, in order to be rational and reflective, must create "striking pictures of virtue rewarded" (Foster *Boarding School* 23). Yet, however much eliminating the logic of physiognomic distinction from writing might relocate discerning character from faces to minds, *Ormond* does not answer how readers are to distinguish the seductive performances of Sinisterus Courtland from those of his namesake: Sophia Courtland. In fact, Sophia blurs the line between dissimulator and author herself when she says, "Forcibly to paint the evil, seldom fails to excite the virtue of the spectator and *seduce* him into wishes, at least, if not into exertions of beneficence" (*O* 237; my emphasis). Or perhaps this is *Ormond*'s point, Constantia kills one dissembling seducer only to run off with another. At least Sophia's lies are ones she can live with.

Ormond's critique of the physiognomic logic of distinction reveals just how central discourses for reading the face—such as physiognomy—and cultural forms for representing the face—such as portraiture—were to the textual and reading practices of the postrevolutionary seduction novel. It is important, however, not to lose sight of what the turn to physiognomy and its conflation of reading and seeing meant for postrevolutionary fiction. Although physiognomy was often specifically identified within these novels, the physical description of a character's face was, as *The Coquette* demonstrated, minimally and at times inconsistently informed by the actual practice of physiognomy. In this sense, these textual practices were related to, but nonetheless distinct from, the more extensive physical description that would be found within Cooper's novels, for instance, or the detailed and frequently phrenologically informed portraits found within later nineteenth-century fiction by authors such as John Davis and Harriet Beecher Stowe. The presence of physiognomy in the postrevolutionary seduction novel therefore matters less as a formal practice of literary characterization than as an alternative social practice for discerning character in the wake of the revolution's social and political transformations.

The transposition in the social perception of character that physiognomy promised—from the voluntary performances of the aspiring individual to the involuntary and permanent features of his face—was presented within these novels as a means to diminish the force of Chesterfieldian civility in the signi-fication of genteel distinction. These novels not only represented the struggle over distinction as one between the cultural capital associated with Chesterfiel-dian civility and the social capital of established elites, they also participated in that struggle by imagining social spaces in which culture, particularly the prac-tice of producing and reading novels, was imagined to work alongside, rather than independent of, prior institutions for genteel distinction (such as the social and familial networks of established gentry). The social spaces and tra-jectories symbolically imagined within these novels as well as the dispositions and ways of looking generated by reading them demonstrate how the post-revolutionary seduction novel enlisted culture to restrict rather than facilitate mobility. Although I have by no means accounted for each novel of seduction, let alone every early American novel, the centrality of the physiognomic logic of distinction to the postrevolutionary seduction novel—from its presence in *The Inquisitor* to its critique in *Ormond*—should invite us to reconsider the social and political aims of the genre. The postrevolutionary seduction novels discussed above certainly complicate those accounts that understand the rise of the novel in America either in terms of a critique of gentility or its democratization.[68] These novels, it would seem, speak more to the social con-sequences of republicanism for the genteel than to the political consequences of its failure for the common, and they spend more time worrying about the relationship of culture to mobility than they do in celebrating it.

Chapter 4

The Face of the Public

> I admit that there is such a thing as being of a bad stock; and the moral qualities are as communicable as the physical constitution of the features. Hence it is, that I would look to the stock in the selection of subjects; but still more to the physiognomy of youth.
> —Hugh Henry Brackenridge, *Modern Chivalry* (1792–1815)

THE PREVIOUS CHAPTER discussed how a number of postrevolutionary seduction novels imagined social spaces in which the visibility of distinction was relocated from the genteel yet voluntary performances of the polite individual to the permanent, involuntary, and unalterable features of his face, and they did so in ways resonant with the cultural practices of physiognomic distinction detailed in Chapter 1. The transposition in the social perception of character that discourses such as physiognomy promised was imagined within these novels as a deterrent to the performances of Chesterfieldian seducers and, by extension, to their promotion of cultural capital in the signification of genteel distinction. If seduction novels such as *The Coquette* dramatized the social consequences of failing to discern character from the face, other postrevolutionary texts specifically addressed the political consequences of locating character in the face. In the volatile political climate of postrevolutionary America, the social perception of character was a matter of some importance since it "was the principal criterion by which to judge the would-be custodians' merit" (Robertson 21).[1]

This chapter explores how the face was used to mediate the political problem of making distinction visible for the public. It seeks to complement recent explanations of the body's relationship to the public in the postrevolutionary period by situating two texts—Philip Freneau's "The Picture Gallery"

(1788) and Hugh Henry Brackenridge's *Modern Chivalry* (1792–1815)—into the contemporary discourses of portraiture and physiognomy that they invoke.[2] Following the recent work of art historians John Barrell, Wendy Bellion, Dorinda Evans, Brandon Fortune, Margaretta Lovell, and Ellen Miles, this chapter explores how postrevolutionary visual culture in America—its public portrait galleries, waxwork figures, prints, sculpture, profile portraits, silhouettes, and printed biographical portrait galleries—utilized the face to represent the abstract ideals of civic virtue and communicate exemplary character and thus participated in the creation of what Robert St. George has called a "visual national imaginary" (302). My analysis focuses specifically on why the rise in postrevolutionary public portraiture would be described as a political liability by Freneau in "The Picture Gallery" and as a possible benefit for the democracy by Brackenridge in *Modern Chivalry*. Freneau's "The Picture Gallery" identifies the rapid expansion in access to portraiture, the growing commercial self-interest of the portrait painter, and the rise of public portrait galleries of distinguished Americans (such as those assembled by Charles Willson Peale, Pierre Du Simitière, James and Ellen Sharples, Charles B. F. Saint-Mémin, and Joseph Delaplaine) as symptoms of a larger generic crisis in the civic function of portraiture. The problem with public portraiture, as Freneau conceives it, is that its emergent political benefit—the representation of abstract republican virtues (such as disinterestedness) to the public—is being undermined by its residual social function, the signification of distinction. As a result, portraits end up identifying civic virtue *with* the faces of particular persons rather than communicating it *through* them. In contrast, Brackenridge defends public portraiture on the grounds that its representations of the face can counter political dissimulation and serve the public interest in the new democracy. Various episodes from *Modern Chivalry* reveal how, on the one hand, the facial features of subordinate groups might be used to exclude them from embodying exemplary public character, while, on the other, physiognomically informed portraits might be used to embody otherwise abstract political ideals in the faces of specific individuals.[3] The asymmetries in *Modern Chivalry*'s application of the logic of physiognomic distinction to the public—individual and politically inclusive for dominant groups, collective and politically exclusive for subordinate groups—provides us with a postrevolutionary precursor to the epistemology of race in America, one in which the representation of racial difference consists not simply in the opposition between white and black or master and slave, but in whether a person's face first identifies the essential features of his individual character or his collective identity.[4]

The Problem of the Postrevolutionary Portrait

When "a person of any condition whatsoever, have he but as much money as the painter asks" can sit for a portrait, "this is a great abuse" (165) wrote the artist Gérard de Lairesse, because portraiture should teach "posterity to emulate the same virtues" (164) as those displayed by the sitter.[5] By the end of the eighteenth century, however, those looking for such virtues in Anglo-American portraits often found themselves staring at the faces of the ordinary and unremarkable. As the earl of Fife observed with respect to the problem in England: "before this century, very few people presented themselves to a painter, except those who were of great families, or remarkable for their actions in the service of their country, or for some other extraordinary circumstance, so that the field for enquiry was not extended, as lately, when every body almost who can afford twenty pounds, has the portraits of himself, wife, and children painted" (Pointon 2). "Since liberty and commerce have more levelled the ranks of society, and more equally diffused opulence," Henry Fuseli complained in 1801, "portrait-painting, which formerly was the exclusive property of princes, or a tribute to beauty, prowess, genius, talent, and distinguished character, is now become a kind of family calendar, engrossed by the mutual charities of parents, children, brothers, nephews, cousins, and relatives of all colours" (449).

While it is hardly surprising that European aristocrats and their painters would be dismayed by the fact that "liberty and commerce" were allowing people "of any condition whatsoever" to enter into the "exclusive" realm of portraiture—thus participate in its embodiment of distinction—it is interesting that the expanded access to portraiture during the last quarter of the eighteenth century should also disturb as ardent and enduring a republican as the American Philip Freneau. As one might expect from an author who occasionally signed himself as "One of the Swinish Multitude," Freneau does not share the earl of Fife's or Fuseli's concern with the deteriorating exclusivity of portraiture. Instead, he is troubled by the fact that wealth was allowing people who were neither "distinguished," "remarkable," nor "extraordinary" to appear in a cultural form historically known for communicating those very qualities to the public.

Freneau's short tale "The Picture Gallery" (1788) addresses the problem of whether the republican ideals of civic virtue and disinterestedness could be communicated through public portraiture. Modeled after Addison's dream essay in *Spectator* 83 (Marsh *Prose* 506), "The Picture Gallery" provides us with a first-person account of one man's initial visit to and subsequent vision about a portrait gallery. After viewing the portraits with a friend during the day, Freneau's narrator falls asleep and imagines encountering "the painter standing in the entrance of his gallery besieged by a number of humble petitioners" (50). The people soliciting portraits in "The Picture Gallery" are clearly identified with a rising, morally suspect, mercantile class whose privileging of personal profit over public interest during the American Revolution resulted in their rapid mobility. Just as portraiture had embodied social power in the faces of the colonial genteel elite, ambitious individuals such as "John Bullskin, cordwainer" (50) seek out portraits in order to substantiate and display their new social position.[6] Their intrusion into and unaccustomed appearance within public portraiture prompts Freneau's narrator to exclaim "who are yonder fat headed animals" when he first enters the portrait gallery, and the only explanation that his equally bewildered friend can muster at the time is that "there are too many placed here who are remarkable for nothing but their wealth" (49).

The prospect of a republican portraiture identified with people remarkable for something other than their wealth, Freneau suggests, is further compromised by the growing commercial self-interest of the portrait painter, who, in accepting the petitions of profiteers, stands to increase his own income as well.[7] If the portrait painter is as upwardly mobile as his clients, Freneau reasons, then why should he be any more inclined to value public over personal interests? When a common shoemaker accused of embezzling seeks to have his portrait painted, Freneau's artist refuses him more on account of his being "a rogue and poor" than on any moral or political principle. The only way his "swarthy visage" will "brighten up . . . my gallery," the painter explains, is if he acquires "five or six thousand pounds" (51). Similarly, after a tailor offers "no less than forty guineas" for his portrait, Freneau's painter suddenly seems unconcerned that this man kept public cloth for his own profit while revolutionary soldiers "perished by the severity of the weather" (52–53). If the portrait painter's refusal to depict the embezzling shoemaker's face hints that commercial self-interest might not necessarily be antithetical to communicating civic virtue, the painter's acceptance of the tailor's cash offer ironically reminds us that the choice of who should appear on the "public cloth" of portraiture is dictated more by personal profit than any sense of public interest.

As shocking as it may be to see the faces of common tailors and shoemakers exhibited in public, it is the immorality of the people depicted more than their social mobility that bothers the narrator as he recollects the picture gallery in his mind. Freneau criticizes the growing commercialization of portraiture not simply, or even primarily, because the particular persons displayed are now wealthy, but rather because their only claim to appear before the public is their wealth.[8] That the social conditions for publicity have been reduced to economic ones upsets Freneau (and his republican politics) less than the fact that the conditions for publicity no longer maintain any relationship to exemplary public character.[9] Freneau hopes to retain portraiture's traditional capacity to publicize distinction in the new republic, but he wants the criteria for the visibility of social reputation to be civic oriented rather than restricted to the genteel or wealthy. Freneau struggles to identify an alternative in "The Picture Gallery" in which the public representation of civic virtue could be communicated through, rather than identified with, the faces of particular persons.

Near the end of his dream, for instance, Freneau's narrator suggests that the public should get to view those nameless "men of real merit and virtue" like "the maimed and unrewarded soldier, and the honest and disinterested patriot" (53). Even though they may be common men, Freneau believes that their virtuous and disinterested conduct distinguishes them and justifies displaying their faces before the public. But this raises a familiar problem. How will the public discern character from the face? How will the public discriminate the portrait of a common, but moral man of public interest from that of a common, but immoral man of self-interest? To put it another way, if cash, not conduct, now determines which faces will appear before the public in the picture gallery, then how can exemplary public character be discerned from portraiture alone?

Ideally, Freneau wants the public to see civic virtue in the faces of the common "unrewarded soldier" or the "disinterested patriot," but when the narrator and his friend "recognize exactly the features" of George Washington's face and proceed to identify the portraits of Generals "Lincoln, Montgomery, and Greene" (49) upon entering the gallery, it seems as though the civic function of the portrait gallery still requires the specific and readily identifiable faces of persons of reputation. Thus, "The Picture Gallery" dramatizes a conflict between Freneau's political desire to model public portraiture according to abstract republican ideals and the historical condition that portraiture embody the social meanings it communicates in the particular people it displays.

This conflict is compounded by the fact that it is the economics of portrait production, not any civic-oriented criteria, that determines who will have their portrait painted. The problem of public portraiture in postrevolutionary America, as Freneau's "The Picture Gallery" conceives it, is that, on the one hand, the newly created democratic political order depends on subordinating the images of particular persons to their capacity to represent civic ideals while, on the other, the residual social order of gentility and its emulative double—the rising mercantile class—demands that the extraordinary character of its social class be made visible through the portraits of particular persons.[10] To put the problem another way, two competing notions of a postrevolutionary public—one defined by an emergent republican political theory, the other by a residual visual cultural form—inhabit the space of the picture gallery. That the latter is compromising the integrity of the former is underscored by Freneau's unsettling conclusion to "The Picture Gallery," in which the "unrewarded soldier" and "disinterested patriot" disappear into a rapacious and undistinguished "crowd" of money-grubbers whose escalating bids eventually overwhelm the painter. As the soldier and the patriot are pushed to "the rear of the throng," the narrator's dog, perhaps sensing his owner's troubled sleep, "suddenly barked at something that disturbed him" and "deprived the world of the remainder of [his] dream" (53). Unable to imagine how portraiture could communicate civic virtue to the public without identifying it with the faces of particular persons, Freneau ends "The Picture Gallery" abruptly and incompletely.

The iconoclastic nature of Freneau's later thinking on the subject suggests that a solution to the problem of the postrevolutionary portrait would remain unimaginable for him. It is extraordinary, for instance, that the man known as the poet of the American Revolution never arranged to have his own portrait painted during his lifetime and, moreover, deliberately refused to sit for one when offered the chance.[11] "There is no portrait of the patriot Freneau," his contemporary, Dr. John W. Francis, explained, because "he always firmly declined the painter's art, and would brook no 'counterfeit presentment'" (Duyckinck *Cyclopedia* 1: 333–34). "The aversion of the poet to sitting for his portrait," Evert Duyckinck surmised, "was one of his peculiarities, for which it is not easy to suggest a sufficient explanation. . . . Whatever the motive, Freneau resolutely declined to have his portrait painted" (xxxi–xxxii).[12] While we may never know the motive behind Freneau's personal renunciation of portraiture, it is worth considering how his decision to remain faceless before the public created a type of visual anonymity analogous to the kind he achieved through pseudonyms in his prose.[13]

If this sort of iconoclasm appears severe, it is entirely consistent with an anonymous November 15, 1797 untitled editorial that Freneau penned for the New York newspaper the *Time Piece*.[14] In the column, Freneau revisits the questions raised in "The Picture Gallery" by asking his readers "whether . . . it be politic or prudent in a free people to erect statues to any human being, dead or living"? The answer, he asserts here, however, is unequivocally no for "it is a sort of self-degradation; it is setting up of images to worship, and appropriating that gratitude and acknowledgement which we owe to the Deity to a vain, frail mortal like ourselves, whom time or a longer life might have discovered to be a tyrant in embryo; and embracing popular opinions, or serving the nation merely from secret, interested designs which would have disclosed themselves at the proper period." Freneau's iconoclasm even included the faces of philosophers since "there are people in the word [*sic*], . . . who would shudder to set up a statue of a general, and admiral, or any of the capital characters in the elevated stations of action, who nevertheless would recommend to be placed in the public squares or building, the busts and statues of philosophers—But even danger lurks here." Evidently wary of dissimulating politicians "embracing popular opinions" for their own "secret, interested designs," Freneau, still unable to resolve the problem of the postrevolutionary portrait, advises the American public that "it would be a good rule therefore in a people who politically act for themselves, to discountenance this species of adoration."

"The Rage for Portraits" and the Visual Culture of Physiognomic Distinction

Freneau had good reason to be concerned. Although he had hoped to divorce the particularization of portraiture from republican civic ideals, the visual culture of postrevolutionary America (with its variety of cheaper portrait forms, portrait galleries, waxwork figures, and public sculpture) was tying them ever closer together. During the 1780s and 1790s, artists such as Charles Willson Peale, Pierre Du Simitière, James and Ellen Sharples, and Charles B. F. Saint-Mémin assembled portrait galleries of distinguished Americans similar to the one described in Freneau's "The Picture Gallery." Starting in the 1780s, for example, Peale exhibited a collection of bust portraits "of

Figure 18. Charles Willson Peale, *Richard Henry Lee*, 1784. Image courtesy of Independence National Historical Park.

various . . . characters of distinction" (Peale *Guide to the Philadelphia Museum* 5) at his Philadelphia Museum (Figure 18) and in 1782 Du Simitière included profile portraits of the leaders of the American Revolution as part of his American Museum (Figure 19).[15] Six years later, between 1798 and 1800, James Sharples displayed his "Collection of Portraits of Distinguished Characters" to the New York public (Gottesman *The Arts and Crafts in New York*

Figure 19. Pierre du Simitière, *General Washington*, engraved by B. Reading from *Thirteen Portraits of American Legislators, Patriots, Soldiers, . . .* (London: W. Richardson, 1783). Image courtesy of the Historical Society of Pennsylvania [Bd 912 D94, case 44, box 79].

1777–99, 19) and the same collection would later tour around the country (Cunningham 9) (Figure 20).

The rationale behind exhibiting or publishing such portrait galleries was partly rooted in the political desire to model the nascent American republic after its Greek and Roman predecessors who had represented the likenesses of their distinguished citizens through painting, portraiture, and sculpture. Peale, for example, believed that his portrait gallery would have a "beneficial

Figure 20. James Sharples, *Thomas Jefferson*, 1797. Image courtesy of Independence National Historical Park.

tendency . . . in a Republic, to instruct the mind and sow the seeds of Virtue" (Fortune 309) and in his 1792 petition to the state of Pennsylvania he pointed to the exemplary function of his hall of portraits as proof of the public utility of his museum. The political function of Peale's Museum was made more apparent after 1802 when it relocated to the State House in Philadelphia. Peale exhibited the faces of exemplary Americans "with a hope that [a] young man may be excited to emulation and labour" after looking at them (Peale *The Philadelphia Museum* 1). Similarly, illustrated biographies and national portrait galleries such as James Hardie's *The New Universal Biographical Dictionary* (1801–5), Joseph Delaplaine's *Repository of the Lives and Portraits of Distinguished American Characters* (1815–16), John Sanderson's *Biographies of the Signers to the Declaration of Independence* (1820–27), and James Herring and James Longacre's *National Portrait Gallery of Distinguished Americans* (1834–39) extended this line of thinking to print. Delaplaine, for instance, likened the "practical morality" (*Prospectus* 12) of his biographical portrait gallery to the notion of emulative virtue found within ancient Greek and Roman biographies.[16] Delaplaine, however, believed that the biographies of the ancients were flawed since "They contained no likenesses of the great men whose lives and actions they so ably recorded. To a delineation of the mind they did not subjoin a portraiture of the body" (*Repository* ii). "The countenance of a Washington," Delaplaine reasoned (Figure 21), "would mark the epoch of its military, and a Franklin, of its philosophical glory; and all the galaxy of genius around them, while furnishing the materials for memory to work upon, would create new heroes, and stimulate new sages, new statesmen, and new orators" (*Prospectus* 12).

The notion that portraits displayed exemplary public character and communicated it to its viewers—in addition to representing individual people— was implicit within eighteenth-century British theories of portraiture from Richardson to Reynolds. As John Barrell has remarked, eighteenth-century civic humanist theories of painting justified the public function of art by claiming that citizens who saw exemplary acts of public virtue in painting would be inspired to perform similar acts of public interest in life (10–23). As the above examples of Peale and Delaplaine would suggest, postrevolutionary American artists and biographers did not abandon the British civic humanist theory of painting or its belief that portraits of the face could promote public virtue. At the same time, it is evident that postrevolutionary American portraiture adapted that civic humanist theory of painting, as did British portraiture of the period, so that a spectator's sense of "public virtue"

Figure 21. From Joseph Delaplaine, *Repository of the Lives and Portraits of Distinguished American Characters.* (Philadelphia, 1815–16), vol. 1, part 1, page opposite 81. George Washington drawn by J. Wood from Jean-Antoine Houdon's 1785 sculpture bust and engraved by William S. Leney. Image courtesy of the Brown University Library.

would be generated by the faces of specific men rather than a representation of their virtuous acts.[17]

Postrevolutionary American painters, like their British counterparts of the same period, believed that a face could communicate virtues to the public, and many artists thought that the emulative power of portraits was specifically "revealed through the particular features" of the countenance (Fortune 318). If late eighteenth-century Anglo-American portraiture differed from portraiture earlier in the century, it was on the question of what kind of face would be best for the job—a general and idealized portrait or a more particularized one. Reynolds, for instance, recommended more idealized portraits in his *Discourses* not because he believed that a person's particular face was incapable of communicating the character of the individual, but rather because he believed that, in some people, it failed to do so. Reynolds reasoned that "The Painter has no other means of giving an idea of the dignity of the mind, but by that external appearance which grandeur of thought does generally, though not always, impress on the countenance; and by that correspondence of figure to sentiment and situation, which all men wish, but cannot command" (58). Since a person's face does not always express "the dignity of the mind," Reynolds thought that it was up to the painter to "deviate from vulgar and strict historical truth" so that "the grace" and "the likeness" of portraits would consist "more in taking the general air, than in observing the exact similitude of every feature" (56–57). By the end of the eighteenth century, however, Reynolds's alignment of the perfection of portraiture with "general ideas" and not individual "particularities" (55) was yielding to the belief that a person's character was visible in their particular facial features.[18] In his lectures delivered before the Royal Academy, for example, Henry Fuseli challenged the suppression of particularity championed by his predecessor and rival Reynolds by boldly stating that physiognomy, "the companion of anatomy," was indispensable for painting the body (500). J. S. Memes would later add that excellence in portraiture now consists in "the happy union of detail and of individual resemblance with greatness and breadth of general power" (194). Memes argued that "in every countenance there is a general impress of thought or feeling, which may be said to constitute the habitual mental likeness of the individual. This it is of the first importance faithfully to transfer to the canvas" (195). Indeed, it was this kind of confidence in the visibility of permanent moral character on the face that led figures such as Peale and Delaplaine to depict specific exemplary persons and display them in portrait galleries before the public.

The theoretical justification for the particularization of postrevolutionary portraiture, as art historians such as Wendy Bellion, Dorinda Evans, Brandon Brame Fortune, Ellen G. Miles, David Steinberg and John Clubbe have argued convincingly in the last fifteen years, had much to do with the rise of Lavaterian physiognomy.[19] "After 1789," Clubbe explains, "physiognomy exerted a pervasive influence on the visual arts, in particular portrait painting" (214). Lavater's *Essays on Physiognomy*, as Chapter 1 demonstrated, was pivotal to understanding how people of the period thought about the relationship between faces and characters. "There is no better way known, of ascertaining a man's intrinsic character," Francis Hopkinson observed, "than by the indication of his countenance: hence the science of physiognomy, and the great encouragement *portrait painting* hath found" (130). The publication of Lavater's lavishly illustrated *Essays* during the 1780s and 1790s—a type of public portrait gallery itself (see Figures 15 and 16)—and the subsequent appearance of various pocket, juvenile, and periodical variants in the following two decades not only distributed the logic of physiognomy widely, it also transformed how faces were represented in portraiture by elevating traditionally low forms, such as the silhouette and profile portrait, above the more expensive oil portrait as the preferred mediums for reading character.[20] "No art comes near the truth of an exact silhouette" (1:177), Lavater reasoned in the *Essays*, because the silhouette facilitates "more than any other kind of drawing this method of measuring and comparing the height and breadth of the head" (1:184).[21] The silhouette offered "positive and incontestable proof of the reality of the science of Physiognomics" (1:178) for Lavater because its profiles captured the unmodifiable features of the face and thus revealed "the impress of character" (1:180) that critics such as Memes would later identify as crucial for portraiture. The American painters Charles, Rembrandt, and Raphaelle Peale, for example, were all familiar with Lavaterian physiognomy; Charles thought the connection between moral character and the face to be so strong that he regretted not preserving the corpse of Benjamin Franklin for public view (Fortune 317).[22] In fact, he told his sons Rembrandt and Rubens that "Collections of profiles are highly interesting, when taken with such accuracy, nay it appears to be a very certain means of studying Characters, to determine the measure of Intulects [*sic*] as well as disposition" (Peale *Papers* 2:537). In a letter reprinted in the *Port Folio*, Rembrandt Peale confessed that: "no one ever was so devoted to the pleasure and reputation of studying to record the physiognomy of learned characters" ("Original" 278) than he was.

If the Peales embraced Lavater's preference for studying character from profiles, others, such as Thomas Sully and Gilbert Stuart, appear to have consulted him in order to model character within their portraits.[23] After comparing Stuart's 1795 Vaughan and 1796 Athenaeum portraits of George Washington with Jean-Antoine Houdon's 1785 life mask, Dorinda Evans has determined that Stuart "made subtle adjustments in Washington's appearance" in an effort "to present not just the likeness but also the essence of the president's character" (66).[24] Similarly, Stuart drew a profile of Washington from one of Houdon's life casts only to trace over it "with a darker pencil, adapting the likeness evidently to Washington as he knew him" (Evans 144). Stuart altered "an arch in Washington's forehead, the indentation between his eyes, a bump at the base of his nose, the slight downturn in the tip of the nose, the heaviness of the eyelids, the saddened expression of the mouth, and the slight projection of a second chin" (144), Evans explains, "at least partly because his most knowledgeable audience was Lavater educated and, whether they agreed with the specifics of Lavater's system or not, they would be especially primed to read character in a portrait of such a famous man" (66). The promise of such physiognomically informed portraits led the *Villager, A Literary Paper* to predict triumphantly in 1819, "Who can tell but in a few hundred years the science of physiognomy may be so far advanced, that the inhabitants of America, in a later century, may possess an exact resemblance of their beloved Washington, collected from an account of his virtuous life and glorious actions" (M. 21). As Stuart's portraits of Washington and these last remarks suggest, the postrevolutionary portrait negotiated what a person looked like visually with what a portrait said physiognomically so that the notion of "exact resemblance" could be as much the product of physiognomical likeness to character as it was perceptual likeness to visible person.

While oil portraitists such as Rembrandt Peale and Gilbert Stuart used physiognomic theory to modify the particular features of sitters into legible types, dozens of itinerant artists such as Saint-Mémin, the Sharpleses, Joseph Sansom, John Wesley Jarvis, William King, William Bache, Raphaelle Peale, and Auguste Edouart encouraged physiognomic readings by producing thousands of profile portraits and silhouettes that emphasized the particularity of the face. One profile, out of the more than eight hundred produced by Saint-Mémin as he traveled up and down the Atlantic coast between 1796 and 1810 (Miles *Saint-Mémin* xiii), prompted a physiognomist to conclude that "this is the kind of man, that, from his countenance, I should choose to associate with" ("Physiognomy. No V." 284). In New England, King advertised that he took profile likenesses with a physiognotrace, having already taken some eight thousand of them by 1805–6 (Jackson 48), while Bache, also a user of the physiognotrace, claimed to have made over two thousand profile likenesses in America (Jackson 79). When Raphaelle Peale brought his physiognotrace to Boston in 1804, he claimed to have "brought with him ten thousand examples of his work—selected from almost three hundred and fifty thousand he had recently taken in Maryland, Virginia, South Carolina, and Georgia" (Benes 138). Eduoart made over 3,800 silhouettes of American citizens from 1839 to 1849 and Charles Willson Peale estimated that 8,800 silhouettes were cut in 1802 at his museum, which David Brigham uses to assert that nearly half of all museum visitors had their silhouettes taken in that year (70). In fact, Peale thought the "rage for profiles" was so extensive in 1805 that he told John Isaac Hawkins that "profiles are seen in nearly every house in the United States of America, never did any invention of making the likeness of men, meet so general approbation as this has done" (Peale *Papers* 2:916). Even as the more affordable versions of portraiture—the silhouette and the profile—extended the capacity to represent oneself to a larger number of people, it also meant that for those without access to such representations of the self, their face would then become the image consulted in order to determine their character.

On the one hand, the explosion in the production of profile and silhouette portraits in early America—what Aaron Burr referred to as "the rage for portraits" (Dickson 25)—compounded Freneau's problem by further expanding access to portraiture without regard to civic virtue or moral character. More mechanized production processes, like the physiognotrace, pantograph, and polygraph, allowed portraits to be taken more quickly (even if it meant eliminating the portrait painter himself), and they dramatically shrunk the amount of leisure time and capital required to have a portrait produced.[25] As Edward Schwarzschild notes, "whereas the portrait painter has to know and converse with his subject at length, in the case of the physiognotrace, the subject can operate the apparatus independently" (60). More important, the mechanical production of portraits in all their particularity upset the notion, espoused in British civic humanist theories of painting, that the public function of portraiture depended on its status as a "liberal" art addressed to the mind rather than a "mechanical" one addressed to the eye (Barrell 12–13). On the other hand, the use of physiognomy to discern character from the face addressed Freneau's concerns about how exemplary character might be displayed to the public by portraiture. As portrait production in early America changed from a system of genteel or state patronage to an early form of mechanization, not only were more people displayed in portraits than before but what those portraits displayed was little more than the face itself. No longer just another agent in the social persuasion of character, the face had become the only agent.[26]

Whereas the pictorial conventions for signifying social status in colonial American portraiture guide a painter like John Singleton Copley in his 1767 portrait of the wealthy merchant Nicholas Boylston (Figure 22), those conventions are noticeably absent in an engraving after a silhouette portrait of George Washington that appeared in the 1788 *Columbian Magazine* (Figure 23).[27] In Copley's portrait, Boylston's "essential person," as Paul Staiti rightly observes, is expressed through "inanimate markers"—his expensive silk clothes, refined pose, and the thick ledger and large ship depicted around him, while his "face is largely inscrutable as a bearer of meaning" (14). Boylston's exotic costume and cultivated pose exude the easy elegance espoused by Chesterfield; the lush drapery hanging behind him was a standard symbol of affluence and abundance in colonial American portraiture.[28] In contrast, Washington appears without any of those external signifiers of gentility. It is his face, specifically his profile, that exhibits his character. The author of *The Columbian Magazine* article in which this engraving appears quotes directly from Lavater's *Essays on Physiognomy* and informs us that Washington's profile "indicates a sound judgment; freedom from prejudices, and a heart that opens itself to truth" (145). The long, receding arch of Washington's forehead, for example, was understood by Lavater as a sign of superior comprehension and intelligence. Likewise, the equal breadth and height of Washington's profile means that he is neither obstinate nor malicious (2.1:183–84). It was impossible to contemplate the character of Washington, Rembrandt Peale insisted, without noting "how far his corporeal features corresponded with his acknowledged mental and moral greatness" (281).

Washington's public appearance in a lower cultural form such as the silhouette suggests that portraiture's signification of distinction was changing in early America. During the last few decades of the eighteenth century, distinguished public figures and wealthy merchants sat for these less expensive and traditionally more private portraits as well as for the more public oil portraits. Charles Willson Peale, for instance, informed Thomas Jefferson that several hundred of his silhouettes were taken away from his museum (Cunningham 124). During 1798 and 1799, James Sharples offered the public not only the chance to see his "collection of portraits of distinguished characters," but the opportunity to purchase them as well (Gottesman *The Arts and Crafts in New*

Figure 22. John Singleton Copley, *Nicholas Boylston*, 1767. Image courtesy of the Harvard Art Museum, Fogg Art Museum, Harvard University Portrait Collection. Bequest of Ward Nicholas Boylston to Harvard College, 1828, H90.

Figure 23. Profiles of George Washington (left) and Benjamin Franklin (right) from *The Columbian Magazine* (March 1788), Philadelphia. Image courtesy of The John Work Garrett Library, The Sheridan Libraries, The Johns Hopkins University.

York, 1777–99 19). Whereas full- or half-length oil portraiture had signified the elite through its expense and size and, therefore, could theoretically confer distinction on the sitter regardless of who they were (as we saw in Freneau), the cost and size of silhouettes and profile portraits were not necessarily an indicator of a lower social position.

The proliferation of the profile portrait and silhouette in early America began to separate the assumed relationship between a portrait's costs of production and its capacity to communicate extraordinary social character in public, and, as I have been arguing, it was able to do so because of the logic of physiognomic distinction. In this respect, a transformation in the production of portraiture coincided with, and was facilitated by, a transformation in the cultural reception of faces. As more and more people began to own and circulate portraits, the kind of face that a portrait depicted and the character that it displayed to its viewers (anticipating the modern notions of personality and publicity) began to matter more than either the costs of a portrait's production or its conventions for representing social station. The face itself became a portrait and what mattered most, as the example of Stuart suggests, was its desired legibility in the social field.[29] Although the idea of the face as a portrait was hardly new, what was new was the idea that the face contained only one essential portrait—its permanent character—and not numerous fleeting ones. To be clear, my claim is not that the face becomes a portrait for the first time, but rather, at this moment in American cultural history, it begins to become a particular kind of portrait—one whose features index a permanent moral character.

The Face of the Public

The belief that a portrait could communicate a person's permanent moral character was not lost on Freneau's Princeton classmate and literary collaborator during the revolution, Hugh Henry Brackenridge, who sensed that the face might be used to stabilize a political order now at the mercy of a newly enfranchised and easily persuaded democratic populace. Unlike Freneau, who initially hoped that a portrait of a common man—such as the "unrewarded soldier" in "The Picture Gallery"—might embody civic virtue to the public, Brackenridge believed that the majority of its viewers, who were common men, were incapable of distinguishing public interest from their own interests. In Brackenridge's more cynical view, such men would more likely see the portrait of an "unrewarded soldier" as representing the interests of unpaid labor rather than the patriotic actions of a disinterested citizen. Brackenridge's intermittently published civic commentary/picaresque novel, *Modern Chivalry* (1792–1815), demonstrates how, on the one hand, the particular physiognomic features of subordinate groups (like those of the Irish servant Teague) could be used to exclude them from embodying exemplary public character, while on the other, physiognomically informed portraits might be used to modify the faces of the dominant group (like those of the president) and identify them with otherwise abstract and disembodied political ideals.

Near the end of volume 2 of *Modern Chivalry*, for example, the quixotic man of letters, Captain Farrago, searches for his perpetually absconding servant, Teague O'Regan. After looking for the rogue at Congress, where he encountered a man that "had . . . the brogue of Teague . . . but nothing of his physiognomy" (123), and the university, where he met a professor of Greek "not wholly unlike him, especially in the tinge of the brogue" (126), Farrago joins "a party of gentlemen" at the theater in order to "cast his eye upon the pit and galleries, and observe if he could anywhere descry the physiognomy of Teague" (132). Like his unsuccessful searches at Congress and the university, Farrago's surveillance of the theater only yields "several that a good deal resembled him; but yet not the identical person" (132). Besides suggesting the ubiquity of the Irish and their indistinguishable brogue in Farrago's mind, these scenes also testify to the efficacy with which physiognomic discernment enables him to discriminate within what he imagines to be an otherwise similarly sounding, similarly featured, homogenous ethnic group.

Brackenridge's reference to physiognomy, however, is more than just another ethnographic instrument. Similar to the function of dialect within the novel—whose graphic particularity not only differentiates one subgroup from the standardized speech of the Captain and the narrator, but also distinguishes them from other subgroups in the novel—physiognomy legitimates social relations by aligning them with "natural" somatic differences.[30] Yet, while physiognomy seems to share dialect's ethnographic function in these scenes, the absence of detailed physical description leads me to suspect that Brackenridge is less concerned with a specific race or nation of men—although the Irish are certainly his primary object—than with two kinds of men: the performances of a dissembler and an undiscerning public. As the narrator reiterates throughout *Modern Chivalry*, the problem with Teague—his capacity to deceive the public and obtain positions for which he is unqualified—is only partially his responsibility. Farrago's discernment of Teague's physiognomy proposes that one method for preventing characters like Teague from continually exceeding their "natural" limitations, and thus escaping their stations in life, might be to imagine the criteria for professional or political employment in terms other than those of the success of their public performances.

It is little wonder then that Brackenridge, that tireless ironist, will set his critique of the performative notion of selfhood inside the theater itself. The theatricality of the self and the social fluidity that its performances could generate in the actual world found one of its strongest metaphors in the secular idea of *theatrum mundi*.[31] Yet, at the same time, late eighteenth-century American theatrical practice paradoxically maintained the social hierarchy that such a metaphor threatened to dissolve. Thus, after nearly two volumes of wandering through the backwoods, the moment when Farrago sits with his gentlemen friends in their box marks an attempt to return to the stability of the existing social order (*MC* 132). Unsurprisingly, it is also at this narrative moment that Farrago finally locates his missing servant, who is neither in Congress nor at the university, but is acting in the very play the Captain has paid to see. Even though Farrago does not recognize Teague at first, the point at which he does is the moment when his run-away servant appears as the low Irish character of Darby. The irony, of course, is that this part is not a part at all, since Teague's performance consists in simply being himself. This scene is important because it is the first time in the novel that Farrago does not persuade Teague to relinquish his newly obtained post. Instead of convincing him to return to a life of servitude, as he has done in previous episodes, Farrago decides to "find another servant who can supply his place" (*MC* 133). It is striking that Farrago's decision to terminate Teague's servitude happens only at the moment when Teague's theatrical character and his physiognomy are identical. It is as if Teague's servitude can only end when his ambition is limited to accepting his "natural" physiognomic part in society, which is defined for him by a shrewd stage manager as a "low character" (*MC* 133). That the restraints against Teague's mobility should end—even if temporarily—at the moment when he learns to act the part his face necessitates demonstrates that Farrago's physiognomic discernment operates not only as an instrument for identifying Teague with precision should he run away, but as one that seeks to regulate his mobility by reference to his face.

As Chapter 3 discussed, a number of postrevolutionary seduction novels imagined how the physiognomic distinction of the face might counter the polite performances of aspirants and restrict their mobility. *Modern Chivalry* invokes this specific literary history by featuring a satirical episode of Chester-fieldian seduction modeled on the plots of contemporary seduction novels. In the episode, Farrago's attempts to refine Teague's appearance for future political appointment result in a bad case of "Teagueomania" (pt. 1, bk. 3): a social disease similar in spirit and effects to Tabitha Tenney's "novel-mania" in *Female Quixotism*. If "novel-mania" demonstrated how reading romances could blind a woman to a dissembling seducer's actual character, "Teagueomania" discloses how reading "Chesterfield" (*MC* 213) can transform an illiterate and uncouth Irishman into a genteel marital prospect and a potential politician. Although it would "seem improbable that the female mind of great delicacy, and refinement, should be captivated by a rough and gross object," the narrator attributes such behavior, just as the seduction novelists did, to "the powers of imagination" (*MC* 229). Teague's newly acquired polite performances enable him to seduce wealthy women away from their professional-class lovers—Mr. Williams, a merchant and Mr. Hardicknute, a lawyer (*MC* 232)—and fathers—Mr. Mutchkin, another merchant, whose daughter is smitten with the "bog-trotter" (*MC* 235). After recounting Mutchkin's story, the narrator laments how "It is a painful thing, having accumulated property, for the sake of a child: and having taken pains to improve and polish, to have her thrown away upon a beast" (*MC* 254). Farrago tries to persuade Teague to stop his seductions, but his rational petitions fail to persuade his servant to abandon his chances for rapid mobility. In fact, Farrago can only prevent Teague from actualizing his mobility through marriage by brute force. Farrago couples the exposure of his actual low status as a servant with the lash of the cowskin as Teague is literally branded for his attempts to conceal his actual character behind a mask of genteel performance.

Yet, what distinguishes Brackenridge's treatment of the dissembling seducer from that of the postrevolutionary seduction novelists is that he is far more explicit in identifying how dissimulation—when coupled with an undiscerning public—poses particular problems for democratic politics and its understanding of public interest. The novel emphasizes this point by having Teague's political dissimulation and his potential candidacy precede and instigate his social dissimulation "among the best families of the city" (*MC* 226). As a result, Teague's Chesterfieldian exploitation of "the power of the imagination" not only threatens the reproduction of wealth and rank among the established gentry, it also menaces the democracy at large. Brackenridge's narrator likens the effects of "Teagueomania" to the days of chivalry when "mere squires had been taken for knights" and the "beginning of the revolution in America" when "taylors and barbers, had slurred themselves for gentry or nobility" (*MC* 229). The direct comparison of "Teagueomania" to such radically egalitarian and unstable political moments extends the danger of Teague's dissimulation from the social leveling of wealthy families to the political destruction of a developing nation during the increasingly tumultuous and oppressive Federalist era, and it prompts the narrator to ask the reader what could hinder men like Teague from being "taken for a person qualified to fill any place in government, from the bare pretending to it?" (*MC* 229). Similar to the anti-Chesterfieldianism discussed in Chapter 2, *Modern Chivalry* understands a performative notion of selfhood in decidedly anti-democratic terms.

• • •

Although the physiognomic distinction of the face is shown to expose the political and professional "pretending" of Teague, *Modern Chivalry* also discloses how the face might be used as an instrument for communicating exemplary public character. Volume 3 of the novel, for example, considers the political value of public portraiture and physiognomy—those notions of emulative virtue and "practical morality" motivating Charles Willson Peale's and Joseph Delaplaine's portrait galleries of distinguished characters—during a scene in which Farrago takes Teague to the president's morning levée.[32] The narrator of the scene opposes the levée, not because it smacks of monarchical state power, but because it turns the president into "a bear at a stake" (*MC* 203) for all the "gaping haubucks" (*MC* 202) to see. Its only value, Brackenridge's narrator informs us, consists in training the idle and "uninstructed" "mass of citizens" not to bother "their chief magistrate" (*MC* 202). If he were president, the narrator explains, he would not have a levée, but "propose in its place to have myself taken off the more abundantly in portraits, and to have innumerable medals struck representing my physiognomy and features . . . to satisfy the curiosity of strangers" (*MC* 203). The narrator justifies substituting his portrait for his actual face since only "weak minds" equate a great man's character with his face, while the "more solid know" that "when they *see* the most distinguished in arts, in letters, or in arms, they will *see* a person that *looks just like another man*" (*MC* 202; emphasis mine).

There seems to be something contradictory about the levée episode. In a novel that has been consistently relying on physiognomy and dialect as instruments for distinction—as we saw in the theater episode—this scene appears to assert the radical visual equality of the faces of men. Has Brackenridge actually changed his mind with respect to physiognomy? Or is this another instance of Brackenridgean irony? While the answer to the latter question is an unsatisfactory maybe, the answer to the former is a definite no. If anything, the later volumes of *Modern Chivalry* assert the logic of physiognomic distinction even more adamantly than the earlier ones do. In part 2, volume 4, chapter 9, for example, the narrator says, "I admit that there is such a thing as being of a bad stock; and the moral qualities are as communicable as the physical constitution of the features. Hence it is, that I would look to the stock in the selection of subjects; but still more to the physiognomy of youth" (*MC* 667).[33] The levée scene does not contradict his earlier position with respect to physiognomy. It qualifies that position. Similar to *Ormond*, *Modern Chivalry* acknowledges the physiognomic fallacy. Yet, the novel also argues for its potential utility for the political management of the common man through public portraiture.

Unlike Freneau, Brackenridge defines public portraiture's political value for the bourgeois public sphere precisely in terms of its ability to depict the faces of particular persons. In Brackenridge's view, the problem of postrevolutionary portraiture is not necessarily the commonality of its sitters, but the commonality of its viewers. If the "mass of citizens" mindlessly equates character and face without any regard to actual conduct, Brackenridge reasons, then a person's portrait might allow the ignorant to identify exemplary public character through the face in a way that they are unable to discern it from conduct alone. When the narrator proposes to have his portrait taken and disseminated, for instance, it is meant to satisfy the desire of those "gaping haubucks" whose "weak minds" can only discern a distinguished man's greatness from his face (*MC* 213–16). The difference between "weak" and "strong" minds in the levée scene, and what distinguishes Brackenridge from Peale and Delaplaine, is that the "more solid" know that there is no *actual* correlation between physical features and character, only one as it might be *made* to exist in public portraiture.

Thus, the theater and levée scenes reveal the asymmetries inherent in *Modern Chivalry*'s understanding of physiognomic distinction. Where the theater scene proposed that the social and political mobility of common men might be regulated by restricting their performances to the subordinate character that their faces assign them, the levée scene acknowledges the inherent fallacy of such a position, but suggests nonetheless, that for those men with access to public portraiture, physiognomy could also be used to substantiate the legibility of their character to a public unable to discern it from their conduct alone. While the particular physiognomic features of the faces of subordinate groups (such as Teague's) bear a negative relationship to embodying public character, the particular physiognomic features of the faces of dominant groups (such as the President's) bear a positive relationship to embodying public character.

As I have tried to show, the profile portrait served a purpose for postrevolutionary public figures. That Federalist and Democratic Republican alike sat for profile portraits and allowed their profiles to be distributed widely (Miller *In Pursuit* 43) suggests that one's social identity did not determine one's political behavior.[34] This 1804 profile portrait of Jefferson by Charles B. F. Saint-Mémin, for instance, was offered to the public as a mezzotint and was later copied by Thomas Gimbrede for an engraved portrait (Figure 24) in which Jefferson's face embodies what the goddess Minerva can only symbolize: wisdom (Cunningham 82–86). Physiognomy's political value, as the distribution of the portraits of George Washington, Thomas Jefferson, and Benjamin Franklin (Figure 25) would seem to confirm, was to make such positive public character visible, so that selecting political representatives would not be reduced to an ignorant public seeking to elect only those whom they saw as themselves.[35] The *New England Galaxy and Masonic Magazine* went so far as to declare that

Figure 24. Thomas Gimbrede, *Thomas Jefferson*. Copy after Charles B. J. F. de Saint-Mémin, 1809. Image courtesy of the National Portrait Gallery, Smithsonian Institution [92–96].

Figure 25. Profile portrait of Benjamin Franklin from *Massachusetts Magazine* 2:5 (May 1790). Image courtesy of the John Carter Brown Library at Brown University.

physiognomy "will have its due weight in the election of the next president" ("Physiognomy"). The magazine reprinted William Leete Stone's physiognomic readings of "six distinguished Americans"—including four presidential prospects—in 1824 ("Physiognomy"). Apparently after viewing Benjamin O. Tyler's engraving of William Harris Crawford's face, Stone recommended to the public that "the best project for preventing his election to the Presidency, would be to exhibit his features throughout the United States" ("Physiognomy"). If British civic humanist theories of painting asserted that the public, in its disinterested sense, was invisible to men of self-interest such as mechanics (Barrell 8), then Brackenridge's *Modern Chivalry* suggests cynically that the physiognomic distinction of the face in public portraiture might restore the visibility of the public to a democratic audience largely composed of self-interested, "gaping haubucks" like Teague O'Regan.

Brackenridge's awareness of the function and force of this type of public visibility and his participation in nearly the same process that his narrator describes during *Modern Chivalry*'s levée scene is evident in a blurb he wrote for the tenth edition of Mason Weems's *The Life of George Washington* (1810).[36] The widespread dissemination of Washington's face during Brackenridge's era created a visual archive from which the visibility of George's public character was made to coincide with the virtuous, paternalistic figure that Federalists were constructing in the visual national imaginary. Dozens of written physiognomic portraits testified to what the Marquis de Chastellux saw as "the perfect union . . . between the physical and moral qualities" in his face (Baker *Character Portraits* 26).[37] In addition, biographies, such as Mason Weems's seminal *The Life of George Washington* offered the public an immediately sensible—since visible (through engravings)—figure for civic virtue and national greatness. In his recommendation for Weems's biography of Washington, Brackenridge wrote: "With regard to biographical merit, the delineation is such to give a view of character not in a parade day; but as independent of command or station; This is the painting which interests; it is that which alone makes a likeness; for a mere outline, wanting the expression, gives no physiognomy. I shall be glad to see more, in this way" (Weems, back matter). Similar to his narrator's discussion of the utility of portraiture in the levée scene, Brackenridge discusses the value of Weems's biography in almost exclusively visual terms. Brackenridge lauds Weems's depiction of Washington since it is neither the performance "of command or station," nor the social self on display during a parade. Neither is it "a mere outline," sketchy and unfinished.

Instead, Weems's Washington is described as a precise portrait that captures the full expression of his character, or what Brackenridge refers to as his "physiognomy." This allows the postrevolutionary reader—imagined in the familiar terms of a viewer before a portrait—to glimpse the permanent character of a man amid the ceremony, convention, and costume. The identification of Washington's greatness with his physiognomy, rather than his performances, not only provides "weak minds" with an exemplary instance of public character—as it was imagined to do in the levée scene—it dismisses the performative model of Washington's professional ascendancy as somehow inauthentic. What makes Washington great is not his costume or military actions—which anybody (including men like Teague) might wear or possibly imitate—but his specific character, made intelligible through the particular physiognomy of his face. Thus, Brackenridge imagines biography in terms of portraiture, readers in terms of viewers, and character in terms of physiognomy, not because those notions are necessarily valid, but because they possess political utility in a new democracy. It is as if the cognitive activity of readers when they read is understood by Brackenridge in the more passive terms of seeing a person rather than the more active process of imagining what he might have looked like. The exemplary function of portraiture for a democratic republic, Brackenridge reasons, is no longer to inspire its citizens to emulate virtuous acts, but is to instruct them to look for and recognize public virtue in the faces of those who will act for them. The culture of physiognomic distinction attracted Brackenridge as it did so many other postrevolutionary novelists because it offered authors an alternative model of reading, one, as the previous chapter demonstrated, based on the presumably less imaginative and more rational act of looking. *Modern Chivalry* illustrates how portraiture was instrumental in articulating the face of the public and how physiognomy encouraged a method of rational vision for discerning such faces. Early republican visual culture and its appearance in *Modern Chivalry* provides us with evidence of how portraiture and physiognomy were imagined as countering the impermanence and impersonation associated with the type of culture of performance on the one hand and the abstraction and disembodiment of the disinterested public sphere on the other.

Yet, *Modern Chivalry's* theater scene not only reveals how the physiognomic distinction of the face might counter such genteel performances of the body, it draws our attention to the fact that the mediating figure between those two prevalent modes of corporeal intelligibility was described in terms of cultural production, or to use Brackenridge's term, a stage manager. Years after publishing that scene, Brackenridge would continue to refer to the political author as "the manager of the drama," a person "disposed not only to choose his own part, but to assign to others, what part they shall act" (Brackenridge *Gazette* 109). Without collapsing Brackenridge into either *Modern Chivalry*'s narrator or Farrago, I do find that the figure of a stage manager could be applied to either character. As I have tried to demonstrate, Brackenridge conceives of the political author as a stage manager for the republic. The parts people choose for themselves and the mobility that the performative self's disassociation of face and permanent moral character enables are regulated by the parts that the stage manager assigns and the immobility that physiognomy's shallow reduction of character to face instills.

Critics, however, have long understood the politics of *Modern Chivalry* as embodied by its two central characters rather than by the position the novel articulates with respect to the use of the corporeal legibility of character. For some, Teague represents the gross inadequacy of the common man to represent himself and the interests of his constituency.[38] For others, Farrago's repeated use of coercion to retain Teague as a servant reflects the hypocrisy of the supposedly disinterested man of classical republicanism.[39] Yet, what Brackenridge satirizes in the novel is not simply Farrago's failure to be disinterested, as many critics have claimed, but rather that he even needs to be disinterested at all. What is archaic, perhaps even chivalrous, about *Modern Chivalry* is Farrago's continued appeal to republican disinterest. If this were not true, Brackenridge's satire of Farrago's alleged disinterestedness in the novel would resemble the political position of his bitter rival in real life, William Findley.[40]

Findley's historical significance, besides defeating Brackenridge politically during the 1780s and inspiring the characters of Traddle the Weaver and Teague O'Regan, lies in the fact that his anti-Federalist arguments anticipate the emergence of the particularized party politics of a competitive democracy. Findley argued that the Federalists had no right to "pass off their support of [a] personal cause as an act of disinterest."[41] Although Brackenridge may have realized that an appeal to disinterestedness was no longer possible in an emergent era of partisan politics, he was not ready to accept the position that all interests were equally well qualified to understand and articulate the public's interest.[42] Despite the complexity of his politics, Brackenridge's anxiety over the capacity of the common man to discern the public's interest remained fairly consistent throughout his career,[43] and contrary to Findley, he believed that "a representative is not supposed to be a mere machine . . . he is sent to hear from others, and to think for himself . . . [for] It is certain that the people do not always know their own interest" (Brackenridge *Gazette Publications* 41).

If the problem of disinterestedness in *Modern Chivalry* is that it fails to persuade in the face of self-interest, and if the problem of self-interest is that it elevates men like Teague O'Regan beyond their "natural" capacities, then Brackenridge struggles to define public interest as best understood and defined by men whose lack of self-interest is a condition of their superior education and discernment (as opposed to their leisure and capital). Yet, in order to define that new sense of public interest without appealing to disinterestedness, Brackenridge can only satirize both the absurdity of Findley's government of unqualified men and Farrago's antiquarian and unsuccessful notion of persuading the masses by appealing to a reason they do not possess.[44] Brackenridge overcomes this impasse, however, by proposing an alternative method for the assertion of public interest. Public interest would no longer be mediated by rational appeals to a disembodied and abstract notion of disinterest, nor would it be reduced to mere public performance. Rather it would be mediated by the more palpable agents of culture—those Brackenridgean stage managers of the American scene, authors and portraitists—who are able to register the distinction between qualified and unqualified men more sensibly for the common man through the emergent logic of physiognomic distinction and its more embodied form of public character. Since the type of knowledge required to participate in defining public interest in Brackenridge's model reduced the substance of critical reason to the mere recognition of moral character in the face, a person's sense of agency in that process would be extended even though that participation would have been narrowed from the act of thinking and debating rationally in public to that of looking and recognizing rationally in public.

Brackenridge is perhaps the first American author to realize that since the legitimacy of political representation was understood increasingly in terms of identifying particular interests with specific faces (in the sense that the interests of mechanics could best be represented only by other mechanics), one could then use the face to calibrate notions of what constituted a political representative and political representation itself.[45] In this sense, Brackenridge renovates the eighteenth-century civic humanist notion of a public—one traditionally defined in opposition to the particularities of personality and self-interest—by defining the public in terms of exemplary public character that is now embodied by a particular person. Unlike Freneau, who worried about how public portraiture's bourgeois form of civic humanism might align public and self-interest in the faces of specific men, Brackenridge saw this convergence as an opportunity to increase the political efficacy of cultural production. If the "public" in public interest had disappeared in a nation of competing self-interests by the end of the eighteenth century, postrevolutionary authors and painters could strive to make the "public" visible again by locating it in the faces of those who were perceived to possess exemplary moral character. Although physiognomy would be complemented and, eventually, overtaken by phrenology as the antebellum period's science of permanent moral character, the persistence of the logic of physiognomic distinction within the works of Cooper, Melville, Hawthorne, and Stowe indicates its centrality to the imagination of social space in the novel in America, and it demonstrates the degree to which that logic and its emphasis on looking at the face as a form of social knowledge worked alongside or resonated with the emergence of racial and ethnographic difference as instruments for social organization in nineteenth-century America. As Brackenridge's example suggests, at the dawn of the era of partisan politics in America rests the notion of a politics of identity as yet unaffiliated with black/white racial distinction, but intricately caught up with, and plotting its logic of, corporeal difference and distinction.

PART II

The Changing Face of the Novel

Chapter 5

The Invisible Aristocrat

Books are, in a great measure, the instruments of controlling the opinions of a nation like ours. They are an engine, alike powerful to save or destroy.
—James Fenimore Cooper, *Precaution* (1820)

The first object of a writer, should be the support of just and honorable sentiments. When an author of fiction has sufficiently respected this imperative obligation, it would seem that he has some right to felicitate himself that his *pictures*, whether of the passions, or of sensible objects, are so like the originals as to be recognized by those who are most familiar with the subjects.
—James Fenimore Cooper, *Letters and Journals* (1830)

It is a trait of American genius to give pictures with astonishing clearness and reality, and Cooper exhibits this trait in its greatest perfection.
—*United States and Democratic Review* (1849)

THE PREVIOUS FOUR chapters traced the face's relationship to the social perception of character in early American culture with particular attention paid to how transatlantic discourses for reading the face (such as civility and physiognomy) and cultural forms for representing the face (such as portraiture) shaped the literary representation of distinction in the fifty years following the revolution. The presence of Chesterfieldian civility and the logic of physiognomic distinction in postrevolutionary literature, I suggested, were part of a more general struggle over how distinction would operate within the social

space of the new republic and, more broadly, how culture, specifically literature, might participate in that struggle. The postrevolutionary seduction novel
imagined the face as a location from which the absence of distinction would
be made visible through physiognomy and, it did so, I argued, in an effort to
minimize the legitimacy of the cultural capital of Chesterfieldian civility in the
signification of genteel distinction. The transposition in the determination of
character that physiognomy promised was central to how the postrevolutionary novel of seduction imagined social space. Moreover, the reading practices
and ways of looking promoted by these novels positioned culture—especially
dispositions to culture—as a means to restrict rather than facilitate social
mobility.

By the second quarter of the nineteenth century, however, the conditions
for understanding the social perception of character had changed from their
original postrevolutionary context. The face remained an important location
for the social perception of character during these years, but physiognomy as
a scientific discourse for understanding its meaning was being challenged by
more quantitative, if equally arbitrary, discourses such as such as crainology,
phrenology, and eventually scientific racism. In addition, the rise of Jacksonian
democracy signaled the transformation of the United States from an elite republic to a democratic republic inclusive of all white men.[1] By the 1820s "state
legislatures across the United States moved toward enfranchising all free white
men regardless of property holdings" (Nelson 127). "White claims to racial
preeminence became more urgent, rigid, and consistent in the 1820s and 30s,"
John Wood Sweet notes, "just as new democratic ideals were becoming established and new class divisions were becoming entrenched" (11). The decade of
the 1820s thus "stands as a crucial decade in marking all sorts of distinctions,"
Mary Kelley observes, "including the distinction signaled by the rise of the
'middling classes'" (27). Refinement, once the exclusive domain of the established gentry, had been democratized into a form of vernacular gentility which
"became an integral part of the aspirations of ordinary men and women in
the first decades of the nineteenth century" (Appleby 43). By the middle of the
century, this vernacular form of gentility had become "the possession of the
American middle class" (Bushman xiii). Yet, as Richard Bushman observes,
"the spread of gentility reminds us that the *ancien regime* still had a grip on
the social imagination of Americans" (408). The perception that America was
politically democratic, but socially aristocratic would persist into the 1820s
and beyond. "From the conflicts between Federalists and their opponents in
the 1790s over the alleged monarchical tendencies of the new government, to

the Jacksonian Democrats' attacks on 'aristocracy' in the 1830s, and Abraham Lincoln's condemnation of 'crowned kings, money-kings, and land-kings,' a quarter-century later still," Christopher Clark notes, "reference was to the model of a hierarchical social order which most Americans claimed to have set aside" (560). The democratization of gentility during the first half of the nineteenth century did not eliminate a more exclusive, aristocratic form of gentility so much as threaten to render its distinction invisible.

The second part of *Discerning Characters* examines how the transposition in the social perception of character imagined within postrevolutionary seduction fiction would continue to shape not only the representation of distinction within the novel, but more broadly, the practices of literary production and reception in nineteenth-century America. My analysis concentrates on the fiction of two authors in particular, James Fenimore Cooper and Herman Melville, in order to examine the ways in which the terms of literary value would remain coincident with the representation and reproduction of genteel distinction during the second quarter of the nineteenth century even as the conditions for the social perception of character were changing in America. The following two chapters consider how the emphasis on the social perception of character shifts within the fiction of Cooper and Melville from discerning the visibility of its absence to addressing the invisibility of its presence. These chapters thus chart a more narrow literary history than the previous four. Where the previous four chapters understood the presence of the physiognomic logic of distinction inside the postrevolutionary novel of seduction within the larger cultural history of the social perception of character in the early republic, the final two chapters consider why the logic of physiognomic distinction would continue to inform novel reading and writing in nineteenth-century America even as the discourse of civility was being democratized and as the discourse of physiognomy was yielding to more modern conceptions of racial difference. Indeed, the supercession of physiognomy by phrenology, ethnology, and the American school of anthropology during the third decade of the nineteenth century is precisely what makes Melville's extended meditation on the physiognomic distinction of the face in *Pierre* so compelling in 1852. Melville's interest in the physiognomic distinction of the face, like that of Cooper, resides not merely in its persistence as a practice in the social perception of character, but more significantly, in how the reading practices and ways of looking promoted by postrevolutionary seduction fiction would continue to shape literary practice during the first half of the nineteenth century.

The second part of *Discerning Characters* explores how the physiognomic logic of distinction as well as the iconotextual practices of the postrevolutionary seduction narrative described in part one would continue to inform the reading and writing of fiction in America. The importance of the physiognomic distinction of the face to the didacticism of the postrevolutionary seduction novel promoted a particularly anti-imaginative relationship between reading and seeing that would become constitutive of the genre and, as the following pages will demonstrate, would eventually serve as one of the hallmarks for distinguishing "American" literature. The pictures that literature, particularly novels, brought before the mind's eye of its readers, I argued in chapter 3, was one of the most significant criteria for determining the value of a literary text in postrevolutionary America and, as the following two chapters will explore, it would remain so well into the middle of the nineteenth century. The final two chapters thus seek to refine our understanding of the relationship between literary and visual culture during the first half of the nineteenth century, first, by elaborating the arguments articulated in part one about how and why visual culture, particularly portraiture, was important to conceptions the literary before the 1830s and prior to the advent of the daguerreotype; and, second, by asking us to move beyond the formalist perspective of comparative approaches to the arts which tend to conceive of the literary in temporal, the visual, in spatial terms.[2] As Part I suggested, intermediality, particularly the intertextual references to portraiture, was a recurrent and significant feature of early American fiction and the equivalence between reading and seeing had been a part of the discourse surrounding the production and reception of the novel in America from at least the last quarter of the eighteenth century. When nineteenth-century critics valued a novel's characterization for its vivid portraiture, as Part II will demonstrate, the reference was not to a generic spatial form, but to a specific visual cultural form with its own histories and practices for depicting character and with its own intermedial presence within the novel itself.

•　•　•

By the time James Fenimore Cooper would begin writing his fiction in the early 1820s, the physiognomic distinction of the face, as Chapter 3 argued, was an important feature of the postrevolutionary seduction novel. This chapter explores how Cooper's early seduction fiction, *Precaution* (1820) and *Tales for Fifteen* (1823), appropriates and transforms the physiognomic logic of distinction found within the postrevolutionary novel of seduction. Cooper's early fiction modifies the didactic structure of postrevolutionary seduction novels such as *The Coquette* so that the face distinguishes the invisible aristocrat hidden among the ordinary rather than identifying the dissimulating seducer masquerading amid the genteel. Reading remains central to the task of picturing men and discerning their character accurately, as it was for postrevolutionary seduction fiction. In Cooper's early fiction, however, those pictures no longer serve to expose the wrong man, but to distinguish the right one. The problem of the illegibility of faces is transformed from one in which a person's presumed lack of moral character does not correspond with his appearance to one in which a person's distinction is itself invisible. Thus, for Cooper, the struggle over culture concerns the fading visibility of distinction within the social space of democracy as much as it does the threat of cultural capital and mobility in defining that social space. "The democratic landscape of society" made it difficult for Cooper "to discern social distinctions" (Gustafson "Natty" 485). Cooper's early fiction (his seduction fiction plus *The Spy* and *The Pioneers*), I contend, confronts the problem of the invisible aristocrat by representing the visibility of distinction in terms of corporeality, especially the face, and by accounting for acts of social judgment in terms of visual discernment. By having the face assert allegedly natural differences rather than deny the imposition of artificial ones, Cooper also becomes one of the first American novelists to integrate the physical features of racial difference as a component to that prior physiognomic logic (Starke 30).[3]

The Invisible Aristocrat

One of the more striking features of James Fenimore Cooper's first novel, *Precaution*, is how it begins. Within the first three pages of the novel, no less than twelve characters quickly pass before the reader as they assemble for dinner at an English country manor, and at least another two are mentioned in conversation. It would be easy to dismiss this crowded and confusing start as a formal mistake, perhaps accounting for it as the clumsy sign of an inexperienced writer—as Cooper himself later did—but to do so would be to miss how markedly *Precaution*'s beginning differs from those of his next two novels: *The Spy* (1821) and *The Pioneers* (1823).[4] As Cooper prepared to write what he called "an American novel professedly" (*Letters* 1:49) for his next work, *The*

Spy, he decided to change more than *Precaution*'s English setting and aristo-cratic character types.[5] He also adopted a different mode of introducing his characters to his readers.

When characters are introduced to the reader in *Precaution*, their names, titles, and familial identities often precede any physical description of them as persons. In Chapter 1, for instance, Mr. Haughton is first described as "a gentleman of landed property in the neighborhood" (*P* 2) and the recently arrived and upwardly mobile Mr. Jarvis is characterized by others as "a capital merchant" (*P* 1) before he even appears physically in the novel. Clara, John, and Lady Anne Moseley first take shape before the reader as the relatives of Sir Edward Moseley, who, in turn, is known principally for having been "de-scended from one of the most respectable of the creations of his order by James" and for having "inherited, with many of the virtues of his ancestors, an estate which placed him amongst the greatest landed proprietors of the country" (*P* 3).

As the readers of *Precaution* listen in on the polite dinner conversation of these country gentlemen and their patrician families, they meet characters who have, for the most part, "long known and esteemed each other" (*P* 13) and who have been (or will be) connected to each other by familial, social, or religious networks. To say that these characters belong to a system of social relations that is independent of what they look like and, as a result, of what the reader's image of them might be, would be putting it too strongly. Yet, the relationship between what these characters look like and who they are socially matters, if it matters at all, mostly in terms of familial resemblance (the vis-ibility of which is routinely questioned in the novel). Consequently, readers of *Precaution* encounter a fictional community where distinction is as likely to be discerned from the features adorning a person's mode of transportation as it is from the features of his face. A "plain travelling chaise," for example, instantly tells Mr. Jarvis's oldest daughter Mary that the owner was "nobody of consequence" (*P* 26). Mary's remarks reveal how signs other than the face—such as a family's armorial ensign or lack thereof—can take precedent in the determination of status in *Precaution*, but the fact that her assessment is even-tually proven to be incorrect demonstrates the inadequacy of such a system of distinction for *Precaution*.

In contrast, when readers first meet characters in Cooper's next two "professedly" American novels, *The Spy* and *The Pioneers*, the reverse occurs. Physical descriptions frequently precede the revelation of social, familial, or even nominal identities. Readers of these two novels must first "see" these characters before they learn what their social identities are. *The Spy*, for instance, begins with an unidentified stranger, "a solitary traveler" (9) looking for lodging during a time when "great numbers . . . wore masks" (10).[6] Before the "averted face[s]" (*S* 10) and suspicious eyes of revolutionary era New Yorkers, the man approaching from a distance initially appears to be a person of "somewhat doubtful character" (*S* 10). Even though the door of the stranger's first potential host "was too nearly closed to admit of a minute scrutiny" (*S* 11), she refuses admittance, telling him that "I can't say I like to give lodgings in these ticklish times" (*S* 11). When the man finally does find lodging, we learn that the house's owner, Mr. Wharton, is forced to conceal his Loyalist sympathies just as his redcoat son, Henry Wharton, is forced to travel home in disguise. The Revolutionary War thus intensifies the opening chapter's profound sense of unfamiliarity and mutual suspicion by transforming the social space and turning virtually everyone into strangers. With home and street indistinguishable in revolutionary America, family members become strangers even to themselves. Yet, before the Whartons or even the reader learn the travelling stranger's name—which turns out to be false anyway—the narrator describes his "manly form" (*S* 11) and, especially his face, in detail: "On taking an extra handkerchief from his neck, and removing a cloak of blue cloth, with a surtout of the same material, he exhibited to the scrutiny of the observant family party, a tall and extremely graceful person, of apparently fifty years of age. His countenance evinced a settled composure and dignity; his nose was straight, and approaching to Grecian, his eye, of a grey colour, was quiet, thoughtful, and rather melancholy; the mouth and lower part of his face being expressive of decision and much character" (*S* 13). In short, "his whole appearance was so impressive and so decidedly that of a gentleman," the narrator tells us, "that as he finished laying aside the garments, the ladies arose from their seats" (*S* 13). That the ladies have read this man's facial features correctly and thus have acted appropriately by their deference is confirmed later when it is revealed that the face of the man before them—who calls himself Mr. Harper in this scene—belongs to none other than George Washington.[7] While the stranger's face is not the only signifier of distinction in this scene—his clothes, hair, and deportment are others—it is certainly the focal point. Unlike *Precaution*, which presents readers with a large group of people connected by prior social networks, *The Spy* begins with a stranger whose distinction is ascertained only after a thorough examination of his countenance. Moreover, the initial unfamiliarity that these characters have for each other in *The Spy* is replicated in the experience of the reader for whom these same characters are equally unfamiliar. Readers of *The Spy* are introduced to characters on the page as they might encounter strangers on the street: by the image that their faces communicate first.

Like *The Spy*, Cooper's third novel, *The Pioneers*, also introduces characters by their faces first, but in this text the initial illegibility of persons is produced (in the opening scene at least) by natural rather than political conditions. Where the instability of the American Revolution created a social space that encouraged characters to conceal their identities at the start of *The Spy*, the winter weather of the North American climate accomplishes the same task in *The Pioneers*. Readers of that novel first meet three unnamed people—a driver, "a negro of apparently twenty years of age"; "a man of middle age" and of "large stature"; and "a female, just entering upon womanhood" (*Pioneers* 16)—riding in a sleigh in the middle of the American wilderness.[8] Before disclosing any of their names, Cooper's narrator describes how the man's greatcoat "enveloped the whole of his figure, excepting the head" leaving "but little of his person exposed to view" (*PI* 16). Yet, "from beneath this masque," the narrator informs us, "were to be seen part of a fine manly face, and particularly a pair of expressive eyes, that promised extraordinary intellect, covert humour, and great benevolence" (*PI* 16). The female is likewise "hid beneath the garments she wore" that "concealed the whole of her head, except a small opening . . . through which occasionally sparkled a pair of animated jet-black eyes" (*PI* 16). Even the subordinate figure of the "driver" is first introduced by his face—or perhaps more precisely, by his servitude and then by his race—before his name.

On the one hand, the wintry New York climate contributes to the initial illegibility of these characters; their bodies are protected so completely from the cold that there is little for readers to apprehend at first. On the other, the freezing weather enables Cooper to isolate the face in particular, just as he did in *The Spy*, as the narrative focal point for discerning character under such circumstances. From the middle-aged man's "expressive eyes," for example, readers learn that he possessed "extraordinary intellect, covert humour, and great benevolence." In contrast, the face of the driver gleams "with a glistening black" and it is so "mottled with the cold" that "his large shining eyes filled with tears" (*PI* 16). His face, the narrator remarks, becomes "a tribute" to nature's "power" for it reveals those features "that the keen frosts of those regions always extracted from one of his African origin" (*PI* 16). Far from commenting on the individual aspects of his particular personality, the driver's countenance reveals "his African origin." His black skin and "large shining eyes" are the superficial marks that the torrid African climate supposedly left on his face and on all other African faces; the tears in his eyes disclose his and his race's physiological unfitness for the temperate North American climate.[9] The representation of racial difference in this scene consists not simply of the opposition between white and black or master and servant, but whether a person's face first identifies the features of his individual character or his collective identity. In either case, nature becomes both the occasion for revealing such differences on the face and its underlying cause.

As opposed to the opening pages of *Precaution*, *The Spy* and *The Pioneers* display an intense interest in scrutinizing faces first.[10] Yet, as distant as the ancient manors and country estates of *Precaution*'s England are from the more unsettled but aspiring bourgeois frontier of America, Cooper presents a similar problem in his first three novels: the visibility of the distinction of men. In addition to the centrality of marriage to their plots, each of these novels, as critics have remarked, revolves around the inscrutability of men and the possible techniques for discerning their character.[11] Cooper reproduces the familiar didactic motif of two women—one exemplary, one not—that was a hallmark of postrevolutionary seduction fiction (such as Julia and Eliza in *The Coquette* or Harriot and Dorcasina in *Female Quixotism*). In *Precaution*, for example, readers watch as two sisters, Jane and Emily Moseley, struggle to determine the character of the two men courting them. Jane fails to detect the polished Colonel Egerton for the immoral Chesterfieldian that he is and she ends the novel alone; whereas Emily is able to marry a duke thanks to her own cautious discernment and her aunt's vigilance. *The Spy* repeats these elements of the plot structure as two more sisters, Sarah and Frances Wharton, are punished and rewarded based on their respective scrutiny of men. Sarah, the "belle of the city" (*S* 25), nearly marries an already-married British Colonel Wellmere, and she ends the novel single, childless, and insane. Her more discerning sister, Frances, whose ocular abilities are emphasized throughout the novel, marries the American Peyton Dunwoodie, whose curious blend of Revolutionary War hero and Virginia aristocrat is reproduced in their son, Wharton Dunwoodie. In *The Pioneers*, the two sisters merge into the lone character of Elizabeth Temple, just as the two male alternatives co-exist inside the same body of the presumed half-breed Oliver Edwards and the genteel Oliver Effingham.

Despite these narrative similarities, Cooper opts for different national solutions to the shared problem of reading men. *Precaution* struggles to make distinction visible from something other than a family's inherited "armorial bearings" (*P* 154) and heraldic symbols (since anyone, even social climbers like the middling Jarvises, can now purchase them), but it fails to do so. By the novel's close, the enigmatic George Denbigh (who has been hiding his true identity throughout the novel) is allowed to marry Emily Moseley only after it is revealed that he is the mysterious Earl of Pendennyss. Yet, *Precaution*'s resemblance to the English novel of manners and its eventual legitimization of Denbigh's distinction through his aristocratic lineage belie the fact that the social problem of the novel is actually more American than English: how can a man who has the kind of distinction associated with aristocracy be recognized as such when the visible signs of aristocracy—heraldry and familial resemblance—are either unavailable or insufficient. Since Denbigh conceals his title, but not necessarily his familial name in *Precaution*, characters must wrestle with the question of whether he is a duke more than is he a Denbigh. Similar to many characters within postrevolutionary American seduction novels, who often had to judge men without recourse to the established social networks that could confirm their status, these characters must somehow discern Denbigh's distinction without recourse to title or familial resemblance since he does "not look in the least" like the man who turns out to be his grandfather, General Denbigh (*P* 65).

For this reason, I believe that *Precaution* is less interested in whether Denbigh looks like his ancestors than it is in whether he looks like a duke in their absence.[12] What makes George Denbigh/Earl of Pendennyss American, then, and what I believe links him to Mr. Harper/George Washington in *The Spy* and to Oliver Edwards/Effingham in *The Pioneers* is his problematic social status as an invisible aristocrat.[13] Of course, what keeps Denbigh and *Precaution* ultimately English is that Cooper's fictional solution—the revelation of his disguised peerage—would be impossible to reproduce in democratic America.[14] Unlike the alleged half-breed Oliver Edwards in *The Pioneers*, George Denbigh has no need to resurrect a member of his ancient family in order to substantiate his claims to distinction, because the system by which his genealogy is distinguished is still in place. In England, he can simply *be* a duke. In contrast, almost as soon as Major Effingham emerges from his sepulchral cave in *The Pioneers*, he dies and is put back into the ground. It is as though Cooper feels compelled to disavow the colonial aristocratic means for legitimating young Edwards's distinction almost as soon as it had been unearthed.

I will come back to *Precaution* in more detail in a moment, but for now I want to point out how the social space imagined within in *Precaution* (one structured by the established hierarchy and deference of English peerage) is anterior to the novel itself. Indeed, the crowded opening scene of the novel makes little sense without it (which may help to explain why it sold so poorly in the United States, but went through five editions in England before 1851).[15] *Precaution*'s characters occupy positions in a social world that precedes the entrance of the reader. Consequently, within the imaginative space of the novel, readers remain at a distance as they look in on, rather than look at, the characters they encounter.[16] In *The Spy* and *The Pioneers*, however, the imagination of a coherent structure for social space is not anterior to the novel. In Cooper's more self-consciously "American" narratives, fictional characters are not presented within an existent social space of aristocratic distinction—although the visibility and legitimacy of that distinction is desired—so much as seen within an emergent social space of corporeal distinction. Here, the imaginative distance between readers and characters is reduced dramatically so that readers confront characters as if standing face to face before them. As I mentioned earlier, the opening scenes of *The Spy* and *The Pioneers* intensify this effect by aligning the initial unfamiliarity of the reader with a character with the initial unfamiliarity that characters may have for each other so that the act of reading duplicates the process by which those characters are first made familiar with each other.

My point is that while all three novels represent the reproduction of social and economic capital through intermarriage, *Precaution* tries to imagine alternative ways to legitimate a marital partner's distinction when the markers of social origin and aristocratic rank are unavailable—namely, through the corporeal legibility of character—even though it ultimately fails to rely entirely on those terms. *The Spy* and *The Pioneers*, however, place far more emphasis on the corporeal legibility of character—with particular attention paid to discerning character from the face. *The Spy*, as Wayne Franklin notes, gives the reader "the sort of physical embodiment of values which *Precaution* lacked" (28). Since many nineteenth-century reviewers and twentieth-century critics have placed Cooper at the origins of American literary nationalism, as an author who was said to have "laid the foundations of American romance," it would seem that one of the features that distinguishes his first two self-consciously American novels from their English predecessor is their greater emphasis on the body, particularly the face, in the visible discernment of character.[17] This is not to say that the face did not matter to British fiction, but rather to attend to its primacy in delineating character in Cooper's early fiction.[18] That is, the face serves as the occasion for a practice of visibility, a way of looking, that operates differently in the social spaces that Cooper identifies as American as opposed to English.

Cooper's early fiction—especially *Precaution* and *Tales for Fifteen*—shares many generic features with postrevolutionary seduction fiction: the appearance of dissimulating, at times, Chesterfieldian seducers; didactically driven marriage plots; the didactic motif of two women (one exemplary, one not); the dangers of female reading; and the corporeal legibility of character.[19] My interest in Cooper's relationship to this genre, however, has less to do with the critical question of literary genealogy—that is, the question of whether Cooper turned to Foster and Tenney as the sources for his early fiction rather than Austen, More, Opie, or Brunton—or with the question of how this genre might have helped him attain an audience for his fiction.[20] Instead, I wish to examine how and why Cooper's early fiction inhabited and modified postrevolutionary seduction fiction's didacticism, generic features, and intense interest in scrutinizing faces. Contrary to the critical tradition that reads *Precaution*, if it reads it at all, as a first failure or an imitative experiment that is similar formally but ultimately unrelated to Cooper's later fiction, I want to claim that *Precaution* inaugurates a set of concerns that he will continue to pursue in his first two "American" novels.[21] *Precaution* represents an attempt, in other words, to resolve the postcolonial problem of the invisible aristocrat within the social space of democracy, but it fails to do so because its solution—the corporeal legibility of character—is imagined within the aristocratic social space of the English domestic novel of manners.[22] In short, the generic structure of *Precaution*'s social space undercuts its attempts to import and legitimate an alternative form of distinction.

By distinguishing men by such "natural" differences, as we saw in the openings of such novels as *The Spy* and *The Pioneers*, Cooper reasserts American national identity in terms consonant with a natural (as opposed to an artificial) social stratification. In Cooper's mind, herein lay the true mission for culture in a democracy; his early fiction attempts to imagine a way for distinction to be visible in a democracy without resorting to the artificial forms of aristocracy. In this sense, Cooper's early fiction continues the instrumental cultural politics that I described as operating within Brackenridge's *Modern Chivalry* in Chapter 4. Similar to Brackenridge, Cooper did not believe in "raising men very far above their natural propensities" and for this reason he, too, thought that cultural forms such as the novel were vital to the health of a democracy (*American Democrat* xxv). "Books are," he wrote in *Precaution*, "the instruments of controlling the opinions of a nation" (162). Cooper thought such social control was necessary in America since "large democracies . . . are unable to scrutinize and understand character with the severity and intelligence that are of so much importance in all representative governments" (*American Democrat* 81).[23] If Cooper thought that the mission of American literature was—as Ross Pudaloff puts it—"the valorization of a culture politically democratic and socially aristocratic" (712), the discernment of character on the face appears to have been a vital component to that cultural project.[24] Cooper's early fiction, in other words, provides us with an opportunity to examine the cultural imagination of distinction within the social space of democracy as literary nationalism emerged in America.

Reading as Seeing: Cooper and His Critics

One rainy day during the month of April in 1823, an apparently bored Cooper decided to pass the time by inspecting Thomas Sully's portrait of Thomas Jefferson (1821) in a nearby library (Figure 26). Although the portrait had been the subject of much praise, Cooper was in no particular hurry to see it for himself. In a now-famous letter, he suggests that only inclement weather could have made him disregard his obdurate "antipathies" to Jefferson and travel to see his image. As Cooper put it in his letter to Charles Kitchel Gardner, "I would have gone twice as far to see the picture of almost any other man" (*Letters* 1:95). This last statement is all the more remarkable considering what happens next, for Cooper proceeds to describe how Jefferson's portrait affected him so profoundly and positively that it has "really shaken my opinions of Jefferson as a man if not as a politician" (*Letters* 1:96).

Cooper's incredibly powerful reaction to the portrait has been read by some critics as a catalyst in his political and social thinking, fusing in Cooper's "mind the figures of the American democrat, the agrarian gentleman and the patrician revolutionary" (McWilliams 45). Yet, what is most important about Cooper's response to Sully's portrait for my purposes is not *what* Jefferson might have embodied for Cooper politically, but rather that his face could disclose his character so immediately, accurately, and forcefully. "Cooper was certain the portrait had revealed to him the essence of Jefferson's character" (3), and, as H. Daniel Peck so aptly expresses it, this experience led Cooper to feel that he had "recognized or discovered (not interpreted) the final and true 'image' of Thomas Jefferson's character" (4). The instantaneous effect of

Figure 26. Thomas Sully, *Thomas Jefferson*, 1821. Image courtesy of the United States Military Academy.

Jefferson's face on Cooper not only resonates with the one that Washington's face had on the Whartons in *The Spy*, but it is an effect, I would like to suggest, that Cooper seeks to replicate within the minds of his readers in an effort to address the problem of the invisible aristocrat.

When the historian William H. Prescott reflected on Cooper's career as an author in 1851, he noted, as so many critics had done before him, the proximity between Cooper's prose and portraiture. He declared with confidence that "surely no one has succeeded like Cooper in the portraiture of American character" (quoted in McWilliams 3). When twentieth-century criticism discusses the particularly visual aspects of Cooper's fiction, however, the genre that is more likely than not to be at the center of that conversation is landscape, not portraiture. For these critics, Cooper's lush literary pictorialism evokes the work of the Hudson River school of painters (especially Thomas Cole) or contemporary practitioners of the picturesque.[25] Yet, the descriptive power of Cooper's early fiction—especially with respect to characterization—was understood by his contemporaries to be equally concerned with producing vivid pictures of men. To place Cooper's early fiction within the context of his contemporary critics, I would like to suggest, is to recover the portraiture of his literary pictorialism.

Cooper, like many postrevolutionary authors, was concerned intensely with the social consequences of reading and like these authors he, too, understood that reading his fiction would produce an imaginative experience similar to seeing. For Cooper, the moral force of a novel was best achieved through its images.[26] As Donald Ringe explains it, Cooper expected his readers "to read descriptive passages as one might view a painting" and "above all to visualize the scene described and discern its thematic significance."[27] Cooper believed in "the veracity and reliability of the visual image" (Peck 5), a faith that was based in Locke, the Scottish Common Sense school, and associationist philosophy. In what has been called his most explicit theory of the American novel (Wallace *Early Cooper* 106), Cooper describes how the moral force of a novel is best attained through the production of "one of those popular *pictures* which find their way into every library, and which, whilst they have attractions for the feeblest intellects, are not often rejected by the strongest" (*A Letter* 13–14). Whether or not Cooper had Jefferson's portrait in mind when he wrote these remarks, his words reveal that he understood the moral force of novels in terms of pictures because of the immediacy and universality of their effect. When "a good novel addresses itself very powerfully to our moral nature," Cooper reasoned that "we feel ourselves, as we look upon a touching *picture*, or as we read of trying situation" (*Early Critical* 99; my emphasis).[28]

The degree to which readers of Cooper's early novels felt as if they were before such vivid pictures can be measured by the language reviewers used to describe him in their criticism. Cooper's nineteenth-century readers consistently describe the success of his narrative technique in predominantly visual metaphors such as "the vivid pencil of the author" or as producing "a good portrait." Balzac declared that "Never did the art of writing tread closer upon the art of the pencil" (240–41). The reality of Cooper's fiction was spoken of in terms of its "almost visual effect" (Review of *The Pioneers, Album* [1823] 165) and the process of reading *The Pioneers* was described as that of advancing from "one of his paintings to another" (Review of *The Pioneers, Album* [1823] 158). "The trial of Bumpo," another reviewer noted, "can hardly be surpassed in strength of delineation and vividness of colouring" (Review of *The Pioneers, Port Folio* [1823] 246). Indeed, *The Pioneers* was celebrated for being "wonderfully graphic and real in its descriptions of both scenery and persons" (Review of *The Pioneers, Album* [1823] 157).

What is important to glean from the enthusiasm that critics had for Cooper's early fiction when it first appeared, however, is that these readers admired his pictorialism for its vivid characterization as much as they did for its rich scenery. One critic, for instance, complimented Cooper for his "graphic and spirited" descriptions and for the "vivacity in his delineations of different characters" ("James F. Cooper" 231). *The Spy* was found to be remarkable for having characters who "are naturally delineated" and "bear the stamp of nature" (Review of *The Spy, Port Folio* [1822] 95). Similarly, Maria Edgeworth identified *The Spy's* Betty Flanagan as "one of the most faithful and exquisite Irish characters I ever saw drawn; with individual characteristic touches, and yet representing a whole class" (Review of *The Spy* 86). Edgeworth's remarks about Flanagan were cited later as proof "Of the truth to nature of this author's portraits from life" (Review of *The Spy* 93). Even when *The Spy* was criticized, it was for having too much detail in its characterization. W. H. Gardiner, for instance, chastised Cooper for his "full length descriptions of the exact tone, look, and gesture, with which something, or nothing, is uttered, the precise graduation of this or that emotion" (65). Cooper's characters were so vivid that one critic even noticed the same change in characterization from *Precaution* to *The Spy* that I described at the beginning of this chapter with respect to their opening scenes. *Precaution* was singled out by this reviewer for lacking the visual force that was so evident in Cooper's other works. The reviewer argued that *Precaution* "has none of the characteristic traits which in his subsequent productions so eminently distinguished Mr. Cooper—none of the fire and fervour—the brilliance of description—the vivid portraiture of character, and the strong power of grouping, which the 'Spy,' . . . and others of that class exhibit" (Review of *Precaution*, *Godey's Lady's Book* 96).

Like *The Spy*, *The Pioneers* was also lauded for its graphic and vivid characterization. Across the ocean, a British reviewer praised Cooper for his "graphic delineation of scenes and manners" and *The Pioneers* for offering "a new picture to an Englishman" ("Remarks on *The Pioneers*" 36). "The graphic powers of this author—perhaps especially with regard to personal appearance," another critic wrote, were superb and "the description of the old hunter is given with almost visual effect" (Review of *The Pioneers*, *Album* [1823] 165). In fact, Cooper's narrative technique was considered so striking and graphic in *The Pioneers* that the novel quite literally demanded the attention of visual artists. "The scene in which Elizabeth is saved from the panther," a reviewer from the *Port Folio* predicted, would make "a fine subject for the painter" and it should "excite the pencil of some one" (Review of *The Pioneers*, *Port Folio* [1823] 243). And it did. The *Port Folio* later reported that *The Pioneers* had "excited a sensation among the artists, altogether unprecedented in the history of our domestic literature" ("Literary Intelligence" 520). American artists such as Henry Inman, Tony Johannot, William Dunlap, Gideon Fairman, Tompkins Matteson, Robert Farrier, John Quidor, and George Loring Brown all depicted scenes from *The Pioneers*. As the images by Inman, Johannot, Fairman, Matteson, and Farrier make clear, Cooper's landscapes appear as a richly rendered, but nonetheless secondary, backdrop for the primary subject matter of the composition: Cooper's characters.

According to contemporary critics, Cooper's literary characters were real or vivid because they were thought to match the type of people one encountered in the actual community. As one reviewer of *Precaution* put it, "None of the characters or incidents are distorted, or out of nature; most of the personages we can recognize in the living groups around us" (Review of *Precaution*, *New York Literary Journal* 39). Another critic, reviewing *The Pioneers*, noticed how the novel's "individuals will all be found in good keeping; not deformed by caricature nor frittered away by extravagance. Each one speaks and acts with perfect fitness and congruity, and they are, as we can testify from personal observation, the very kind of persons who may be expected to be found in such situations" (Review of *The Pioneers*, *Port Folio* [1823] 231). What these reviewers admire here is how the actuality of the characters helps to foster that type of immediate and virtually face-to-face encounter that I described earlier as characteristic of Cooper's narrative technique in the openings to both *The*

Spy and *The Pioneers*. The force of Cooper's characters on readerly visualization was so strong that its immediacy and actuality could have an inverse effect. As one English critic described it, the "impressions are so vividly stamped upon the imagination, that it is difficult to persuade ourselves that we have not met them under some extraordinary, but forgotten circumstances" ("Living Literary Characters" 360).

Cooper's Seductions: *Precaution* and *Tales for Fifteen*

Of course, the capacity of fiction to produce such vivid pictures in the imaginations of its readers was a feature of the early American novel that was condemned as much as it was admired. As I argued in Chapter 3, the postrevolutionary seduction novel sought to distinguish itself from continental romances on precisely this point: that the kinds of pictures produced by reading its novels would edify, not seduce the imaginations of its readers. These novels not only represented the struggle over distinction as one between the cultural capital associated with Chesterfieldian civility and the social capital of established elites, they also participated in that struggle by imagining social spaces in which culture, particularly the practice of producing and reading novels, was imagined to work alongside, rather than independent of, prior institutions for genteel distinction (such as the social and familial networks of established gentry). Cooper's first novel *Precaution* and his little known *Tales for Fifteen* transform the problem of the postrevolutionary seduction novel from countering the polite performances of the Chesterfieldian dissimulator to visualizing the allegedly natural differences of the man of distinction. Since Cooper seeks to resolve a different type of illegibility, the invisible aristocrat, his seduction fiction—similar to the second book of the *Female Quixotism*—deemphasizes the agency of the Chesterfieldian seducer. In *Precaution* and *Tales for Fifteen*, reading books remains as instrumental to combating the problem of discerning men as it had been in postrevolutionary seduction fiction, but for Cooper such reading now facilitates a person's (specifically a woman's) capacity to discern from the face those supposedly natural, but clandestine, features that will testify to a man's distinction rather than expose its absence.

The different reading habits and the conflicting quality of the imaginations formed by those reading habits, for instance, account for the unequal marital outcomes of the two Moseley daughters in *Precaution*. The negative exemplar of how to read books and picture men in *Precaution* is Jane Moseley.

Like Dorcasina in *Female Quixotism*, she is described as having "a mind more active than her father, and more brilliant than her mother; and if she had not imbibed injurious impressions from the unlicensed and indiscriminate reading she practiced, it was more owing to the fortunate circumstance that the baronet's library contained nothing extremely offensive to a pure taste, nor dangerous to good morals, than to any precaution of her parents against the deadly, the irretrievable injury to be sustained from ungoverned liberty in this respect to a female mind" (*P* 163). It is clear from this passage that Jane's practice of "unlicensed and indiscriminate reading" will result in "deadly" and "irretrievable injury" to her mind. It is also clear that if Jane had somehow failed to imbibe "injurious impressions" from such unregulated reading, it was owing more to the largely inoffensive moral quality of the baronet's library than to any type of precaution exercised by her parents. What is uncertain, however, is whether Jane has been injured by her injurious practice. It appears as though Cooper wants Jane to be seduced by her reading without exposing her to any seductive reading. His narrator condemns Jane's "unlicensed and indiscriminate reading," yet applauds the good taste of the baronet's library as being perhaps the only resource that might have prevented such injury from happening. The narrator struggles to distance Jane's reading from all reading by suggesting that books, while not entirely innocent, are also not the sole cause of her ungovernable imagination. According to Cooper's reasoning, reading books simply elicits or subdues features of a person's natural state just as they can "save or destroy" a nation.

Reading the right books matters for Jane not because it could have altered the natural disposition of her mind, but rather because it could have regulated it. Without a well-governed mind (*P* 13), Jane's indiscriminate reading leaves her unable to discipline her passions to moral principle: "Principles such as are found in every-day maxims and rules of conduct sufficient to restrain her within the bounds of perfect decorum she was furnished with in abundance; but to that principle which was to teach her submission in opposition to her wishes, to that principle that could alone afford her security against the treachery of her own passions, she was an utter stranger" (*P* 83). Conduct books are insufficient for women like Jane, Cooper's narrator suggests, because they can only regulate her performances in public, not her natural passions. Conduct books fail her because they only supply her body with behavioral models to copy in particular situations. What she needs, Cooper believes, are books that address the moral principles that form the mental source of and motivation for such behavior in the first place. In other words, Jane's course of reading turns a natural weakness into a tragic vulnerability. As *The Minerviad* warned its readers in 1822, "It is in the continual feeding of the imagination in which the great danger of novels consists . . . the imagination, once deceived, becomes itself the deceiver" ("Opinions Upon Novel Reading, No. 1" 45). Without moral principles to regulate her mind in private, Jane indulges "her own passions" and "dwells so much upon imaginary perfections" that "the man who flatters her delicately will be sure to win her esteem" (*P* 47). This, of course, happens when the smooth talking, novel-reading, Chesterfieldian, Colonel Egerton seduces her.

Although Egerton resembles the Chesterfieldian male seducer found within postrevolutionary seduction fiction, his dissimulation factors less in Jane's seduction than she does. Almost from the onset of the novel, the seducer in Jane's affair, as far as Mrs. Wilson is concerned, has been Jane herself: "That the imagination of Jane would supply her lover with those qualities she most honored herself, she believed was taken as a matter of course, and that when the veil she had helped throw before her own eyes was removed, she would cease to respect, and of course cease to love him, when too late to remedy the evil, she greatly feared" (*P* 83). Of course, Egerton is hardly passive in Jane's seduction, but his dissimulation seems almost secondary to how Jane quixotically idealizes "his form" and "his face" in her mind (*P* 136). Had Jane "possessed a matured or well-regulated judgment to control that fancy," the narrator explains, Egerton's physical features "might possibly have assumed a different appearance" (*P* 136). For this reason, dissimulation, while hardly endorsed in *Precaution*, seems almost inevitable rather than preventable. In fact, it is more or less exonerated as a social practice since none other than the duke himself, the Earl of Pendennyss, spends most of his time in the novel masquerading as George Denbigh. It seems as though Jane's real "danger existed in her imagination" (*P* 82) as opposed to the performances of her seducers.

In contrast to Jane, whose "indiscriminate reading" and "ungoverned" mind prevent her from discerning Egerton's character, her sister Emily Moseley represents the exemplary reader of books and men. "Emily," we learn, "had never read a book that contained a sentiment or inculcated an opinion improper for her sex or dangerous to her morals" (*P* 84). If "books were the entertainers of Jane," then they were "the instructors of Emily" (*P* 162). Her vigilant aunt, Mrs. Wilson "had inculcated the necessity of restraint, in selecting the books for her perusal, so strenuously on her niece, that what at first had been the effects of obedience and submission, had now settled into taste and habit; and Emily seldom opened a book, unless in search of information; or if it were the indulgence of a less commendable spirit, it was an indulgence chastened by a taste and judgment that lessened the danger, if it did not entirely remove it" (*P* 163). Unlike Jane, Emily's reading is guided by restraint and not led by passion. She reads for information and displays how "obedience and submission" can turn into "taste and habit." Their near interchangeability suggests how close literary taste and social submission were understood to be. Emily's history of discretionary reading enables her to repel the advances of the culturally fluent Egerton in a way that her sister cannot. Egerton, for instance, first tries to seduce Emily by speaking of his knowledge of the fashionable world and "novels" (*P* 36), but this failing he soon turns his attention to Jane. In Jane, the narrator tells us, Egerton "found a more willing auditor . . . and in works of the imagination she found her greatest delight. An animated discussion of the merits of their favorite authors now took place" (*P* 36).

Emily's reading is exemplary, however, not only because it allows her to see through the mask of the wrong suitor in *Precaution* but, more important, because it helps her to discern the otherwise obscure features of the invisible aristocrat, George Denbigh. Denbigh's superior, pure, and impressive reading of Campbell's poems, for example, affects Emily's imagination and her heart (*P* 116). What is interesting about Emily's reaction to Denbigh's reading of literature is that she listens to how he reads books, and through that listening, she is able to notice things about his character (*P* 116). In contrast, her sister Jane reads books and then imaginatively projects those characteristics onto the men before her.

For Emily, books do not create the artificial characters that men become; rather, they disclose the "natural" characters that men presumably already possess. What moves Emily as Denbigh reads Campbell's poetry is the quality of his voice. Here books, specifically literature (poetry), serve as a vehicle from which the distinction of a man might be felt (although it might still be performed) just as a Jefferson's or Washington's face might affect its beholder. Thus, *Precaution* distinguishes between the effects of two modes of reading, each associated with one of the sisters, but it rewards only one. Jane's unregulated reading and undisciplined mind leave her unable to distinguish men from her own imaginative projections, which makes her vulnerable to a conspiracy of culture, performance, and seduction. In contrast, Emily's discriminate reading makes her attentive to more embodied forms of distinction, which enables her to discern studied performances from allegedly natural features. That is, Emily not only spies the rake behind Egerton's facade, but she is able to detect the invisible aristocrat, Denbigh, from his masquerade.

Even if *Precaution* falls back on its English logic of aristocratic distinction—in that Denbigh's peerage, not his face or voice, ultimately authorizes him for marriage—Emily's discernment of Denbigh begins to articulate an alternative, more corporealized form of distinction that would figure prominently and distinguish Cooper's next two novels.

Emily not only exemplifies proper reading habits to the reader of *Precaution*, she becomes an exemplary reader of *Precaution* itself by literally painting a picture immediately after one of the novel's more dramatic and memorable scenes. Almost halfway through the novel, Emily's good-natured but thoughtless brother John playfully points his gun at her. Unaware that the weapon is loaded, thanks to the carelessness of Captain Jarvis (who hastily supplied the gun with ammunition only a moment earlier), he inadvertently fires at Emily. The bullet, however, never reaches its accidental target because the novel's mysterious hero, George Denbigh, miraculously throws his body between John and his sister, suffering a wound in her place (*P* 130). The scene would be quintessential Cooper if its action, gunfire, life-threatening wound, fainting women, and apparently selfless sacrifice were set somewhere in the backwoods of the American frontier—as it would be in a different context at the beginning of *The Pioneers*—instead of the romantic arbor of an English estate. Yet, the English setting cannot hide what is quintessentially Cooper about the scene: it produces a picture.

In fact, the nearly calamitous gunshot scene of *Precaution*'s chapter 18 is immediately followed by and becomes the subject of a picture by Emily Moseley in chapter 19. As the more discerning and less imaginative of the two unwed daughters, Emily "had early manifested a taste for painting" and her "vivid perception" (*P* 139) leads her to sketch the incident "with neatness and accuracy" (*P* 139). Emily's painting of the gunshot scene doubles the original narrative event of Chapter 18; this repetition aligns the two narrative moments as if the point of the gunshot scene is to produce just such a vivid picture in the mind of the novel's readers (as it does evidently for Emily, who visualizes it as a drawing). It also reveals the extent of Cooper's didacticism in that his concerns over the effect of the initial fictional incident impel him to include its reception in the following chapter.

At this moment, at least, *Precaution* seems to be fantasizing about its own fictional effects. According to its logic, the effect of the novel on readers should be identical to the effect of the incident on Emily. The novel should create a vivid picture from which we might glimpse a person's permanent character from his unpremeditated actions (like those prompted by such an accident) as opposed to his studied performances. It is important to note that Emily does not simply sketch Denbigh, she scrutinizes his face while she thinks it is at rest (a moment, incidentally, that Lavater had singled out as ideal for studying the face). Believing that he is asleep, Emily seizes on this "favorable moment to complete his . . . resemblance" (*P* 139) and concentrates on finishing "the face of the sleeper" (*P* 139). By drawing his face at rest—at a moment when his own masquerade is at least temporally suspended—Emily's painting attempts to capture Denbigh's permanent moral character from his face as transparently as his heroic, yet transient, action did. The difference is that her drawing attempts to defeat the transience of the image generated by his actions by aligning it with the permanence of his facial features. The episode encapsulates the larger mission of *Precaution*, which is to help its readers produce such pictures of men just as Emily is able to capture Denbigh's "true" character visually without yet knowing the complete details of his illustrious aristocratic family. Through Emily's portrait, Cooper fantasizes about the capacity of the novel to create an image of the face that could exhibit character as legibly as it would be from the performance of a heroic action. Just as Washington's face disclosed his character despite his performance as Mr. Harper in *The Spy*, and just as Jefferson's portrait communicated his character to Cooper despite his prejudices, Emily's portrait of Denbigh offers a model for how such fiction should be read: as a picture, to be sure, but in this instance, at least, as a portrait of a man with distinction in particular.

Sometime in the middle of composing his second novel, *The Spy*, Cooper decided to return to the ideas set forth in *Precaution*. Convinced by his publisher, Charles Wiley, he published two short pieces together as *Tales for Fifteen: or, Imagination and Heart* under the female pseudonym Jane Morgan.[29] The book's first tale, "Imagination," relates the near seduction of a genteel orphan, Julia Warren, by an imaginary man named Edward Stanley who, as it turns out, has been invented in a series of letters written to her by her best friend, Anna Miller. Julia becomes so enthralled with Anna's image of this man that she spurns Charles Weston (her one legitimate flesh-and-blood suitor) and nearly runs off with a common carriage driver whom she believes is Stanley in disguise.

Anna's letters describing Stanley furnish Julia with "the outlines of a picture" that her "imagination . . . completed" (*I* 7). Julia's unrestrained imagination embodies Stanley in her mind, his "eyes, his nose, his countenance were avowed to be handsome; and her fancy soon gave a colour and form to each" (*I* 7). She even renames him "Antonio" (*I* 7) and her mind is described as "constantly employed in canvassing the qualities of the unseen Antonio" (*I* 9). Julia's seducer is, as it was for Jane in *Precaution* and as it was for Dorcasina in the second book of *Female Quixotism*, mostly the creation of her own mind and imaginative reading.

Julia, like Emily in *Precaution*, also paints a portrait of her lover, yet hers is quite different. Julia's imagination negatively affects her ability to separate idealized forms from "natural" ones. She sketches "an outline of the figure of a man that answered to Anna's description, and satisfied her own eye" (*I* 10). The drawing satisfies her because "without being conscious of the theft, she had copied [it] from a print of the Apollo" (*I* 10). Cooper insists that the imaginative effects of reading can be so severe that Edward Stanley's face (even if he did exist) is entirely irrelevant to her imaginative projection of him. The triumph of imagined over actual faces is complete when "The face of Apollo" and "the image of Antonio" coalesce in Julia's mind at precisely the moment she spurns the marriage proposal of her only embodied lover in the tale, Charles Weston.

Julia's imagination and Anna's letters not only cause her to fall in love with and to paint a portrait of a fictional person—nothing more than a literary character if you will—they encourage her to seek him out in the flesh of the actual community. Herein lies the real danger of such writing and reading for Cooper—as it was for postrevolutionary Anglo-American moral critics—since Julia's imagination not only turns Edward Stanley's face into that of the Apollonian Antonio, it also locates that idealized image of Antonio (disguised, of course) onto the face of her social inferior: a lower-class coachman. In chapter 4, Anna tells Julia of Antonio's intentions to come to New York "in a mask" (*I* 14) and she goads Julia into believing that she would not be "able to penetrate his disguise" (*I* 14). This challenge only intensifies Julia's romantic imagination and she is soon looking everywhere "in quest of an unknown figure" (*I* 14). Even though "Julia had so long associated the idea of her hero with the image in her bosom, that she had given it perfect identity" (*I* 14), she eventually decides that her beloved Antonio could only appear in disguise "as a servant" and she "confidently expected to see him in the character of a coachman" (*I* 14).

During her trip up to Niagara Falls, Julia's imagination embodies her fictional and incognito Antonio in the person of her own carriage driver: "everything about him equalled her expectations—even at a distance, she had easily discerned the noble dignity of his manners—his eye gave assurance of his conscious worth—his attitude was that of a gentleman" (*I* 16). The joke here is that Julia has mistaken a whiskered, one-eyed carriage driver for her beloved

Antonio. Indeed, her imagination is so strong that it obliterates even the ide-alized image of Antonio—the Apollo Belvedere—whose portrait should look nothing like the carriage driver. Instead, Julia privileges his "manners" and "attitudes" in her assessment of his distinction.

Yet, even if this scene dramatizes Julia's inability to discern a gentleman from a carriage driver, the tale does not reject the face's legibility as an in-strument for making such distinctions. In fact, the opposite occurs. Cooper's narrator emphasizes the fact that it is Julia's mind—her quixotic imagination—that overrules what her eyes should be telling her about this person: that he has the face of an ordinary carriage driver. As a result, the reader sees what Julia cannot: that a whiskered, one-eyed carriage driver who does not look like the Apollo Belvedere is not a gentleman in disguise. For the man is described as having a "complexion dark near to blackness; his face was buried in whiskers" (*I* 15) and his eye was "large, black, and might be piercing" (*I* 15). In short, as the narrator says, "he did not resemble Apollo" (*I* 15).

When Anna finally reveals to Julia that she has invented Edward Stanley/Antonio in order to have something to write about in her letters, the story does not end immediately, but continues as if to make another point. Know-ing now that her driver Anthony/Tony is not her imaginary Antonio, Julia boards her carriage only to witness "a fluid that was discoloured with tobacco fall on her shoe and soil her stocking. Raising her eyes with disgust, she per-ceived that the wind had wafted it from the mouth of Antonio, as he held open the door—and the same blast throwing aside his screen of silk, discovered a face that was deformed with disease and wanting an eye!" (*I* 21). The soiling of Julia by Tony's foul fluid hints at the sexual union that might have ensued had Julia continued to let her imagination get the best of her. In addition, it demonstrates just how far Julia's reading has perverted her imagination and just how far her imagination has disabled her eyes. Cooper does so by recourse to the carriage driver's face. Now that Julia is enlightened to the true nature and identity of Anthony—an inferior and subordinate carriage driver—she discerns what supposedly everyone else sees: a disfigured face (*I* 21). Similar to the physiognomic logic of distinction found in the postrevolutionary seduc-tion novel, the ineradicable legibility of the face stands in opposition to the transformative power of Julia's imaginative reading.

Yet, unlike the seduction novelists who at least recognized the potential agency of the seducer to conceal his lack of distinction, Cooper seems to sug-gest that the supposedly natural differences between a "gentleman" and his "in-ferior" are so transparent as to be incapable of being hidden. The transparency of distinction on the face of the servant seems to be Cooper's default position. By eliminating the agency of the seducer in his apparent dissimulation, it is as if Cooper suggests that the only way an ordinary carriage driver could possibly be mistaken for a gentleman would be through this dangerous conspiracy of imaginative female writers and imaginative female readers. It is as if Cooper wants to underscore just how disastrous this combination can be on the minds of women. That Cooper situates his tale of the potentially catastrophic effects of imaginative reading in a series of letters composed by one woman and read by another mocks, even as it invokes, the epistolary tradition of the postrevolutionary seduction novel that continued to be reproduced in the pages of scores of sentimental novels of the nineteenth century.

For this reason, Cooper's cautionary tale on the dangers of unregulated imaginative reading ultimately departs from postrevolutionary versions such as Tabitha Tenney's *Female Quixotism* because Cooper is less interested in Chesterfieldian dissimulation than he is in the problem of making allegedly natural differences visible. Unlike the first book of *Female Quixotism*, in which male dissemblers such as Patrick O'Connor are characterized by their aggressive, manipulative deception, Cooper's male dissembler in "Imagination" is a carriage driver who does not intentionally take advantage of Julia's imaginative reading at all, but rather becomes the unknowing projection of it. Although the success of the imagined seduction still depends on disguise and deception, the male figure's (Anthony's) agency is entirely removed from that deception. Since volitional dissimulation is missing from "Imagination," so is the threat of mobility behind such dissimulation and for this reason, I believe "Imagination" is able to excuse its exemplary female reader, Julia Warren, in a way that *Female Quixotism* cannot. Thus, "Imagination" is able to provide Julia with a proper marriage resolution, whereas *Female Quixotism* punishes Dorcasina for her novel reading with eternal spinsterhood. Cooper's point in varying the seduction tale in this way is not meant to counter the dissimulation of performing Chesterfieldians, but to dramatize how imaginative reading can obscure the otherwise irreducible features of the face.

• • •

As I argued at the beginning of this chapter, *Precaution* is distinct from *The Spy* and *The Pioneers* in that it attempts to imagine an alternative form of distinction for the problem of the invisible aristocrat, but ultimately fails to do so. In the end, it decides to legitimate Denbigh as a proper genteel marriage partner by revealing his identity as a duke. In addition, I observed that *Precaution*'s characterization, in general, relies less on the physical description of persons, especially their faces, than it does on the social space of aristocracy to visualize such distinction—even though it struggles to imagine a new way to picture men with such distinction—than Cooper's next two novels do. From that observation, I hypothesized that the more embodied form of characterization found within his more self-consciously nationalist novels *The Spy* and *The Pioneers* was a significant feature of his attempt to resolve the problem of the invisible aristocrat in the social space of the early republic.

I want to close by discussing one of the many pictures that Cooper's fiction literally produced in the early nineteenth century. It is an engraving of one of the opening scenes with which I began this chapter. Henry Inman's 1823 engraving for the *Port Folio* (Figure 27) depicts the moment after Judge Temple (the man at the far left) has shot Oliver Edwards (the man in the middle foreground) in the first chapter of *The Pioneers*.[30] What is fascinating about Inman's image is his decision to imagine the significance of this scene in terms of Oliver's wound rather than in the novel's terms of the dispute over property. In the novel, the conversation between Natty Bumpo and Judge Temple occupies center stage as they argue over whose bullet killed a deer and thus who rightfully owns it. The as yet unidentified Oliver stands a mysterious stranger, all but silent behind a tree (*PI* 22), until he resolves the dispute by revealing that his wound had come from Temple's gun. In Inman's engraving, however, Oliver's wound becomes the focal point of the composition and the episode. The diagonal lines of the arms of both the Judge and Oliver direct our eyes to the wound and the eye lines of all the figures except Oliver point to its bullet hole. As for Natty, so talkative in the novel, he retreats quietly so far to the rear of the composition that he stands behind his dog, Hector.

I mention Inman's picture and his decision to center the scene on Oliver's wound because I believe it foregrounds both the invisible aristocrat as the central problem in the novel and the corporeal inscription of character as one of the practices to be used for resolving that problem. At first glance, the engraving displays three men (Judge Temple, Oliver, and Natty) who wear relatively similar winter clothes, hats, and visages. Upon further inspection, however, one discovers not only slight differences between the figures in clothing, but in their features as well. The judge's large eyes, slightly arched eyebrows, and capacious forehead, for example, denote his superior intellect in a manner that matches the initial description given by the narrator in which his "expressive

Figure 27. Henry Inman and Frances Kearney, *Edwards Showing His Wound to Judge Templeton*. *Port Folio* (August 1823), 256. Image courtesy of the American Antiquarian Society.

eyes," indicated his "extraordinary intellect, covert humour, and great benevolence." Moreover, Inman's decision to depict Temple from the profile enables viewers to discern the perfect proportion of the breadth and height of his head (as an imaginary line traversing his head from the tip of his nose to the back of his head is almost exactly the same length as an imaginary line running from the bottom of his chin to his hat's headband).

In addition, Oliver's social illegibility, as represented by Inman, follows the logic of the novel. Oliver resembles Natty only superficially, as in his dress, whereas his physical appearance is much closer to that of the Judge than that of Natty (an affinity the novel plays out and validates in the end by Oliver's marriage to Temple's daughter Elizabeth). Natty is distinguished from the others in Inman's drawing just as Cooper distinguished him: hardly heroic, but "skinny" and "thin almost to emaciation" (*PI* 21). In short, Inman did not simply illustrate the opening scene from *The Pioneers*, he also reproduced its model for making character visible by communicating Judge Temple's character through his face on the one hand and representing Oliver's affinity to him by his physical, but not familial, resemblance on the other.

As I mentioned above, Oliver is the George Denbigh of *The Pioneers* in that he, too, is an invisible aristocrat. Like Denbigh, Edwards alone decides when his hybrid status as a "half-breed" will end. Yet, Edwards differs from Denbigh in that he was not the only person responsible for when his social invisibility should begin. Unlike Denbigh, who assumes his illegibility voluntarily and then throws off his mask when the heroic moment arises, Oliver's illegibility is not solely his own choice, but the product of the man who has shot him. That man, Judge Temple, is the same person who is responsible for inflicting his metaphoric wound from the past (Temple's theft of his family's social and economic capital during the American Revolution).

Temple's wounding of Oliver, however, does resemble Denbigh's gunshot wound in *Precaution* in that the visibility of their distinction is associated with inscriptions made on their flesh. The bodies of neither one of these characters can remain inviolate if they are to be recognized as men of distinction. Oliver's injury, however, is different than Denbigh's since it refers to what he has lost—his aristocratic status and wealth—rather than to what he has been disguising. Oliver's pointing to the bullet hole, as Inman's illustration so wonderfully captures, acknowledges not only his loss, but also the loss of an entire system of genteel distinction. His wound represents both the loss of a pre-revolutionary system of civility associated with colonial gentility and its replacement with a postrevolutionary system of corporeal distinction in the new democracy. Thus, it refers to this loss at the same time it imagines the terms for its compensation (Downes 131). The metaphoric wound of his missing distinction and wealth is acknowledged, disavowed, and then compensated for by his eventual integration into the family that has displaced him: the Temples. As I have been trying to suggest throughout this chapter, Cooper relocates the artificial distinction of hereditary aristocracy onto the bodies, and in particular the faces, of his invisible aristocrats. He does so in a way in which violence and accident serve as the occasions to make such distinctions visible and natural. Thus, even if Denbigh and Oliver share gunshot wounds that create situations for them to act with distinction—as critics such as John McWilliams and James Wallace suggest—those situations also target their bodies as the sites for reimagining the visibility of distinction.[31]

More than twenty years after Inman's engraving, the experience of reading *The Pioneers* continued to be described in terms of seeing such pictures.[32] The literary pictorialism and vivid characterization that I described as distinguishing Cooper's early fiction in the minds of its initial readers remained a significant feature for criticism of those same novels throughout the 1840s and 1850s. In 1847, for example, Rufus Griswold's *The Prose Writers of America* reproduced the terms by which Cooper's fiction had been valued a generation earlier. Griswold, one of America's first literary nationalist critics, lauded Cooper for "giving to his pictures an astonishing reality" (269) and for creating characters who "rise before the mind, each in his clearly defined and peculiar lineaments, as striking original creations, as actual coherent beings" (30).[33] Two years later, *Holden's Dollar Magazine* concurred, noting how Cooper's "continuity of character," "bold dash of description," and "interesting method . . . of detail" made each of his Leatherstocking novels "a well-executed picture" ("Living Pictures" 90).[34] In fact, reviewers often criticized Cooper's later novels, especially those published after 1840, for failing to produce the kind of pictures that distinguished his early fiction. In an 1850 review of *The Ways of the Hour*, the *North American Review* called Cooper "the ghost of his former self" and accused him of having "committed literary suicide at least ten years ago" (121).[35] They found the "feeble delineations of character" in *The Ways of the Hour* as proof that this novel was "not written by the author of *The Spy*" (121). *The Ways of the Hour* lacked the "descriptive power" that had earned for Cooper "the title of *the* American novelist" (121).

While admiration for Cooper's capacity to generate strong visualizations in his readers (particularly of persons) remained constant during the 1840s and 1850s, what changed was the way in which critics now started to use Cooper's pictorialism to identify American literature.[36] By the 1850s, the native settings and enormous international popularity of the Leatherstocking novels had made Cooper an icon for American literary nationalism. Periodicals such as the *United States Magazine and Democratic Review* celebrated Cooper for rejecting the cultural secondarity of America. They argued that Cooper had "struck a new course. He made himself independent; possessed himself of American ideals, and threw his picture before the public with original clearness and impressive force seldom equaled" ("Cooper's Works" 54). Yet, it was not simply that Cooper's novels were American in *what* they depicted, they were American in *how* they depicted. "It is a trait of American genius to give pictures with astonishing clearness and reality," the *United States Magazine and Democratic Review* remarked, "and Cooper exhibits this trait in its greatest perfection. His actors are living breathing men" ("Cooper's Works" 54). What characterizes American literature, in other words, is its capacity to present pictures, especially those of "living breathing men." While it is true that picture-writing was a critical value for all novels during the nineteenth century, not just American ones, the pictorialism, corporeal legibility of character, and rational model of reading that had differentiated the seduction novel from the continental romance at the end of the eighteenth-century was now being recognized, at least in the eyes of America's first generation of literary nationalists, as a constitutive feature of American literature itself.

Chapter 6

The Physiognomic Fallacy

"There is a physiognomy in the title page of books," says old Butler,
and we are more than ever inclined to believe the saying from this
new work by the author of *Typee*.
    —*Anglo-American Magazine* (1847)

As for the Dauguerreotype [*sic*] . . . that's what I can not send you,
because I have none. And if I had, I would not send it for such
a purpose, even to you.—Pshaw! you cry—& so cry I.—"This is
intensified vanity, not true modesty or anything of that sort!"—
Again, I say so too. But if it be so, how can I help it. The fact is,
almost everybody is having his "mug" engraved nowadays; so that
this test of distinction is getting to be reversed; and therefore, to
see one's "mug" in a magazine, is presumptive evidence that he's a
nobody. So being as vain a man as ever lived; & beleiving [*sic*] that
my illustrious name is famous throughout the world—I respectfully
decline being obliviated by a Daguerre[o]type.
    —Herman Melville to Evert Duyckinck (1851)

This is a long letter, but you are not at all bound to answer it.
Possibly, if you do answer it and direct it to Herman Melville, you
will missend it—for the very fingers that now guide this pen are not
precisely the same that just took it up and put it on this paper. Lord,
when shall we be done changing?
    —Herman Melville to Nathaniel Hawthorne (1851)

THE PREVIOUS CHAPTER explored how the physiognomic distinction of the face in the social perception of character was appropriated and transformed in the early fiction of James Fenimore Cooper. Cooper's seduction fiction reproduced the transposition in the social perception of character to the physiognomic features of the face, but where those features had served primarily to unmask the dissimulating seducer in postrevolutionary seduction fiction, they now served to distinguish the invisible aristocrat. As a result, the purpose of discerning character from the face had changed from detecting the visibility of its absence to addressing the invisibility of its presence. I would like to conclude *Discerning Characters* by reading one of the nineteenth-century's most complex treatments of faces, Herman Melville's novel *Pierre* of 1852. *Pierre* offers a critique of the structuring effect of the physiognomic fallacy—that opposition between a model of character read from performance and one read from the face discussed in Chapter 1—on the genre of the novel, its model of reading, and on the representation of distinction in early America. Unlike Cooper's seduction fiction, which reproduced the structure and physiognomic logic of the postrevolutionary seduction narrative only to modify its function, Melville's seduction novel is similar to Brockden Brown's *Ormond* in that it inhabits the form to expose the fallacy of its physiognomic logic. As the following pages will demonstrate, *Pierre*, in astonishingly precise terms, inverts the tragedy of the postrevolutionary seduction narrative—which, as I argued in Chapters 2 and 3, ensues from not reading character from the face—by dramatizing the consequences of reading character from the face. Melville's extensive discussion of faces, portraits, and physiognomy in *Pierre* is all the more remarkable considering that by the time the novel was published 1852, the prevailing science for ascertaining character from the face was phrenology, not physiognomy. Physiognomy, of course, remained a residual component of phrenology and, at times, it periodically generated new books such as James Redfield's *Outlines of a New System of Physiognomy* (1849) and his *Comparative Physiognomy* (1852), but its scientific purchase had clearly diminished in light of phrenology's allegedly more quantitative and less synthetic methods.[1] Phrenology was an extension of physiognomy in the sense of reading moral qualities from the head, yet it was a far less visual practice than physiognomy, involving more empirical methods of cranial measurement (such as skull volume measurements, tactile readings, calipers, and other such devices). Yet, physiognomy did not simply disappear. Physiognomy's quasi-scientific practice of judgment from observation rather than from measurement and analysis, I suspect, enabled it to persist in a residual fashion—as a practice of visibility—long after phrenology's scientific theories and methods had been discredited. *Pierre's* interest in faces, however, has less to do with physiognomy's standing as a valid scientific practice than it does with its historical role in the transposition of the social perception of character and the continuing effect of that transposition on visual and literary practice of the first half of the nineteenth century. It is to this cultural persistence that this final chapter now turns.

"An Eccentricity of the Imagination": Reading and Seeing *Pierre*

It would seem rather uncontroversial to assert that Herman Melville's *Pierre* is a novel about looking at faces. After all, several recent studies have pointed to the faces and portraits that pervade the novel as the keys to unlocking its meaning.[2] The chair portrait of Pierre's father, for instance, serves as "the nodal point of the text" (144) in James Creech's decoding of *Pierre's* closeted homosexual content. In many of these accounts, however, the significance of the visual apparatus identified in *Pierre*—its complex discussion of faces, portraits, and the practices and histories that shape looking at them—is explained in terms of cultural forms or discourses related to reading and writing rather than looking and picturing.[3] Sacvan Bercovitch, for example, contends that "the central problem" of *Pierre* is "the interpretation of a portrait or rather a series of portraits" (262). Nonetheless, he finds those interpretations as ultimately participating in the novel's critique of the "rhetoric of authority" and "the authority of rhetoric" (278).[4] In a similar fashion, Elizabeth Renker identifies the face as "the force whose pressure presides over the events of the novel" (24).[5] Yet, for Renker, *Pierre's* "haunting and persistent faces" are motivated by "the institution of a destructive regime of writing" (25).[6] On the one hand, recent criticism insists on the primacy of portraiture and faces for understanding *Pierre*, on the other, it tends to understand that importance in terms that privilege verbal over visual representation. Or, perhaps to put it more precisely, the importance of portraiture and faces to *Pierre* has been articulated by recent critics according to notions of rhetoric, reading, and cultural production that subordinate the visual to the verbal.

Despite the subordination of image to word within these readings of *Pierre*, to which I will return in a moment, the centrality of faces and portraits within recent criticism differs dramatically from what nineteenth-century readers saw in the novel. It is striking, for example, that nineteenth-century reviewers scarcely mention the portraits or faces that so many recent critics identify as *Pierre*'s most crucial elements. If nineteenth-century reviewers routinely used the language of painting to write about the novel as a picture, as Nina Baym has shown, then how could they overlook *Pierre*'s emphasis on portraits, faces, and looking?[7] Do twentieth-century readers see something in *Pierre* that nineteenth-century readers do not? Or are they both looking at the same thing, but in different ways? I believe these questions are worth pursuing because their answers will help us understand what has often been a matter of disagreement in *Pierre* criticism: the subject of the novel's critique.[8]

Before we can begin to address these questions, however, it seems useful to revisit the initial nineteenth-century reception of *Pierre*. After the novel was first published, it was, as is well known, almost universally despised by critics.[9] While the contemporary reviews of *Pierre* vary in the severity of their criticism, most register the same five complaints: (1) *Pierre* violates generic norms, largely through its improbability and use of unnatural descriptions, characters, or events; (2) *Pierre* is immoral;[10] (3) *Pierre* is unsuccessful because of its style, specifically, its opaque and, at times, invented language;[11] (4) *Pierre* represents a "new" kind of writing for Melville that critics usually, but not always, dislike; and (5) *Pierre* represents the exhaustion of Melville as an author. Here reviewers situate *Pierre* in terms of Melville's previous and more popular sea novels and conclude, as one did, that "Melville has written himself out" or, worse, has lost his mind.[12]

Twentieth-century criticism has often understood these complaints, especially the last three, as signs of Melville's literary individualism and modernism, as evidence of his negotiation with and, for some, his rejection of popular nineteenth-century literary genres—most notably, the sentimental romance.[13] Yet, when nineteenth-century reviewers described *Pierre* as repudiating generic norms, one of their main points of contention was not particular to any one genre. *Pierre* failed, many noted, because it failed to provide the kind of pictures that nineteenth-century readers had come to expect from reading fiction in general. "Where," the *New York Herald* asked, "did Mr. Melville find an original for the portrait of Isabel?" (*HMCR* 437). Nineteenth-century critics understood *Pierre*'s refusal of genre, in large part, in terms of its indistinct or unreal characterization. Review after review reiterated the point that *Pierre*'s characters were, as the Boston *Evening Traveller* put it, "exceedingly unnatural" and bear " but little resemblance to living realities" (*HMCR* 426).[14] In fact, the same features that literary nationalists had praised in Cooper's novels and had begun to identify as "American"—their strong delineation of character, and the vivid, rational pictures they elicited in the minds of their readers—were precisely the grounds for condemning *Pierre*. One of the leading voices of that Young American movement, Evert A. Duyckinck, specifically criticized *Pierre* for "the indefiniteness of its characters, and want of distinctness in its pictures" (*HMCR* 431). Despite his familiarity with Melville's fiction, Duyckinck struggled to make sense of *Pierre*: "The object of the author, perhaps, has been, not to delineate life and character as they are or may possibly be, but as they are not and cannot be. We must receive the book, then, as an eccentricity of the imagination" (*HMCR* 430).

What shocked some nineteenth-century reviewers of *Pierre*, or appeared new to others, I want to argue, was the fact that Melville's previous work indicated that he was not only capable of such pictorialism and distinct characterization, but had in fact built his literary reputation on it. The contemporary reviews of Melville's earlier novels (especially *Typee, Omoo, Redburn*, and *White-Jacket*) suggest that his vivid power of description was a significant feature by which his critical reception was determined. The success of Melville's fiction was frequently defined in terms of its distinct pictures of people and places, its failure, in terms of their absence. Reviewers applauded Melville's pictorialism not simply because it was vivid, but because it displayed to the reader's mind the right kind of images. *Typee*, for instance, avoided boring or, worse yet, overheating a reader's imagination, because its pictures possessed all the veracity of actual eyewitness observation without its tedium, on the one hand, and all the interest of a romance without its improbability on the other.[15] Like *Typee*, *Omoo* also walked this fine line of readerly visualization as it, too, was lauded for its "very good picture-writing" (*HMCR* 103).[16] What most distinguished *Omoo*'s pictures, however, was Melville's "rare pen for the delineation of character" (*HMCR* 148).[17] According to critics, *Omoo*'s lifelike characterization transformed readers into viewers and narrative description into living portraiture.[18] "The vraisemblance is so perfect, the details so minute, the incidents are so natural, the portraitures of character and life so very graphic," the *United States Catholic Magazine and Monthly Review* remarked, "that fiction seems out of the question" (*HMCR* 173). As the reviews of *Typee* and *Omoo* suggest—and one can find similar remarks for *Redburn* and *White-Jacket*—Melville's early fiction was valued for its pictorialism, its lifelike characterization, and its capacity to generate strong visualizations in the minds of its readers.[19] Although *Mardi* and, to a lesser extent, *Moby-Dick*, were not perceived to be as successful in this regard as *Typee, Omoo, Redburn*, and *White-Jacket* were, they too generated similar, if noticeably fewer, commendations.[20]

As Jennifer Toner has argued, *Pierre*'s "radical difference from his previous works" undoubtedly "assaulted the genealogical continuity of the Melville canon" (254) that nineteenth-century critics had identified with his sea novels. I would add, however, that that canonical continuity was rooted strongly in generic expectations of characterization and pictorialism that Melville strayed from in *Mardi* (and to a much lesser extent in *Moby-Dick*), but unequivocally failed to meet in *Pierre*.[21] *Pierre* not only assailed what critics had come to expect from Melville as author-function and what they had expected to see from his novels, it assaulted what they had expected to see from *any* novel. *Pierre*, as William Spengemann succinctly notes, "is not so much a novel as an anti-novel" (ix).

To put the matter another way, *Pierre* is an antivisual novel in nineteenth-century terms, which is precisely why it is a visual novel in twentieth-century terms. What makes *Pierre* anti-visual in nineteenth-century terms is the way in which its relationship to genre self-consciously invokes and denies the type of conflation between reading and seeing which, as I have argued throughout this book, was associated with postrevolutionary fiction in America from Hill Brown to Cooper and which was, in fact, central to establishing Melville's own reputation as an author. What makes *Pierre* visual in twentieth-century terms—"oppressively visible" (26) to use Elizabeth Renker's phrase—is the materiality of writing in the novel. Henry Murray was among the first twentieth-century critics to notice how "visualizations are weak, because appearances are not in focus" in *Pierre*, suggesting that Melville had "given up his long standing interest in 'presentational immediacy.'" Even though Murray finds *Pierre* to be comprised of a "miscellany of grammatical eccentricities, convoluted sentences, neologisms, and verbal fetishisms" (xciv), he does not connect the notorious materiality of *Pierre*'s prose style to the novel's refusal of readerly visualization. From this point of view, nineteenth-century readers were all too observant and their reactions more than understandable, for what they saw when they read *Pierre* was the thickness of Melville's participial nouns and adverbs rather than the transparency of words, which were supposed to generate distinct images in the mind. In this sense, as William Spengemann and others have noted, Melville shares much with the modernists.[22] Yet, what is important about *Pierre*'s style, for my purposes, is not so much its proleptic value for literary modernism, but the way in which its refusal of visualization reveals the dominance of picture-writing as a critical value for nineteenth-century fiction. What *Pierre* offers its readers, I would like to suggest, is more metapicture than picture.[23]

The initial nineteenth-century and more recent twentieth-century critical receptions of *Pierre* suggest that the discourses informing antebellum fiction and its pictorialism occupy the novel as much as, if not more than, any particular genre of nineteenth-century fiction. For this reason *Pierre*'s relationship to genre appears to be less a question of literary classification—that is, less a question of whether it parodies or emulates a particular genre—than it is a question of which discourses were shaping fiction itself. In this respect, I am interested, as Samuel Otter is, in how *Pierre* "inhabits antebellum discourse" (209). Otter's sensitivity to Melville's language and his analysis of Melville's probing of "the rhetorical structures and ideological functions of antebellum discourse" (4) seem a particularly rich way to confront *Pierre*. Yet, the discourses that I find Melville to be inhabiting are not exactly the same ones that Otter identifies. To be sure, sentimentalism, phrenology, and racial ethnology inform *Pierre*, but the novel is interested in seduction, faces, and portraits at least as much as it is in skulls and hearts. So the question remains: why would a novel so widely discussed in terms of genre ultimately be a novel so obsessed with faces?

The answer, I contend, can be found in the subject of the novel's critique: the physiognomic distinction of the face.[24] Faces dominate *Pierre* because, as we have seen, they were instrumental to the representation of distinction in early American visual culture in general and to the didacticism of the post-revolutionary seduction novel in particular. Part of *Pierre*'s complexity comes from the fact that it engages this critique on both of these registers at the same time (examining both early American visual culture and the novel's relationship to that visual culture). On the one hand, the trajectory of *Pierre* reproduces this visual cultural history within itself by moving as it does from the portraiture of the colonial aristocratic world to the physiognomic portraits of the postrevolutionary generation before closing with the daguerreotypes, frontispieces, and picture galleries of the urban democratic present. The novel's plot details how the various Glendinning portraits, Pierre's docile and idolatrous relationship to them, and his physiognomic method for reading them contribute to a culture in which distinction is read from the face. On the other, *Pierre* inhabits the postrevolutionary seduction narrative—the genre that arguably structures the novel's characters and plot most strongly—not to emulate or parody it, but to expose the physiognomic fallacy at the heart of its imagination of distinction and to measure the residual force of that logic on the cultural representation of distinction in America. As John Carlos Rowe suggests, Melville knew how powerfully literary forms (such as the romance and the novel) "contribute to the very social forces of domination they so often claim to contest" (64).

Over the course of *Pierre*'s critique of the physiognomic logic of distinction, the novel maps the social space of two aristocracies: the aristocracy of the face and the aristocracy of the brain, with particular attention paid to how the cultural forms of each signify distinction through the face.[25] The aristocracy of the face unfolds during the first half of the novel, documenting how the reproduction of genteel distinction in America depends on the cultural forms for representing it (such as the portrait and the novel), the dispositions that structure a person's relationship to those forms (such as docility and idolatry), and the discourses used to read those forms (such as physiognomy) as much as actual economic capital or social origin (the very things Pierre will renounce before leaving his ancestral home). Part of what makes Melville's analysis so compelling is the complex way in which he identifies not simply the cultural forms that reproduce distinction, but the dispositions that structure a person's relationship to those forms. Where the first half of *Pierre* examines the cultural forms, dispositions, and discourses of the aristocracy of the face, its transformation and persistence into democratic America, and the contradictions generated by that transformation and persistence, the second half of the novel (especially books 17 and 18) explores the relationship between that residual aristocracy of the face and what Melville describes elsewhere as "the aristocracy of the brain" (*Correspondence* 191). Despite the fact that the aristocracy of the brain—which coincides with the novel's discussion of Pierre's relationship to authorship—is represented as distant from the social origin and economic capital of the aristocracy of the face, the novel explores how representations of the locations of cultural production—such as authorship—might reproduce rather than renounce the cultural forms and dispositions of that residual aristocracy of the face.[26] Pierre's acts of defiance in the novel do not overthrow the distinction associated with his aristocratic past so much as unwittingly dramatize the conversion of its practices of reproduction from the artificial and external signifiers of gentility to the allegedly more natural physiognomic distinction of the face.

As I mentioned earlier, twentieth-century criticism has often understood *Pierre* as Melville's repudiation of popular nineteenth-century literary genres, most notably, the sentimental romance. Some have read Pierre's complaint that "when every body has his portrait published true distinction lies in not having yours published at all," as part of Melville's assertion of a particular type of literary individualism where distinction is associated with obscurity and not the commercial success and publicity that accompanied the sentimental authors of the nineteenth-century literary marketplace.[27] Alternatively, I want to suggest that what is driving Melville's rejection of publicity is not merely its ties to the literary marketplace of sentimentalism, but its ties to the residual forms, discourses, and dispositions of distinction. Unlike Cooper's seduction fiction, which reproduced the structure and physiognomic logic of the postrevolutionary seduction narrative only to modify its function, Melville's seduction novel, similar to Brockden Brown's *Ormond*, inhabits the form to expose the fallacy of its physiognomic logic.

Distinction and the Imagination of the Social Space of Democracy

Pierre begins with a question that we have encountered throughout this study: how might distinction be recognized within the social space of democracy? By the middle of the nineteenth century, the subject of this question had changed from its original postrevolutionary context. The emphasis on the social perception of character, as the previous chapter demonstrated, had been transformed from discerning the visibility of its absence to addressing the invisibility of its presence. Within the first ten pages of the novel, the narrator reformulates this familiar question in the following terms: "The monarchical world very generally imagines, that in demagoguical America the sacred Past hath no fixed statues erected to it, but all things irreverently seethe and boil in the vulgar caldron of an everlasting uncrystalizing Present. This conceit would seem peculiarly applicable to the social condition. With no chartered aristocracy, and no law of entail, how can any family in America imposingly perpetuate itself?" (8–9). The narrator asks how a family can distinguish and reproduce itself in "demagoguical America" without relying on the "fixed statues," "chartered aristocracy," and "law of entail" of its colonial genteel past on the one hand, or being reduced to the "vulgar" melting pot of its democratic present on the other. The temporal terms ("sacred Past" and "everlasting and uncrystalizing Present") reposition the familiar tension between the cultural and social forms of genteel distinction and the social leveling implied by democratic politics so that our attention is drawn to how distinction might be reproduced in the future. How, in other words, can a family remain distinguished under the American social condition?[28]

This passage, however, also implies that America has no current cultural or social forms of distinction. The fact that this conceit is articulated by "the monarchical world" suggests that it may be only from an aristocratic point of view that "demagoguical America" appears to have no system of distinction. In contrast to earlier novels in this study, which took the visibility or invisibility of distinction on the face as its subject, *Pierre* opens by addressing the perceived invisibility of America's social and cultural forms of distinction, its notorious classlessness. The opening pages of *Pierre* quickly confront the validity of this conceit of "the monarchical world" through two related claims. First, there is the suggestion that the political ascendancy of democracy has not removed the cultural forms of distinction ("fixed statues") so much as broadened their access and shortened their duration to "an everlasting uncrystalizing Present." Using terms that evoke the chemistry of that more democratic form of por-traiture, daguerreotypy, the narrator explains how "the democratic element operates as a subtile acid among us," seemingly "forever producing new things by corroding the old" (9).[29] Yet, the "new" is less a replacement of the "old" than a transformation and reproduction of it. Even if "in America the vast mass of families be as the blades of grass," the narrator confesses that there are still "some few" who "stand as the oak; which, instead of decaying, annually puts forth new branches" (9). The conflation of the genealogical with the nat-ural brings us to the second claim: that the political ascendancy of democracy has not eliminated the vestiges of aristocratic distinction in America so much as transformed the artificiality of that aristocracy, "producing new things by corroding the old."[30] Despite the democratization of formerly aristocratic cul-tural forms (such as portraits) on the one hand, and the political termination of its social forms (such as chartered aristocracy, law of fee entail) on the other, one of the reasons aristocracy has managed to survive, the narrator suggests, is because the artificiality of its social and cultural forms of distinction has been naturalized.[31]

Melville's narrator explains how such an invisible aristocracy has managed to persist in a democracy through a complicated comparison of the English and American aristocracies. The narrator describes the artificiality of the Brit-ish peerage system and resents how recent social climbers have "manufactured nobility" (10). "In England this day, twenty-five hundred peerages are extinct; but the name survives," the narrator remarks, "so that the empty air of a name is more endurable than a man, or than dynasties of men" (10). As John Carlos Rowe explains, "the difference between these American aristocrats and the English is that the former stake their claims to nobility on the property they possess, whereas the English gentry make vain appeals to the past, often to fictionalized lineages" (77). Yet, the fictionalized lineages that Rowe identifies as distinguishing British and American models of aristocracy are also what connects them. At least part of the reason the artificiality of British peerage is mentioned is to demonstrate that American claims to aristocratic distinction, like the Glendinnings, are not as laughable as "the monarchical world" would have us believe. As the narrator explains, if England has witnessed a flood of aristocracy and manufactured nobility then "our America will make out a good general case with England in this short little matter of large estates, and long pedigrees" (11). In terms of lineage, we "can compare pedigrees with England, and strange as it may seem at the first blush, not without some claim to equality" (9). In this sense, as Samuel Otter remarks, "America out-Englands England" (196).[32]

While it is true, as Rowe and others have argued, that these moments are part of Melville's contention that "the rise of the bourgeoisie . . . does not lead to authentic democracy, but merely to the manufacture of new and explicitly arbitrary titles in the place of those social institutions that would transcend the family and thereby realize a larger human community" (Rowe 77), the English and American models of aristocracy differ in that the explicit artificiality of English social forms (the empty "air"/heir of British peerage) has been transformed into the seemingly more natural, if no less artificial, corporealized forms of American aristocracy. As Melville's narrator observes, "political institutions, which in other lands seem above all things intensely artificial, with America seem to possess the divine virtue of a natural law" (9). "In countries like America," the narrator explains, "where there is no distinct hereditary caste of gentlemen, whose order is factitiously perpetuated as race-horses and lords are in kingly lands; and in especially, in those agricultural districts, where, of a hundred hands, that drop a ballot for the Presidency, ninety-nine shall be of the brownest and the brawniest; in such districts, this daintiness of the fingers, when united with a generally manly aspect, assumes a remarkableness unknown in European nations" (98). With "no distinct hereditary caste of gentlemen," the color of a person's hand and the shape of his face obtain a social power "unknown in European nations." Embodied forms of distinction, such as race and physiognomy, are said to possess so much more power in America than they do in Europe because they reinscribe, in an apparently natural way, the artificial forms of aristocracy that supposedly ended when democratic laws abolished entails and the privilege of primogeniture established under colonial monarchical rule.[33] In a country where so many people labor, the power of corporeal signifiers of distinction—such as the "daintiness of fingers" and "generally manly aspect"—is further magnified by the perceived rarity of the signifiers. Yet, this passage also discloses the ways in which the face might maintain intraracial distinction within racial homogeneity. On the one hand, race includes and politically empowers those white hands to "drop a ballot." On the other, race is shown to displace class as the contrast between the hands of leisure ("this daintiness of fingers") with those of labor ("the brawniest") is simultaneously represented as one between "daintiness" and "the brownest." The asymmetries that were operative in Brackenridge's application of the logic of physiognomic distinction to the public—individual and politically inclusive for dominant groups, collective and politically exclusive for subordinate groups—and that were reproduced within Cooper's representation of racial difference are shown to be operating intraracially in Melville's account. For those whose race includes them politically, the distinction of the face and hands remain a potential site of social exclusion and stratification.

That the novel's introduction to the subject of how distinction might be reproduced in America is coincident with its introduction to the character of Pierre, I would like to suggest, aligns the question of reproducing distinction in a democracy with the subsequent fictional trajectory of Pierre. The point of "asserting the great genealogical and real-estate dignity of some families in America," the narrator tells us, is to "establish the richly aristocratic condition of Master Pierre Glendinning" (12). Readers are told that Pierre's claims for "some special family distinction" will be "important . . . with reference to the singularly developed character and most singular life-career of our hero" (12). While the narrator undoubtedly "stresses the European character of the Glendinning family" to remind "democratic Americans that they might be working to produce a society that will merely repeat the hierarchical class systems of Europe" (70), as John Carlos Rowe contends, the narrator also reminds us of Pierre's status as a character within a novel. Thus, Pierre embodies not only the residual presence of aristocratic forms of genteel distinction in America ("the richly aristocratic condition of Master Pierre Glendinning"), but one of the cultural forms for reproducing it ("our hero").

The Aristocracy of the Face

The first half of *Pierre*, the Saddle Meadows section of the novel, discusses what I referred to above as the aristocracy of the face in early America. These pages demonstrate how Pierre's docility before a number of faces, including those of his grandfather, his father, and their portraits, structure his idolatrous relationship to the Glendinning past and suggest how dispositions to cultural forms might be as integral to the visibility of distinction as the forms themselves.[34] The portrait of Pierre's grandfather, for example, not only embodies the social power of the colonial past in his face, but it becomes the icon from which Pierre can practice a model of docile, idolatrous looking on which the distinction of his grandfather's portrait depends.[35] His grandfather's portrait is almost certainly a full-length military portrait that is designed to project an exemplary image of a genteel, yet resolute, Christian to the public. The portrait hung on the wall, the narrator informs us, so that it could declare "to all people" that old Pierre embodied all that was good in man. The narrator explains how the ferocity of a man who bludgeoned Indians and kept slaves is buried beneath the "heavenly persuasiveness" of an image that depicts him with a "majestic sweetness" (30): "Never could Pierre look upon his fine military portrait without an infinite and mournful longing to meet his living aspect in actual life. The majestic sweetness of this portrait was truly wonderful in its effects upon any sensitive and generous-minded young observer. For such, the portrait possessed the heavenly persuasiveness of angelic speech; a glorious gospel framed and hung upon the wall, and declaring to all people, as from the Mount, that man is a noble, god-like being, full of choicest juices; made up of strength and beauty" (30). The "sensitive and generous-minded young observer" aptly describes the youthful Pierre, whose generosity consists in reading his grandfather's face as the natural sign of his "god-like being" (30).[36] Rather than see the man who "had annihilated two Indian savages by making reciprocal bludgeons of their heads," Pierre beholds "the mildest hearted, and most blue-eyed gentleman in the world . . . the gentlest husband, and the gentlest father" (30).[37]

Yet, what is striking about Pierre's idolatry is that its terms are oddly verbal. Pierre's unselfconscious construction of the mythical Glendinning is the product of his "sensitive and generous-minded" listening. The portrait speaks to him (a feature that will characterize Pierre's relationship to portraits and faces throughout the novel and that will eventually prove tragic for him). He does not see his grandfather's portrait so much as hear its "glorious *gospel*" and "the heavenly persuasiveness of" its "angelic *speech*" (emphasis added). Thus, Pierre's initial relationship to portraiture in the novel is one in which he listens to the story of a face and that story, as it turns out, mystifies the colonial violence and dispossession funding his aristocratic condition. That the mystification of the old General's participation in Native American genocide and transatlantic slavery features auditory rather than visual terms also suggests the submission of image to ideology.[38] While critics have tended to interpret this passage ironically, in a way that doubts the existence of any kind of gentleness in the old General, I believe that the passage also invites us to consider how docility—the docility of image to words and of viewers to those images—can also serve as the very means of domination.

The dispositions and conditions for viewing his grandfather's colonial portrait and the codes informing its image are also found in his father's drawing-room portrait. Like his grandfather's portrait, the drawing-room portrait of Pierre's father is a large, expensive painting intended to project his "marked reputation as a gentleman and a Christian" (68). Having paid "many hundred dollars for it" (80), Pierre's mother displays it prominently "in the great drawing-room" where it occupied "the most conspicuous and honorable place on the wall" (72). According to her, only this portrait of Pierre's father could "correctly . . . convey his features in detail, and more especially their truest, and finest, and noblest combined expression" (72). For much of his life, Pierre shares his mother's view that this portrait was "the more truthful and life-like presentation of his father" (72). The drawing-room portrait's embodiment of virtue confirms Pierre's childhood remembrances of his father as a man "without blemish, unclouded, snow-white, and serene" (68).

As was the case with his grandfather, Pierre constructs "gothic oratories" in his mind in which his father's image is made legible by "all those innumerable scrolls" that crown its shrine. While the imagery used to describe Pierre's paternal memories is spatial, as Peter Bellis suggests, Pierre's unambiguously virtuous image of his father is again the product of what he hears more than what he sees. The "talk" between Pierre and his mother stamps in his "soul the cherished conceit, that his virtuous father . . . was now uncorruptibly sainted in heaven" (69). In fact, Pierre's recollection of his father "as a gentleman and a Christian" is not even his own, but comes from "the general voice of the world" (68). These secondhand stories continue to mold Pierre's image of his father until they attain the "marbleized" permanence of those more durable cultural signifiers of aristocratic distinction—the "unchangeable and eternal" aspect of the "fixed statues" and portraits of the sacred past.[39]

Pierre's veneration of his father differs from that of his grandfather by the fact that the reproduction of his idolatry is metaphorically aligned with nature itself. With the aid of his mother's "green memory," Pierre would hang in his "fresh-foliaged heart" "fresh wreaths of a sweet and holy affection" until his annual "votive offerings" made his father's shrine "one green bower" (68). From the top of this shrine "radiated all those innumerable sculptured scrolls and branches, which supported the entire one-pillared temple of his moral life" and within which "stood the perfect marble form of his departed father" (68). The "scrolls" and "branches" blend word and nature into one idolatrous image as they support the seemingly natural "branches" of the Glendinning lineage. The language recalls the narrator's earlier distinction between the artificial aristocracy of England and the natural aristocracy of America, suggesting how the naturalization of aristocratic distinction might facilitate its reproduction in America. The Saddle Meadows pages of the novel document the aristocracy of the face and disclose how portraiture, docility, and idolatry reproduce distinction within the world that Pierre inhabits. Part of what makes Melville's analysis so compelling is his attention to the practices of consumption as well as the more obvious forms of production. The survival of genteel distinction like that of the Glendinnings, he suggests, depends not merely on the cultural forms that embody it, but on the dispositions and discourses that reproduce the legibility of those forms.

"The Story of the Face": *Pierre*'s Seduction

The dispositions structuring Pierre's relationship to the faces of his aristocratic past inform nearly all of his subsequent relationships to faces in the novel, including what is perhaps the most significant countenance in *Pierre*: Isabel's face. When Pierre first sees Isabel, the narrator emphasizes that "it was mostly the face—the face, that wrought upon" him (48), for hers was "one of those faces, which . . . appear to a man, and without one word of *speech*, still reveals some fearful *gospel*" (43; emphasis added). The same aural terms—"gospel" and "speech"—that characterized Pierre's relationship to his grandfather's portrait are used to describe his relationship to Isabel's face, but now whatever her face says to Pierre, it says "without one word of speech." If Pierre habitually listens when he looks at the faces of his fathers, then he hears nothing when he first looks at Isabel's face. "What, *who* art thou?" he asks, "Oh! wretched vagueness—too familiar to me, yet inexplicable,—unknown, utterly unknown!" (41). Pierre's exasperation at the initial obscurity of Isabel's face reflects his chronic inability to see faces without words. "I conjure ye to lift the veil," he demands, "I must see it face to face" (41). Pierre fails to recognize, however, that his desire to see Isabel "face to face" would be to see her without words, which is precisely how he first sees her. Thus, Pierre misrecognizes the veil he seeks to remove. What prevents him from seeing Isabel "face to face" is not her face's initial inscrutability, but rather Pierre's disposition to subordinate faces to words.[40]

Isabel's face, however, does not remain wordless. She tells Pierre a mysterious tale of her mother's seduction by his father and her effusive words—in a letter and in person—eventually persuade him to see her formerly nameless face in terms of familial resemblance. Yet, the seduction story that Pierre hears when he looks at Isabel's face—"the story of the face" (37)—is not her story so much as a conventional one. As Robert Miles explains, Isabel's "story bears not the ring of truth, but the ring of romances" (168).[41] While the resemblance between Isabel's "story of the face" and any seduction tale is consistent with the mediated nature of all signification within the novel, as critics such as Edgar Dryden note, certain aspects of her seduction narrative—such as the significance of her face, her emotionally charged letter, and Pierre's enthusiastic reception of it—recall the postrevolutionary seduction narratives examined earlier in this book.

In fact, *Pierre* reproduces a remarkable number of elements particular to the postrevolutionary seduction narratives discussed in Chapters 2 and 3. Besides rakish men, ruined women, and the disruption of patrilineal inheritance, *Pierre* features the presence of physiognomy, portraiture, and dissimulation in the seduction plot; the embodiment of distinction in the face; the appearance of emotionally laden, sentimental writing and enthusiastic, overly imaginative reading; and the inclusion of commentary on the social effects of reading novels. The conventional plot of seduction, impregnation, and abandonment appears at least three times within *Pierre*: through the seduction of Isabel's mother, Delly Ulver, and, arguably, Pierre himself. If it seems strange to speak of Pierre's seduction, then consider how many attributes he shares with the typical postrevolutionary seduction narrative victim: his family is distinguished in terms of social origin and capital; he is the sole inheritor of that capital; one of his parents is either dead or otherwise incapacitated; a prearranged engagement with someone of equivalent social origin and sanctioned by his remaining family is discarded in preference for a sexual relationship with someone of an unknown or inferior social origin; and, after keeping no secret from his mother, Pierre, like Susanna Rowson's Charlotte Temple, fails to tell his mother about his seducer.[42] By the novel's end, Pierre also shares the conventional fate of the seduced: he ends up disowned by his family, uncertain of the legitimacy of his new partner's identity, and dead from one of postrevolutionary moral criticism's more common metaphors for the negative effects of reading novels: a vial of poison.[43]

Pierre's seduction, however, is distinct from the other two seduction sub-plots in the novel, not simply because of his sex but because he is seduced by a sentimental tale of seduction as much as he is by a person.[44] In this sense, Pierre is—as Hill Brown's Harrington, Tenney's Dorcasina, and Cooper's Julia Warren are—both a character within and a reader of seduction fiction. Pierre is a "New York Werther."[45] Like Harrington, Dorcasina, and Julia, he is characterized by an enthusiastic disposition, an early and unregulated history of novel reading, and a preference for the imaginative and romantic in literature. As a result, Pierre exemplifies, as his predecessors do, a negative model of reading (one understood as an overly imaginative form of seeing that was found to facilitate the performances of dissimulating seducers). Yet, what distinguishes *Pierre* from its postrevolutionary antecedents is that he also embodies aspects associated with the conventional positive model of reading (one that was understood as a rational, at times physiognomic, model of seeing, which was supposed to oppose to such Chesterfieldian performances). As we shall see, Pierre is ultimately betrayed by the same discursive logic—the physiognomic distinction of the face—that those earlier seduction narratives proposed would detect imposition, prevent seduction, distinguish their novels from romances, and diminish the force of cultural capital in the signification of genteel distinction. Thus, Melville's interest in reproducing so many features of the post-revolutionary seduction narrative derives less from the particularity of its form than from the structuring effects of genre. *Pierre* explores how the postrevolutionary seduction narrative's imagination of distinction, its physiognomic logic, and its didactic models for reading as seeing might continue to structure antebellum fiction. *Pierre* reproduces the postrevolutionary seduction narrative, in other words, not so much to emulate or parody its sentimentalism, but to inhabit and, at times, invert its generic features and discourses.[46]

Isabel's "tear-mingled" letter to Pierre, for instance, is the apotheosis of the kind of overly enthusiastic, emotionally laden writing—full of the "unquenchable yearnings" of a "bursting heart" (64)—that postrevolutionary moral critics and seduction novelists had found so dangerous in romance reading and that numerous antebellum authors continued to reproduce in sentimental novels.[47] In P. D. Manvill's popular sentimental novel, *Lucinda, or, The Mountain Mourner* (1807), for example, Mrs. Manvill writes to her sister that "The conclusion of our child's narrative, has quite overcome me. Indeed, I do not know but my tears have rendered it quite illegible; for as I had no command over my feelings, while committing it to writing, they have flowed almost incessantly through the whole course of it" (89).[48] As Chapter 3 demonstrated, *Lucinda* locates truth in the body, whether it be in the tears of its supposed author or through the physiognomic logic she promotes. Similar to Mrs. Manvill's tear-drenched letter, Isabel's pulpy letter, which "gushed with all a sister's sacred longings" and "painted the anguish of her life" (142), is, as more than one critic has remarked, "a sentimental spectacle" on which "Pierre builds a fantasy of false feeling."[49] It was "stained . . . with spots of tears, which chemically acted upon by the ink, assumed a strange and reddish hue—as if blood and not tears had dropped upon the sheet—and so completely torn in two by Pierre's own hand, that it indeed seemed the fit scroll of a torn, as well as bleeding heart" (65). Similar to the depiction of Harrington's irrational reading practice near the end of *The Power of Sympathy*, Pierre hangs "half life-less" (65) in his chair and presses Isabel's letter to his own wounded heart in a dramatic and utterly generic act of sympathetic identification. "Nothing but Truth can move me so," he sighs and as a result is convinced that "this letter is not a forgery" (66). Pierre's certainty, however, appears to be grounded in the letter's form—in how the materiality of its ink and tears assume the hue and force of blood—more than its lachrymose content.[50] The truth of Isabel's seduction tale as well as the legitimacy of the social origin she claims is thus guaranteed by the discursive association of truth with the materiality of the body, be it the actuality of her tears, the imagined presence of her blood, or the presumed legibility of her face. The narrator underscores this point by compar-ing Isabel to a novelist and her tearful letter to epistolary fiction. "Impostors are not unknown in this curious world," the narrator warns Pierre, "the brisk novelist, . . . will write thee fifty such notes, and so steal gushing tears from his reader's eyes; even as thy note so strangely made thine own manly eyes so arid; so glazed, and so arid, Pierre—foolish Pierre!" (70). What is remarkable about Isabel's heartrending epistolary fiction, the narrator asserts, is that it fails to make Pierre cry. This is not to say that he is emotionally unaffected by Isabel's letter, but rather that its power over him derives more from its sentimental typology of the body than from his actual emotional response to its content.[51] Through such commentary, the narrator encourages us as readers to suspect the letter's authenticity and the corporeal signifiers of its legitimacy even if Pierre as a character has already accepted them as genuine. In doing so, the narrator distinguishes the logic of Pierre's validation of Isabel's letter from the logic of the novel he is chronicling and, it is in this sense, that *Pierre* inhabits the form of the postrevolutionary seduction narrative.[52] Readers see, in a way that Pierre cannot, how the truth of Isabel's seduction narrative might be con-fused with the discursive structures that lend her story its truth.

The generic familiarity of Isabel's seduction narrative not only compensates for its factual obscurity, it solicits Pierre's eager and enthusiastic reception of it. If Pierre's docility and idolatry structure his relationship to faces, his enthusiasm—so generic a characteristic of the seduced in postrevolutionary fiction—structures his relationship to the words he reads (whether they belong to Shakespeare or Isabel) and to the stories he hears (whether they come from the mouth of Isabel or Aunt Dorothea). "The strangest feelings" and "coincidence" that would have "little power" to affect "less susceptible . . . and poetic beings" strike Pierre with "the lightning's flash" (111). As Wyn Kelley notes, "Melville's ironic narrator, repeatedly stresses Pierre's mistaken enthusiasm," and his mocking cynicism "underscores Pierre's naive eagerness to believe Isabel's sensational story" (155). Pierre's enthusiasm not only disposes him to be seduced by Isabel's face, "tear-mingled" letter, and seduction tale, it is repeatedly linked to his fateful decision to renounce his aristocratic social origin and its capital (106, 166, 172). Like Dorcasina in *Female Quixotism*, Pierre is depicted as willing to sacrifice the benefits of his genteel social condition on the basis of his own forceful enthusiasm and overheated imagination. In fact, whatever suspicion he might have had of Isabel, we learn, he attributes to "the distrust of his intellect" (167). Thus, Pierre's conviction in the legibility of the face is represented in opposition to his reason rather than the product of it. While Melville reproduces the mistaken enthusiasm so typical of the postrevolutionary seduction narrative, he inverts this feature's didactic function—as Brockden Brown did in *Ormond*—by showing how the perception of physiognomic resemblance might be the product of an enthusiastic disposition and a culturally shaped imagination rather than the rational vision of a disciplined mind.

Besides deconstructing the opposition between overly imaginative vision and physiognomic discernment, *Pierre* reproduces the terms commonly found within postrevolutionary debates about reading novels, its perceived social effects, and the relationship between the fictional and the actual in order to invert the positions that were characteristic of seduction narratives such as *The Power of Sympathy* and *Female Quixotism*. The terms used to describe Pierre's novel reading, for instance, replicate the typical postrevolutionary model of negative reading. Similar to Dorcasina in *Female Quixotism*, Pierre is described as having "read more novels than most persons of his years" (141) and as having been "a profound emotional sympathizer with them" (244). We learn, for instance, that in his "romance-engendering" youth Pierre "spent long summer afternoons in the deep recesses of his father's fastidiously picked and decorous library" (6). His course of novel reading, like that of Dorcasina, fans the "imaginative flames in his heart" (6) just as postrevolutionary critics warned that "the warm representation painted in the novel" would "naturally prepare[s] the mind for the admittance of vicious ideas."[53]

Melville, however, reverses the consequences that postrevolutionary critics had come to expect from such an enthusiastic, overly warm reading practice. Unlike Dorcasina, Pierre's reading adversely affects his mind not because novels confuse fictional and actual worlds, but rather because they fail to do so. For Pierre, fiction fails to imitate life's mysteries closely enough. "Like all youths," the narrator explains, "Pierre had conned his novel-lessons . . . but their false, inverted attempts at systematizing eternally unsystemizable elements; their audacious, intermeddling impotency, in trying to unravel, and spread out, and classify, the more thin than gossamer threads which make up the complex web of life; these things over Pierre had no power now" (141). Such novels have no power over Pierre, Melville's narrator suggests, because they "spin vails of mystery" only to "clear them up" in the end, whereas "the profounder emanations of the human mind . . . never unravel their own intricacies, and have no proper endings" (141). Pierre finds such novels false because they lack the mystery and unformulaic endings that he identifies with "the complex web of life" (141).

The transformative power of the imagination that postrevolutionary moral criticism negatively identified with reading romance novels and that the postrevolutionary seduction novel associated with seduction, dissimulation, and the loss of distinction thus comprise the very foundation of Pierre's notion of literary value. His excessive novel reading teaches him to value novels for precisely the reason that postrevolutionary moral critics had criticized them. His complaint that "the countless tribes of common novels laboriously spin vails of mystery, only to complacently clear them up" (141) recalls the terms, but not the argument, of Reverend John Bennett's anti-novel criticism in his enormously popular *Letters to a Young Lady* (1791).[54] Unlike Pierre, Bennett laments the fact that "novels and romances" (2:43): "lead young people into an *enchanted* country, and open to their view an *imaginable* world, full of inviolable friendships, attachments, ecstasies, accomplishments, prodigies, and such visionary joys, as never will be realized in the *coarseness* of common life. The romantic turn, they create, indisposes for every thing that is *rational* or substantial. They corrupt all *principle*. Fortitude they unnerve, and substitute, in its place, a *sickly* sensibility, that cannot relish *common* blessings or *common* things" (2:43). That the terms of Pierre's sense of literary value are nearly identical to Bennett's sense of its absence is striking. Harriett, Bennett's negative exemplar of a novel reader in the passage, like Pierre, was "deeply read in novels and romances" (2:43), and the "inviolable friendships, attachments, ecstasies, accomplishments, prodigies, and . . . visionary joys," in which she indulges could very well describe the enthusiastic and ecstatic nature of Pierre's relationship to literature, Isabel's letter, and her face. In fact, the "naturally poetic" Pierre will later dismiss any lingering doubts he still might have concerning the validity of Isabel's seduction story by accepting its "all-controlling and all-permeating wonderfulness" (139) as the "intuitive certainty" of her sisterhood (139). That Isabel's mysterious life appears as "an unraveled plot" to Pierre makes her story unlike any "common" novel he has read and thus, in his mind, more like the actual world.

By identifying life in the actual world with mystery and obscurity, and life in the fictional one with its demystification, Pierre's literary criticism also inverts the conventional postrevolutionary critique of imaginative literature. In fact, Pierre's tragedy is preceded by his distinguishing between reading fiction and reading life rather than his failure to do so. The "enchanted country" and "visionary joys" of Bennett's novels and romances are taken by Pierre to be a positive model for fiction and for life. In the critical moments preceding Pierre's fateful decision to renounce his aristocratic social origin and leave Saddle Meadows, Pierre, "his mind . . . wandering and vague" (168) sifts through the pages of such literature and displays the same conventional overly enthusiastic response that he did when reading Isabel's letter. The *Inferno* falls dramatically onto the floor after he reads Dante and, after reading Shakespeare, *Hamlet* drops from his hand as "his petrifying heart dropped hollowly within him" (168).[55] The destructive, burning metaphor behind Bennett's account of "an imagination, inflamed with the rhapsodies of novels" (2:44) is inhabited by Melville as its negativity is erased within the mind of Pierre. Such intense light does not mislead Pierre, at least as far as he is concerned, but rather it reveals the extent to which "the intensest light of reason and revelation combined, cannot shed such blazonings upon the deeper truths of man" (169). Such overly affected, irrational reading is in fact what distinguishes Pierre's mind and allows him to see "all objects through a medium which is mere blindness to common vision" (169). The transformative power of the imagination that Pierre values in literature such as the *Inferno* and *Hamlet* is the same power that the seduction novel associated with seduction, Chesterfieldianism, and the loss of genteel distinction and that moral criticism—such as Bennett's— found rampant in the romance novel. The narrator suggests that Dante and

Shakespeare taunt Pierre to the point that he begins to question why he has failed to act and publicly acknowledge Isabel. "What more was there to learn," he asks (170). Isabel's "magnetic contact," her face, and her "marvelous story" (173), the narrator discloses, "unconsciously left their ineffaceable impressions" (173) on "the impulsive Pierre" (176) and, when combined with his own "enthusiastic virtue," they persuade him to renounce his family and pose as his alleged half-sister's husband.

It is extraordinary that much of the evidence of Isabel's supposed familial legitimacy—such as her "magnetic contact" and her "marvelous story" (173)—is nearly identical to the "false, over-strained ideas"—such as the *similarity of souls, and involuntary friendship*" (2:44)—that postrevolutionary moral critics such as Bennett found circulating within novels and identified as leading "many a poor girl to *ruin*" (2:44). Such similarities have undoubtedly encouraged readers to understand Pierre's enthusiasm and the novel's sentimentalism in terms of emulation or parody. Yet, what prevents *Pierre* from either becoming or parodying the postrevolutionary seduction narrative it inhabits is the fact that Melville disaligns the face from the genre's didacticism. Unlike *The Coquette*, *The Inquisitor*, or *Female Quixotism*, the face confirms, rather than refutes, the claims of the seducer. The power of Isabel's face is not denied, but its force is redirected and associated with the same enthusiasm that surrounds her "magnetic contact," tear-stained letter, and "marvelous story" in Pierre's mind. In doing so, Melville shows, as Brockden Brown did before him, how the enthusiastic, irrational vision of an overheated imagination might be the same one that immediately recognizes his father's visage in a nameless stranger's face.

• • •

The perception of familial resemblance, Melville suggests, is mediated more by past cultural forms and their viewing and reading practices than by the existence of any actual physiognomic features. Pierre's initial look at Isabel's face would be the "first and last fraternal inquisition of the person the mystic girl," and from this "one instant," he concludes that "this being is thy sister; thou gazest on thy father's flesh" (112). Yet, the physical similarity that Pierre sees so strongly and instantaneously is one between a face and a portrait (specifically, the smaller "chair" portrait of his father). For when Pierre looks at Isabel's face and accepts her as a Glendinning, he sees "not only the nameless touchingness of that of the sewing-girl, but also the subtler expression of the portrait of his then youthful father, strangely translated, and intermarryingly blended with some before unknown, foreign feminineness" (112). Once more, the perceived similarity between his alleged sister's face and his father's chair portrait is undermined by the narrator's evocation of namelessness in the very words he uses to describe that resemblance ("nameless" and "unknown"). Isabel's face is associated with namelessness throughout the novel: from the "nameless sadness" (37) and "nameless beauty" (49) of her face to the "nameless wonderings" (118) and "nameless melancholy" (167) of her tale.[56] Even in the final chapter of the novel, Isabel is described as "namelessly glancing at Lucy" (349).

While the narrator's association of namelessness with Isabel would seem to challenge her claims to be a Glendinning, such namelessness turns out to be the basis of their resemblance since the portraits of Pierre's father are also marked by namelessness. Pierre's mother, for instance, finds something "namelessly unpleasant" (72) in her husband's chair portrait. She perceived "that the glance of the face in the portrait, is not, in some nameless way, dedicated to herself, but to some other and unknown object" (82). Perhaps most memorably, in the moments before Pierre burns the chair portrait, his father's portrait faces him with its "ever-nameless, and ambiguous unchanging smile" (196). Even the drawing-room portrait of Pierre's father "seemed to possess all the nameless and slightly portly tranquilities, incident to that condition when a felicitous one" (73). Consequently, Isabel's namelessness, rather than dismiss her claim to the name of Glendinning, actually becomes the foundation for it. The namelessness of both Isabel's face and the portraits of Pierre's father simultaneously questions the legitimacy of Isabel's sisterhood and the legitimacy of familial resemblance itself. By articulating familial resemblance in terms of namelessness, *Pierre* questions the legitimacy of names like Glendinning and the distinction they possess.[57] That Isabel's resemblance to Pierre's father is grounded in namelessness underscores the novel's insistence that the legitimacy of any perception of physical resemblance may owe more to the mediation of cultural forms and discourses than any actual visual or phenotypical features. Moreover, those cultural forms most intimately connected with corporeality—such as the embodiment of portraiture or the sentimental novel's typology of the body—can mask the mediated nature of their images or effects behind the supposed naturalness of the face or feelings. Since Isabel's "story of the face" is a generic one of seduction and since that story is put into an homologous relationship to the stories surrounding the faces of Pierre's ancestors, the genre of the postrevolutionary seduction narrative is thus put in a homologous relationship to that of the portrait in *Pierre*. This homology between seduction narrative and portrait in *Pierre* suggests how the seduction narrative (and, by extension, the novel) might convert the practices and discourses of the aristocracy of the face by reproducing the embodiment of distinction in the face.

The Physiognomic Fallacy

The nameless power of Isabel's face and Pierre's enthusiastic reception of her seduction narrative produce a crisis in the idolatrous image of "his virtuous father" (69). This crisis is expressed through a transformation in the relationship that the two portraits of Pierre's father have in his son's mind. The first is the full-length "drawing-room portrait" of Pierre's father as a middle-aged man—the second, a smaller, physiognomically informed "chair portrait" of him as a youth. In the past, Pierre had understood the chair portrait as depicting the younger, more carefree side of the aristocratic figure his father would later become in the public drawing-room portrait, but after hearing Isabel's tale, these two portraits come to represent two different people for Pierre. The transformation in the relationship between the two portraits in Pierre's mind and the subsequent value he assigns to them, I would like to suggest, correspond with a more general transformation in the representation of distinction in early America. *Pierre* reproduces the transformation of the representation of distinction in early American portraiture from the aristocratic social masks of colonial portraiture to the physiognomic details of the face featured in many postrevolutionary portraits, and exposes the false opposition on which this transformation is premised: the false opposition between a model of character associated with self-fashioning and performance and one associated with the involuntary and permanent features of the face. This opposition—or what I referred to in Chapter 1 as the physiognomic fallacy—distinguished physiognomy from prior discourses for reading the face, such as pathognomy, on the grounds that its assessment of character was neither temporary nor subject to individual manipulation. The term physiognomic fallacy, however, does not mean that the opposition between a model of character read from performance and one read from the physiognomic features of the face was somehow false in historical practice, but rather that the theoretical opposition informing this historical practice was false.

As we saw earlier, the drawing-room portrait of Pierre's father reproduces the colonial model of portraiture associated with the aristocracy. Like his grandfather's portrait, the drawing room portrait is a large, expensive painting intended to project his father's virtuous image and, as such, is conspicuously hung in the most visible part of the house. In contrast to the large size and carefully constructed public persona of the drawing-room portrait, the chair portrait is "a small portrait in oil" painted by his father's cousin, Ralph Winwood. It is associated with privacy, intimacy, solitude, and secrets. Shrouded in the mystery of Aunt Dorothea's "romance," the chair portrait remains hidden in a closet where "the sometimes solitary" Pierre "had many a time trancedly stood" (71). According to the "romantic and imaginative" (73) Aunt Dorothea, the chair portrait depicted Pierre's father as the wooer of a young, impoverished, and presumably noble French lady. Unlike the deliberate manufacture of the drawing-room portrait, Aunt Dorothea describes how Ralph "stole" the chair portrait. Ralph had to trick Pierre's father into sitting long enough to capture his likeness since he "was always in motion" (75). The terms of the chair portrait's production, in Aunt Dorothea's account, are similar to those found in the portrait of the sleeping Denbigh in Cooper's *Precaution*; they recall the Lavaterian distinction between the voluntary nature of pathognomy and the involuntary nature of physiognomy that we have been tracing throughout this study. That the production of the chair portrait is also discussed in terms of theft—Aunt Dorothea says Ralph "slyly picked his portrait"—links the unauthorized chair portrait of Pierre's father not only with economic loss, but with a loss of volition. The implication is that when Ralph stole the face of Pierre's father, he caught him with his mask off. The chair portrait, in other words, captures a countenance that is neither the scripted but fleeting face of social performance nor its fixed façade (like the mask depicted in the drawing-room portrait).

Yet, what clearly makes the chair portrait so powerful in Aunt Dorothea's "romance" and subsequently in Pierre's mind is its presumed physiognomic legibility.[58] After Pierre's father confronts Ralph about having his portrait involuntarily taken and asks him to destroy it, Ralph decides to give the "secret portrait" (78) to Aunt Dorothea. When Pierre asks Dorothea why his father did not want Ralph to paint his picture, she replies:

> But cousin Ralph had a foolish fancy about it. He used to tell me, that being your father's room some few days after the last scene I described, he noticed there a very wonderful work on Physiognomy as they call it, in which the strangest and shadowiest rules were laid down for detecting people's innermost secrets by studying their faces. And so, foolish cousin Ralph always flattered himself, that the reason your father did not want

his portrait taken was, because he was secretly in love with the French
young lady, and did not want his secret published in a portrait; since the
wonderful work on Physiognomy had, as it were, indirectly warned him
against running that risk. (79)

Similar to how the portrait of Peter Sanford functions in *The Coquette*, the
physiognomic legibility of the chair portrait, if we believe Aunt Dorothea's
"romance" about it, threatens to expose Pierre's father as a seducer. "Should
I honor my father," Pierre later wonders, "if I knew him to be a seducer?"
(103).[59] *Pierre* reproduces the intermediality of postrevolutionary seduction
fiction—including the centrality of portraits to its plots—in order to expose
the corporeal legibility of character at its core. The same physiognomic logic
that convinces Julia Granby that Sanford is a Chesterfieldian in *The Coquette*
or that persuades Mr. Sheldon that O'Connor is a fortune hunter in *Female
Quixotism* causes Pierre's father to fear Winwood's portrait. It is this logic that
also persuades Pierre that the face of the chair portrait might be his "real father" (83) underneath the mask of the drawing-room portrait.

Besides its smaller size and supposed physiognomic legibility, the chair
portrait is also distinguished from the drawing-room portrait in that the conditions for viewing each—the closet versus the parlor—correspond with the
supposedly private and public selves of Pierre's father. The narrator, however,
muddies any distinction between private and public selves by imagining what
critics might have written about the chair portrait had it been "hung in any
annual public exhibition" (72). The narrator suggests that:

Had this painting hung in any annual public exhibition, and in its
turn been described in print by the casual glancing critics, they would
probably have described it thus, and truthfully: "An impromptu portrait
of a fine-looking, gay-hearted, youthful gentleman. He is lightly, and, as
it were, airily and but grazingly seated in, or rather flittingly tenanting
an old-fashioned chair of Malacca. One arm confining his hat and cane
is loungingly thrown over the back of the chair, while the fingers of the
other hand play with his gold-watch-seal and key. The free-templed head
is sideways turned, with a peculiarly bright and care-free expression. He
seems as if just dropped in for a visit upon some familiar acquaintance.
Altogether, the painting is exceedingly clever and cheerful; with a fine,
off-handed expression about it. Undoubtedly a portrait, and no fancy-
piece; and, to hazard a vague conjecture, by an amateur." (72)

What is striking about this passage is the narrator's reluctance to describe the painting himself. The elaborate conditional construction of what these "casual glancing critics" might have printed about the painting removes us, as readers, from the portrait as a visual object and instead places us before the portrait as a discursive construct. The narrator does not want us to see this portrait so much as read how others might have seen it and described it for a reading public. Even as the privacy associated with the chair portrait is opposed to the public persona depicted in the drawing-room portrait, the mediated nature of seeing either one is demonstrated. The ekphrasis offered, besides being imaginary, is thus twice mediated: once through the narrator and a second time through how the narrator imagines how critics "would probably have described it" in print. Yet, the point of the double mediation is not merely to draw attention to the mediated nature of the portrait, as Edgar Dryden contends, but rather to expose the tendency to naturalize the supposedly more private and physiognomically revealing chair portrait despite its mediation.[60] The emphasis on "published" in the discussion of the chair portrait—both in its odd, conditional ekphrasis and in Ralph's speculation that Pierre's father "did not want his secret published in a portrait"—demonstrates how father and son both understand portraits as images of the self subject to the verbal, at times physiognomically informed, descriptions of its viewers. The narrator demonstrates how even the most natural and apparently private, solitary, and embodied cultural forms, like the chair portrait, are nonetheless the product of how they are read.

Despite the length and mediated nature of the chair portrait's ekphrasis and given the importance of physiognomy to Aunt Dorothea's "romance" regarding the chair portrait, it is extraordinary that the description of the portrait itself says relatively little about the physiognomy of Pierre's father. As was the case with the postrevolutionary seduction novel, there is virtually no physical, let alone physiognomic, description. Instead, the imagined critics refer to his father's pose, his possessions, and his overall expression: the position of his body, his fingers, and the air of the painting—the combination of which E. H. Gombrich calls "the mask" (10). We learn that Pierre's father appears "gay-hearted," "youthful," "bright," "care-free," and "cheerful" (72), but what is the shape of his nose, mouth, or lips? What color is his hair or eyes? Other than the reference to his "free-templed head" (72), all of the physiognomic details that supposedly matter so much to his father's and Pierre's own response to the portrait are unavailable to us as readers (just as they were in Foster's *The Coquette*). If the legitimacy of the chair portrait for Pierre depends, to some degree, on its physiognomic truth and its nameless resemblance to Isabel, then the narrator describes that portrait in terms of its "mask" qualities rather than its presumed "face" ones. Pierre's confidence in the chair portrait's transparency is questioned by the narrator, who notes how it only appeared "as if there was nothing kept concealed" (80). The narrator's remarks point to how cultural forms can naturalize their own mediation by conflating their meaning with the body they depict just as physiognomically informed portraits such as the chair portrait might reduce a sitter's character to his or her face.

Although the "face" of the chair portrait has the effect of challenging the "mask" of the drawing-room portrait as the true image of his father in Pierre's mind, the former perpetuates the aristocracy of the face by reproducing the dispositions and conditions for viewing colonial portraiture even as it transforms the codes for representing distinction within it. Like the aristocratic images of his grandfather and father, the chair portrait speaks to Pierre, telling him not to "believe . . . the drawing-room painting" (83). "Look again," the chair portrait says, "I am thy father as he more truly was. In mature life, the world overlays and varnishes us, Pierre; the thousand proprieties and polished finenesses and grimaces intervene, . . . in youth we *are*, Pierre, but in age we *seem*" (83). Always eager to listen to what images might have to say, Pierre soon imagines that the drawing-room portrait is nothing more than a social mask that conceals the essential self disclosed by the physiognomically transparent face of his father's chair portrait (the "*seem*" versus the "*are*"). The same docile, idolatrous disposition that structured Pierre's relationship to the faces of his ancestors continues to structure his relationship to the "face" of the chair portrait. The chair portrait solicits from Pierre the same kind of idolatrous "reveries and trances" that the "mask" of the drawing-room portrait did. "In his sober, cherishing memories, his father's beatification remained untouched" (85), the narrator observes, and the "strangeness of the portrait only served to invest his idea with a fine, legendary romance" (85). Just as Pierre sees Isabel's face in terms of her seduction narrative (and mistakenly understands that face in terms of a familial relation rather than his own erotic desire), he also understands the chair portrait in terms of "romance" (and mistakenly understands that face in terms of his father's erotic desire). In each, a tale of seduction strongly shapes how Pierre sees each face and, as a result, structures what he sees.

In the past, Pierre had accounted for the dissimilarity between his father's two room portraits as the product of time. One depicted a youthful bachelor, the other, a married middle-aged man. Recalling two of his own portraits—one painted when he was four and the other when sixteen, Pierre reasons, "If a few years can have in *me* made all this difference, why not in my father?" (73). Just as the "pensively smiling youth" had grown out of the "loud-laughing boy" (73), Pierre sees the traces of the youthful bachelor in the married middle-aged man. As such, Pierre engages in what E. H. Gombrich calls "perceptual fusion." "The experience of likeness," Gombrich explains, "is a kind of perceptual fusion based on recognition, and here as always past experience will colour the way we see a face" (7).[61] Pierre's two portraits of himself represent different likenesses rather than different people in his mind, because a consistent, but "nameless" facial trait allows him to see both portraits as equivalent, if discrete, images of himself. He is able to reconcile the different likenesses he sees in his own portraits—and, by extension, in his father's portraits—by the appearance of "an indestructible, all-surviving something in the eyes and on the temples" (73). While this "something" is unspecified, it is, nonetheless, identified with the face. Gombrich refers to this kind of recognizable "something" in the face as "physiognomic likeness" (8). Pierre's portraits resemble each other and he comes to resemble them in his mind because he sees this physiognomic "something" in each. On the one hand, Pierre senses that differences in physical appearance might indicate different selves. He apprehends that the continuity of the self from moment to moment might be a willful fiction. On the other, he is unable to recognize these differences as salient because of the unifying power of that physiognomic "something" in the face. That physiognomic something, for Pierre, remains consistent over time and this facial feature is what establishes the continuity of a self (and a family) over time. What Pierre fails to see at this point in the novel, but what he will learn by its end, is that "logically . . . anything can be said to be like any other thing in some respect" (Gombrich 7). Thus, for Pierre, the continuity of self can be independent of the differences in its physical appearance so long as there is a visible resemblance between the represented selves. As Gombrich has argued, the equivalence of portraits often resides in this perceived physiognomic likeness.

It is precisely this kind of physiognomic likeness that Pierre comes to see between Isabel's face and his father's chair portrait. Their resemblance—that nameless look—is mediated as much by Isabel's "tear-mingled" letter and his aunt's "romance" (85) as by any shared physical facial feature. In fact, the perceived physical resemblance between Isabel's face and his father's chair portrait is described in the same enthusiastic, overly imaginative terms of romances. "All that had been inexplicably mysterious to him in the portrait, and all that been inexplicably familiar in the face" (85), the narrator explains, merge to create the "lineaments of an added supernaturalness" (85). The certainty of the "intuitively certain, however literally unproven fact of Isabel's sisterhood" (139) in Pierre's mind is largely the product of this nameless look, this physiognomic "something." "Why do I believe it?" (139), he asks himself, because "I have seen her," he replies, because of "the portrait, the chair-portrait" (139). Pierre mistakes his father's chair portrait as his face, in part, because he sees it as opposed to the mask of the drawing-room portrait, and, as a result, he sees Isabel's face as equivalent to his father's face when it is actually equivalent to a look. Isabel's resemblance to the chair portrait of his father, however, does not prompt Pierre to question the nameless physiognomic "something" that unites them. Instead, he grants, as early American culture had, that look or physiognomic "something" the force of blood. *Pierre* shows how the fiction of physiognomic likeness becomes the fact of familial resemblance.

In fact, this physiognomic "something" also leads Pierre to destroy the chair portrait. In the moments before he burns the chair portrait of his father, Pierre obsesses over that "certain lurking lineament in the portrait, whose strange transfer, was visible in the countenance of Isabel" and which was "now detestable" to him (196). This "new hatefulness had its primary and unconscious rise," the narrator explains, "in the strange relativeness, reciprocalness, and transmitedness, between the long-dead father's portrait, and the living daughter's face" (197). The irony of the narrator's description suggests that the truth of the chair portrait's resemblance and the "lurking lineament" from which it derives is clouded by "strange relativeness, reciprocalness, and transmitedness." As if to emphasize the way in which such visual and apparently unmediated notions of physiognomic resemblance—that nameless look—are contingent on the discourses informing them and their viewers, the narrator remarks that "Pierre could not recall any distinct lineament transmitted to Isabel, but vaguely saw such in the portrait; therefore, not Pierre's parent, as any way remembrable by him, but the portrait's painted *self* seemed the real father of Isabel; for, so far as all sense went, Isabel had inherited one peculiar trait nowhither traceable but to it" (197). The physiognomic truth of the chair portrait's face and its nameless resemblance to Isabel, it turns out, are no less of a construction than the public persona of the drawing-room portrait.

Unable to reconcile what the face of the chair portrait says with what the mask of the drawing-room portrait proclaims, Pierre decides to destroy the former in order to preserve the virtuous image of the latter. His decision to burn his father's chair portrait is perhaps the most significant incident in *Pierre*: it not only separates the first half of the novel from the second—the

Saddle Meadows Pierre from his urban counterpart, the aristocracy of the face from the aristocracy of the brain—it reflects the ascendancy of the physiognomic distinction of the face over the external signifiers of gentility as the more legitimate model for representing moral character. Pierre's rationale for destroying the chair portrait—that its depiction of moral character renders the drawing-room portrait's image false—thus stages a false opposition between a model of character read from the face and one read from social performance.

Although Pierre's decision to burn the chair portrait coincides with his legitimization of the nameless Isabel and the renunciation of his economic and social capital, his act is less revolutionary than it appears because it ultimately works to preserve his aristocratic social origin more than it does to repudiate it. Pierre destroys "the one great, condemning, and unsuborned proof" of his father's alleged seduction because he is "resolved to hold his public memory inviolate" (198). As Ann Douglas observes, Pierre's discovery of Isabel "does not disillusion Pierre with his father" (375). He remains "determined at all hazards to hold his father's fair fame inviolate from any thing" (172). With the "sacredness and the indissolubleness of the most solemn oath," Pierre abides by an "enthusiastic . . . resolution to hold his father's memory untouched" (177). His decision to help Isabel, whatever his motives, is not an attempt to amend the social order the novel represents, but rather an effort (however futile) to get that social order to recognize her (Jehlen 200). "Pierre leaves precisely to maintain the symbolic order of Saddle Meadows," Priscilla Wald contends, "his fictitious marriage is not specifically intended as an act of defiance, but rather as an attempt to 'legitimize' Isabel, to bring her into the realm of social conventions from which she has felt excluded" (115). The recognition of Isabel's legitimacy as a Glendinning, in Pierre's mind, depends on keeping his father's scandal unknown and his public image sacrosanct. If Pierre runs off with Isabel with the declared intention of legitimating her, then he burns the chair portrait in order to uphold the public image of his father. What Pierre repudiates when he burns the chair portrait, legitimates Isabel, and renounces his past, is his relationship to, but not the reputation of, his social origin. Pierre's act does not overthrow the distinction associated with his aristocratic past so much as unwittingly dramatize the conversion of its practices of reproduction from the artificial and external signifiers of gentility to the physiognomic distinction of the face.

Pierre's inability to subordinate the face of the chair portrait to the mask of the drawing-room portrait thus marks a transformation in the aristocracy of the face. Where the drawing-room portrait projected the public image of his father—an image substantiated by wealth, social rank, and familial legend—the authority of the chair portrait legitimates its image, in Pierre's mind, through an actual face—Isabel's—and the seduction narrative that speaks to it. The means for representing distinction have shifted from the conventions and practices of the colonial portrait associated with the aristocracy to the allegedly more natural and thus supposedly more democratic actualities of the face and the corporeal discourses used to understand it. It is a moment that runs parallel to the visual cultural history implied by the two portraits of his father, a moment in which the colonial model of the aristocracy of the face has been converted into the postrevolutionary model of the aristocracy of the face. The fact that the image that survives—the drawing-room portrait—was painted after the chair portrait symbolically suggests how the alleged truth of the chair portrait's physiognomic "something" might work to extend that colonial aristocracy of the face into the social space of democracy.

Pierre inhabits the genre of the postrevolutionary seduction novel in order to expose the physiognomic fallacy at the heart of that genre's imagination of distinction and that fallacy's structuring relationship to the novel itself. On the one hand, the cultural form of portraiture, the dispositions that structure Pierre's relationship to that form (docility and idolatry), and the discourses used to understand that form (physiognomy) demand that Isabel's face speak to him. On the other, the cultural form of the novel (the seduction genre), the dispositions which structure Pierre's relationship to that form (enthusiasm), and the discourses used to understand that form (sentimentalism) provide the legibility he seeks. The point is to emphasize that the connection between the demand that faces speak or that pictures tell stories and the words they speak or the stories they tell is arbitrary. The story of Isabel's face asserts that the arbitrary, culturally determined resemblance between her and Pierre is actually a natural one of familial resemblance, blood relation, and genetic identity. *Pierre* suggests that the perception of visual resemblance is mediated by cultural rather than natural forces. It is not simply the naturalness of the sign that the novel questions through Pierre's relationship to portraits and faces, but rather how the naturalness of the sign depends on the stories surrounding it. As both the ground to which cultural forms and the dispositions associated with them might apply and the actual corporeal object from which such stories generate significance, Isabel's face encapsulates the dialectic of how cultural forms might shape experience and how experience might shape cultural forms.

The Aristocracy of the Brain

Where the first half of *Pierre* examines the cultural forms (portraits), dispositions (idolatrous and docile), and discourses (physiognomy) of the aristocracy of the face, its transformation and persistence into democratic America, and the contradictions generated by that transformation and persistence, the second half of the novel (especially books 17 and 18) explores the relationship between that residual aristocracy of the face and what Melville describes elsewhere as "the aristocracy of the brain" (*Correspondence* 191). On the one hand, the second half of the novel finds Pierre fleeing the stratified, aristocratic, and rural world of Saddle Meadows for the fluid, democratic, and urban streets of New York. On the other, it also finds Pierre embracing a profession—authorship—that, according to the narrator, is deeply informed by and reproduces the aristocratic genteel world that Pierre departs.[62] During the idyllic days of his youth, Pierre had published as a wealthy man of letters, but now, thrust into the economic realities of the antebellum present, he struggles to write as a professional author. Pierre's past and present experiences as an author, as many critics have remarked, reflect a tension between thinking about authorship as the belletristic pursuit of leisured gentlemen and thinking about it as the market-driven activity of commercial authors.[63] While Pierre's obscure and impoverished career as a professional author during the second half of the novel resists both models of authorship—belletristic and commercial—it also exposes the ways in which the latter model converts and reproduces the former. Less alternative than transformation, the commercial model of authorship of Pierre's antebellum present contains traces of the belletristic model of the colonial past within itself and, chief among these, the novel suggests, is the way in which authorship itself is informed by and reproduces the physiognomic distinction of the face.

Even though Pierre descends socially from the wealth and celebrity of manorial littérateur to the destitution and anonymity of urban author by the end of the novel, the apparent opposition between these two models of authorship belies their mutual engagement with the cultural forms of the face (engravings, portraits, daguerreotypes), its dispositions (idolatrous and docile), and discourses (physiognomic). The contradictions involved in the transformation of authorship from an aristocratic and belletristic model to a supposedly democratic and commercially driven one during the second half of the novel, I would like to suggest, are thus placed in a homologous relation to the contradictions involved in the transformation of the aristocracy of the face from an artificial, colonial model for representing distinction to a physiognomic, postcolonial one during the first half. Moreover, these two different phases of Pierre's career as an author—belletristic and commercial—register the shifting relationship between culture and distinction in antebellum America. The former addresses how culture might signify other forms of capital and contribute to their reproduction. Pierre's past experience as a genteel author, for example, demonstrates how literature might signify capital by virtue of the leisure required to produce and appreciate it. The latter explores how culture itself, its producers, and the dispositions toward it can all act *as* capital. The second half of the novel, in other words, is interested in the ways in which culture as symbolic capital can be converted into a form of capital itself.

The significance of Pierre's social origin—"that fine social position and noble patrimony" (260) to his past literary reputation is emphasized throughout the second half of the novel. If the "aristocracy of letters" can be divided into two kinds of authors—those who "are noble from genius, or from family: by the birthright of natural gifts, or the claims of descent and hereditary title," as the *United States Magazine and Democratic Review* declared in 1843—then Pierre's early literary career clearly belongs to the latter kind ("Noble Authors" 479). In one of the few moments in the novel when the narrator promises "to drop all irony" (257), readers learn that Pierre's juvenile writing amounted to nothing more than "the veriest common-place" (257). Hardly the work of genius, it is valued instead for the ways in which it reproduces the genteel world of Saddle Meadows. Pierre's past publications in "polite periodicals" win him "not only the vast credit and compliments of intimate acquaintances, but the less partial applauses of the always intelligent and extremely discriminating public" (245). Yet, the object of satire in passages like these is not merely the inferiority of the literature that receives the deferential nods of cultivated critics and the reading public whom they guide, but the way in which the terms of literary value are coincident with the representation and reproduction of genteel distinction.[64] The critical value of Pierre's writing consists in its "genteelness" and "perfect taste" (245). Young Pierre receives the easy accolades of "parlor society" (250) because his literature has successfully "translated the unruffled gentleman from the drawing-room into the general leveé of letters" (245).

While Pierre's youthful writing reproduces the world of genteel refinement, the "popular literary enthusiasm" (246) generated by his "literary celebrity" (252) demonstrates how the aristocracy of the brain participates in the
same cultural forms, dispositions, and discourses for representing distinction
that were found in the aristocracy of the face. Although the sudden revelation of Pierre's past literary career in book 17 ("Young America in Literature")
has often troubled readers for the way in which it appears to compromise
the novel's formal unity, its discussion of literary authorship's relationship to
distinction is consistent with the novel's sustained meditation on portraiture's
relationship to distinction.[65] Where the first half of the novel traced how portraits embodied the distinction of Pierre's aristocratic past, the second half
considers how portrait engravings, daguerreotypes, and autographs embody
the distinction of literary authorship in the democratic present. As Meredith
McGill notes, "it was the fiercely competitive reprint publishers who pioneered
American book marketing techniques, trumpeting the names and fortifying
the reputations of authors as a means of distinguishing their editions from
rival reprints" including the use of "engraved portrait frontispieces, prefatory
statements, and florid authorial signatures" as markers for authorized editions
(17). Portraits of distinguished authors were a staple of periodicals associated
with the group of literary nationalists known as the Young Americans. During
the 1840s and 1850s, New York literary periodicals such as Rufus Griswold's
International Monthly Magazine and Evert and George Duyckinck's *The Literary World* and *Holden's Magazine* reproduced numerous portraits of distinguished authors. When the Duyckincks took over *Holden's Dollar Magazine*
in 1851, for instance, they planned to include "an original Portrait and Biography of a Distinguished American in Public Life" in each issue as part of
the magazine's featured series "Our Portrait Gallery."[66] One prominent Young
American, Cornelius Matthews, was said "to have sat for a portrait in every
American novel, fable, satire, and poem, published in the last five years" ("The
Moral for Authors" 475). Many of the same visual elements of antebellum
book marketing that McGill identifies and that the Young Americans used figure prominently in books 17 and 18 of *Pierre*.[67] Pierre's early literary celebrity,
we learn, was not fueled by merit but "by publishers, engravers, editors, critics, autograph-collectors, portrait-fanciers, biographers, and petitioning and
remonstrating literary friends of all sorts" (255). "The bill-stickers of the Gazelle Magazine," for instance, "every month covered the walls of the city with
gigantic announcements of his name" so that "the whole universe knew him"

(249). When admiring readers demand somatic traces of "the high-prestiged" Pierre (autographs and portraits), he responds by giving them an even more corporealized mark in return: "lipographs" straight from his mouth (251).

The cultish demand for and the reverential display of author portraits, names, and autographs by Pierre's early readers and publishers cultivate the same idolatrous and docile disposition with which Pierre beheld the portraits of his aristocratic ancestors. The connection between the aristocracy of the brain and the aristocracy of the face is made explicit by the narrator when he notes how some of the literary petitioners for Pierre's portrait failed to "remember that the portrait of any man generally receives, and indeed is entitled to more reverence than the original man himself" (253). For the portrait, the narrator explains, "is better entitled to reverence than the man; inasmuch nothing belittling can be imagined concerning the portrait, whereas many unavoidably belittling things can be fancied as touching the man" (253). The idolatry that young Pierre receives from his readers is no less apparent in the admiration he receives from the supposedly more discerning literary critics and publishers. It is striking, for instance, that the terms of critical admiration for Pierre's early literature are nearly identical to those found within Pierre's assessment of Isabel's legitimacy (and her resemblance to his father). The narrator explains how "with one instantaneous glance" (245) critics expressed "their unqualified admiration for the highly judicious smoothness and genteelness of the sentiments and fancies expressed" (245). If "one instant" (112) is all that Pierre needs to determine that Isabel's face was that of his sister, then literary critics require only "one instantaneous glance" to determine his literary reputation. In each, the visuality and immediacy of such superficial judgments are emphasized (and implicitly criticized by the narrator) along with their relationship to sustaining legitimate forms of distinction (whether they involve social origin, capital, or cultural capital). Just as there is a physiognomy of the face, "there is," as the *Anglo-American Magazine* put in 1847, "a physiognomy in the title page of books" (*HMCR* 103).[68] "A reader seldom pursues a book with pleasure," one author remarked in *The Emerald*, "till he has a tolerable notion of the physiognomy of the author" (Echoe 97). In fact, the *American Whig Review* went so far as to suggest that some authorial portraits "served sometimes to neutralize the text for one saw at a glance . . . that the attributed work, the books, (if any), written were quite beyond the capacities" of the faces and heads depicted ("Literary Prospects" 149).

Although the juvenile Pierre acquiesces to the demands of publicity in certain forms—allowing his name, autograph, and lipograph to promote his literary celebrity—he oddly refuses to participate in others. Unlike his fellow contributors to the Gazelle Magazine, who "had their likenesses all taken," Pierre did not. "This highly celebrated and world-renowned Pierre—the great author . . . the world had never seen," the narrator remarks, "for had he not repeatedly refused the world his likeness?" (262). Pierre refuses on the grounds that "when every body has his portrait published true distinction lies in not having yours published at all" (254). Pierre's unwillingness to have his portrait taken as a young author seems less a celebration of obscurity—as his eager submission to the other forms of literary celebrity would seem to suggest— than a calculated delay of submitting his face to the world of publicity.[69] Pierre declines to have his portrait taken because he believes that his face fails to embody the public's image of an author. He considers himself but "an infant" (250) who lacks "the most noble corporeal badge of . . . the illustrious author," "a flowing beard" (253).[70] Not only does Pierre worry that his image might not conform to that of an "illustrious author," it might not even be consistent with itself. Pierre frets that the changing nature of his "boyish features and whole expression" (253) might allow his face to be considered imposture. So when magazine editors solicit Pierre's "portrait in oil, in order to take an engraving therefrom, for a frontispiece to their periodicals" (253), he refuses, it would seem, not because he recognizes and repudiates the public image of literary authorship and its physiognomic logic of its distinction, but rather because he believes that he fails to embody it consistently.[71]

The same line of thinking also prompts Pierre to reconsider all those autographs he hastily signed as a young author. He regrets signing them because "the very youthful and quite unformed character of his handwriting, his signature did not possess that inflexible uniformity, which . . . should always mark the hand of illustrious men" (253). In Pierre's mind, the chirographic fluidity of his immature signature contradicts the "inflexible uniformity" associated with "the hand of illustrious men."[72] With "so many contradictory signatures of one supereminent name . . . posterity would be sure to conclude that they were forgeries all; that no chirographic relic of the sublime poet Glendinning survived" (253). Just as Pierre believes that his boyish features might not conform to the fixed face of an illustrious author, he wonders whether the fluidity of his handwriting might prevent the formation of a "chirographic relic." As these passages suggest, the idolatry and distinction associated with Pierre's literary celebrity (the visuality of Pierre's author function) depends on a stable and legible image of the authorial body—whether it is of his face or his hand—that is consistent with the permanent facial features on which physiognomy based its readings of moral character. The aristocracy of the brain, it would seem, mystifies the same physiognomic fallacy of the aristocracy of the face. The false opposition between a notion of the self whose model of character is fluid, voluntary, and read from performance and one that is permanent, involuntary, and read from the face—an opposition epitomized by the two portraits of Pierre's father—also underwrites the logic informing Pierre's refusals of literary portraiture.

Yet, the physiognomic fallacy implicit within the representation of literary authorship in *Pierre* is only one facet of the problem with literary celebrity. The democratization of residual cultural forms such as portraiture by more available and more transient variants such as daguerreotypy has further eroded the distinction formerly associated with appearing in a portrait itself. When Pierre refuses to have his daguerreotype taken for the literary magazine, the *Captain Kidd Monthly*, he marvels at the realization that now "the most faithful portrait of any one could be taken by the Daguerreotype, whereas in former times a faithful portrait was only within the power of the moneyed, or mental aristocrats of the earth. How natural then the inference, that instead of, as in old times, immortalizing a genius, a portrait now only *dayalized* a dunce. Besides, when every body has his portrait published, true distinction lies in not having yours published at all. For if you published along with Tom, Dick, and Harry, and wear a coat of their cut, how then are you distinct from Tom, Dick, and Harry?" (254). No longer restricted to the "moneyed" or "mental aristocrats," a portrait no longer ensures that only a genius will be immortalized. While the above passage may also be questioning the degree to which portraits *ever* immortalized genius (for what they usually immortalized was wealth and social power), it also appears genuinely to lament the present condition of publicity in which portraits "*dayalize* a dunce." It is the indiscriminate faces of dunces, not geniuses, who appear in portraits and their faces are not there for eternity, but for a day. The exclusivity of who portraits preserve and the duration of that distinction have been transformed. The expansion of access to portraiture and the rapidity and affordability of its production have devalued the cultural form and made it more difficult for distinction (whether defined as gentility or genius) to be preserved across generations. Publicity has become a facile structure for reproducing the recognition of distinction in antebellum America.

The problem with the proliferation of portraiture in *Pierre*—one that da-guerreotypes exacerbate, but, as we saw in Chapter 4, did not initiate—is as much a matter of distinction as it is a fear of circulation (the market).[73] Melville recognized that distinction owed as much to a set of practices and dispositions toward cultural forms as it did to the consumption and economic patterns of those cultural forms. So when Pierre reasons that "true distinction lies in not having yours published at all," his iconoclasm draws attention to the fact that what matters to and now erodes the representation of distinc-tion is not the cultural form (portrait) itself or its circulation so much as the publicity of that form (i.e., the circulation of what it says, what it "publishes"). To a certain extent, Melville addresses the same transformation in the relation-ship between distinction and portraiture that was identified by Freneau in "The Picture Gallery" (one in which the form of the postrevolutionary portrait could no longer signify distinction by itself). Melville, however, departs from Freneau in that he also recognizes that there is something (a physiognomic resemblance or a look) within the portrait that continues to associate a par-ticular named individual with distinction. For this reason, Melville seems less interested in celebrating Pierre's turn to obscurity, as some critics suggest, than he is in revisiting what Freneau had feared about culture, the social order of gentility, and the political order of democracy: the impossibility of distinction and namelessness.

The second half of the novel also suggests that Pierre's turn from the pub-licity of authorship might be a conversion strategy similar to that expressed by his renunciation of inherited social and economic capital. Just as Pierre's deci-sion to destroy his father's chair portrait preserved the image of the drawing-room portrait and, as a result, reflected a transformation in how distinction would be represented in the aristocracy of the face (from an artificial and colonial model to a physiognomic one), Pierre's decision to renounce both his former literary celebrity and any present commercial opportunities reflects a transformation in how culture and distinction will intersect in antebellum America. In *Pierre*, the struggle over whether culture will convert gentility into symbolic capital or by that very process of conversion come to serve as capital itself is represented as a struggle between a residual aristocratic and emergent middling culture. *Pierre* documents how cultural forms such as portraiture and literature went from converting gentility into cultural capital to generat-ing capital itself by that very process of conversion. Yet, the contradiction that Melville probes in *Pierre* is how the transformation of authorship from belletristic to commercial models—one aligned with a shift from aristocratic to middling culture—also preserves the forms, dispositions, and discourses of the face.

The Face and the Look

Given the connections between the aristocracy of the face and the aristocracy of the brain, it should hardly be surprising that the face that haunts Pierre during the second half of the novel is no longer that of his alleged sister Isabel but that of an enigmatic author, Plotinus Plinlimmon. "By-and-by the blue-eyed, mystic mild face" of Plinlimmon, the narrator informs us, "began to domineer in a very remarkable manner upon Pierre" (292). Yet, unlike Isabel's face, which is eventually supplied with a tale of seduction and familial resemblance, Plinlimmon's face remains unknowable. More than any other attribute, Plinlimmon's appearance is characterized by "a certain floating atmosphere [that] seemed to invest and go along with this man. That atmosphere seems only renderable in words by the term Inscrutableness. Though the clothes worn by this man were strictly in accordance with the general style of any unobtrusive gentleman's dress, yet his clothes seemed to disguise this man. One would almost have said, his very *face*, the apparently natural glance of his very *eye* disguised this man" (emphasis mine; 290). Plinlimmon's "very face" and "the apparently natural glance of his very eye" disguise rather than disclose the man. In a novel in which the single most important decision Pierre makes is based on his unequivocal but mistaken belief in the legibility of such faces, Plinlimmon's countenance strikes him as impossibly confused and unreadable. Plinlimmon's face, "that remarkable face of repose" (291), contests the physiognomic logic underwriting Pierre's knowledge of faces and persons throughout the novel. "One adequate look at that face," the narrator explains, "conveyed to most philosophical observers a notion of something not before included in their schemes of the Universe" (291). In Pierre's world, this paradigm-shifting "something" could only be a face without words, without a story. Isabel's generic seduction narrative—"the story of the face"—enables Pierre to disavow his initial recognition that faces might be wordless.

The "strange mystery" of Plinlimmon's inscrutable face begins the process of dismantling all of Pierre's practices (his dispositions and discourses) for viewing and reading faces, ones that had hitherto led him to see physiognomically grounded equivalences in terms of identity, to read faces as signs of blood, and to accept Isabel as his sister. Without "family or blood ties of any sort" (290), Plinlimmon's face embodies the absence of social origin. As Pierre plunges further into "depression and despair" (292), he imagines hearing Plinlimmon's face speak to him even though it "did not respond to any thing" (293). It "was something separate, and apart, a face by itself" (293) and the "malicious leer" (293) it wears, the narrator remarks, "was a subjective sort of leer in Pierre" (293). "The face knows that Isabel is not my wife" (293), Pierre shudders, because its inscrutable visage challenges the physiognomically grounded equivalence he sees between Isabel and his father. Confronted with the fact that the things "men think they do not know, are not for all that thoroughly comprehended by them; and yet, so to speak, though contained in themselves, are kept a secret from themselves" (294), Pierre's disavowed erotic desire for Isabel returns to him in the form of Plinlimmon's malicious leer. Unable to look at the face any longer, Pierre "procured some muslin for his closet-window; and the face became curtained like any portrait" (293). Pierre cannot bear Plinlimmon's face because he refuses to admit that a face might be nothing more than a look. By turning his window into a portrait, Pierre literalizes what the narrator describes about his vision. He enacts the impossibility of "seeing" naturally by making window and portrait indistinguishable. In contrast to the physiognomic coherence of his father's portrait—whose face supposedly divulged the secret of his seduction—the physiognomic incoherence of Plinlimmon's face discloses the secret of Pierre's seduction. The malicious leer, a look, which takes the place of Plinlimmon's inscrutable face exposes the false physiognomic premises on which Pierre legitimated Isabel as his sister and took her as his wife.

●　●　●

The opposition between the face and the look at the heart of *Pierre* culminates in the final picture gallery scene of the novel. The novel closes with one last encounter with portraiture as Pierre, Isabel, and Lucy visit "a gallery of paintings, recently imported from Europe" (349). The gallery described in Book 26 is consistent with the antebellum art world of New York City where art "galleries were known to be full of European fakes" (Sten 12). Christopher Sten contends that "the central ambiguity that Melville's hero faces, the question of whether the mysterious Isabel is in fact Pierre's half-sister, is mirrored in the ambiguity of the various portraits" in the picture gallery (12). Yet, Pierre's relationship to the picture gallery portraits, however ambiguous it may be, is less ambiguous for the reader. What unfolds during the picture gallery episode, I would like to suggest, has less to do with the truth of Isabel's story and her status as Pierre's sister—which has been questioned by the narrator all along—than it does with the particularly visual and physiognomic logic by which Pierre legitimated her in the first place. Just as "one instant" (112) was sufficient for Pierre to see that Isabel's face was that of his sister, "one hurried, comprehensive glance" (349) at the gallery catalogue persuades him that he must see painting "No. 99. A stranger's head, by an unknown hand" (349).

In a gallery full of forgeries in which "Rubens, Raphael, Angelo, Domenichino, and Da Vinci" (349) are "shamelessly" promoted by the catalogue as "undoubted" (349), Pierre's sudden, superficial, and idolatrous vision—his "headlong enthusiastic admiration" (350)—somehow leads him to the one authentic painting in the gallery. "By some mere hocus-pocus of chance, or subtly designing knavery," the narrator explains, "a real Italian gem of art had found its way into this most hybrid collection of impostures" (350). It is remarkable that what constitutes the "real" in this scene—"a stranger's head by an unknown hand" (349)—is exactly what characterizes Isabel throughout the novel: namelessness. Unsurprisingly, when Isabel stands before the anonymous painting of a stranger, she sees herself. "Only my mirror has ever shown me that look before!," she cries, "see! see!" (350). Since painting no. 99 is the only "real" painting in a room full of fakes, the resemblance between the anonymous portrait of an unknown person and Isabel should not be considered ironic. The look that Isabel and the portrait share, in other words, is the "real." What Pierre finally comprehends in the picture gallery scene is that the knavery of the "real" lies in its incapacity to be named. He gradually comes to realize that the reality of the look that he and Isabel share is not Glendinning, but namelessness.

The equivalence or physiognomic resemblance that Pierre formerly believed could only be the product of inherited facial features is now shown to be nothing more than "a pervading look" (351). Unlike Isabel, who spots "in the eye and on the brow . . . certain shadowy traces of her own unmistakable likeness," Pierre sees in the anonymous portrait "the resurrection of the one he had burnt at the Inn" (351). "Not that the separate features were the same" as the chair portrait of his father, the narrator observes, "but the pervading look of it, the subtle interior keeping of the entirety, was almost identical" (351). Whereas Isabel sees "her own unmistakable likeness" in a portrait of a stranger's head by an unknown artist, Pierre sees only a "pervading look" that bears no relation to any actual person, let alone his father, but can be applied to make any face express the same type of interior character. Once more, the anonymity of the sitter and the painter make the portrait particularly well suited to affect Pierre so profoundly. As a portrait without words, without a story, painting no. 99 confounds Pierre's disposition to see images according to the stories that accompany them.

Isabel's resemblance to the stranger's portrait causes Pierre to doubt her resemblance to the chair portrait, leaving him to wonder if her claims, and perhaps any claims, to blood identity are nothing more than imposture. As Elizabeth Renker observes, "this restaging of Pierre's earlier confrontation with his father's portrait throws into question the presumed blood relationship the earlier scene helped to establish" (25). "How did he *know* that Isabel was his sister?," he asks himself after seeing the portrait: "Nothing that he saw in her face could he remember having seen in his father's. The chair portrait that was the entire sum and substance of all possible, rakable, downright presumptive evidence, which peculiarly appealed to his own separate self. Yet here was another portrait of a complete stranger . . . which was just as strong an evidence as the other. Then, the original of this second portrait was as much the father of Isabel as the original of the chair portrait" (353). Pierre finally and tragically recognizes that the physiognomic distinction and corporeal legibility of his father's chair portrait—on which he had based his legitimacy of Isabel and for whom he had sacrificed his family, wealth, and social status—might be more the product of a look than a face. It is at this moment that the opposition guiding Pierre throughout the novel, the opposition between the physiognomic distinction of the face and the performative, social mask of the portrait, is exposed as a false one.

That the painting which Pierre and Isabel see with such "an accumulated impression of power" (350) might be less the product of an empirical reality— the representation of an actual face—than of a look "seen" only by them is confirmed by Lucy's response to the portrait. Unlike Pierre and Isabel, Lucy "passed the strange painting, without the least special pause" and with apparent "uninterestedness" (351). Instead, she is absorbed by the Cenci of Guido, whose face represents the illicit desires—parricide and incest—associated with Pierre throughout the novel. Although Pierre will come to recognize the falsity of the opposition between face and look in the picture gallery scene, he will not recognize the motives—parricide and incest—that may have prompted him to accept that opposition as true. Yet, the apparent social radicalness of those two motives is undermined by the fact that these acts, in *Pierre* at least, do not threaten the social order that the false opposition between face and look was designed to preserve and reproduce (the aristocracy of the face), for the parricide Pierre commits symbolically actually makes him more of a Glendinning than less and the incest he might have committed may not have been incest after all. Instead, the two portraits around which *Pierre* closes—the stranger's portrait by an unknown hand and the Cenci—draw attention to how dispositions to and discourses about cultural forms might structure our knowledge of those forms as much as the forms themselves. The portraits of the stranger and the Cenci hang high in the picture gallery and "exactly faced each other" so that "in secret they seemed pantomimically talking over and across the heads of the living spectators below" (351). On the one hand, the "secret" conversation of painting no. 99 and the Cenci portrait symbolizes the totality of knowledge that is unavailable to Pierre, but is made available to us as readers. On the other, the inaccessibility of what the portraits say to the living—they hang high and talk to each other "over and across the heads of the living spectators"—serves as a perfect analogue for the practices (those dispositions and discourses) that prevent living spectators from hearing them.

Pierre's formulaic ending with "the usual vial of poison" (*HMCR* 446), as George Washington Peck unsympathetically called it in 1852, recalls the postrevolutionary novels with which this study began. The irony of *Pierre*'s formulaic ending is that the typical imbiber of poison—the seduced and abandoned female of compromised virtue—ends up the sole survivor of the novel. While Lucy, Isabel, and Pierre meet their predictably tragic ends, Delly Ulver survives. If Pierre's sex prevents him from having the child whose death would conventionally symbolize the nonreproduction of family and its capital, then what dies with Pierre is the opposition between the physiognomic distinction of the face and the look and idea that imaginative reading—understood as distinct from a rational model of reading as seeing—is poisonous. Where *The Power of Sympathy* and others aligned the dangers of seduction and reading through their mutually poisonous effects, *Pierre* severs this connection. *Pierre* inverts the tragedy of postrevolutionary didactic seduction novels such as *The Coquette* and *Female Quixotism*—which ensues from *not* reading character from the face—by dramatizing the consequences *of* reading character from the face.

The opposition that I have been tracing throughout *Discerning Characters* is epitomized by the distinction that Melville draws between the face and the look in *Pierre*. The final picture gallery scene exposes the physiognomic fallacy—that false opposition between the supposed essentialism of the face and transience of the look—and undercuts the physiognomic logic underwriting Pierre's decisions in the novel, the genre *Pierre* inhabits, and the model of distinction that genre reproduces. By challenging both assumptions of the logic of physiognomic distinction—that a person has one essential character over time and that a face can express it—*Pierre* exposes the false opposition between a model of character read from performance and one read form the face. This is an opposition that, as I have been arguing through this book, was foundational to how the postrevolutionary novel in particular and early American culture in general imagined its social space.

Epilogue

> Daguerre by the simple but all abounding sunlight has converted
> the planet into a picture gallery. . . . men of all conditions may see
> themselves as others see them. What was once the exclusive luxury
> of the rich and great is now within reach of all.
> —Frederick Douglass, "Pictures and Progress" (1861)

THE PHYSIOGNOMIC FALLACY—that opposition between a model of character read from performance and one read from the permanent and involuntary
features of the face—would find new life within the context of the performative and corporeal components of racial identity in nineteenth-century
America. The asymmetries found operating in Brackenridge's and Cooper's
application of the logic of physiognomic distinction to the public—individual
and politically inclusive for dominant groups, collective and politically exclusive for subordinate groups—provide us with a post-revolutionary precursor
to how the epistemology of race would be imagined in nineteenth-century
American culture, one in which the representation of race consists not simply
in the opposition between white and black or master and slave, but in whether
a person's face first identifies the essential features of his individual character
or his collective identity.

Published in the same year as *Pierre*, Harriet Beecher Stowe's *Uncle Tom's
Cabin* suggests how the physiognomic features of the face would continue to
inform the literary imagination of social space even as racial difference emerged
as the primary determinant of the social order in nineteenth-century America.
The residual importance of physiognomic distinction to the social perception
of character is acknowledged in *Uncle Tom's Cabin*, yet it ultimately proves
insufficient to the novel's eventual imagination of social space. In Chapter 11

of the novel, for example, the runaway mulatto slave George Harris enters a Kentucky hotel passing as the distinguished white gentleman, Henry Butler. George's performance as Butler—that is, his performance of whiteness—is accompanied by all the attributes of genteel distinction. He arrives in a buggy with "a genteel appearance" (Stowe 180) and walks in as "a well-dressed, gentlemanly man" (Stowe 180). Yet, the irony of George's performance of whiteness is that it is not entirely a performance. He is, of course, half white. In fact, when George first enters the hotel, the narrator focuses our attention to the corporeal foundation of George's whiteness by describing his physical appearance in general and his face in particular. He was "very tall, with a dark, Spanish complexion, fine, expressive black eyes, and close-curling hair, also of a glossy blackness. His well-formed aquiline nose, straight thin lips, and the admirable contour of his finely formed limbs, impressed the whole company instantly with the idea of something uncommon" (180). According to his physiognomic facial features—George *is* white. His "well-formed aquiline nose" and "straight thin lips" communicate his distinction, and facilitate his "performance" as the white gentleman Henry Butler.

Yet, Stowe's narrator also makes it clear that a physiognomic description of George's race is insufficient for precisely these reasons. If the social space of America is to be imagined primarily on the basis of race, then the physiognomic distinction of the face cannot be its corporeal basis or else mixed-race individuals such as George can disguise their blackness through a calculated performance of the acquired practices of gentility and the inherited features of a white physiognomy. George, in other words, does not simply pass as white in the scene, he passes as a white gentleman. If, in the postrevolutionary era, the physiognomic distinction of the face had opposed the performances of the self in the transposition in the social determination of character and in an effort to counter the mobility of social aspirants, now, in Stowe's imagination, the physiognomic distinction of the face was facilitating not only George's performance of whiteness, but his mobility from propertyless slave to masterless gentleman. According to this logic, for mixed-race individuals like George to remain black, he must be faceless. He must, in other words, disappear as an individual into the collectivity of his race.

This is, of course, precisely what happens by the novel's end. George privileges his racial identity not only at the expense of his national identity as an American, but at the expense of his personal identity as an individual. Before returning to Africa, George proclaims, "No, not as an individual; . . . let me go and form part of a nation" (Stowe 610). "It is with the oppressed, enslaved

African race that I cast my lot; and if I wished anything," he says, "I would wish myself two shades darker" (Stowe 608). Whereas in the passing scene, George's darker skin color facilitates his mobility in a world of physiognomic distinction—"a little walnut bark has made my yellow skin a genteel brown" he admits (Stowe 182)—by the novel's end and in a social space organized by race, his darker skin color signifies his collective identity as part of the African race. Stowe reproduces the physiognomic fallacy even as it is transformed by the terms of racial difference; for the mixed-race person like George Harris, his claims to whiteness, individuality, and gentility are understood as performative and supposedly mask an essential blackness characteristic of his race. As the determination of the social perception of character shifted from face to race, a new figure of dissimulation would emerge in the history of the novel in America—the passing mulatto—whose hidden race status and potential for upward mobility would reproduce a familiar social dynamic in American culture that attempts to control mobility and the instability it brings to the social order by turning to corporeality in general and the face in particular. The reproduction of the physiognomic fallacy from the seduction novels of the early republic to the facial recognition systems of biometrics of today reflects the persistence of the idea that the body does not change and suggests the degree to which our notions of a person's essential character or unique identity have been grounded historically in that idea of the body's permanence.

Pierre's critique of the physiognomic fallacy might appear somewhat belated given that the conditions for understanding the social perception of character had changed from their original postrevolutionary context. By the 1850s new discourses for reading the face, such as phrenology, ethnology, and the American school of anthropology, and new forms for representing it, such as the daguerreotype, were not only present but ascendant within American culture. The force of *Pierre's* critique of the physiognomic fallacy, however, seems directed at the history of the novel in America more than at the history of the social perception of character in America—or perhaps to put it more precisely, it is directed at the relationship of the latter to the former. It is in this direction that I would like to point my closing remarks. While my discussion of *Pierre* suggests that the physiognomic logic of distinction as well as the iconotextual practices of the postrevolutionary seduction narrative would continue to inform the reading and writing of fiction in America, much more can and should be said about the intermediality of literary practice after the first quarter of the nineteenth century. *Pierre's* extensive iconotextual references to the portraiture of the colonial aristocratic world, the physiognomic portraits of the postrevolutionary generation, and the daguerreotypes, frontispieces, and picture galleries of the urban democratic present reflect how important cultural forms for representing the face and the discourses used to read the face were to the imagination of social space within the novel in America. The iconotextual practices of early American fiction, as I have argued throughout *Discerning Characters*, provide us with singular opportunities to consider how the production and consumption of cultural forms (such as writing and reading novels as well as drawing and looking at portraits) were imagined as mediating social space. At the very least, I hope the preceding pages demonstrate how our notions of reading, literacy, and the novel are altered and enlarged when we move beyond the formalist perspective of comparative approaches to the arts and consider the complicated intersections of visual and literary culture.

Notes

1. Franklin 27. Hereafter cited parenthetically in the text and abbreviated *F.* For an alternative reading of this famous scene, see Erkkila 722.

2. Franklin's tale of necessity not only emphasizes the ease he will attain later in life (his distance from practical necessity in terms of capital), but demonstrates his luxury to be able to have a second distance from that moment (the first is material, the second cultural). This "objective distance from necessity and from those trapped within it combines with a conscious distance which doubles freedom by exhibiting it" (Bourdieu *Distinction* 55).

3. Michael Warner contends that "access to the public came in the whiteness and maleness that were then denied as forms of positivity, since the white male qua public person was only abstract rather than white and male" ("Mass" 383). For Warner, the "rhetorical strategy of personal abstraction is both the utopian moment of the public sphere and a major source of domination" ("Mass" 382) since the "bourgeois public sphere has been structured from the outset by a logic of abstraction that provides a privilege for unmarked identities: the male, the white, the middle class, the normal" ("Mass" 383).

4. Warner argues that Franklin valued the personal only insofar as it could be socially reproducible, and it is for this reason that he "envisions writing as the scene of pure socialization" (*Letters* 87). For alternative accounts of the personal in Franklin's *Memoirs*, see Baker 71–95 and Kennedy.

5. For the centrality of politeness to Franklin's *Autobiography*, see Harris, Shurr, and Chaves.

6. On the different forms of capital, see Bourdieu "Forms of Capital" 243–48. Bourdieu criticizes traditional mobility studies for ignoring how social space is transformed by the conversion of one form of capital (economic) into another (cultural or educational) and for disregarding how these conversions may impact the distribution of capital itself (*Distinction* 141). He contends that the exchange rate between economic, social, and cultural capital is exactly what is at stake in the struggle over the dominant principle of domination as different fractions of the dominant class struggle to determine the dominant form of capital and its exchange rate. See Bourdieu *Distinction* 124–25.

7. Burroughs 224. Hereafter cited parenthetically in the text and abbreviated *B.*

8. Henry Fielding remarked some seventy years earlier, "that an open disposition, which is the surest indication of an honest and upright heart, chiefly renders us liable to be imposed on by craft and deceit" (178); see also Fliegelman 37 and Tytler *Physiognomy* 147.

9. For more on the relationship between Burroughs's *Memoirs* and Franklin's *Memoirs*, see Downes, Williams 120, and Mihm 35.

10. On the theatricality of the commercial self, see Agnew.

11. On how Franklin's *Autobiography* transformed the status of mobility, see Wood *Americanization* 240.

12. Stephen Mihm understands Burroughs similarly as someone who represents "the promise and peril of an emergent market economy" (23).

13. My sense of the term "social space" is shaped by, but not identical to, the work of Pierre Bourdieu. Social space, as Bourdieu defines it, is the invisible reality that "organizes agents' practices and representations" ("First Lecture" 635). For Bourdieu, individuals occupy a position in a multidimensional social space; they are not defined by social class membership, but by the amounts and kinds of capital they possess. These are "economic capital (in its different kinds), cultural capital and social capital, as well as symbolic capital—commonly called prestige, reputation, renown, and so forth—which is the form in which different types of capital are perceived and recognized as legitimate" (Bourdieu "The Social Space" 724). Individuals do not move about social space in a random way, because they are subject to the forces that structure the space and because they resist these forces according to their specific properties—dispositions (habitus in embodied form) and goods/qualifications (in its objectified form) (Bourdieu *Distinction* 110). Bourdieu's theory of social space departs from traditional Marxist theories of class in its attention to how relationships and other forms of capital (such as cultural or social) structure social space as much as material substances and economic capital do. He maintains that the identity of class with capital distribution renders the social space more durable and stable than it actually is ("The Social Space" 726). My understanding of social space differs from Bourdieu in that it does not seek to analyze postrevolutionary social space and the general social field that shapes it, but rather it attempts to understand how social space was articulated by particular cultural producers. I am especially interested in how novelists imagined social space as a site of struggle between social aspirants and their superiors and between contending forms of cultural and social capital. On Bourdieuian social space, see Bourdieu *Distinction* 110–68; Bourdieu "The Social Space"; and Bourdieu "First Lecture." For an alternative account of democratic social space, see Fisher. On Bourdieu's relationship to the study of literature, see Loesberg, Guillory, Moi, and Litvak. On Bourdieu as a starting point for thinking about social class in early American historiography, see Middleton and Smith, Kelley *Learning*, and Rockman "Contours."

14. My use of the term "distinction" in this book refers primarily to its historical meaning at the end of the eighteenth century—generally understood as the condition of being highly distinguished, of the highest rank, order, status, sort, or station. This meaning was usually applied directly to individuals and only indirectly as a category of individuals who share that rank or station. I use "distinction" secondarily in reference to its theoretical

meaning in Bourdieu's writings, where it is defined as a misrecognized, legitimate form of social class—an aesthetic outlook or a set of perceptual practices bearing a relationship to rarity and indicative of a freedom from necessity, which then leads to specific judgments of taste. For Bourdieu, distinction is "a certain quality of bearing and manners, mostly considered innate (one speaks of distinction *naturelle*, 'natural refinement')" that "is nothing in fact but difference, a gap, a distinctive feature, in short, a relational property existing only in and through its relation with other properties" (Bourdieu "First Lecture" 631). Distinction is "the difference inscribed in the very structure of the social space when perceived through categories adapted to that structure" (Bourdieu "Forms of Capital" 731) and it "only exists through the struggles for the exclusive appropriation of the distinctive signs which make 'natural distinction'" (*Distinction* 250). Thus distinction can refer to both an individual attribute and a social/cultural practice.

I am less interested, however, in understanding distinction in terms of an aesthetic outlook than I am in what Bourdieu identifies, following Durkheim, as the cultural means that every group uses to perpetuate itself beyond the finite individuals in whom it is incarnated (*Distinction* 72). These means include "representation, the portrait or statue which immortalizes the person represented (sometimes, by a sort of pleonasm, in his own lifetime); and memorials, the tombstone, the written word, *aere perennius*, which celebrates and 'hands on to posterity,' and, in particular, historical writing, which gives a place in legitimate history" (*Distinction* 72). This book studies the cultural means, specifically postrevolutionary seduction narratives and portraits, by which distinction was represented, recognized, and reproduced through the face. On how literary characters supply readers with the means to implement the work of cultural classification and stratification, see Lynch.

15. The debate as to when class identity and conflict emerged in America has made it difficult to discuss preclass relations in the eighteenth-century Atlantic world. Even though the social world of early America was marked by sharp divisions and material inequalities, most early Americans "did not use 'class' to describe social divisions, but rather spoke of 'ranks,' 'orders,' 'degrees' or . . . 'interests, . . . using 'class' as a general term for any group" (Rosswurm 18). The stratified and hierarchic social order of the eighteenth-century Atlantic world was organized primarily around the distinction between the gentry and the common. Initially, the development of the social designation "sorts" (as in "middling sorts") during the eighteenth-century indicated a weakening of hierarchic social distinctions and "a transition away from the more formalized authority of and deference to the classifications of 'Rank.' Ranks were determined by birth, education, manners, and to a less visible degree wealth" (Bledstein and Johnston 5). Stuart Blumin characterizes "the structure of eighteenth-century society on both sides of the Atlantic" as "organized primarily into vertically arranged interests (religious and political as well as economic) rather than into horizontally layered and antagonistic classes; that 'ranks' identified the flow of influence, patronage, and deference within this system of interests, rather than the experiences and consciousness of separate classes; and that society as a whole was profoundly elitist in its recruitment of political leadership and in its assignment of social prestige. Within this aristocratic and preindustrial world there was, to be sure, a recognizable 'middling rank'

that was not yet, however, a 'middle class'" (Blumin 17). On the history of the emergence of "class" as a category as well as an overview of the historiography of class, particularly the middle class, in America, see Bledstein and Johnston 1–25. On the social structure of eighteenth- and early nineteenth-century Britain, see Berry and Brooks, Smail, Hunt, Klein "Politeness," Wahrman, and Davidoff and Hall. On the social structure of eighteenth- and early nineteenth-century America, see Appleby, Bledstein and Johnston "Introduction," Blumin, and Smith *Down and Out*.

16. Seth Rockman, for example, contends that historians need "to define an appropriate vocabulary to express class as materially real in a world of cultural and social constructions" ("Contours" 95). "What makes social class," Simon Middleton and Billy Smith argue, "are the relationships between individuals and groups that derive from differential access to various forms of capital—economic, cultural, symbolic—and social power" (10). On the need for a greater understanding of the material consequences of the cultural assumptions, social practices, and legal structures organizing social relations, see Smail, Rockman "Contours," Middleton and Smith, Newman, Clark, and Rockman *Scraping By*.

17. On physiognomy and European culture, see Graham "Lavater," Graham "Character Description," Tytler *Physiognomy*, Weschler, Cowling, Flavell, McMaster, Stafford, Shookman, Rivers, Benedict, Tytler "Lavater," Judson, Juengel, Lynch, Percival, Meijer, Bindman, Hartley, Gray, Tytler "Faith," Percival and Tytler, Porter, Wheeler "Racial Legacies," and Wahrman 294–305. On physiognomy and American literary culture, see Fliegelman, Brown *Sentimental Novel* 189–96, and Stoehr.

18. On physiognomy and American art history, see Verheyen, Crawford, Evans "Survival," Benes, Steinberg, Miles *Saint-Mémin*, Miles "1803," Evans *Genius*, Schwarzschild, Bellion, and Clubbe.

19. Although historians have shown how the elite on either side of the Atlantic shared many of the same codes and manners of a transatlantic gentility (see Rozbicki and Hemphill), the North American elite of colonial and postrevolutionary America were, strictly speaking, gentry rather than nobility and aristocracy. North American gentry were usually aristocrats in the sense of "manufactured nobility" rather than established peerage. "All the topmost tiers of English society were missing in America," Gordon Wood explains, "there were no dukes, no marquesses, no court, and nothing like the fabulous wealth of the English nobility" (*Radicalism* 112). "Although real and substantial distinctions existed in colonial America," Wood contends that "the colonial aristocracy was never as well established, never as wealthy, never as dominant as it would have liked" (*Radicalism* 113). The distinction between elite and nonelite grew even more tenuous during the early republic as laws abolishing primogeniture and fee tail tenure (a system of heritable ownership that forbade the selling of the land on the market) were passed and property shifted from landed to mobile models. In the postrevolutionary American context, it should be understood as emphasizing the aspiration of those to which the term applies on the one hand and the illegitimacy of the distinction to which they lay claim on the other.

20. On the necessity of theorizing race in a way that accounts for its emergent character

and on the novel as a textual climate conducive to the integration of racial taxonomy and physiognomy, see Wheeler "Racial."

21. My reference to the terms "aristocracy" and "democracy" in this study deserves some additional comment since their social and political connotations shift throughout the eighteenth and nineteenth centuries. Throughout most of the eighteenth century, the term "aristocracy" had more of a political than a social connotation: "it referred to a system of government more than to a well-defined body of people" (Wahrman 151). Following the work of Paul Langford, Dror Wahrman notes that "it was only from the American revolutionary crisis onward . . . that the meaning of 'aristocracy' shifted to denote primarily a social group rather than a political system" (151). The specific political meanings of aristocracy and democracy, however, concern me less than how their social meanings were imagined by postrevolutionary American culture. I am interested in exploring how postrevolutionary culture imagines social space in a democracy whose founding political revolution had terminated the political, but not necessarily the cultural and social, forms of aristocracy. That is, my interest is similar to what Richard Bushman refers to as "the perplexing contradiction of a democratic government presiding over the spread of an aristocratic culture" (411), but I would reformulate the contradiction as the continuing cultural reproduction of an aristocratic social space within the political sphere of democracy.

22. The centrality of performance and orality to early American culture has been well documented in recent scholarship. On the culture of performance in early America, see Bushman, Fliegelman, Looby, Shields, Gustafson *Eloquence*, Ruttenberg, and Wahrman. On performance as a dominant critical paradigm in American eighteenth-century studies, see Breitwieser.

23. On the need to consider politics as an arena of culture rather than culture as an arena of politics, see Wahrman and Slauter.

24. Physiognomy provides a scheme of perception for the face and functions as one of those allegedly natural, but nonetheless "historically constituted and acquired categories which organize the idea of the social world in the minds of all the subjects belonging to that world and shaped by it" (Bourdieu *Distinction* 469). As Bourdieu notes, even today "there are no merely 'physical' facial signs, the colour and thickness of lipstick, or expressions, as well as the shape of the face or the mouth are immediately read as indices of a 'moral' physiognomy, socially characterized, i.e., of a 'vulgar' or 'distinguished' mind, naturally 'natural' or naturally 'cultivated'" (*Distinction* 193).

25. Amy Lang notes the "uneasy elision of class" (5) in nineteenth-century American literary criticism. For Lang, "the contests over the meaning of class . . . over both the anterior social reality the language of class seeks to capture and the social prospect to which it points—frame the novelistic representation of class difference" (6). For studies attentive to the representations of class within early American literature, see Rigal, Dimock and Gilmore, Smith-Rosenberg "Black Gothic," Lang, Fichtelberg, Tennenhouse, Merish, Simpson, and Dow.

26. As John Guillory observes with respect to Bourdieu, "The experience of reading a fiction (or the experience of any work of art) is itself the model for social action, in that it

combines belief and disbelief, *illusio* and *disillusio*. Bourdieu is saying neither that calculation is all that there is nor that calculation is really unconscious, but that social action is
complex in the same way that making or consuming art is complex" (397).

27. For accounts of literacy attentive to visual as well as verbal culture in early America, see Rigal, Crain *The Story of A*, McGill, Brückner, St. George, and Slauter.

28. On the need for literary critical practice to acknowledge "the competitions and
alliances that divided and united these media prior to the age of literature" rather than
engaging with each medium in isolation, see Lynch (77).

29. Over the past twenty years, a number of critics—including W. J. T. Mitchell,
Norman Bryson, and Peter Wagner—have "forged radical links between the disciplines of
literary analysis and visual art theory in order to rethink the interrelations between verbal
and visual representation" (Aikins 465). The image/text problem, Mitchell claims, "is not
just something constructed between the arts, the media, or different forms of representation, but an unavoidable issue within the individual arts and media. In short, all arts are
'composite arts' (both text and image); all media are mixed media" (*Picture* 94–95). As such
interdisciplinary work attempts to move beyond the comparative methods of sister arts
criticism, some scholars have called for "practical interpretations that take into account the
intermedial nature" of literary texts (Wagner 18). Mitchell calls for the study of "vernacular
forms of representation" or "mixed media" in which the image/text problem is already
necessitated (*Picture* 89). He insists that the study of language and visuality should be one
of "mediums" rather than semiotic or narratological systems since image/text relations are
not "univocally coded schemes open to scientific explanation," they are discursively heterogeneous (*Picture* 94–95). "No theory of media can rise above the media themselves," he
contends, "what is required are forms of vernacular theory, embedded in media practices"
(*What* 210). On applying the methodologies of semiology and narratology to media other
than the traditional, text-based one of literature, see Bryson, Bal, and Meister, Kindt, and
Schernus. On intermediality as an alternative to the comparative study of the arts, see
Wagner and Homem and Lambert.

30. Lynch follows Bourdieu in identifying distinction with taste so that the cultural
capital of the late eighteenth-century British novel is a product of the literariness of texts
and the "depth" associated with its reading practices. Alternatively, I find that the novel
in postrevolutionary America sought to define itself against cultural capital as a primary
means of signifying distinction initially. Its reading practices were resonant not with psychological depth, but with physiognomic legibility.

31. On physiognomy and the novel in England, see Graham "Character Description,"
Tytler *Physiognomy*, McMaster, Tytler "Lavater," Wheeler *Complexions*, Benedict, Tytler
"Faith," Lynch, and Wheeler "Racial Legacies." On physiognomy and the novel in France,
see Rothfield and Rivers.

32. On the early American novel's relationship to the development of a middling
culture of vernacular gentility, see Bushman. On the novel and middle-class formation
in early America, see Fiedler, Douglas, Tompkins, Smith-Rosenberg "Subject," Merish,
Smith- Rosenberg "Black Gothic," Lang, Shapiro, Rust, and Knott. See also Watt and

Armstrong. On how the early American novel articulated a critique of the existing social order of gentility, including empowering individual readers and assaulting social authority, see Davidson, Tompkins, Smith-Rosenberg "Domesticating," and Stern.

33. By physiognomic fallacy, I refer to the opposition produced by Lavater's subordination of pathognomy to physiognomy: an opposition between an assessment of character read from performance and one read from the permanent and involuntary physiognomic features of the face. This opposition distinguished physiognomy from pathognomy (and a culture of performance) on the grounds that a person has one essential, permanent moral character that the face involuntarily and visibly discloses. The term "physiognomic fallacy," however, should not be taken to mean that the opposition between a model of character read from performance and one read from the physiognomic features of the face was somehow false in historical practice. It was, as the following pages will document, widely distributed, reproduced, and debated in early America as it was elsewhere. Rather, my purpose in using the term "physiognomic fallacy" is to acknowledge that the theoretical opposition informing this historical practice was false.

CHAPTER I. DISCERNING CHARACTERS

1. On physiognomy and European culture, see Graham "Lavater," Graham "Character Description," Tytler *Physiognomy*, Weschler, Cowling, Flavell, McMaster, Stafford, Shookman, Rivers, Benedict, Tytler "Lavater," Judson, Juengel, Lynch, Percival, Meijer, Bindman, Hartley, Gray, Tytler "Faith," Percival and Tytler, Porter, Wheeler "Racial Legacies," and Wahrman 294–305.

2. Meijer contends that twentieth-century critics have "unconsciously and unwillingly perpetuated nineteenth-century interpretations of Camper" (2) that imagine him as one of the founders of racist anthropology. Camper's facial angle, she argues, should be understood in its eighteenth-century context, as his attempt "to prove empirically that all the races were equal" (3).

3. Dror Wahrman is one of the few scholars to consider physiognomy in the North American context and he does so only indirectly. He understands the rise of physiognomy in England at the end of the eighteenth century as part of a more general transformation from *ancien* to modern regimes of identity brought about by the imperial crisis in America. Wahrman claims, however, that "the late eighteenth-century transformation that brought an end to the English *ancien régime* of identity did not affect the new republic in North America in quite the same way and at quite the same time as it did the mother country" (250). "The same events that signaled the retreat of a flexible understanding of identity in England," he adds, "spelled for the Americans the beginnings of an unprecedented period of experimentation—lasting for at least a couple of decades—with the full, albeit daunting, potential of such flexibility" (251). On physiognomy's relationship to visual culture in America, see Verheyen, Crawford, Evans "Survival," Benes, Steinberg, Miles "1803," Evans *Genius*, Schwarzschild, Bellion, and Clubbe.

On physiognomy and literary culture in America, see Fliegelman, Brown *Sentimental Novel* 189–96, and Stoehr.

4. On the complexities of race in early America, see Dain, Sweet, and Roediger.

5. Michael Warner reminds us that "modern notions of race and nation took shape only gradually in colonial practice; they did not drive colonization consistently" ("What's Colonial" 53). From the late seventeenth century to the Revolutionary period, "skin tones—either too light or too dark—were only one among many perjorative features of creolization," Susan Scott Parrish observes, "and natives and African slaves were viewed inconsistently" (102).

6. At a time when the origin and unity of the human species was being debated, physiognomy was utilized to support both polygenist and monogenist positions. On the one hand, polygenists found physiognomy's attention to the fixed and essential nature of a person's identity attractive as a counterargument to environmental accounts of human variety. Abraham Rees, for example, proposed aligning physiognomy and race as early as 1805 in his *Cyclopedia* entry for the word "Physiognomy." On the other hand, monogenists such as Samuel Stanhope Smith would use Lavaterian physiognomy to defend the ultimate unity of the human species. Inspired by the Mosaic doctrine of a single creation, Smith's 1810 *An Essay on the Causes of the Variety of Complexion and Figure in the Human Species* quoted Lavater as seeing "no greater difference between the skulls of a German and an East-Indian, than between that of a German and a Hollander." Moreover, Smith added that "we often see among the children of Africa both in insular and continental America, heads as finely arched, and persons as handsomely formed as are ever seen among the descendants of Europeans" (Smith *Essay* 1965 160). Of course, after 1825, the polygenist arguments of the American school of anthropology (especially Louis Agassiz and Samuel George Morton's 1838 *Crania Americana*) would begin to align physiognomy and race even among those who opposed slavery, such as Hermann Burmeister.

7. On physiognomy as an occult practice, see Porter, Tytler *Physiognomy*, Rivers, and Shortland.

8. Despite Lavater's success in revitalizing and legitimating physiognomy during the 1770s and 1780s, versions of occult physiognomy persisted in early America well into the nineteenth century reproduced largely in the pages of widely distributed almanacs such as Erra Pater's *Book of Knowledge* and *The Complete Fortune Teller*. The coexistence of occult and scientific physiognomy in early America is remarkable not simply for the struggle between their competing practices and the kinds of knowledge they produce (the occult as opposed to the scientific), but for the way that the struggle over the legitimacy of physiognomy as a practice was intimately related to the status of its practitioners (gypsy, vagabond, servant, and slave on the one hand, or a "liberal" and "enlightened" people on the other).

9. As late as 1800, the state of New Jersey still declared "all persons, who shall use, or pretend to use, or have any skill in physiognomy, palmistry, or like crafty science, or who shall pretend to tell destinies or fortunes, and all runaway servants or slaves, and all vagrants or vagabonds, common drunkards, common night walkers, and common prostitutes, shall

be deemed and adjudged to be disorderly persons" (*Laws* 410). On the persistence of these "obsolete laws of our ancestors" (Ulpian 1), see Ulpian.

10. On Lavater's role in the transformation of physiognomy from an occult to a "scientific" practice, see Shortland and Gray.

11. Theoretically, the neo-Platonic tradition of *kalokagathia*—in which beauty expresses virtue and ugliness exposes vice—was part of the moral philosophy of Shaftesbury and Hutcheson, and the natural expression of the body was fundamental to the Scottish philosophy of Lord Kames, James Beattie, and Dugald Stewart. This is particularly relevant for late eighteenth- and early nineteenth-century America where "the philosophy of the Common Sense school was . . . the philosophy which professors of philosophy in America were as likely as not to be teaching" (Grave 4). On *kalokagathia* and physiognomy, see Bindman 48–58.

12. On "the marginal position of pathognomy in Lavater's work" and its subordination to physiognomy in Lavater, see Delaporte 35–48; see also Zelle 45. For an alternative account of Lavater's position in the history of physiognomy, see Percival, especially Chapters 1 and 8.

13. See Shookman 3 and Weschler 113.

14. By 1810, "there had been published 16 German, 15 French, 2 American, 1 Dutch, 1 Italian, and no less than 20 English versions" of Lavater's *Essays*—"a total of 55 editions in less than 40 years" (Graham *Lavater* 62). See also Miller 431.

15. Between 1789 and 1826, booksellers regularly advertised Lavater's *Essays* in newspapers, and various French, English, and German editions appeared in the catalogues for the Library Company of Philadelphia, the New York Society Library, the Boston Library, the Salem Bookstore & Circulating Library, Hocquet Caritat's Circulating Library (New York), Blake's Circulating Library (Boston), the New Haven Library Company, Harwood's Circulating Library (Philadelphia), Nash's Circulating Library (New York), Union Circulating Library (Boston), the Library of Congress, Charles Whipple's Circulating Library (Newburyport, Mass.), New Castle Library Company (New Castle, Del.), and the Mercantile Library Association (New York).

16. As early as 1800, the works of Lavater had found their way as far west as Lexington, Kentucky (Pochman 359).

17. In 1790s America, the *Essays* were targeted "to the lovers of polite learning" and "friends of virtue" ("Literary Article" 1). On the importance of leisure to physiognomic discernment, see Lavater *Essays* 91, [Carey] 401 (1796), "Narrative of Mrs. Dholson" (1797), "Symptoms" (1805), "Familiar Letters on Physiognomy" (1809), "British Biography" (1810), and "Familiar Letters" (1820).

18. Searches of the collections at the American Antiquarian Society, the Massachusetts Historical Society, the Library Company of Philadelphia, the Historical Society of Pennsylvania, the Library of Congress, the Winterthur Library and Museum, Johns Hopkins University Special Collections, and Harvard University Library, as well as the American Periodical Series (APS), Early American Imprint series 1 and 2 (EAI 1 and EAI 2), Early American Newspaper (EAN), Nineteenth-Century United States Newspaper

(19CUSNEWS), and Sabin Americana (SABIN) digital databases identified no fewer than 110 different imprints, 308 newspaper articles, and 369 periodical articles discussing physiognomy in American publications in the years between 1775 and 1826. The total number of 787 references excludes bookseller advertisements and catalogues, library catalogues, and any references in which "physiognomy" appears merely as a synonym for "face" rather than as a system for reading faces. Since some of the digital databases (such as EAN) are still evolving; the total number of 787 references is preliminary and should be understood as a first step in assessing the reception of physiognomy in early America. Nevertheless, only 7.5 percent of these published references to physiognomy discuss people of specifically non-European descent (typically Native Americans, Africans, Asians, the indigenous peoples of South America and the Pacific Islands, and peoples belonging to the Jewish and Gypsy diasporas).

19. According to early modern humoral theory, complexion "denoted the balance of humors and could include the colors of the skin but was not limited to that symptom" (Parrish 79). On the multiple understandings of complexion during the seventeenth and eighteenth centuries, see Parrish chap. 2, and Wheeler *Complexion*.

20. See note 18.

21. The article is an excerpt from Humboldt's *Political Essay on the Kingdom of New Spain* (1811).

22. See Williamson, 12, 25–26, 28, 59.

23. On the face's significance in the development of commercial society, see Lynch and Wheeler *Complexion*. On the importance of the face to commercial transactions before the emergence of bank notes in America, see Mihm 15.

24. This anecdote was also reproduced in the *Star* (1809) and Philadelphia's *Port Folio* (1814). On physiognomy's use in commercial transactions, see Mercier 71 (1788), Roberts (1803), and "Old Times" (1824).

25. This quotation was probably reprinted from the English *Gentleman's Magazine* and also appeared in the article "Lavater" in 1801 in the *Lady's Monitor*. On physiognomy and discerning the character of servants, see De Monde (1816).

26. On the physiognomy of politicians, see Philo (1785), Webster 14–15 (1791), "Miscellany" 1796, D'Argenson 373 (1797), "Physiognomy" (*Kenebac Gazette* 1802), "Physiognomy" (1802) 3, "Miscellany. Portrait of Burr" (1807), "Hon. Elias Boudinot" (1822), and "Sketches" (1824).

27. On physiognomy and homosocial affiliation, see Carey (1796), "Narrative" (1797), "Eugenio" (1797), "Old Nick" (1802), "Extracts" (1803), "Physiognomical Anecdotes" (1804), "Eugenio" (1805), "Alphonso and Emily" (1807), Marmontel (1807), Observator (1810), "Extracted" (1812), "The Following" (3 October 1817), "The Following Little" (8 October 1817), [Godwin] (1818), "Banking" (1819), [Godwin] (1822), Harlan (1822), "From the State" (1824), and "Original Anecdote" (1824). On affiliation in the new republic, see Waterman, Schweitzer, and Nelson *National*.

28. For reprints of this anecdote, see *Daily National Intelligencer* (1817) and *American Monthly Magazine and Critical Review* (1817).

29. For reprints of this anecdote, see the *Freeman's Journal* (1790), the *New York Packet* (1790), *Essex Journal* (1790), *The Farmer's Journal* (1790), Albany's *American Mercury* (1790), the *Vermont Gazette* (1790), *Concord Herald* (1790), *United States Chronicle* (1790), and the Norwich *Courier* (1800).

30. The letters from the soldier's family are reproduced in later reprints, but not in the *Cumberland Gazette* version.

31. When physiognomy's prejudicial nature was specifically criticized in American publications, the critique typically followed the moral objections raised by Addison in *Spectator* 86 (published long before Lavater's *Essays* in 1711) or by Lavater's most outspoken antagonist, Georg Lichtenberg. Thomas Fessenden, for example, reproduced Lichtenberg's prediction that "when physiognomy arrives at the perfection expected by Lavater, we shall hang children before they have committed the crimes which deserve the gallows" (*Modern* 46). For additional objections see "The Gleaner. No. II" (1806), Musaeus (1808), "Article 1" (1808), and Grito (1815). Alternatively, the value of physiognomy's prejudicial function was frequently discussed. On the face of slander, see "Miscellany. Slander" (1804) and "From the Charleston Courier" (1804). On the face of murder, see "A Concise Account of Mr. Lavater" (1814), "Physiognomy of Murderers" (1823), Geryn (1824), and "Execution" (1824). On the face of theft, see "The Attributes of God Displayed. Diversity of Features in the Human Face" (1819). On the physiognomy of criminals in general (thieves, murderers, and adulterers), see "Article 1" (1808).

32. For reprints of this anecdote see "Anecdotes" in Boston's *Herald of Freedom* (1789), "Anecdotes" in the *New Hampshire Spy* (1789), and *Carlisle Gazette* (1790).

33. For reprints of this anecdote, see "Physiognomy" in New York's *Weekly Museum* (1796) and "Physiognomy" in the *Philadelphia Minerva* (1796).

34. This newspaper article was an extract from Louis-Sébastien Mercier's *The Night Cap* (first American edition in 1788).

35. On physiognomy as a means of detecting cunning impostors, see "To the Printer" (1787). For reprints of "To the Printer," see Newburyport's *Essex Journal* (1787), Philadelphia's *Freeman's Journal* (1787), the *New Haven Gazette* (1787), and Philadelphia's *Pennsylvania Packet* (1787).

36. John Graham identifies an 1808 "Musaeus" letter as being first published in Germany in 1778–1779 and translated by Anne Plumtre in 1800. The satirical letter "had a curious tone for all of its critical attitude, revealing clearly the disappointment of the author over the lack of system in the science" (Graham 1961, 570).

37. On tracing dissimulation on the face, see M. "Physiognomy" (1819) and "Art. IV" (1821).

38. This article was reprinted in Philadelphia's *Independent Gazetteer* (1786). For articles skeptical of physiognomy's ability to detect dissimulation and imposture, see "Essay on Fraud" (1791), which was reprinted in the *Massachusetts Spy* (1791), *Worcester Magazine* (1791), *Windham Herald* (1792), *Morning Ray* (1792), and *Eastern Herald* (1792). See also Miller (1803) 434.

39. The problem of dissimulation was not restricted by gender. On physiognomy's

failure to uncover "true dispositions" among "women of breeding" (228), see "Artificial Courtesy."

40. This article was reprinted in the *Newburyport Herald* (1802).

41. On the material and symbolic coordination of class identity and whiteness in America during the nineteenth century, see Roediger, Lang, and Nelson *National*.

42. On the volatility of the postrevolutionary era, see Wood *Radicalism*, Kelley, and Bushman.

43. On the postrevolutionary culture of performance see Fliegelman, Bushman, Looby, Ruttenberg, and Gustafson.

44. "If birth was a primary (but in America not necessary) ingredient of gentility," Margaretta Lovell notes, "performance was its absolute (and necessary) essence" (91) "Hierarchy, especially among males," Lovell observes, "was marked by the minute observation of degree (and, therefore, one suspects the ritualized avoidance of conflict) for strangers and family as well as acquaintances in terms of who sat where in the coach, who walked next to the wall and who the open street, who walked a half-pace behind whom, and who read a letter in the presence of whom. These rules pertained to strangers as well as to acquaintances and were used as cues to appropriate behavior when 'true' status was unknown" (88). On the history of manners in colonial and nineteenth-century America, see Hemphill, Bushman, Bullock, Rozbicki, Zuckerman, Haltunnen, Fliegelman, Wood *Radicalism*, Lockridge, Kasson, and Pocock.

CHAPTER 2. READING AND BREEDING

1. On the importance of a culture of honor and character to early national politics, see Freeman and Daniel.

2. Although historians have shown how the elite on either side of the Atlantic shared many of the same codes and manners of a transatlantic gentility (see Rozbicki and Hemphill), the North American elite of colonial and postrevolutionary America were, strictly speaking, gentry rather than nobility and aristocracy. North American gentry were usually aristocrats in the sense of manufactured nobility rather than established peerage. The distinction between elite and nonelite grew more tenuous during the early republic as laws abolishing primogeniture and fee tail tenure (a system of heritable ownership that forbade the selling of the land on the market) were passed and property shifted from landed to mobile models. As Joyce Appleby notes, "land ownership and wealth distribution were much more equitable in the United States than in any other country" (34). On the history of manners in colonial and nineteenth-century America, see Hemphill, Bushman, Bullock, Rozbicki, Zuckerman, Haltunnen, Fliegelman, Wood *Radicalism*, Lockridge, Kasson, and Pocock. On genteel sociability in early America, see Shields and Allgor.

3. On politeness as a mode of cultural discourse that provides conceptual organization to various forms of social and cultural life in eighteenth-century England, see Klein *Shaftesbury*.

4. John Kasson notes how "Established codes of behavior have often served in unacknowledged ways as checks against a fully democratic order and in support of special interests, institutions of privilege, and structures of domination" (3). See also Wood *Radicalism*, Warner, and Grasso. On the development of the discourse of politeness in eighteenth-century England, see Klein "Politeness."

5. Philip Gould contends that "the category of manners allows us to think about the rise of commercial capitalism outside of the tired binary between 'republicanism' and 'liberalism' that once dominated eighteenth-century American studies" (5).

6. On how middling young men used literary practices to fashion a complex sense of self suited to the dislocations of capitalism in antebellum America, see Augst.

7. On Chesterfield's particular appeal to a middling American reading audience, see Dean "Authorship" 699–701. See also Haltunnen, Gulick, and Newton.

8. For examples, see *Letters* (1775) 1:127; 1:180; 2:64–65; 3:60; 3:83–85; 3:168–69; 3:211–13; 3:238–40, and 4:183.

9. By the end of the seventeenth century, the capacity to dissemble one's own facial features and to discern it in others was considered integral to the education of a young gentleman. In the self-fashioning world of the Renaissance court, for instance, the advantage of concealing one's own thoughts, paradoxically enough, was "to discover the Mind of another. . . . For to him that opens himselfe, Men will hardly shew themselves adverse" (Bacon 22). Dissimulation thus avoided the appearance of intentional dishonesty because it was meant to solicit social intimacy. The courtier might feign openness, for instance, so that others would disclose more knowledge to him than otherwise. Even the third earl of Shaftesbury, who opposed the "dazzle" of the courtly world, accepted dissimulation as a practice when it facilitated sociability (Klein *Shaftesbury* 92). Although dissimulation appeared to meet civility's declared intention to accommodate others, it could also, as Chesterfield recognized, mask one's own interests. For this reason, educators such as John Locke recommended that a young gentleman "should be instructed how to know and distinguish men; where he should let them see, and when dissemble the knowledge of them" (83). The genteel tutor, he suggests, "should be able to . . . teach him skill in men, and their manners; pull off the mask which their several callings and pretences cover them with; and make his pupil discern what lies at the bottom, under such appearances" (Locke 80–81). On the tension between sociability and egoism in the discourse of politeness, see Klein *Shaftesbury*.

10. On the use of deception in early American commerce, see Ditz and Mihm.

11. On politeness and commerce, see Klein "Politeness" 372, Bushman, and Zabin 81–106.

12. On the tension between virtue and politeness, see Klein *Shaftesbury*, Grasso 285–326, and Warner 132–38.

13. Of course, anti-Chesterfieldianism was not limited to America. Samuel Johnson famously declared that Chesterfield taught "the morals of a whore, and the manners of a dancing master." In England, anti-Chesterfield literature included Pratt's *The Pupil of Pleasure* (1776; 1777), Clara Reeve's *The Two Mentors* (1783) and Ann Berkeley's *The Contrast* (1791) and the negative responses ranged from the gentle mockery of William Woty's

burlesque *The Graces* (1774), G. M. Woodward's *Chesterfield Travestie* (London, 1808; Philadelphia, 1812), and *Chesterfield's Maxims* (1808–15?) to the more sustained and scathing criticism of William Crawford, Thomas Hunter, and John Bennett. See Gulick.

14. The 1792 *American Museum* reprinted "Letter XII: On Politeness" from John Bennett's didactic *Letters to a Young Lady*.

15. For more on the identification of Chesterfieldianism and self-interest, see "Extracts" (1808) and "Men of the World" (1817).

16. Catherine Kelly claims that the urgency that suffused discussions of postrevolutionary reading speaks to the circulation of texts and ideas in a protean consumer market and the "near impossibility of regulating that circulation" (128).

17. See Hemphill 74, Bullock 254.

18. Karin Calvert, however, reminds us that while the genteel elite abandoned the sartorial code of privilege around 1700 (and its sumptuary laws), a "new code of genteel dress that was more complex, subtler, and more difficult for the uninitiated to master" emerged and did not reach its full elaboration until the 1820s (260–61).

19. See [J.] 4. On the rising emphasis on white men's social crimes of seduction and how the perceived status of men was integral to the way they could force sex, see Block 37–52 and 211–218.

20. *The Gubernatocial Collection* associates the social mobility of "upstart gentry" (7), such as the allegorically named seducers, Mr. Pomposity and Count Dipper Dapper, with a Chesterfieldian attention to the graces. Pomposity asks Count Dipper Dapper, "You have read Chesterfield, I suppose" (9).

21. Sans Souci, Kate Davies explains, "was the name associated with the tea assembly where it was proposed Boston's fashionable elite might meet every other week for an evening of cards, music, and dancing. The intention was to establish Boston as the centre of American metropolitan sociability. At the Sans Souci, the polite and the aspirant of both sexes would be able to display their urbanity and taste, their accomplishments and conversation" (221). On the debate surrounding the Boston Sans Souci during the 1780s, see Davies 235–47.

22. See Tennenhouse on the need to separate the idea of "the nation as a political entity from the nation as a culture" (9) in order to understand the meaning of "American" and "English" in postrevolutionary culture.

23. On Chesterfield and *The Contrast*, see Borkat, Siebert, Pressman, and Rinehart.

24. On the similarity between the sentimental novel and *The Contrast*, see Kierner 25.

25. The downward distribution of Chesterfield's *Letters* from master to servant first appears in Samuel Pratt's anti-Chesterfieldian novel, *The Pupil of Pleasure* (London, 1776; Boston, 1780). In Pratt's novel, Philip Sedley is criticized for "exposing the volumes . . . to the plebeian eyes of thy valet" Thomas (Melmoth 1:131).

26. Tyler would have been painfully aware of the limitations of Chesterfieldianism. His courtship of John Adams's daughter Abigail was compromised by young Nabby's suspicions that Tyler was "practicing upon Chesterfield's plan" (Carson and Carson 17).

27. Trish Loughran contends that the work of *The Contrast* "strongly resembles the

cultural work that federalism would eventually do everywhere else in the republic" (196). Tyler studied with the conservative elite while at Harvard, unsuccessfully courted John Adams's daughter during the 1780s, and eventually fought for them in 1787 when, as an aide-de-camp in the Massachusetts state militia, he helped to suppress Shays's Rebellion, see Pressman, 91. No less of a Federalist icon than George Washington was one of *The Contrast*'s first subscribers.

28. Jeffrey Richards suggests that Tyler's prior knowledge of the bodies of the original cast for *The Contrast* would have given him "a good sense of who could do what" on stage (Tyler 2).

29. *The Contrast* premiered in New York in 1787 and was followed by performances in Baltimore (August 1787), a staged reading in Philadelphia (December 1787), revivals in Baltimore (August 1788) and New York (June 1789) and publication in 1790. By 1800, "a total of thirty-eight recorded performances had taken place in locations ranging from Boston to Charleston" (Shaffer 169). Although the theater was associated with American's elite—Trish Loughran identities it as "an essentially nonpopulist activity" (203)—Michael Gilmore explains that, "Going to see a play in the eighteenth and nineteenth centuries entailed interacting with people, from players to other members of the audience. Seating arrangements physically separated the classes, with servants and slaves in the gallery, the 'middling sort' in the pit, and gentleman and their families in the costly boxes" (575).

30. On Jonathan's centrality to the 1790 frontispiece engraving as well as to *The Contrast* in general, see Loughran 190–93.

31. For additional seducers either specifically identified with Chesterfield or associated with the cultural capital of Chesterfieldian civility, see Philip Sedley and Thomas Traverse in Samuel Pratt's *The Pupil of Pleasure* (Boston, 1780), Lord Ernoff in Susanna Rowson's *The Inquisitor* (1793), Sir George Lovemore in Rowson's *Mentoria* (1794), Peter Sanford in Hannah Foster's *The Coquette* (1797), the military captain who seduces Julianna in Foster's *The Boarding School* (1798), Sinisterus Courtland in Judith Sargent Murray's *The Story of Margaretta* (1798), Patrick O'Connor and Philander in Tabitha Tenney's *Female Quixotism* (1801), Evander Ebbert and Edward Somerset in Caroline M. Warren's *The Gamesters* (1805), and Melvin Brown in P. D. Manvill's *Lucinda, or The Mountain Mourner* (1807). For additional references to Chesterfield in early American seduction fiction, see Brown *Sentimental* 45.

CHAPTER 3. THE FACE OF SEDUCTION

Note to epigraph: Sarah Anderson Hasting. *Poems on Different Subjects* . . . (Lancaster, Pa.: William Dickson, 1808), 101–2.

1. On the politics of the sentimental novel of seduction in early America, see Douglas, Davidson, Smith-Rosenberg "Domesticating," Tompkins, Warner 173–76, Barnes, Burgett, Stern, Samuels, Chapman and Hendler, Merish, Brown *Sentimental Novel* 123–76, Dillon, Castiglia, and Rust. On the politics of sensibility in early America, see Ellison and Knott. On social mobility and the early American education novel, see Gilmore.

2. Winfried Fluck notes how the seducer in the sentimental novel of seduction is almost always "a man of the world" ("Novels" 97). For examples of dissimulating seducers either specifically identified with Chesterfield or associated with the cultural capital of Chesterfieldian civility, see Philip Sedley and Thomas Traverse in Samuel Pratt's *The Pupil of Pleasure* (Boston, 1780), The Honorable Harrington in William Hill Brown's *The Power of Sympathy* (1789), Lord Ernoff in Susanna Rowson's *The Inquisitor* (1793), Sir George Lovemore in Rowson's *Mentoria* (1794), Lord Ossiter and Mr. Savage in Rowson's *Rebecca* (1794), Peter Sanford in Hannah Foster's *The Coquette* (1797), the military captain who seduces Julianna in Foster's *The Boarding School* (1798), Sinisterus Courtland in Judith Sargent Murray's *The Story of Margaretta* (1798), Patrick O'Connor and Philander in Tabitha Tenney's *Female Quixotism* (1801), Edward Somerset and Evander Ebbert in Caroline Warren's *The Gamesters* (1805), and Melvin Brown in P. D. Manvill's *Lucinda* (1807). For alternative accounts of the male seducer in postrevolutionary fiction, see Traister and Tennenhouse. See also Fiedler 88–89.

3. The seducers (and their imagined social trajectories) at the center of so many seduction novels correspond with Margaret Hunt's description of the amorphous category of eighteenth-century gentlemen: "The middling may not have been a huge group, but in sheer numerical terms they dwarfed the gentry and the aristocracy. There were 173 peers in 1700 and 267 in 1801. The gentry were more numerous, of course, and are also more difficult to pin down as a category. G. E. Mingay estimates that in the eighteenth century there were some one thousand families in the upper gentry, perhaps two thousand in the lesser gentry, and as many as ten thousand in that more amorphous—and expanding— group who called themselves "gentlemen": lesser esquires, men of respectable lineage who had lost their estates, the better class of professional men, retired military officers, former merchants, and the like" (17).

4. On the significance of faces and character to the emergence of the novel in British print culture and to the formation of the category of literature and the disciplinary divisions that sustain it, see Lynch. For alternative accounts on physiognomy and the novel outside America, see Graham "Character," Tytler *Physiognomy*, Rivers, McMaster, Benedict, and Wheeler "Racial."

5. For how the distinctions of class were rendered in mid-nineteenth-century novels, see Lang. Lang notes how "the contests over the meaning of class . . . over both the anterior social reality the language of class seeks to capture and the social prospect to which it points—frame the novelistic representation of class difference" (6).

6. Ideas and images were indistinguishable for many eighteenth-century intellectuals. "For eighteenth-century Americans, authorities as diverse as John Locke, Cotton Mather, Jonathan Edwards, Isaac Watts, François Fénelon, and Jean-Jacques Rousseau, . . . , advance the cause of the image, whether they intend to or not, and further erode Puritan and evangelical iconoclasm" (Crain *The Story of A* 57).

7. "Reading," Elizabeth Barnes notes, is one of the ways Adam Smith sees identification being established, for in reading, our imaginations allow us to " 'become the very person whose actions are represented to us' " (141).

8. The eighteenth-century novel was often imagined in terms of "a spectacle before readers who are pictured as spectators" (Marshall *The Surprising Power* 2). Diderot, for example, praises Richardson for picturing characters who bear an immediate and visible relation to persons found on the street. After reading Richardson's novels, Diderot explains, "I have formed a picture for myself of the characters the author has brought before us; their faces are there: I recognize them in the street, in public places, in houses; they inspire affection or aversion in me" (89). He lauds Richardson for producing characters where "each one has his own ideas, his own facial expressions, his own tone of voice" (90), so that he can "seek out the honest folk and . . . avoid the wicked" (89).

9. See, for example, "Character and Effects of Modern Novels" (1792) 225; D.S. 141; "Character and Effects of Modern Novels" (1798), 184–85; "Literature and Criticism," 7; "Tendency of Novels," 122; "Commentator. No. 11," 238.

10. That reading was understood in terms of seeing made intermediality central to Anglo-American discussions of the postrevolutionary novel. By intermediality, I refer to what Peter Wagner calls the intertextual use of one medium (such as painting) within another (such as prose fiction) which can include iconotexts as well as "the actual insertion of an illustration into a printed verbal text" (quoted in Aikins 466). "Acknowledging intermediality as a constitutive element in fiction," Janet Aikins explains, "enables us to perceive that the reader of any verbal narrative is also a spectator to narrated action, and most especially so when in the presence of an actual 'iconotext,' a verbal narrative that makes use of an image, either by reference or allusion (real or imaginary)" or explicitly, as in the case of an illustrated edition (471).

11. On anti-fiction sentiment in early America, see Orians and Mulford.

12. Mary Kelley's fascinating study of the letters, commonplace books, journals, and diaries of early American women finds that while "the majority did read widely in poetry, history, biography and travel literature" "no reading appealed to them more than fiction" (179). She suggests that "it was fiction's power to shape a more expansive subjectivity that gave cultural arbiters pause" (*Learning* 182). On the popularity of novels, see "The Ubiquitarian No. XV" (1798), "Commentator. No. 11" (1801), "On Novels" (1803), Thoughtless (1803), Brown (1807), and "On the Moral Tendency of Novel Reading" (1823).

13. The injunction against reading romances, of course, had been standard fare for Puritan ministers and was sustained throughout the eighteenth century by Anglo-American moralists who worried about fiction's capacity to lead the female sex astray (Reilly and Hall 408–10). Increase Mather, for example, warned that "He that can read is able to read the Scripture, and Books which promote Godliness in the power of it, but a Sinful Creature chuseth rather to mispend his time reading Vain Romances, or it may be worse Books" (from "Awakening Truth Tending to Conversion" [Boston, 1710] quoted in Miller and Johnson 339).

14. Although "all the material evidence available . . . attests that men as well as women read even the most sentimental novels" during the postrevolutionary period (Davidson 98), novels frequently coded "the reader—whether male or female—as feminine" (Barnes 41). For examples of male readers whose minds "had become diseased by an assiduous study of those Romances" (A.Z. 71) and thus served as examples "of the fatal effects of addicting

the undisciplined mind to books" (A.Z. 72), see Harrington from William Hill Brown's *The Power of Sympathy*, Archibald from A.Z.'s [Charles Brockden Brown] "A Lesson on Sensibility," and Eugenio from Reverend William Roberts's *Too high a pitch may be given to the mind in early life. Story of Eugenio and Amelia.*

15. This passage was reprinted from Bennett's *Letters to a Young Lady*, see Bennett 2:44.

16. For an alternative account of the early American novel and dissimulation, see Rice 147–72.

17. On how the proliferation of newspapers and libraries introduced new habits of reading and learning in the early republic, see Grasso 281–486.

18. Eighteenth-century epistolary novels, Jürgen Habermas contends, "fashioned for the first time a new kind of realism that allowed anyone to enter into the literary action as a substitute for his own, to use the relationships between the figures, between the author, the characters, and the reader as substitute relationships for reality" (50).

19. On how novels give readers erroneous ideas of mankind, see also *The Lady's Pocket Library* (1792), 144–45 and Philalethes, "Letter 2," 80.

20. On how novel-reading disrupted station or rank, see also "The Gossip No. XIII" (1803), "Miscellany" (1811), and "On Novel-Reading" (1823).

21. For examples of how novel reading was described as poisonous, see Hitchcock 2:186; "Hints; Addressed to Both Sexes" (1793), 231; *Hapless* 1:56–57; Philalethes "Letter 2" (1794), 242; Stanford (1796), 161; "The Ubiquitarian. No. XV" (1798), 112; "Commentator, No. 11" (1801), 238; Miller (1801), 178; "Novel Reading A Cause" (1817), 717; "On the Moral Tendency of Novel Reading" (1823), 223.

22. On how novel reading left "the mind so softened," see also D.S., 141. On the importance of "rational discernment" to postrevolutionary notions of sensibility and fiction, see Kelley *Learning* Chaps. 1 and 5.

23. For an astute reading of quixotic narratives as key media in the shaping of liberal consent in early America, see Brown *Consent.*

24. On how novels provide a "true picture of life," see "Literature and Criticism" 5; "The Novelist, No. 1. On Novel Reading" 5; and Warren iv.

25. On how novels provide "an idea of the characters of men," see "The Dreamer. No. II." 101 and "On The Moral Tendency" 223.

26. For additional dissimulating seducers either specifically identified with Chesterfield or associated with the cultural capital of Chesterfieldian civility, see Philip Sedley and Thomas Traverse in Samuel Pratt's *The Pupil of Pleasure* (Boston, 1780), Lord Ernoff in Susanna Rowson's *The Inquisitor* (1793), Sir George Lovemore in Rowson's *Mentoria* (1794), Peter Sanford in Hannah Foster's *The Coquette* (1797), the military captain who seduces Julianna in Foster's *The Boarding School* (1798), Sinisterus Courtland in Judith Sargent Murray's *The Story of Margaretta* (1798), Patrick O'Connor and Philander in Tabitha Tenney's *Female Quixotism* (1801), Edward Somerset and Evander Ebbert in Caroline Warren's *The Gamesters* (1805), and Melvin Brown in P. D. Manvill's *Lucinda* (1807).

27. On how the ubiquitous presence of deceivers and coquettes in literature reflects a social problem, see Lewis "The Republican Wife," see also Bell.

28. On how Rowson not only survived "the democratization of American genteel sociability" but "taught her readers how to partake of what was left of it," see Rust 42.

29. Rowson, 10. Hereafter cited parenthetically in the text and abbreviated *I*. All quotations from *The Inquisitor; or, Invisible Rambler* are taken from the first American edition (1793) from the Electronic Archive of Early American Fiction at the University of Virginia.

30. See also "The Professing Friend," in which the inquisitor observes a "little man" "whose features, however plain, and, to the generality of the world, uninteresting, immediately prepossessed me in his favour" (*I* 24).

31. As Elizabeth Barnes notes, "sentimental literature teaches a particular way of reading both texts and people that relies on likeness and thereby reinforces homogeneity" (4).

32. Cogdie first seduces Olivia, then Melissa, and finally Madame L'Estrange. In fact, Cogdie's chronic disposition to seduction and theft are instrumental to the novel's transformation of Lord Ernoff from noble rake to noble victim. Cogdie's conspiracy with Ernoff's "infamous strumpet" (*I* 83), Madame L'Estrange, to seduce and "rob the Earl" (*I* 94) is only disrupted by the inquisitor's invisible efforts.

33. *The Inquisitor* was dedicated to Lady Cockburne, "a society woman who had taken a generous interest in the author, and who may be seen in the flattering portrait of Lady Allworth in the book" (Brandt 34). In "The Dressing Room," the inquisitor scrutinizes the face of Lady Allworth (Lady Cockburne) and concludes that: "her face had a benignity about it that diffused itself over all her features, and seemed enlivened by a ray of celestial light; her fine black eyes were of that sort that would pierce the inmost recesses of a guilty soul, but withal, tempered with so much benevolence that to the innocent they seemed to beam only with humanity and compassion" (*I* 112). The alignment of a superior visage with the face of the aristocracy and the fictional face of the aristocrat funding the novel discloses for whom these discursive logics are directed.

34. Despite his performances, Wouldbe's "affected air and gait" (*I* 121) declare him to be "a finished coxcomb" just as clearly as Cogdie's face does to the inquisitor.

35. By habitus I refer to Pierre Bourdieu's sense of an almost unconscious set of practices—a disposition or set of behaviors that is internalized, embodied capital. It is acquired, but not necessarily self-consciously so. It is the principle that generates all the group's properties, but also their judgments of other groups' properties (*Distinction* 170). The habitus is internalized and converted into a disposition that generates meaningful practices and meaning-giving perceptions (*Distinction* 170). Different conditions of existence produce different habituses (*Distinction* 170). Habitus is a structuring framework that organizes perceptions and practices (*Distinction* 170). Vincent Leitch likens the habitus to "ways of being, habits, and generative social codes" (95). "Each social agent acts within the context of her or his habitus, a cultural unconscious common to his or her particular historical community," Leitch explains, "Members of different social classes and groups share different habitus" (95).

36. "What is particularly interesting in Sartre's phenomenology," George J. Stack and Robert W. Plant note, "is that he constructs the gaze as signifying that we are objects of

evaluation and judgment for conscious subjects" (370), see also Sartre, 252–303. They add that "in the experience of shame or pride, an individual attests to an awareness of the other individual as a consciousness that is judgmental, a consciousness that expresses itself through 'the look.' Shame and pride imply our relationship to others as objects for their awareness, their judgment, their approval or disapproval. When I look at others, Sartre claims, I measure my power. And when others look at me they measure their power" (Stack and Plant 370).

37. Foster, *The Coquette*, 194. Hereafter cited parenthetically in the text and abbreviated *C*.

38. Sarah Wood notes how Eliza's downfall is attached not only to what she reads (plays or novels), but to why she reads (amusement rather than edification); see 169. Christopher Castiglia understands the characterization of Eliza's reading as "romance" as symptomatic of her friends' attempts to accentuate the print basis—as opposed to the embodied context—of her melancholia and thus neutralize her critique of the managed interiorities of liberal character.

39. Foster's lack of physical description of the face departs from the literary practice of the eighteenth-century British novel (which typically describes the features of a generically European face and associates them with positive character attributes); see Wheeler "Racial."

40. See Davidson, Smith-Rosenberg "Domesticating," and Harris "Hannah." See also Stern who proposes an alternative reading of *The Coquette* that refuses the traditional conduct book reading of the novel (where Eliza serves as the negative exemplar), but retains the force of the socially conservative inflection of the book all the same.

41. Sarah Emily Newton also reads Foster and Rowson within the tradition of "usable fiction" whose works placed the responsibility for seduction on the failure of independent women to judge men for themselves (138–67).

42. Julia's active, if still limited, agency is consistent with what Gillian Brown has identified as the structure of liberal consent found within seduction stories like *The Coquette*. "Women's participation in the social compact," Brown argues, "does not necessarily serve the rights of women, particularly if female members of society espouse only long-standing androcentric views of class, courtship, marriage, and family" (*Consent* 143). As Lori Merish puts it, "the constitutive condition of female subjectivity, gaining agency in a state of subordination, is a model for the formation of all liberal political subjects" (24). Alternatively, Christopher Castiglia reads *The Coquette* more optimistically, suggesting that although "Eliza negatively defines the virtues that constitute the discourse of liberal character, she also constitutes the deconstructive uncertainty within that discourse" (53).

43. For critics who read the novel as a political allegory on the threats to or limitations of the new nation, see Frost, Arch, Harris "Hannah," Brown *Consent*, and Wood *Quixotic Fictions*.

44. Brown, however, still foregrounds the national and political in her reading of the novel. "The pervasive stories about quixotic readers in early American fiction and cultural criticism," she notes, "serve the nationalist project of advancing a different habit of readerly identification" (*Consent* 160).

45. On quixotic narratives as key media in the shaping of liberal consent in early America, see Brown *Consent*.

46. Tenney, 14. Hereafter cited parenthetically in the text and abbreviated *FQ*.

47. See also *FQ* 61.

48. The attribution of quixotism to the father rather than the mother, Sarah Wood notes, distinguishes Tenney's quixotic fiction from its British source, Charlotte Lennox's *The Female Quixote*; see 178.

49. The trope of turning heads is used frequently in *Female Quixotism* to express how novels obscure or distract "rational" vision. Mrs. Stanly, for example, criticizes Dorcasina for "having that propensity so common to youth, to peruse every novel she could lay hands on, and unfortunately obtaining as many as she wished, her head, has been, for many years, completely turned, and she has been by turns the dupe of knaves and fools" (*FQ* 181).

50. Cultural capital can exist in three forms: in the embodied, objectified, and institutional states. Cultural capital in its embodied state takes the form of "long-lasting dispositions of the mind and body" (Bourdieu "Forms of Capital" 243). Cultural capital in its objectified state takes "the form of cultural goods (such as pictures, books, dictionaries, instruments, machines, etc.) which are the trace or realization of theories or critiques of these theories, problematics, etc," (Bourdieu "Forms of Capital" 243). "Cultural capital in its objectified state," Bourdieu explains, "presents itself with all the appearances of an autonomous, coherent universe which, although the product of historical action, has its own laws, transcending individual wills, and which, as the example of language well illustrates, therefore remains irreducible to that which each agent, or even the aggregate of agents, can appropriate (i.e. to the cultural capital embodied in each agent or even in the aggregate of the agents)" ("Forms of Capital" 247). On the different forms of capital, see Bourdieu "Forms of Capital" 243–48.

51. On the importance of books as a source of cultural capital for actual early American women, see Kelley *Learning* 165–76. Tenney's *Female Quixotism* is among the novels specifically identified by early American women readers in their letters, commonplace books, journals, and diaries (Kelley *Learning* 164–65 and 184).

52. See Bourdieu, *Pascalian Meditations*, 185 and Simpson xxiii.

53. One female reader understood *Female Quixotism* in precisely these terms. Elizabeth Payson found Tenney's novel "valuable" for "being a reverse burlesque upon novel readers" (quoted in Kelley *Learning* 184). She added, in terms remarkably similar to those used by critics of the novel, that "fiction raise[s] expectations of bliss which are never, can never be realized thus prepare[s] the mind engrossed by them for continual disappointments" (quoted in Kelley *Learning* 184).

54. Mischelle Booher claims that *Lucinda* "is not a nineteenth-century text even though its reprints continue through 1868 with more than seven separate versions" (287).

55. Manvill 27. All quotations come from the third 1817 edition. Hereafter cited parenthetically in the text and abbreviated *L*.

56. Although the function of physiognomic discernment is primarily negative in *Lucinda*, like *The Inquisitor*, it also operates positively in the novel. The face serves as the foundation of sympathy and the index of familial relation. Mrs. Manvill, for instance, is able to

recognize a son whom she has never seen because she felt "an unaccountable emotion and interest in the countenance of the young man" (*L* 28).

57. On how the repetition of disguise, misrecognition of characters and class, and the deceptiveness of surfaces in *Ormond* participates in "the late eighteenth/early nineteenth-century anxiety about physiognomy" (242), see Smyth.

58. See Levine, Verhoeven, Schieck, Watts, Stern, and Richards, respectively.

59. See also Bell and Ringe 34.

60. Brown *Ormond* 37. Hereafter cited parenthetically in the text and abbreviated *O*.

61. See Bushman, Shields.

62. For *Ormond*'s relationship to contemporary discussions of education, gender, religion, and politeness, see Waterman 118–29.

63. See Stern 174; see also Hinds and Smyth.

64. For another example of how physiognomy and portraiture might facilitate rather than deter irrational vision, see Brockden Brown's "A Lesson on Sensibility" (1798). This short tale chronicles the disastrous effects of reading romances on the mind of Archibald and provides "an example of the fatal effects of addicting the undisciplined mind to books" (72). Archibald's accidental encounter with a young woman of social origin (but not wealth) inspires an enthusiastic rather than a rational attachment. Confident that he was "profoundly skilled in the language of features and looks" from the "aid of certain German writers" (72), Archibald draws a portrait of his beloved lady and idolizes it. Besides reversing the gender roles typically assigned to reading romance novels, the tale suggests, as *Ormond* does, how discourses such as physiognomy and cultural forms such as portraiture might be shaped by the irrational sensibility and imagination of their practitioners. For the attribution of Brown as the author of "A Lesson on Sensibility," see Bell.

65. On the relationship between Benjaminian aura and Lavaterian physiognomy, see Lyon 260–61.

66. As Sidney Krause notes, "the only certain instance of Brown's going back to pick up earlier material" for *Ormond* "occurs with his appropriating half of the fourth and almost all of the fifth number of his 'Man at Home' series for chapter seven of *Ormond*" (242); see also Russo 210–11 and Hinds 42–44.

67. For more on the unreliability or inconsistency of Sophia's narration, see Nelson; Rodgers 17–19; Krause 244; Russo 205; Schieck 133–37; Grabo 31; Verhoeven 212–13; and Waterman 127–28.

68. There has been long-standing association of the novel with individualism, the rise of the middle class, and the processes of democratization and market expansion in the American context. On the early American novel's relationship to the development of a middling culture of vernacular gentility, see Bushman. On the novel and middle-class formation in early America, see Fiedler, Douglas, Tompkins, Smith-Rosenberg "Subject," Merish, Smith-Rosenberg "Black Gothic," Lang, Shapiro, Rust, and Knott. On how the early American novel articulated a critique of the existing social order of gentility, including empowering individual readers and assaulting social authority, see Davidson, Tompkins, Smith-Rosenberg "Domesticating," and Stern.

CHAPTER 4. THE FACE OF THE PUBLIC

1. On the importance of the public presentation of a person's "real" character to early republican politics, see Grasso 386–459, Roberts, and Freeman.

2. There is an extensive critical literature on embodiment and early American print culture. On how print culture forms a public by negating the body whose relationship to a particular person compromises the disinterestedness of republicanism, see Warner, *Letters*. On how print culture creates a public through a shared discourse of affective experience in which the body is managed by the "natural" expressions necessary for a sincere social performance, see Fliegelman, Klein *Shaftesbury*, Shields and Ruttenberg. On how texts of the early republic utilized the more somatic discourses of affective experience, sympathy, and sentimentalism to define or disrupt the idea of a community for their readers, see Samuels; Stern; Burgett; Barnes; Ellison; Crain *American Sympathy*, and Coviello. On how oratorical performance became a crucial site from which national identity became concretely embodied, see Gustafson *Eloquence*, especially 170–99. For accounts of the literary public sphere in which female embodiment figures prominently, see Dillon, Cima, Merish, and Kelley *Learning*. On the importance of voluntary association and transnational intellectual culture to the public sphere, including the visible signs of moral character, see Waterman.

3. On how nineteenth-century photographic portraiture simultaneously degrades the existent tradition of portraiture (its ceremonial presentation of the bourgeois self) by extending the honorific conventions of portraiture downward in the social order and creates a criminal or "social" body by establishing and delimiting the terrain of the other, see Sekula 6–7.

4. This claim is not meant to overlook the important work done on race in early American culture by Dana Nelson, Jared Gardner, Bruce Dain, and others, but rather to analyze alternative forms of embodying social difference for the period.

5. For the importance of De Lairesse's *The Art of Painting in All Its Branches* for eighteenth-century colonial American portraiture, see Craven, "Colonial American Portraiture," 113.

6. Before the revolution, Anglo-American portraits had historically documented the visibility of the monarchical nation and reproduced its genteel social relations through the faces of particular persons. Margaretta Lovell observes that eighteenth-century portraiture in America was distinguished by recording "a specific social strata: the gentry, merchant, and professional classes (not the court on the one hand or the laboring classes on the other)" ("Reading Eighteenth-Century American Family Portraits" 243). According to Wayne Craven, what characterizes colonial American portrait style during the eighteenth century, in distinction to English portraiture of the same period, is its more pronounced individualism and naturalism. Rather than impose a class ideal on the depiction of a face, for instance, Craven finds that colonial American artists tended, in general, to preserve individual likeness. While Craven is correct to suggest that the colonial American mercantile aristocracy's mode of portraiture was not as ostentatious and idealized as that of the eighteenth-century English aristocracy, its pictorial conventions were in large measure derivative of formal Georgian portraiture, replete with a full vocabulary of gestures, poses, faces, and settings

that would be as recognizable to its informed spectators as the face itself would be as a likeness; see Staiti and St. George, *Conversing by Signs*, chap. 4.

7. Freneau's fictional portrait painter, like many actual portrait painters from the period, uses portrait painting as an opportunity for upward mobility. Eighteenth-century British-American portrait painters such as Benjamin West, Charles Willson Peale, John Singleton Copley, Gilbert Stuart, "and others—were, by and large, born into and raised in artisan, often quite impoverished, and certainly ungenteel environments." "They were," in short, "actively upward mobile themselves" (Lovell "Reading Eighteenth-Century American Family Portraits" 46). See also Lovell "Painters and Their Customers" 303.

8. For an account of Freneau's criticism of America's growing materialism, see Elliott *Revolutionary Writers* 128–70 and Watts *Republic Reborn* 79. Freneau's desire to reconcile the economic conditions of culture with its civic function in "The Picture Gallery" addresses what Michael Gilmore identifies elsewhere in his poetry as the characteristic contradiction of the era, a tension between a "devotion to the common-weal" and "an individualistic spirit" ("The Literature of the Revolution and Early National Periods" 609).

9. Freneau's apprehension over the effects of the transformation of cultural production from political and public motives to economic and individual ones corresponds with Grantland Rice's characterization of the period as marked by "the gradual but continuous replacement of a political understanding of authorship with an exclusively economic one" (11).

10. Gisèle Freund has made similar remarks concerning the rise of mechanized portraiture in France. More and more people decided to have their portrait taken, Freund argues, because by doing so "an individual of the ascending classes could visually affirm his new social identity to himself and to the world at large" (9). "The bourgeoisie," he claims, "still modeled itself after the aristocracy, which continue to set standards of taste even though it was no longer the dominant economic or political force" (10).

11. Evert Duyckinck claims that Freneau "was once waited upon by the artist, Rembrandt Peale, with a request for this purpose, by a body of gentlemen in Philadelphia; but he was inexorable on the subject. On another occasion, the elder Jarvis, with a view of securing his likeness, was smuggled into a corner of the room at a dinner party, at Dr. Hosack's, to which the poet had been invited; but the latter detected the design and arrested its accomplishment" ("Introductory Memoir" xxxi–xxxii).

12. Duyckinck explains how "the portrait prefixed to this volume has been sketched by an artist, at the suggestion and dictates of several members of the poet's family, who retain the most vivid recollection of his personal appearance" (*Poems* xxxi).

13. In this sense, Freneau embodies the contradiction that Michael Warner identifies with Franklin and republican statesmen in general. "The republican statesman," Warner observes, "is in some measure a contradiction in terms: he is the embodiment of that which, by definition, cannot be embodied" (*Letters* 73). Warner claims that this contradiction was mediated or disguised by print.

14. Although published anonymously, Philip Marsh designates Freneau's authorship of this article as "certain" (Marsh *Bibliography* 118).

15. See Du Simitière. It is worth noting that Freneau was in and out of Philadelphia

throughout the early 1780s and possibly could have viewed either Peale's portrait gallery, Du Simitière's portrait gallery, or both. See Miles, *Saint-Mémin*.

16. See also Casper and Marshall "The Golden Age" 29–83.

17. See Barrell 58–63.

18. On the increasing importance of physiognomic particularity to late eighteenth-century discussions of portraiture (including James Barry, Archibald Allison, and Charles Bell), see Wahrman 301.

19. My arguments are particularly indebted to the recent work of Bellion, Evans, Fortune, Miles, Steinberg, Verheyen, and Clubbe, who have demonstrated the importance of physiognomy to the interpretation of American portraiture during this period. Miles, for example, claims that "the study of physiognomy undoubtedly played an important role in the way people looked at portraiture" during this period (" 'Memorials" 157), and notes that "comments about people or portraits between the 1730s and the 1860s often indicate that people continued to be aware of prevailing theories of physiognomy or, later, phrenology" (24). See also Colbert, Stafford, and Crawford.

20. The profile portrait was a feature of classical state portraiture (particularly on "official" representations such as coins or medallions) and its revival during the end of the eighteenth century, I would like to suggest, had as much to do with the rise of physiognomy as it did with the prevailing neoclassical aesthetics.

21. Quotations are from Lavater, *Essays on Physiognomy*, trans. Henry Hunter, with engravings by Thomas Holloway, 3 vols. in 5 (London: John Murray et al., 1789–1798) unless otherwise noted.

22. For Rembrandt Peale's relationship to physiognomy, see Miller 43–46.

23. On physiognomy's influence on Sully's portrait practice, see Clubbe 204–25.

24. Stuart's 1796 Athenaeum portrait of Washington, for example, "diminished the size of the eye sockets and the prominence of the cheekbones" in order to avoid making Washington look "more sensitive looking" (Evans 67). For how Rembrandt Peale used Lavaterian physiognomy to discredit Stuart's Vaughan portrait and establish his own portrait of Washington as closest to his character, see Verheyen 131–37.

25. See Bellion, Miles "1803" 118–38 and Benes 138–51.

26. See Staiti 20. Dorinda Evans contends that the Federal-era artist sought a new form of idealization that "depended not on props or a symbolic background, but rather on the representation of the head alone" ("Survival and Transformation" 130).

27. Washington's engraving was copied from the French edition of Lavater (*Essai sur la physiognomie, destiné à faire connaître l'homme et le faire aimer*, trans. M. E. de La Fité, A. B. Caillard, and Henri Refner, 4 vols. [The Hague, 1781]).

28. Staiti contends that "Copley knew firsthand the codes of polite behavior because he was himself trained by his English-born stepfather, Peter Pelham, who taught classes in manners in Boston. Pelham, in turn, would have been familiar with, and sensitive to, the contemporary English behavioral theory that reached its culmination in Lord Chesterfield's *Letters to His Son*" (20); see also Craven *Colonial American Portraiture* 172.

29. Although contemporary accounts of portraiture are rare (Hood 84–91), the degree

to which one's face was negotiable is evident in a 1797 letter Judge Cushing wrote to his niece Esther Parsons about a James Sharples portrait and in the travel diary of the profile portrait cutter James Guild. For the former, see Knox 15; for the latter, see McCourbrey 29.

30. On Brackenridge's depiction of "a multilingual American society" at risk of disintegration, see Looby 223.

31. See Agnew and Fliegelman. For the applicability of this metaphor to 1760s prerevolutionary British America, see Wood *The Radicalism of the American Revolution* 59. John Evelev finds Royall Tyler's postrevolutionary play, *The Contrast*, supporting Agnew's assertion that "the metaphorical use of the world as theater, *theatrum mundi*, functioned within Anglo-American theater as a representation of the radically defamiliarizing effects of that new system of exchange" (85).

32. The ceremonial practices of the levée and the couchée were associated with the European courts, particularly Louis XIV, and they allowed nobles or courtiers access to the monarch while he dressed and undressed for the day. Since the royal body was a sign of power, intimacy with the monarch indicated a sign of privilege among those who were present. The practice continued in the United States under the Federal administrations of Washington and Adams; see Bushman 42.

33. See also the swindled lawyer Otterborn's ballad "Tom Rascal, or Rascal Tom" in which he praises "Lavater" for his "happy knack / Of telling to help clear / Of such as might impose themselves / Like Monsieur Braganeer / Cou'd read the faces, and take a hint / From brow, or lurid eye / And make a book, and called it, of / The physiognomy" (*MC* 769).

34. On the shifting relationships between one's social and political positions at the end of the eighteenth-century, see Wahrman 150–51.

35. On how revolutionary oratory equated the elite white male body with the figure for the nation, see Gustafson *Eloquence* 171–99. For more on the graphic distribution of the character of Washington, see Reaves. For Washington's written character portraits, see Baker's dated, but encyclopedic *Character Portraits of Washington as Delineated by Historians, Orators, and Designers*.

36. See also the ninth 1809 edition of Mason Weems's *The Life of George Washington* (Philadelphia: Mathew Carey, 1809), 3.

37. Marquis de Chastellux's physiognomic portrait of Washington was included in his *Travels in North America, 1780–1782* and was reprinted in America frequently; see "American Intelligence" (1787), "The Following Animated Portrait" (*Daily Advertiser* 1787), "The Following Animated Portrait" (*Massachusetts Gazette* 1787), "New York, March 2" (1787), "Of General Washington" (1787), "Extracts" (1789), "The Following Portrait" (1790), and "Portrait of General Washington" (1800).

38. See Newlin and Nance.

39. See Elliott 171–217 and Patterson. Patterson finds *Modern Chivalry* to be centrally concerned with uncertainty, one that he reads as representational (in its formal philosophical sense). Yet, like Gilmore ("Eighteenth-Century"), Hoffa, and later Looby, representation means linguistic representation and so linguistic arbitrariness is a sign for political or social arbitrariness. I differ from Gilmore's and Patterson's account of the novel since I find

that Teague's success in signifying what he was not has less to do with formal problems concerning the nature of the signifier than in broader problems in the visibility of distinction.

40. The election of William Findley, an Irish weaver without formal education, to the Constitutional Convention prompted Brackenridge to ridicule the popular anti-Federalist in the *Pittsburgh Gazette* (1787) with a rhymed satire featuring none other than Teague O'Regan. Some critics have read Brackenridge's *Pittsburgh Gazette* satire as evidence that William Findley was the historical referent for Teague O'Regan.

41. Wood *The Radicalism of the American Revolution* 257. For more on Findley's politics, see Wood "Interest."

42. See Elkins and McKintrick 257–303.

43. Brackenridge's role in the Whiskey Rebellion, for example, provides some indication of just how complicated his politics were. While originally a staunch Federalist, Brackenridge began to voice his opposition to the Federalists in the 1790s, and eventually became a Jeffersonian Republican in 1798, only to turn around and oppose Jefferson's policies on judicial reform a year later. In contrast to such political inconstancy, Brackenridge remained fairly consistent in his suspicion of lower-class political enfranchisement. The preface and "Introduction" to his optimistic but unsuccessful republican periodical, *The United States Magazine* (1779), provides an excellent example of his simultaneous faith that "the honest husbandman who reads this publication will rapidly improve in every kind of knowledge" ("Introduction" 10) and "be qualified to be a Magistrate" and his nervousness that Americans might degenerate back into men without taste—like "so many Ouran-Ourans of the wood" (preface). Michael Warner reads this periodical similarly, seeing it as both an example of print's rhetoric of diffusion—its erasure of the differences of political status—and a reinscription of "those differences by enabling the reader to attain distinction" (*Letters* 139).

44. See Rice, chap. 6. Rice argues that Brackenridge feared the power of a democratic print culture to consolidate a coercive public opinion, and worried that such power would eradicate the critical individualism necessary to a viable liberal republic. I find Rice's larger claims concerning Brackenridge's skepticism about the expanding print sphere in *Modern Chivalry* to be misplaced. Brackenridge's skepticism, for me, is much more concerned with an expanding and illiterate/uneducated populace than with a democratic print culture in which Brackenridge consistently participated throughout his life.

45. Marlon Ross has recently identified "the politics of identity" with what he calls "the politics of face/ts" (832) and he believes that it is "a monstrous mistake to think that the politics of identity is something that happened only recently" (833).

CHAPTER 5: THE INVISIBLE SRISTOCRAT

Note to epigraphs: Cooper, *Precaution* (1820), 162; Cooper, *Letters and Journals* (1830), vol. 2, 34–35; "Cooper's Works," *United States Magazine and Democratic Review* 25 (July 1849): 54.

1. On the transformation of America following the War of 1812, see Sellers and Howe.

2. Nina Baym, for instance, claims that the prevalence of the visual within much

antebellum literary criticism should be understood as the means by which reality might be recognized as a value for the novel without disclosing the rules by which the real was produced (Baym *Novels* 154). She contends that reviewers insisted on the spatial, static form of the novel, because they wanted to both separate novels from "their powerful emotional affect in favor of a more measured, intellectual response" and "enforce through the novel a particular idea of reality and the human situation within it" (*Novels* 154). While antebellum literary and moral critics were undoubtedly drawn to a visual language in order to enforce a particular idea of reality and a certain mode for representing it as a literary value, the question as to when and why this begins to matter for critics of fiction needs to be reconsidered. As I argued in chapter 3, the equivalence between reading and seeing had been a part of the discourse surrounding the production and reception of the novel in America well before 1830. Moreover, the conversation was one in which the pictures produced by novels were both criticized and celebrated so it is not clear how turning to the visual would necessarily downplay "the emotional affect of the novel" when that emotional affect had been understood historically in terms of pictures. Whether a novel is valued for its temporal (plot) as opposed to its spatial (picture) form matters less than what kind of pictures the novel produces in the minds of its readers. For sister arts approaches that consider the relationship between the visual and the literary after 1830, see Baym and Williams.

3. Kay Seymour House also states that "Cooper was the first American author to characterize repeatedly, and in some depth, the American Negro" (73). For how Cooper's fiction participates in the cultural work of constituting a more modern, "interior" notion of race, see Tawil.

4. In his 1839 preface to the revised edition of *Precaution*, Cooper admitted that "the medley of characters . . . no doubt will appear a mistake in conception" and that "the novel's faults were attributable to haste and to the awkwardness of a novice" (*Precaution* v). Hereafter cited parenthetically in the text and abbreviated *P*.

5. For more on Cooper's characterization, see House.

6. Hereafter cited parenthetically in the text and abbreviated *S*.

7. The physiognomic distinction of Washington's face, as we saw in Chapter 4, was well documented in the print and visual culture of postrevolutionary America. Cooper's description of Mr. Harper/George Washington's physical appearance recalls that of William P. Carey, who found Washington's "person is majestic and striking, his physiognomy prepossessing, and strongly expressive of the noble qualities of his soul: the dignity of his appearance inspires an awe, which keeps the unacquainted beholder at a respectful distance, until the easy politeness of his manners, formed to gain the affections without artifice, and the modest frankness of his conversation, fraught with judicious reflections, . . . insensibly banish the coldness of reserve" (686). For reprints of Carey's physiognomic portrait of Washington in America, see "Extract from" (1789), "Miscellanist" (1789), and "The Following" (1789). Washington's face was considered so physiognomically distinct that it made the scene implausible in the eyes of some critics; see Gardiner.

8. Hereafter cited parenthetically in the text and abbreviated *PI*.

9. On environmentalist accounts of human variety and the complexities of race

theory in the early republic, see Dain 40–80. See also Bindman, Meijier, and Sweet. On the nineteenth-century racial science's inversion of eighteenth-century climate theory, see Wheeler *Complexion* 296. On how the representation of race in *The Pioneers* serves as a bridge between eighteenth-century notions of human variety and the emerging racialist discourse of the nineteenth century, see Tawil 80–91.

10. In fact, Cooper routinely introduces characters for the first time through descriptions of their face or by how other characters observe their face (even before revealing their names) in *The Pioneers*. See, for example, the descriptions of Richard Jones, Old Major Fritz Hartman, Monsieur Le Quoi, and Parson Grant in the sleigh scene, or better yet, that of Temple's domestic servant, Benjamin Penguillan (*PI* 59).

11. On the centrality of marriage to Cooper's fiction, see Baym "The Women," Lawson-Peebles, Darnell, and Dean "Marriage."

12. In Chapter 5, for instance, Mrs. Jarvis doubts Sir Edward Moseley's suggestion that Denbigh is "the family name of the Duke of Derwent" because "neither the old man nor his son looked much like a duke" (*P* 35).

13. For an alternative reading of invisibility in Cooper's *The Spy*, see Downes 168.

14. Similarly, the sudden revelation of Gerty's respectable social origin in Maria Cummins's *The Lamplighter* (1854), as Amy Lang notes, transforms her story from a rags-to-riches tale of social mobility to one of social stasis, of recovering "her 'real' but invisible class origins" (Lang 27).

15. See Wallace 43.

16. On how eighteenth-century British novelists used the physical description of the body's exterior features to establish relationships between readers and characters, see Wheeler "Racial."

17. See Gardiner. More recently, Michael Gilmore describes Cooper as an author who self-consciously wrote to found a national literary tradition and who, in the process, re-conceptualized the novel as a genre from the civic-humanist paradigm (where fiction was "truth" or history) to one where history was fiction, laying the foundations for the American romance ("Cooper" 676).

18. On physiognomy and the British novel, see Graham "Character," Tytler *Physiognomy*, McMaster, Benedict, Lynch, and Wheeler "Racial."

19. On how Cooper's later fiction relies on the language and conventions of literary sentimentalism, see Tawil 129–51.

20. Cooper actively cultivated and attained a novel-reading audience by writing within and eventually modifying familiar literary genres and their conventions. Cooper read widely as a child and was familiar with Opie, More, Wilberforce, and Austen as an adult. For more on how Cooper's familiarity with English novelists helped him to create an audience for his fiction, see Wallace's *Early Cooper*, especially 63–116. More recently, critics have resituated Cooper's *Precaution*, claiming that he did not begin his career as the American Austen, but as the American Brunton. For some, *Precaution* "is more nakedly driven by the demands of the conduct genre than *Persuasion*" (Lawson-Peebles 65). See Alliston and Schirmeister, "Taking Precautions," 45 and "James Fenimore Cooper: Entrepreneur of the Self." For arguments identifying Austen as the source of *Precaution*, see Scudder and Hastings.

21. James Grossman finds *Precaution* "very bad" and "an overloaded overtold tale" (21). He cannot explain how Cooper "made the mistake of beginning his career as the American Austen" (21). Ezra Greenspan calls *Precaution* "an unoriginal novel of manners" (109). My own position is closer to that of Michael Gilmore, who characterizes early Cooper (through 1823) as an author torn between gender-encoded models of authorship, torn between the feminine novel of manners and courtship and a masculine civic-oriented fiction ("Cooper" 679). Although Gilmore's account is somewhat heavy-handed with respect to gender, I share his view that *Precaution* was very much in the civic republican/didactic vein of novel writing. However, Gilmore reads Cooper as renouncing postrevolutionary fiction's subordination of the novel to social purpose in favor of an aestheticized version of the novel that values the imaginary as much as the actual ("Cooper" 684). In contrast, I believe that Cooper's early fiction remains suspicious with respect to the imaginative capacity of its readers, thus resembles the didactic novel in terms of its characterization more closely than Gilmore would have it.

22. On Cooper's participation in the creation of a postcolonial culture, see Gustafson "Natty."

23. Later in life, Cooper became so embittered about the intellectual and cultural capacity of the American public that he warned the sculptor Horatio Greenough to expect little from his countrymen. Cooper's June 14, 1836 letter to Greenough is worth quoting at length since it reveals how Cooper's belief in the aesthetic limitations of the American public was coincident with his ethnic racism: "You are in a country in which every man swaggers and talks, knowledge or no knowledge; brains or no brains; taste or no taste. They are all *ex nato* connoisseurs, politicians, religionists, and every man's equal, and all men's betters. In short, you are to expect your own matured and classical thoughts will be estimated by the same rules as they estimate pork, and rum, and cotton. . . . Alas! my good Greenough, this is no region for poets, so sell them your wares and shut your ears. The foreigners have got to be so strong among us that they no longer creep but walk erect. They throng the prisons, control one or two of the larger cities, and materially influence public opinion all over the Union. By foreigners, I do not mean the lower class of Irish voters, who do so much at the polls, but the merchants and others a degree below them, who are almost to a man hostile in feeling to the country, and to all her interests, except as they may happen to be their interests" (*The Correspondence* 1:358–59).

24. Much of Cooper's early fiction contrasts artificial with natural forms of distinction even as it seeks to merge them in something called "natural aristocracy."

25. See Jones, Beard, Ringe "James Fenimore Cooper and Thomas Cole," Callow, Ringe, *The Pictorial Model*, and Nevius.

26. Scottish Common Sense philosophy led nineteenth-century American writers to believe that "the visual image . . . was the basic means by which they could reach the minds of their readers" (Ringe *The Pictorial Mode* 8). "Because the visual image could serve approximately the same purpose as the corresponding object in the external world," Ringe explains, "the writers could use such images in their prose and verse to elicit from their readers a response fundamentally the same as that aroused by the physical objects themselves" (*The Pictorial Mode* 8); see also Wallace *Early Cooper* 20.

27. Ringe *The Pictorial Mode* 15. Ringe contends that Scottish theoreticians such as Archibald Alison and Dugald Stewart not only prompted writers such as Cooper to develop their literary pictorialism, but they also led them to include the moral associations that can be inspired by such images so that "we might 'read' this type of imagery" (*The Pictorial Mode* 11). The key point of this congruence (one that Ringe acknowledges but does not stress) was that verbal images affected the imagination as a graphic image would. How nineteenth-century theory conflated the imaginative with the visual is a topic too large for discussion here. Although Ringe and I both acknowledge that part of the attraction of Cooper's literary pictorialism was its moral force on the imagination of the viewer or reader, he situates his discussion within a sister arts analysis of themes common to Cooper and the Hudson River School of landscape painters.

28. Fiction was most effective and valuable, Cooper insisted in the introduction to *The Pioneers*, when it tried to "represent a general picture" "of characters in their classes" (*PI* 7).

29. See James Franklin Beard's "Introduction" in Cooper's *Tales for Fifteen: or, Imagination and Heart*. All subsequent references to "Imagination" come from the online text edition of *Tales for Fifteen* found at the James Fenimore Cooper Society web site (http://www.oneonta.edu/~cooper/texts.html) and will be cited parenthetically and abbreviated *I*.

30. Henry Inman drew and Francis Kearney engraved the image for the *Port Folio* (August 1823); see Beard, "Illustrations," xiv. Inman and Cooper were fellow members of the Bread and Cheese Club, which met regularly in New York City during the 1820s. For more on the New York City Bread and Cheese Club, see Marckwardt and Callow 52–62, 158–63, 188–90, and 192–215. For more on Henry Inman and his mentor John Wesley Jarvis, see Dickson *John Wesley Jarvis*, Gerdts, Lipton, and Colbert 160–66. For more on Cooper's relationship to Inman, Jarvis, and other contemporary American artists, see Beard 112–27.

31. See McWilliams 100–29 and Wallace 130–69.

32. For an alternative account of the novel as picture, see Baym *Novels* 152–73.

33. A nearly identical assessment was reprinted in 1851 in Griswold's *The International Magazine of Literature, Art, and Science*.

34. For similar admiration of Cooper's "vivid narration, descriptive power," and "vigorously delineated character," see "Harvey Birch and The Skinners" 40.

35. See also "Cooper's Last Novel" 438.

36. Even the cosmopolitan literary toryism of the *North American Review* shared this position: "let an American author make a living character . . . nationality will take care of itself" (quoted in "Nationality" 12). See also the *North American Review*'s 1850 review of Cooper's *Ways of the Hour*.

CHAPTER 6. THE PHYSIOGNOMIC FALLACY

1. Physiognomy and phrenology shared an innatist psychology, although they accounted for it in different ways. For Lavater, the mind was not a product of the body, but rather the body revealed the dispositions of the mind. The body made the mind visible

and intelligible at first glance; Lavater constructed a lexicon for such legibility. Spurzheim's 1826 *Phrenology, In Connexion with the Study of Physiognomy*, provides a clear sense of how and why phrenology would differ from physiognomy. In short, where Lavater read the component parts of the face in order to construct a synthetic, comprehensive account of a person's moral character, Spurzheim's phrenology inverts this method, and reads character by its component parts—its moral and intellectual faculties—as they manifest themselves on the head. What this change in method allows Spurzheim to do is to avoid the problem of heterogeneous faces that troubled Lavaterian physiognomy from the start.

2. See Bercovitch *Rites*, Creech, Renker, Robillard, Williams *Confounding*, Otter, Taggart, and Spanos. See also Dryden "Entangled" and *Melville's Thematics*. "Even more than *Moby-Dick*," Christopher Sten observes, "*Pierre* shows Melville's ever-deepening interests in the visual arts, in the range of allusions and in the way the visual arts are integrated into the book's plot and theme" (12). For more on Melville's relationship to the visual arts in general, see Sten, Robert K. Wallace "Melville's Prints" and *Melville's Prints*.

3. See Dryden "Entangled." Bercovitch *Rites*, Renker, Williams *Confounding*, and Spanos.

4. Bercovitch argues that Pierre's "first attempts to interpret the Chair Portrait undermine the rhetoric of authority; the closing impasse of meaning at the Counterfeit-Art Gallery dissolves the authority of rhetoric" (*Rites* 278). Bercovitch suggests that the novel "builds upon a series of questions of fact which are never resolved because the issues they pose only matter" as ambiguities, as mysteries that open into the problematics of rhetoric (*Rites* 303).

5. See also Hillway, Dillingham, Smith *Melville's Science*, and Dryden "Entangled."

6. Renker argues that faces are metonymically associated with "the imprisoning force of the page" (37) throughout *Pierre* and that Melville's fear of faces is his fear of the materiality of writing, the lurking force of the white page (41).

7. See Baym *Novels* 152–53.

8. *Pierre* has been variously understood as subverting contemporary models of authorship (Brodhead *Hawthorne*, Dimock *Empire*, Brown *Domestic*, Toner), paternal authority (Sundquist), the reliability of knowledge (Dimock "*Pierre*"), literary nationalism (Bercovitch "How," Reynolds *Beneath*, Wald), self-reliance (McWilliams *Hawthorne*, Elliott "Art, Religion," Bercovitch *Rites*), ideology (Rowe), or the possibility of critique itself (Rogin, Jehlen).

9. "The six longest American reviews," Leon Howard and Herschel Parker note, "denounced *Pierre* in terms excessive even in the journalism of that day" (381).

10. In fact, critics "were more often distressed by *Pierre* as an outrage against morality than as an artistic failure" (Howard and Parker 389).

11. Reviewers often explain this feature in terms of a variety of negative literary or philosophical influences such as Carlyle, Transcendentalism, Goethe, or German literature in general.

12. *Herman Melville: The Contemporary Reviews*, 419. Hereafter cited parenthetically in the text and abbreviated *HMCR*.

13. For those who read *Pierre* as either emulating or parodying sentimentalism, see Braswell, Douglas, Rogin, Brown *Domestic*, Williams *Confounding*, Silverman, Otter, Penry, and Colatrella. For those who read *Pierre* as engaging with the gothic novel, see Parker *Herman Melville: A Biography, Volume 2* and Miles "Tranced." For those who identify the novel of sensation, especially urban fiction, see Reynolds *Beneath*, Kelley *Melville's City*, Post-Lauria, and Colatrella. See also Tochlin, Baym "Melville's Quarrel," Milder, and Canaday.

14. The reviewer for the *Southern Literary Messenger*, for instance, explained that "It should be the object of fiction to delineate life and character as it is around us or as it ought to be. Now, Pierre never did exist, and it is very certain that he never ought to exist" (*HMCR* 436). See also the August 1852 New York *Commercial Advertiser* (*HMCR* 424).

15. Nineteenth-century reviewers, for instance, admired *Typee*'s "spirited pictures" ([Margaret Fuller], *New York Tribune* [4 April 1846]; *HMCR* 38) and praised the novel for being "a veritable picture of life among the cannibals" (*Cincinnati Morning Herald* [3 April 1846]; *HMCR* 38). "The pictures it presents," Boston's *Universalist Review* noted "are vivid, and seem to bring the objects before our eyes" (*HMCR* 51). "Clearly," the Washington *National Intelligencer* remarked, "Mr. Melville has a great warmth and beauty of the imagination: to describe and relate as he does one must have the faculty which makes pictures in the mind—which recalls and re-embodies at pleasure all that has passed before the mind or the eyes, and at will 'raises a world of gayer tint and grace' out of every thing" (Washington *National Intelligencer* 27 [May 1847]; *HMCR* 74). See also [Nathaniel Hawthorne] Salem *Advertiser* (25 March 1846, *HMCR* 22); *Western Continent* [Baltimore], May? 1846 (*HMCR* 48); *Merchants' Magazine and Commercial Review* [New York], 14 (May 1846), 491 (*HMCR* 48); and *Universalist Review* [Boston] 3 (July 1846), 326–27 (*HMCR* 51).

16. See New York *Christian Inquirer* (8 May 1847, *HMCR* 103). "The general features of the picture are evidently drawn from the life" (*HMCR* 149) and were vivid enough for the *Times* of London to recommend "the picture to Edwin Landseer" (*HMCR* 152). For more critical admiration of *Omoo*'s pictures, see *Spectator* [London] 20 (10 April 1847), 351–52 (*HMCR* 89); *Critic* [London] 5 (17 April 1847), 308–11 (*HMCR* 92); [Evert A. Duyckinck] *Literary World* [New York] 14 (8 May 1847), 319–21 (*HMCR* 104); G[eorge] W[ashington] P[eck] *American Whig Review* [New York] 6 (July 1847), 36–46 (*HMCR* 132); [Jedediah B. Auld] *New York Evening Mirror* (21 July 1847, *HMCR* 143); *Times* of London (24 September 1847, *HMCR* 149); Honolulu *Polynesian* (18 March 1848, *HMCR* 182).

17. "There are some vivid descriptions of natural scenery that seem as though touched by the pencil of the painter," *Godey's Magazine and Lady's Book* declared, "but we think the great talent of the author is in his sketches of character" (*HMCR* 142). As another reviewer put it in the New York *Evening Mirror*, "If you wish to read the details of forecastle life they are to be found in other works; but if you desire a vivid and masterly picture of a whale ship, inside and outside, fore and aft, with living, moving, wide-awake characters, . . . read 'Omoo.'" (*HMCR* 111). The specific praise for Melville's "rare pen for the delineation of character" in *Omoo* was reprinted elsewhere (and with respect to other novels), see William Cramer, "An American Author in England," Milwaukee *Wisconsin* (18 November 1847, *HMCR* 160); the Philadelphia

Dollar Newspaper (21 November 1849, *HMCR* 280); and the *Literary World* 4:115 (14 April 1849), 348. For more on Melville's graphic characterization, see Troy [New York] *Whig* (5 May 1847, *HMCR* 101) and *Albion* [New York] 6 (8 May 1847, *HMCR* 102).

18. "Every individual" in *Omoo*, New York's *Columbian Magazine* observed, "is made to sit (or stand) for his portrait" (*HMCR* 125). "Eminently truthful to the eye" (*HMCR* 102), *Omoo* placed "every subject distinctly before the reviewer" (*HMCR* 93, Boston *Evening Transcript* [6 May 1847] "truthful"; London *John Bull* [17 April 1847] "every subject"). In fact, the New York *Evening Mirror* reported how one reader "actually imagined himself on the spot—so graphic are the sketches of life and scenery interspersed throughout that work" (*HMCR* 109). See also *Athenaeum* [London] 1015 (10 April 1847), 382–84 (*HMCR* 85); "Pacific Rovings." *Blackwood's Magazine* [Edinburgh] 61 (June 1847), 754–67 (*HMCR* 121); "Protestantism in the Society Islands." *United States Catholic Magazine and Monthly Review* [Baltimore] 7 (January 1848), 1–10 (*HMCR* 173).

19. With *Redburn*, Melville was applauded for "the life-like portraiture of his characters at sea, . . . the fidelity to nature, and, in combination of all of these, the thorough impression and conviction of reality" ([Evert A. Duyckinck] *Literary World* [New York] 146 [17 November 1849], 418–20 [*HMCR* 276]). "The life-like manner in which every event is brought to the reader is most astonishing," Nathaniel Willis pronounced in the New York *Home Journal*, "one actually thinks, when arising from the perusal, that of these occurrences he was actually a witness, so vividly is the mind impressed with their truthfulness" (*HMCR* 283). For additional praise of *Redburn*'s pictorialism, see London *John Bull* (27 October 1849, *HMCR* 257); *Spectator* [London] 1113 (27 October 1849), 1020–21 (*HMCR* 258); London *Morning Post* (29 October 1849, *HMCR* 260–61); London *Morning Herald* (30 October 1849, *HMCR* 261); *Blackwood's Edinburgh Magazine* 66 (November 1849), 567–80 (*HMCR* 271); *Bentley's Miscellany* [London] 26 (November 1849), 528–30 (*HMCR* 273); London *Home News: A Summary of European Intelligence for India and the Colonies* 7 (November 1849, *HMCR* 274); Boston *Post* (20 November 1849, *HMCR* 279); Philadelphia *Dollar Newspaper* (21 November 1849, *HMCR* 280); *Albion* [New York] 8 (24 November 1849), 561 (*HMCR* 281); *Literary American* [New York] 3 (24 November 1849), 419 (*HMCR* 284); *United States Magazine and Democratic Review* [New York] 25 (December 1849), 575 (*HMCR* 286); R. [George Ripley]. New York *Tribune* 1 (December 1849, *HMCR* 288); *Holden's Dollar Magazine* [New York] 5 (January 1850), 55–56 (*HMCR* 290).

Like *Redburn*, *White-Jacket* elicited a similar response from reviewers. Nathaniel Willis, for instance, called the novel "a series of highly finished pictures, each more or less complete, the effect of which, on the reader's mind, is like that of a gradually unrolling panorama; so distinct, so life-like is the scene presented" (*HMCR* 334). For Willis, as for many other reviewers, *White-Jacket* epitomized the Melville canon and reaffirmed his descriptive power as an author in terms of his fiction's vivid yet not improbable pictures. "White Jacket contains a picture of the American Naval service, so minutely graphic," London's *John Bull* noted, "that he who has spent a few hours as a reader in this 'World in a Man-of-War,' is as much at home in the ways and manners of the Yankee Navy, as if he had himself served his time under Commodore Bougee and Captain Claret" (*HMCR* 298). *White-Jacket* was frequently said to place readers before "a gallery of pictures" (*HMCR* 304), what Evert Duyckinck would call "this great portrait-gallery of the man-of-war" (*HMCR* 313); *Literary Gazette* [London] 1725 (9 February 1850), 102–5 (*HMCR* 304); [Evert A. Duyckinck]. *Literary World* 163 (16 March 1850), 271–72 (*HMCR* 313). See also New York *Evening Mirror* (29 March 1850). The *Evening Mirror* argued that *White-Jacket*'s "picture of actual life on board an American man-of-war" was "so evidently veritable, honest, and drawn with a steady hand, for a serious and generous purpose, that, we are inclined to think, it shows the author in a better light than any of his former works, good as they confessedly are, in their several ways" (*HMCR* 319). By the time critics were finished reviewing *White-Jacket*, Melville was being referred to as "the De Foe of the Ocean" (*HMCR* 275); see [Evert A. Duyckinck]. "Passages from New Books." *Literary World* [New York] 145 (10 November 1849), 395–97 (*HMCR* 275). Philadelphia's *Graham's Magazine* agreed with the comparison to the extent that Melville "has De Foe's power of realizing the details of a scene to his own imagination, and of impressing them on the imagination of others, but he has also a bit of deviltry in him which we do not observe in De Foe, however much raciness it may lend to Melville" (*HMCR* 290). Its "graphic sketches" were "painted with such consummate skill and intense energy of expression," that the *Biblical Repository and Classical Review* described how "its horrible features glare upon you like a living being, and can never be effaced from the mind. In this line lies its chief value; and for power in this respect its surpasses any book we ever read" (*HMCR* 347). "For vigorous and graphic descriptions," Nathaniel Willis went so far as to "match 'White Jacket' against the world" (*HMCR* 335). "The great charm of Mr. Melville's books," Willis explained, "is in their vividity and truthfulness. The thoughts are whole ones; no indistinctness or obscurity is there about them. Seen clearly and forcibly, his objects are as clearly and forcibly presented to others. It is a singular union of gifts, is that clearness of eye and tongue" ([N. P. Willis] "American Literature." New York *Home Journal* (13 April 1850, *HMCR* 335).

For additional praise of *White-Jacket*'s pictorialism, see London *Sun* (28 January 1850, *HMCR* 296); *Athenaeum* [London] 1162 (2 February 1850), 123–25 (296); London *Atlas* (9 February 1850, *HMCR* 302); *Bentley's Miscellany* [London] 27 (March 1850), 309–10 (*HMCR* 309); *Literary World* [New York] 164 (23 March 1850), 297–99 (*HMCR* 317); Boston *Evening Transcript* (25 March 1850, *HMCR* 318); Boston *Evening Traveller* (27 March 1850, *HMCR* 318); New York *Evangelist* (28 March 1850, *HMCR* 318); *Saroni's Musical Times* [New York] 1 (30 March 1850), 317–18 (*HMCR* 322); Springfield [Mass.] *Republican* (30 March 1850) (*HMCR* 325); *Christian Register* [Boston] 29 (6 April 1850), 55 (*HMCR* 330); *Spirit of the Times* [New York] 20 (6 April 1850), 79 (*HMCR* 331); Boston *Post* (10 April 1850, *HMCR* 331); Washington *National Era* (25 April 1850, *HMCR* 342); *Holden's Dollar Magazine* [New York] 5 (May 1850), 314–15 (*HMCR* 343); *Knickerbocker* [New York] 35 (May 1850), 448 (*HMCR* 344); *Southern Quarterly Review* [Charleston, S.C.] 1 (July 1850), 514–20 (*HMCR* 348); *Methodist Quarterly Review* [New York] 32 (July 1850), 478–79 (*HMCR* 349).

20. *Mardi*'s "pictures leave traces on the memory," Evert A. Duyckinck remarked, which "are reproduced in our thoughts, pointing many a significant moral" ("Mardi" 334). The New York *Evening Mirror* celebrated *Mardi*'s "graphic descriptions" on which "the

mental eye can never weary of gazing" (*HMCR* 207). The New York *Tribune's* claim that Melville "has the eye of a painter" (*HMCR* 226) in *Mardi* was seconded by the Albany *Argus*, which admired how "all these things rise up before our mind's eye" (*HMCR* 211). Similarly, *Harper's* lauded *Moby-Dick's* "frequent graphic and instructive sketches" (*HMCR* 392) and described how the introductory chapters provide "a succession of portraitures, in which the lineament of nature shines forth" (*HMCR* 392). All of *Moby-Dick's* crew "stand before us in the strongest individual relief, presenting a unique picture gallery, which every artist must despair of rivaling" (*HMCR* 392). "The portraits of these men," London's *Morning Advertiser* reasoned, "must have been taken from the life" (*HMCR* 355). "So natural are the features, and so clear the outlines" in *Moby-Dick* that "every character seems pictured by a daguerreotype," the Newark *Daily Advertiser* observed (*HMCR* 393). After reading *Moby-Dick*, New York's *Spirit of the Times* called Melville one of the few writers "living or dead, who describe the sea and its adjuncts with such true art, such graphic power, and with such powerfully resulting interest" (*HMCR* 395). Like Dickens, Melville creates books "which are living pictures" (*HMCR* 395). Even a negative review from the *Methodist Quarterly Review* admired how *Moby-Dick* "displays the same power of dashing description, of vivid picture-painting, which characterizes all the other works of this writer" (*HMCR* 411).

21. The Concord New Hampshire *Congregational Journal* understood this perfectly when they suggested that "Mr. Melville should feel almost as much ashamed of the authorship of 'Pierre' as he has a right to be proud of his 'Typee'" (*HMCR* 433).

22. See Spengemann vii. Priscilla Wald makes a similar point, reading *Pierre's* literary failure as a successful formal experiment; see Wald 101.

23. W. J. T. Mitchell identifies a metapicture as "a picture that is used to reflect on the nature of pictures" (57); see Mitchell *Picture Theory* 35–82.

24. Melville's knowledge of physiognomy and phrenology has been documented by several critics (Hillway, Dillingham, Robillard, Sealts, Creech). Most believe that Melville was skeptical of the science, but at least one (Robillard) disagrees. On November 7, 1849, Melville saw J. R. Planché's play, *Lavater, The Physiognomist; or, Not a Bad Judge*, performed in London at the Royal Lyceum Theater (*Journals* 13). The play's subject matter and long run testifies to physiognomy's endurance and Lavater's fame by casting Lavater as its detective hero. Two weeks later, Melville purchased a copy of Lavater's *Essays* in London on November 21, 1849 (*Journals* 24). However, Melville could have read them much earlier since his father owned a copy in his library (James Creech notes that Allan Melville had a copy of Lavater's *Essays* in his library [quoted Dillingham, 150]) and since Melville refers to Lavater as early as 1847. References to physiognomy and phrenology (particularly Lavater) are scattered throughout Melville's writing. Nearly all of these physiognomic/phrenological references have been identified (see Smith *Melville's Science*). Tyrus Hillway claims that while Melville "scoffed at these studies as unscientific, he knew and apparently admired the work of Lavater, was reasonably familiar with Gall and Spurzheim, and alluded frequently to the principle of physiognomy and phrenology in his works" (145). Unlike others of his time, Melville "recognized the limitations of their methods and theories" (Hillway 150). Howard Horsford is less hesitant about Melville's repudiation of physiognomy. In the

editorial appendix to Melville's *Journals*, Horsford argues that "Several allusions to Lavater and the pseudoscience of physiognomy, both earlier and later than this purchase, and usually facetious, occur in Melville's writings, including *Mardi* and *Moby-Dick*" (*Journals* 317). William Dillingham concurs, "That Melville considered physiognomy a totally erroneous mode of looking at life is clear from the numerous references to it and its sister science, phrenology, in his works" (154). In contrast to Hillway, Horsford, and Dillingham, Douglas Robillard contends that while "Melville took a somewhat jesting attitude toward phrenology . . . his comments based on physiognomy are more serious" (118). "His lecture on 'Statues in Rome,' delivered about six years after publication of *Pierre*, seems to have been based almost entirely on physiognomical considerations" (118).

25. Although historians have shown how the elite on either side of the Atlantic shared many of the same codes and manners of a transatlantic gentility, the North American elite of colonial and postrevolutionary America were, strictly speaking, gentry rather than nobility and aristocracy; see note 2, Chapter 2. North American gentry were usually aristocrats in the sense of "manufactured nobility" (Melville *Pierre* 10) rather than established peerage. My usage of the term aristocracy over gentry, while less accurate historically, follows Melville's usage in the novel (which I understand as emphasizing the aspiration of those to which the term applies on the one hand and the illegitimacy of the distinction to which they lay claim on the other). For a contemporary assessment of America's "bubble-aristocracy," see "American Aristocracy," 117.

26. Of course, this is not to deny the dominant critical position that characterizes the mid-nineteenth-century novel as "speaking both from and to the middle class" in America (Lang 8). Rather it is to explore how, in the case of *Pierre*, the representation of the kind of distinction associated with antebellum authorship in the second half of the novel might reproduce forms of distinction associated with the aristocracy of the face represented in the first half of the novel.

27. See Brown *Domestic*, Williams *Confounding*.

28. For a similar query into the challenges of reproducing distinction in the apparent social volatility of America, see "American Character," which notes "as there are no entails, nor any rule of primogeniture, to prevent estates from being dissevered, and dissipated, and as the field for enterprise and industry, has been prolific and extensive, changes of fortune are peculiarly frequent" (418).

29. Acids (such as nitric or hydrochloric) were among the chemicals used in daguerreotypy; see Humphrey. The affordability, accessibility, and French origins of the daguerreotype made it a more democratic form of representation in the eyes of many nineteenth-century critics and authors, see, for example, Hawthorne's depiction of Holgrave in *The House of the Seven Gables*. Lydia Maria Child referred to the daguerreotype as "the democracy of drawing . . . it levels all distinctions" (64). By 1851, 21 million daguerreotype plates a year were produced in the city of Paris alone. In 1855, over 400,000 were made in Massachusetts alone. By 1856, Americans spent over 15 million dollars annually on daguerreotypes (Davidson "Photographs"). Despite these staggering numbers, daguerreotypes still resembled previous forms of portraiture (such as the oil portrait) in that its images were unique

and would not be capable of mass reproduction until the perfection of Talbot's negative/positive process.

30. See Toner 247–49. Melville's position seems less an "assault on hereditary stasis" (249) as Toner describes it, than a recognition of its transformation.

31. The narrator's description of aristocracy here is distinct from Thomas Jefferson's famous notion of a natural aristocracy based on "virtue and talents" (1305) that was to replace—not reproduce—an "artificial aristocracy founded on wealth and birth" (1306). Jefferson conceded, however, that a natural aristocracy might be hereditary since "experience proves that the moral and physical qualities of man, whether good or evil, are transmissible in a certain degree from father to son" (1305).

32. See Giles 66.

33. For a deconstruction of the opposition between democracy and monarchism in early American culture, see Downes.

34. For more on Pierre's docility, see Dryden "Entangled." For a more Foucauldian reading of Pierre's docility, see Spanos 23.

35. See Spanos and Otter. Bourdieu contends that "whereas the holders of educationally uncertified cultural capital can always be required to prove themselves, because they are only what they do, merely a by-product of their own cultural production, the holders of titles of cultural nobility—like the titular members of an aristocracy, whose 'being,' defined by their fidelity to lineage, an estate, a race, a past, a fatherland, or a tradition, is irreducible to any 'doing,' to any know-how or function—only have to be what they are, because all their practices derive their value from their authors, being the affirmation and perpetuation of the essence by virtue of which they are performed" (*Distinction* 24). Bourdieu's characterization of the aristocracy by "being" as opposed to "doing" describes Pierre's relationship to his aristocratic past in the first half of the novel. Yet, "being" a Glendinning, Melville shows, means not simply embodying the perceived essence of the name (in terms of resemblance) but practicing the dispositions for looking at Glendinnings.

36. For more on idolatry in *Pierre*, see Porte 181 and Dryden "Entangled." W. J. T. Mitchell claims that "the idolater has 'forgotten' something—his own act of projection" (*Iconology* 197).

37. If Pierre's docility departs from that of his grandfather it may be in accepting his mother's antithetical reading of docility and domination, since Pierre "through the unavoidable weakness of inexperienced and unexpanded youth, was strangely docile to the maternal tuitions" (16).

38. Melville invokes ideology both as false consciousness and as "the structure of values or interests that inform any representation of reality" (Mitchell *Iconology* 4). See also Mitchell *Iconology* 151–208.

39. Bellis 70.

40. It is in this sense that the perceived opposition between the Frankfurt School's idea of culture as reification and Bourdieu's Veblenesque notion of culture as symbolic capital is false; see Gartman 422. Culture neither mystifies social relations, nor does it make them transparent. Rather, what mystifies social relations is not culture, but those things

that structure our relationship to culture. Of course, since one's relationship to culture is informed by culture itself, there is a tendency to conflate it with cultural form and reduce culture to symbolic capital.

41. See also Parker, who notes how "*Pierre* looked like nothing so much as a belated gothic-romance, more akin to sensational books from the turn of the century than the latest novels" (2002 2:54). Melville himself acknowledged that "*Pierre* would be "a regular romance, with a mysterious plot to it, & stirring passions at work, and withall, representing a new and elevated aspect of American life" (*Letters* 150 quoted in Sundquist 154).

42. Nicholas Canaday goes so far as to label the Saddle Meadows Pierre "a daughter, a sister" (398). For alternative comparison of *Pierre* to Rowson, see Charvat 251.

43. The vial of poison was a common postrevolutionary metaphor for the negative effects of reading romance novels, and recalls the frontispiece engraving for *The Power of Sympathy*. *Pierre*, like *The Power of Sympathy*, is as much about the reception of a past tale of seduction (one committed by a father) as it is about a present seduction (involving that father's children). Moreover, *Pierre* invokes, like *The Power of Sympathy* does, incest alongside its seduction plot. In *The Power of Sympathy*, Harrington is powerfully and erotically attracted to a woman who turns out to be his sister, although initially he thought she was not his sister. In *Pierre*, Pierre is powerfully and erotically attracted to a woman who might not be his sister, although initially he thought she was his sister. In Hill Brown's novel, incest was punitive for act of seduction committed by an allegedly honorable father and, as I argued in Chapter 3, the novel fantasized that the social problems of libertinism and seduction, as well as the model of reading that was said to facilitate both practices, would extinguish themselves as if naturally. In contrast, in Melville's novel, incest fails to prohibit the attraction between brother and sister. The revelation of a past tale of seduction—the seduction of Isabel's mother by Pierre's allegedly honorable father—brings Isabel and Pierre together rather than separating them. Despite the number of similarities between *Pierre* and *The Power of Sympathy*, I would argue that their relationship is more structural, thus generic, than allusive and specific. For other comparisons of *Pierre* to *The Power of Sympathy*, see Young 27–28 and Dill. For more on incest in *Pierre*, see Murray and Sundquist.

44. The relationship of Pierre's sex to his seduction is provocative since, as a man, he can neither become pregnant (the sign of his seduction) or lose the child, which would normally punish him for it (the inability to reproduce himself within the imagined social order of the novel). As a result, Melville suggests that what might be lost with Pierre's death is not his capacity to reproduce himself, but rather the capacity of the genre to reproduce such fiction.

45. "The Editor's Shanty" 273; quoted in Hetherington 234.

46. Cindy Weinstein suggests that "*Pierre* is neither a sentimental nor an antisentimental novel yet it is both" (160). For arguments on reading *Pierre* as a parody of sentimental literature, see Braswell, Milder, Douglas, Parker, Higgins "Reading," Canaday, Reynolds *Beneath*, Brown *Domestic*, Williams *Confounding*, and Colatrella. For arguments on reading *Pierre* as emulating the genre, see Hetherington, Thomas, Otter, Penry, and Silverman. On *Pierre*'s intertextual dialogue with British culture, particularly the British domestic novel, see Giles 64–67.

47. My use of the term "seduction narrative" does not intend to deny the sentimentality of postrevolutionary seduction novels but rather to draw attention to the role of seduction in their sentimentalism. Seduction, as Chapter 3 discussed, was a staple of early American sentimental fiction; see Davidson *Revolution* 106, Tennenhouse *Importance* 45, and Rust 34. As Elizabeth Barnes notes, Hill Brown's *The Power of Sympathy* is "a model of American sentimental literature" (145) that "denotes more than the natural sentiments that blood kinship calls forth: it alludes the pedagogical model by which sentimental literature claims its own authority over the hearts and bodies of its readers" (145).

48. After its initial publication in 1807, *Lucinda, or, The Mountain Mourner*, was published at least six more times in nineteenth-century America; see Booher.

49. Penry 234.

50. Cindy Weinstein rightly suggests that "Blood is everywhere in the novel, functioning as a metonymy for the family relations which persist in spite of the text's continuous bloodletting" (181), but here that metonymy seems to be depend on the sentimental conflation of tears and ink.

51. Karen Sanchez-Eppler identifies sentimental fiction "as an intensely bodily genre'" in which "bodily signs are adamantly and repeatedly presented as the preferred and most potent mechanisms both for communicating meaning and for marking the fact of its transmission" (27). See also Haltunnen's description of the antebellum era's "sentimental typology of conduct" (40–42). For more on the relationship between the sentimental novel and physiognomy see Brown *Sentimental* 189–96.

52. This inhabitation of the genre is intensified by Melville's decision to have the narrator, at times, ironically address Pierre as if he is a person in a novel that the narrator is reading about as opposed to a character in one that he is actively narrating. In Book IX, for instance, the narrator reminds readers that "the thoughts we here indite as Pierre's are to be very carefully discriminated from those we indite concerning him" (167).

53. "Character and Effects of Modern Novels" 225. Reverend Holmes reminds readers in *The Power of Sympathy* that in those novels written "in a easy, flowing style . . . the imagination is apt to get heated" (22).

54. The passages are reproduced from the 1791 Hartford edition of Bennett's *Letters to a Young Lady*, which went through no fewer than thirteen editions before 1841. Versions of Bennett's anti-romance novel criticism circulated well into the 1840s as anti-sentimentalist criticism. In 1849, *The Literary World*, for instance, complained of "the disproportionate quantity of sentiment: of weak, effeminate, trashy romance" in " 'popular' literature" ("What Is Talked About" 231). The author relates the familiar postrevolutionary anecdote of how one female reader could have avoided criminality by reading something else. "Had her mind been trained in a vigorous course of reading, she could never have been so ready a dupe of herself, and of the ridiculous letters which were sent her" ("What Is Talked About" 231). What differentiates the antebellum strain of anti-novel criticism is that it is "sentimental culture" rather the romance, which is responsible for leading female readers to criminality. For a defense of imaginative culture, see "The Culture of Imagination."

55. *Pierre*, like William Hill Brown's *The Power of Sympathy*, is a seduction novel about

reading seduction novels. The overly enthusiastic Harrington dies clutching his copy of Goethe's *Werther*, unable to read the past tale of his father's seduction rationally or abandon his love for a woman who turns out to be his sister. The 1852 *Anglo-American Magazine* spotted the resemblance, calling Pierre a "New York Werther" (quoted in Hetherington 234). Again, my point is not to assert literary allusion. I do not mean to suggest that Melville was influenced by Hill Brown or Goethe, but to draw attention to how *Pierre* inhabits the discursive structure of those novels that discuss the dangers of reading novels; see Hill Brown 97.

56. See also 51. Isabel's letter to Pierre is preceded by "a nameless presentiment" in him (61) and augurs "nameless forebodings of ill" (62).

57. Melville encourages this interpretation by including a third instance of nameless-ness in which the social positions of Pierre's father and Isabel's mother as manorial lord and feudal tenant are expressed: "regular armies, with staffs of officers, crossing rivers with artillery, and marching through primeval woods, and threading vast rocky defiles, have been sent out to distrain upon three thousand farmers-tenants of one landlord, at a blow. A fact most suggestive two ways; both whereof shall be nameless here" (11). For how this passage alludes to the Anti-Renter conflict of the 1830s and 1840s and brings America's supposedly distant aristocratic past into its democratic present, see Otter 197–99.

58. William Dillingham claims that "Pierre's tragedy can be traced in part to his affinity for the principles of physiognomy" (150). Had Pierre not had a "tendency to follow Lavater's principles of physiognomy," Dillingham speculates, "he might have questioned more seriously Isabel's claim to be his half-sister" (162).

59. For alternative discussions of the importance of physiognomy to *Pierre*, see Hillway, Dillingham, Smith *Melville's Science*, and Otter.

60. See Dryden "Entangled."

61. Pierre's initial decision to account for the discontinuity of portrait likenesses through temporal progression recalls Gombrich's discussion of two portraits of Bertrand Russell, one at the age of four, the other at the age of ninety. Gombrich explains how a viewer may look for facial features from one portrait in the other and vice versa. Melville departs from Gombrich, I would add, by insisting, as Pierre Bourdieu does, that a person's primary perception of the world is almost always an act of cognition related to the recognition of the social order.

62. John McWilliams notes that Pierre "burns his heritage before leaving Saddle Meadows, but remains obsessed with that heritage in New York" (*Melville* 172).

63. For some, Pierre's impoverished and obscure literary career during the second half of the novel appears to renounce both of these models. For these critics, Pierre's complaint that "when every body has his portrait published true distinction lies in not having yours published at all," is understood as part of Melville's assertion of a particular type of literary individualism in which distinction is associated with obscurity and not the commercial success and publicity that accompanied the sentimental authors of the nineteenth-century literary marketplace; see Brown *Domestic*, Williams *Confounding*.

64. On *Pierre*'s depiction of how the professional literary criticism of the Young

American movement reproduced rather than repudiated the practices of genteel amateur-ism, see Evelev *Tolerable* 147–54. On the political aspects of the Young America movement, see Eyal.

65. Hershel Parker, for instance, insists that "it is folly to look for ways of seeing the Pierre-as-author pages as unified with the rest of the book." (*Herman Melville: A Biography, Volume 2* 87).

66. Note 7 in *Letters* 120. The first of the Duyckincks' projected "Our Portrait Gallery" series featured a full-page profile portrait of William Prescott in his study (May 1851). See also Yanella.

67. See Geary and Avallone.

68. See also "Living Pictures of American Notabilities." According to the author, America is "essentially a nation of hero-worshippers" who are prepared "at any moment, to fall down and worship almost any brazen image which some democratic Nebuchadnezzar the king may set up" ("Living Pictures" 89). Cooper's literary celebrity, for example, has placed him in the pantheon that formerly had belonged only to "military chieftans and political orators" ("Living Pictures" 89).

69. For accounts that read Pierre's iconoclasm as part of Melville's assertion of a par-ticular type of literary individualism, see Brown *Domestic* and Williams *Confounding*.

70. While many antebellum portraits of authors lacked the "flowing beard" that Pierre longed for as a youth, it was part of the public image of antebellum authorship. Such beards figure prominently, for instance, in the portraits of such distinguished authors such as John Saxe, Dr. Starbuck Mayo, George Dewey, George Kendall, and Richard Kimball in Rufus Griswold's *International Magazine*. See *International Magazine* 4:3 (1 Oct. 1851) [Saxe]; *International Magazine* 3 (1851), 442 [Mayo]; *International Magazine* 3 (1851), 286 [Dewey]; *International Magazine* 3:2 (1 May 1851) [Kendall]; and *International Magazine* 2 (1851), 156 [Kimball].

71. See Bellis 155.

72. In November 1851, Melville wrote to Hawthorne: "This is a long letter, but you are not at all bound to answer it. Possibly, if you do answer it and direct it to Herman Melville, you will missend it—for the very fingers that now guide this pen are not precisely the same that just took it up and put it on this paper. Lord, when shall we be done changing?" (Mel-ville to Hawthorne, November 1851, *Correspondence*, 213).

73. See Williams *Confounding*.

Bibliography

Addison, Joseph. *Spectator* 86 (8 June 1711). In *The Works of Joseph Addison*, 3 vols. New York: Harper and Brothers, 1850.

[Advertisement for *Redburn*]. *Literary World* 5:147 (24 Nov. 1849): 42.

Agnew, Jean-Christophe. *Worlds Apart: The Market and the Theater in Anglo-American Thought, 1550–1750*. Cambridge: Cambridge University Press, 1986.

Aikins, Janet E. "Picturing 'Samuel Richardson': Francis Hayman and the Intersection of Word and Image." *Eighteenth-Century Fiction* 14:3–4 (April–July 2002): 465–505.

Allgor, Catherine. *Parlor Politics: In Which the Ladies of Washington Help Build a City and a Government*. Charlottesville: University Press of Virginia, 2000.

Alliston, April, and Pamela J. Schirmeister. "Taking Precautions: Gender Masquerade and Authorial Persona in James Fenimore Cooper." In *Biography and Source Studies*. New York: AMS Press, 1997. 39–54.

———. "James Fenimore Cooper: Entrepreneur of the Self." *Proceedings of the American Antiquarian Society* 107:1 (1997): 41–64.

"Alphonso and Emily." *Pittsfield Sun; or Republican Monitor* 7:363 (5 Sept. 1807): [1]. EAN.

"American Aristocracy." *United States Magazine and Democratic Review* 8:27 (Aug. 1840): 113–35.

"American Biography: Extracted from Dr. Ramsay's *History of South Carolina . . .* Henry Laurens." *Star* 1:45 (7 Sept. 1809): 177. EAN.

"The American Character. Defence of the American Character, or an Essay on Wealth as an Object of Cupidity or The Means of Distinction in the United States." *Port Folio* 7:5 (May 1819): 412–21.

The American Chesterfield, or Way to Wealth, Honour and Distinction; Being Selections from the Letters of Lord Chesterfield to his Son, And Extracts from other eminent authors on the subject of politeness: with alterations and additions suited to the youth of the United States. By a Member of the Philadelphia Bar. Philadelphia: John Grigg, 1827.

"American Intelligence." *Independent Gazetteer* 6:384 (6 March 1787): [2]. EAN.

"Anecdotes." *Herald of Freedom* [Boston] 3:22 (27 Nov. 1789): [85]. EAN.

"Anecdotes." *New Hampshire Spy* (8 Dec. 1789): [n.p.]. EAN.

Anheier, Helmut K., Jurgen Gerhards, and Frank P. Romo. "Forms of Capital and Social Structure in Cultural Fields: Examining Bourdieu's Social Topography." *American Journal of Sociology* 100:4 (Jan. 1995): 859–903.

Anthony, Mischelle. "'I Trust Every Feeling Heart': Reader History and P. D. Manvill's *Lucinda; Or, The Mountain Mourner.*" *EAL* 42:2 (2007): 285–303.

Appleby, Joyce. "The Social Consequences of American Revolutionary Ideals in the Early Republic." In *The Middling Sorts: Exploration in the History of the American Middle Class.* New York: Routledge, 2001. 31–49.

Arch, Stephen Carl. "'Falling into Fiction': Reading *Female Quixotism.*" *Eighteenth-Century Fiction* 14:2 (Jan. 2002): 177–98.

Armstrong, Nancy. *Desire and Domestic Fiction: A Political History of the Novel.* New York: Oxford University Press, 1987.

"Art IV . . ." *Port Folio* 12:1 (Sept. 1821): 42. APS.

"Article 1—No Title; Answer." *The Literary Mirror* 1:10 [Portsmouth] (23 April 1808): 37–38.

"Article VI. Tracts published by the Christian Tract Society, London, and republished by Wells and Lilly." *The Christian Disciple and Theological Review* 2:8 [Boston] (March–April 1820): 146. APS.

"Artificial Courtesy." *Weekly Visitor, or Ladies' Miscellany* 3:29 [New York] (20 April 1805): 228. APS.

"The Attributes of God Displayed. Diversity of Features in the Human Face." *Methodist Magazine* 2 [New York] (1819): 62–63. APS.

Augst, Thomas. *The Clerk's Tale: Young Men and Moral Life in Nineteenth-Century America.* Chicago: University of Chicago Press, 2003.

Avallone, Charlene. "Calculations for Popularity: Melville's *Pierre* and *Holden's Dollar Magazine.*" *Nineteenth-Century Literature* 43 (1988): 82–110.

A. Z. [Brown, Charles Brockden] "Lesson on Sensibility." *Weekly Magazine* 2 (1798): 71–76.

Bacon, Francis. "Of Simulation and Dissimulation." *The Essays or Counsels, Civill and Moral* (1625). Ed. Michael Kernan. Cambridge, Mass.: Harvard University Press, 1985.

Baker, Jennifer. *Securing the Commonwealth: Debt, Speculation, and Writing in the Making of Early America.* Baltimore: Johns Hopkins University Press, 2005.

Baker, William Spohn. *Character Portraits of Washington as Delineated by Historians, Orators, and Designers.* Philadelphia: Robert M. Lindsay, 1887.

Bal, Mieke. *Reading "Rembrandt": Beyond the Word-Image Opposition: The Northrop Frye Lectures in Literary Theory.* Cambridge: Cambridge University Press, 1991.

Balzac, Honoré. "Fenimore Cooper et Walter Scott" from *Oeuvres Completes,* vol. 23. Paris, 1879. Trans. T. R. Lounsbury in *James Fenimore Cooper.* Boston, 1882.

"Banking; The Paper-Mill." *Niles' Weekly Register* 15:390 [Baltimore] (20 Feb. 1819): 7+. APS.

Barnes, Elizabeth. *States of Seduction and Democracy in the American Novel.* New York: Columbia University Press, 1997.

———. "Natural and National Unions: Incest and Sympathy in the Early Republic." In *Incest and the Literary Imagination.* Ed. Elizabeth Barnes. Gainesville: University Press of Florida, 2002. 138–55.

Barrell, John. *The Political Theory of Painting from Reynolds to Hazlitt.* New Haven: Yale University Press, 1986.

Baym, Nina. "The Women of Cooper's Leatherstocking Tales." *American Quarterly* 23:5 (1971): 696–709.

———. *Novels, Readers, and Reviewers: Responses to Fiction in Antebellum America.* Ithaca, N.Y.: Cornell University Press, 1984.

———. "Melville's Quarrel with Fiction." *PMLA* 94:5 (1979): 909–23.

Beard, James Franklin. "Cooper and His Artistic Contemporaries." *New York History* 35 (Oct. 1954): 480–95.

———. "Illustrations." In James Fenimore Cooper. *The Pioneers, or the Sources of the Susquehanna. A Descriptive Tale.* Historical Introduction and Explanatory Notes by James Franklin Beard. Text established by Lance Schachterle and Kenneth M. Andersen, Jr. Albany: State University of New York Press, 1980.

Beattie, James. "Of the Passions, as they display themselves in the Look and Gesture. (From Dr. Beattie's *Elements of Moral Science*, lately published)." *Universal Asylum and Columbian Magazine* 6:1 (Jan. 1791): 12.

Bell, Michael Davitt. "'The Double-Tongued Deceiver': Sincerity and Duplicity in the Novels of Charles Brockden Brown." *EAL* 9:2 (1974): 143–63.

Bellion, Wendy. "Heads of State: Profiles and Politics in Jeffersonian America." In *New Media, 1740–1915.* Ed. Lisa Gitelman and Geoffrey Pingaze. Cambridge, Mass.: MIT Press, 2003. 31–59.

Bellis, Peter. *No Mysteries Out of Ourselves: Identity and Textual Form in the Novels of Herman Melville.* Philadelphia: University of Pennsylvania Press, 1990.

Benedict, Barbara. "Reading Faces: Physiognomy and Epistemology in Late Eighteenth-Century Sentimental Novels." *Studies in Philology* 92 (1995): 311–28.

Benes, Peter. "Machine Assisted Portrait and Profile Imaging in New England After 1803." In *Painting and Portrait Making in the American Northeast.* Ed. Peter Benes. Boston: Boston University Press, 1995. 138–50.

Benjamin, Walter. *Illuminations.* Trans. Harry Zohn. New York: Schocken Books, 1968.

Bennett, John. *Strictures on Female Education: Chiefly as it Relates to the Culture of the Heart.* Norwich, Conn.: Ebenezer Bushnell, 1792.

———. "Letter XII: On Politeness." *American Museum* 11:4 (April 1792): 139–40.

———. *Letters to a young lady, on a variety of useful and interesting subjects . . .* 2 vols. Hartford, Conn.: Hudson and Goodwin, 1791.

Bercaw, Mary. *Melville's Sources.* Evanston, Ill.: Northwestern University Press, 1987.

Bercovitch, Sacvan. "How to Read Melville's *Pierre*" (1986). In *Herman Melville: A Collection of Critical Essays.* Ed. Myra Jehlen. Englewood Cliffs, N.J.: Prentice Hall, 1994. 116–25.

———. *Rites of Assent.* New York: Routledge, 1993.

Berland, K. J. H. "Reading Character in the Face: Lavater, Socrates, and Physiognomy." *Word and Image* 9:3 (1993): 252–68.

Berry, Jonathan and Christopher Brooks, eds. *The Middling Sort of People: Culture, Society and Politics in England 1550–1800.* New York: St. Martin's Press, 1994.

Bindman, David. *Ape to Apollo: Aesthetics and the Idea of Race.* Ithaca, N.Y.: Cornell University Press, 2002.

Bledstein, Burton J. and Robert D. Johnston, eds. Introduction to *The Middling Sorts: Exploration in the History of the American Middle Class*. New York: Routledge, 2001. 1–25.

Block, Sharon. *Rape and Sexual Power in Early America*. Chapel Hill: University of North Carolina Press, 2006.

Blumin, Stuart. *The Emergence of the Middle Class: Social Experience in the American City, 1760–1900*. Cambridge: Cambridge University Press, 1989.

Booher, Mischelle. "P. D. Manvill and the Feminist Companion; Some Corrections." *ANQ* 16:3 (Summer 2003): 26–30.

Borkat, Roberta. "Lord Chesterfield Meets Yankee Doodle: Royall Tyler's *The Contrast*." *Midwest Quarterly* 17:4 (1975–76): 436–39.

Bourdieu, Pierre. *Distinction: A Social Critique of the Judgment of Taste*. Trans. Richard Nice. 1979; Cambridge, Mass.: Harvard University Press, 1984.

———. "First Lecture. Social Space and Symbolic Space: Introduction to a Japanese Reading of Distinction." *Poetics Today* 12:4 (Winter 1991): 627–38.

———. "Forms of Capital." In *Handbook of Theory and Research for the Sociology of Education*. Ed. John G. Richardson. New York: Greenwood Press, 1986. 240–59.

———. *Pascalian Meditations*. Trans. Richard Nice. Stanford: Stanford University Press, 2000.

———. "The Social Space and The Genesis of Groups." *Theory and Society* 14:6 (1985): 723–43.

Brackenridge, Hugh Henry. *Modern Chivalry*. Ed. Claude M. Newlin. New York: Hafner, 1962.

———. *Gazette Publications*. Lancaster, Pa.: Alexander and Phillips, 1806.

———. *A Hugh Henry Brackenridge Reader, 1770–1815*. Ed. Daniel Marder. Pittsburgh: University of Pittsburgh Press, 1970.

Branagan, Thomas. *The Charms of Benevolence and Patriotic Mentor . . .* Philadelphia: W. Spence & E. Jones, 1814.

Brandt, Ellen B. *Susanna Haswell Rowson, America's First Best-Selling Novelist*. Chicago: Serba Press, 1975.

Braswell, William. "Early Love Scenes in Melville's *Pierre*." *American Literature* 22 (1950): 283–89.

Breitwieser, Mitchell. "Commentary: Afterthoughts." *American Literary History* 5:3 (Autumn 1993): 588–94.

Brigham, David. *Public Culture in the Early Republic: Peale's Museum and Its Audience*. Washington, D.C.: Smithsonian Institution Press, 1995.

"British Biography. Editor." *Port Folio* 4:1 [Philadelphia] (July 1810): 17+. APS.

Brodhead, Richard. *Hawthorne, Melville, and the Novel*. Chicago: University of Chicago Press, 1976.

———. *The School of Hawthorne*. Oxford: Oxford University Press, 1986.

[Brown, Charles Brockden Brown]. "Novel-Reading." *Literary Magazine and American Register* (March 1804): 403.

———. "On The Cause of the Popularity of Novels." *Literary Magazine and American Register* 7:45 (July 1807): 410–12.

Brown, Charles Brockden. *Ormond*. Ed. Mary Chapman. Peterborough, N.H.: Broadview, 1999.

———. "The Man At Home, No. IX" (31 March 1798). *The Rhapsodist and Other Uncollected Writings*. Ed. Harry Warfel. New York: Scholars Facsimiles, 1943.

Brown, Gillian. *The Consent of the Governed*. Cambridge. Mass.: Harvard University Press, 2001.

———. *Domestic Individualism: Imagining Self in Nineteenth-Century America*. Berkeley: University of California Press, 1990.

Brown, Herbert Ross. *The Sentimental Novel in America, 1789–1860*. Durham, N.C.: Duke University Press, 1940.

Brown, William Hill. *The Power of Sympathy*. In *The Power of Sympathy and The Coquette*. New York: Penguin, 1996.

Brückner, Martin. *The Geographic Revolution in Early America: Maps, Literacy, and National Identity*. Chapel Hill: University of North Carolina Press, 2006.

Bryson, Norman. *Vision and Painting: The Logic of the Gaze*. New Haven: Yale University Press, 1983.

Bullock, Stephen. "A Mumper Among the Gentle: Tom Bell, Colonial Confidence Man." *William and Mary Quarterly* 55:2 (1998): 231–58.

Burgett, Bruce. *Sentimental Bodies: Sex, Gender, and Citizenship in the Early Republic*. Princeton, N.J.: Princeton University Press, 1998.

Burmeister, Hermann. *The Black Man: The Comparative Anatomy and Psychology of the African Negro*. Trans. Julius Friedlander and Robert Tomes. New York: William C. Bryant & Co., 1853.

Burroughs, Stephen. *Memoirs of Stephen Burroughs*. 1811; Boston: Northeastern University Press, 1988.

Burton, John. *Lectures on Female Education and Manners*. 1st American edition. New York: [Samuel Campbell], 1794. EVANS.

Bushman, Richard. *The Refinement of America*. New York: Vintage, 1992.

Callow, James. *Kindred Spirits: Knickerbocker Writers and American Artists, 1807–1855*. Chapel Hill: University of North Carolina Press, 1967.

Calvert, Karin. "The Function of Fashion in Eighteenth-Century America." In *Of Consuming Interests: The Style of Life in the Eighteenth Century*. Ed. Cary Carson, Ronald Hoffman, and Peter J. Albert. Charlottesville: University Press of Virginia, 1994. 253–83.

Canaday, Nicholas. "Pierre in His Domestic Circle." *Studies in the Novel* 18 (1986): 395–402.

[Carey, Mathew]. "A Fragment. By M. Carey." *New York Magazine* (Aug. 1796): 401–3. APS.

Carson, Ada, and Herbert Carson. *Royall Tyler*. Boston: Twayne, 1979.

Casper, Scott. *Constructing American Lives: Biography and Culture in Nineteenth-Century America*. Chapel Hill: University of North Carolina Press, 1999.

Castiglia, Christopher. *Interior States: Institutional Consciousness and the Inner Life of Democracy in the Antebellum United States*. Durham, N.C.: Duke University Press, 2008.

[Cento]. *Literary Magazine and American Register* 4:22 (July 1805): 7–8.

Chapman, Mary and Glenn Hendler, eds. *Sentimental Men: Masculinity and the Politics of Affect in American Culture*. Berkeley: University of California Press, 1999.

"Character and Effects of Modern Novels." *Universal Asylum and Columbian Magazine* 9 (1792): 225.

"Character and Effects of Modern Novels." *Weekly Magazine* 1 (1798): 184–85.

Charvat, William. "Melville and the Common Reader." In *The Profession of Authorship, 1800–1870*. Columbus: Ohio State University Press, 1968. 262–82.

Chaves, Joseph: "Polite Mentors and Franklin's 'Exquisite Pleasure': Sociability, Prophylaxis, and Dependence in the *Autobiography*." *Early American Literature* 42:3 (2007): 555–71.

Chesterfield, Philip Dormer Stanhope, Earl of. *Letters Written by the late right Honourable Phillip Dormer Stanhope, Earl of Chesterfield . . .* New York: J. Rivington and H. Gaine, 1775. EVANS.

———. *Principles of Politeness, and of Knowing the World by the late Lord Chesterfield with Additions by the Reverend Dr. John Trusler . . .* Philadelphia: Mathew Carey, 1800.

———. *Lord Chesterfield's Letters to his Godson* (1761–1770). 2nd edition. Oxford: Clarendon Press, 1890.

———. *Letters*. Vol. 2. Ed. Bonamy Dobrée. 6 vols. London: Eyre and Spottiswood, 1932.

———. *Chesterfield's Letters*. Philadelphia: J. B. Lippincott, n.d.

Child, Lydia Maria. *Letters from New York*. 2nd series. 11th edition. New York: C. S. Francis, 1850.

Cima, Gay Gibson. *Early American Women Critics: Performance, Religion, Race*. Cambridge: Cambridge University Press, 2006.

Clark, Christopher. "Comment on the Symposium on Class in the Early Republic." *Journal of the Early Republic* 25 (Winter 2005): 557–64.

Clubbe, John. *Byron, Sully, and the Power of Portraiture*. London: Ashgate, 2005.

Colatrella, Carol. *Literature and Moral Reform: Melville and the Discipline of Reading*. Gainesville: University of Florida Press, 2002.

Colbert, Charles. *A Measure of Perfection: Phrenology and the Fine Arts in America*. Chapel Hill: University of North Carolina Press, 1997.

Columbian Magazine (March 1788): 145.

"Commentator, No. 3." *Philadelphia Repository and Weekly Register* 1:20 (28 March 1801): 4.

"Commentator. No. 11." *Philadelphia Repository and Weekly Register* 1:30 (6 June 1801): 238.

"A Concise Account of Mr. Lavater." *Christian Disciple* [Boston] 2:11 (Nov. 1814): 319–27.

Cooper, James Fenimore. *Precaution*. Boston: Houghton Mifflin, 1876–84.

———. *The Spy*. New York: Penguin, 1997.

———. *The Letters and Journals of James Fenimore Cooper*. Ed. James Franklin Beard. 5 vols. Cambridge, Mass.: Harvard University Press, 1960.

———. *The Pioneers*. New York: Library of America, 1985.

———. *Tales for Fifteen: or, Imagination and Heart.* Gainesville, Fla.: Scholars' Facsimiles and Reprints, 1977.

———. *The American Democrat.* Indianapolis, Ind.: Liberty Classics, 1931.

———. *The Correspondence of James Fenimore Cooper.* Ed. James Fenimore Cooper III. 2 vols. New Haven: Yale University Press, 1922.

———. *A Letter to His Countrymen.* New York: John Wiley, 1834.

———. *Early Critical Essays (1820–22).* Ed. James F. Beard. Gainesville, Fla.: Scholars' Facsimiles and Reprints, 1955.

"Cooper's Last Novel." *United States Magazine and Democratic Review* 21 (Nov. 1847): 438–47.

"Cooper's Works." *United States Magazine and Democratic Review* 25 (July 1849): 51–55.

Coviello, Peter. *Intimacy in America: Dreams of Affiliation in Antebellum America.* Minneapolis: University of Minnesota Press, 2005.

Cowling, Mary. *The Artist as Anthropologist: The Representation of Type and Character in Victorian Art. Cambridge*: Cambridge University Press, 1989.

Coxe, W. "Visit to Lavater." *Massachusetts Magazine* 7:1 (April 1795): 21.

Coyne, Joseph Stirling. *Did You Ever Send Your Wife to Brooklyn? An Original Farce, in One Act. Correctly Printed from the Most Approved Acting Copy. . . . Performed in the Principal Theatres.* New York, Philadelphia: Turner & Fisher, 18+. Proquest Lion. American Drama.

Crain, Caleb. *American Sympathy: Men, Friendship, and Literature in the New Nation.* New Haven: Yale University Press, 2001.

Crain, Patricia. *The Story of A: The Alphabetization of America from* The New England Primer *to* The Scarlet Letter. Stanford: Stanford University Press, 2000.

Craven, Wayne. "Colonial American Portraiture: Iconography and Methodology." In *The Portrait in Eighteenth-Century America.* Ed. Ellen G. Miles. Newark: University of Delaware Press, 1993. 102–15.

———. *Colonial American Portraiture.* Cambridge: Cambridge University Press, 1986.

Crawford, John S. "Physiognomy in Classical and American Portrait Busts." *American Art Journal* 9:1 (1977): 49–60.

Crawford, William. *Remarks on the late Earl of Chesterfield Letters to His Son.* London: T. Cadell and John Sewell, 1776. ECCO.

Creech, James. *Closet Writing, Gay Reading: The Case of Melville's Pierre.* Chicago: University of Chicago Press, 1993.

"Criticism in America." *United States Magazine and Democratic Review* 15 (Sept. 1844): 241–49.

"The Culture of Imagination." *United States Magazine and Democratic Review* 22 (Jan. 1848): 33–45.

Cunningham, Jr., Noble E. *The Image of Thomas Jefferson in the Public Eye: Portraits for the People, 1800–1809.* Charlottesville: University Press of Virginia, 1981.

D.S. "Extract of a Letter from a Lady in Jamaica, to her Friend in Pennsylvania; On Novel Reading." *Universal Asylum and Columbian Magazine* 6 (March 1791): 141–42.

Dain, Bruce. *A Hideous Monster of the Mind: American Race Theory in the Early Republic.* Cambridge, Mass.: Harvard University Press, 2002.

Daniel, Marcus. *Scandal and Civility: Journalism and the Birth of American Democracy.* Oxford: Oxford University Press, 2009.

[D'Argenson, Marquis]. "The Countenance an Indication of the Interior Character. By the Marquis D'Argenson." *American Universal Magazine* 3:5 [Philadelphia] (4 Sept. 1797): 373–75. APS.

Darnell, Donald. *James Fenimore Cooper: Novelist of Manners.* Newark: University of Delaware Press, 1993.

Darwin, Erasmus. *A Plan for the Conduct of Female Education.* Philadelphia: J. Ormond, 1798.

Davidoff, Leonore and Hall, Catherine. *Family Fortunes: Men and Women of the English Middle Class, 1780–1850.* Chicago: University of Chicago Press, 1987.

Davidson, Cathy. *Revolution and the Word.* Oxford: Oxford University Press, 1986.

———. "Photographs of the Dead: Sherman, Daguerre, Hawthorne." *South Atlantic Quarterly* 89:4 (1990): 667–70.

Davies, Kate. *Catherine Macaulay and Mercy Otis Warren: The Revolutionary Atlantic and the Politics of Gender.* Oxford: Oxford University Press, 2005.

Dean, Ann C. "Authorship, Print, and Public in Chesterfield's Letters to His Son." *SEL: Studies in English Literature, 1500–1900* 45:3 (Summer 2005): 691–706.

Dean, Janet. "The Marriage Plot and National Myth in *The Pioneers.*" *Arizona Quarterly* 52:4 (1996): 1–29.

Delaplaine, Joseph. *Prospectus of Delaplaine's National Panzographia: For The Reception of The Portraits of Distinguished Americans.* Philadelphia: W. Brown, 1818.

———. *Repository of the Lives and Portraits of Distinguished American Characters.* Philadelphia, 1815–16.

Delaporte, François. *Anatomy of the Passions.* Trans. Susan Emanuel. Stanford: Stanford University Press, 2008.

Delbanco, Andrew. "Melville in the 80s." *American Literary History* 4 (1992): 709–25.

[De Monde, Horace]. "The Club-Room. By Horace De Monde, Esq. No. II." *The Portico, a Repository of Science and Literature* 1:3 [Baltimore] (March 1816): 234–41. APS.

"A Dialogue." *The Nightingale* 1:19 [Boston] (June 21, 1796): 217–221.

Dickson, Harold. *Arts of the Young Republic: The Age of William Dunlap.* Chapel Hill: University of North Carolina Press, 1968.

———. *John Wesley Jarvis: American Painter, 1780–1840.* New York: New-York Historical Society, 1949.

Diderot, Denis. "In Praise of Richardson." 1761. From *Selected Writings on Art and Literature.* Trans. Geoffrey Bremner. New York: Penguin, 1994.

Dill, Elizabeth. "That Damned Mob of Scribbling Siblings: The American Romance as Anti-Novel in *The Power of Sympathy* and *Pierre.*" *American Literature* 80:4 (2008): 707–38.

Dillingham, William B. *Melville's Later Novels.* Athens: University of Georgia Press, 1986.

Dillon, Elizabeth. *The Gender of Freedom: Fictions of Liberalism and the Literary Public Sphere*. Stanford: Stanford University Press, 2004.

Dimock, Wai-Chee. *Empire for Liberty: Melville and the Poetics of Individualism*. Princeton, N.J.: Princeton University Press, 1989.

———. "*Pierre*: Domestic Confidence Game and The Drama of Knowledge." *Studies in The Novel* 16:4 (1984): 396–409.

Dimock, Wai-Chee, and Michael Gilmore, eds. *Rethinking Class: Literary Studies and Social Formations*. New York: Columbia University Press, 1994.

Ditz, Toby. "Secret Selves, Credible Personas: The Problematics of Trust and Public Display in the Writing of Eighteenth-Century Philadelphia Merchants." In *Possible Pasts: Becoming Colonial in Early America*. Ed. Robert B. St. George. Ithaca, N.Y.: Cornell University Press, 2000. 219–42.

Douglas, Ann. *The Feminization of American Culture*. New York: Knopf, 1977.

Douglass, Frederick. "Pictures and Progress: An Address Delivered in Boston, Massachusetts, on 3 December 1861." In *The Frederick Douglass Papers: Series One: Speeches, Debates, and Interviews*. Ed. John W. Blassingame. 5 vols. New Haven: Yale University Press, 1979.

Dow, William. *Narrating Class in American Fiction*. London: Palgrave, 2009.

Downes, Paul. *Democracy, Revolution, and Monarchism in Early American Literature*. Cambridge: Cambridge University Press, 2002.

"The Dreamer. No. II." *Massachusetts Magazine* 1 (Feb. 1789): 101.

Dryden, Edgar. *Melville's Thematics of Form*. Baltimore: Johns Hopkins University Press, 1968.

———. "The Entangled Text: Melville's *Pierre* and the Problem of Reading." *Boundary 2* 7:3 (1979): 145–73.

———. "The Entangled Text: Melville's *Pierre* and the Problem of Reading." (1979). In *Herman Melville: A Collection of Critical Essays*. Ed. Myra Jehlen. Englewood Cliffs, N.J.: Prentice Hall, 1994, 100–15.

Dunlap, William. *The Father; Or American Shandyism*. New York: Publications of the William Dunlap Society, 1879.

Du Simitière, Pierre. *Thirteen Portraits of American Legislators, Patriots, and Soldiers, who Distinguished Themselves in Rendering Their Country Independent . . . drawn from the life by Du Simitière . . . and engraved by Mr. B. Reading*. London: W. Richardson, 1783.

Duyckinck, Evert. *Cyclopedia of American Literature*. 2 vols. New York: Charles Scribner, 1855.

———. "Introductory Memoir." *Poems Relating to the American Revolution By Philip Freneau*. New York: W. J. Widdleton, 1865.

[Duyckinck, Evert A.] Review of *Mardi*. *The Literary World* 4:115 (14 April 1849): 333–35.

———. Review of *Mardi*. Second Paper. *The Literary World* 4:116 (21 April 1849): 351–53.

———. Review of *Redburn*. *The Literary World* 5:146 (17 Nov. 1849): 418–20.

Dwight, Timothy. *A Sermon Preached at Northampton, on the twenty-eighth of November,*

1781: occasioned by the capture of the British Army, under the command of Earl Corn-
wallis. Dedicated to the subscribers. Hartford, Conn.: Nathaniel Patten, 1781. EVANS
Series 1.

Echoe, Proteus. "Essays, Proteus Echoe." *Emerald, or, Miscellany of Literature, Containing*
Sketches of the Manners, Principles and Amusements of the Age 1:9 [Boston] (19 Dec.
1807): 97.

Edgeworth, Maria. "Letter 'to an American Lady.'" *Port Folio* 16 (1823): 86; reprinted in
Fenimore Cooper: The Critical Heritage. Ed. George Dekker and John P. McWilliams.
London: Routledge, 1973, 67–68.

———. Review of *The Spy. United States Magazine and Literary and Political Repository* 1:1
(Jan. 1823): 92–93.

"The Editor's Shanty." *Anglo-American Magazine* [Toronto] 1 (September 1852): 273.

Elias, Norbert. *The Civilizing Process: The History of Manners and State Formation and Civi-*
lization. Trans. Edmund Jephcott. Oxford: Blackwell, 1994.

Elkins, Stanley, and Eric McKintrick. "The Emergence of Partisan Politics: 'The Republican
Interest.'" *The Age of Federalism: The Early American Republic, 1788–1800.* New York:
Oxford University Press, 1993, 257–303.

Elliott, Emory. *Revolutionary Writers: Literature and Authority in the New Republic, 1720–*
1810. New York: Oxford University Press, 1981.

———. "Art, Religion, and The Problem of Authority in *Pierre.*" In *Ideology and Classic*
American Literature. Ed. Sacvan Bercovitch and Myra Jehlen. Cambridge: Cambridge
University Press, 1986, 337–51.

Ellison, Julie. *Cato's Tears and the Making of Anglo-American Emotion.* Chicago: University
of Chicago Press, 1999.

"English Writers." *Aeronaut* 6:113 (1817): n.p.

Erkkila, Betsy. "Franklin and The Revolutionary Body." *ELH* 67:3 (2000): 717–42.

"An Essay on the Modern Novel." *Port Folio* 2:14 [Philadelphia] (10 April 1802): 106. APS.

"Essays. On Physiognomy." *Lancaster Hive* [Lancaster, Pa.] 2:35 (13 Feb. 1805): 137. APS.

Evans, Dorinda. *The Genius of Gilbert Stuart.* Princeton, N.J.: Princeton University Press,
1999.

———. "Survival and Transformation: The Colonial Portrait in the Federal Era." In *The*
Portrait in Eighteenth-Century America. Ed. Ellen G. Miles. Newark: University of
Delaware Press, 1993, 123–37.

Evelev, John. "The Problem of Theatricality and Political Social Crisis in Post-Revolutionary
America." *Early American Literature* 31 (1996): 74–97.

———. *Tolerable Entertainment: Herman Melville and Professionalism in Antebellum New*
York. Amherst: University of Massachusetts Press, 2006.

"Eugenio." [William Roberts]. *Philadelphia Minerva* 3:146 (18 Nov. 1797): [4]. EAN.

"Eugenio." [William Roberts]. *Philadelphia Repository and Weekly Register* 5:5 (2 Feb. 1805):
35. APS.

"Execution . . ." *National Advocate* [New York] (27 Sept. 1824): col. D. 19C US NEWS.

"Extract." *Philadelphia Minerva* 2:67 (14 May 1796): n.p.

"Extract from a periodical publication, entitled 'Miscellanist,' written in Dublin, by W. P. Carey—P. 337." *American Museum* 5 [Philadelphia] (May 1789): 467–68. SABIN.

"Extract of a Letter from Dr. M-R Albany, 27th Dec. 1778." *Concord Herald* 1:37 (18 Sept. 1790): [4]. EAN.

"Extract of a Letter from Dr. M-R Albany, 27th Dec. 1778." *Cumberland Gazette* (6 Sept. 1790): [1]. EAN.

"Extract of a Letter from Dr. M-R Albany, 27th Dec. 1778." *United States Chronicle* 7:354 (7 Oct. 1790): [1]. EAN.

"Extracted. From The Foundling of Belgrade." *Lady's Miscellany: or, Weekly Visitor, and Entertaining Companion for the Use and Amusement of Both Sexes* 14:18 [New York] (22 Feb. 1812): 273–77. APS.

"Extracts from An Unpublished Tour on the Continent, &c. The Monastery of La Trappe." *Christian Observer, Conducted By Members of the Established Church* 2:6 [Boston] (June 1803): 357. APS.

"Extracts from Mrs. Carter's Letters. Lord Chesterfield's Letters. 1774." *Monthly Anthology and Boston Review* (Oct. 1808): 532–33.

"Extracts from the travels of the Marquis De Chastellux, in this country, lately published in two volumes. State of New-Jersey." *Christian's, Scholar's, and Farmer's Magazine* 1:1 [Elizabeth-town, N.J.] (April–May 1789): 76–78.

Eyal, Yonatan. *The Young American Movement and the Transformation of the Democratic Party, 1828–1861*. Cambridge: Cambridge University Press, 2007.

"Familiar Letters From an Englishman in this Country to His Friend at Home. No II." *Rural Magazine and Literary Evening Fire-Side* 1:2 [Rutland, Vt.] (Feb. 1820): 51–54. APS.

"Familiar Letters on Physiognomy." *Visitor* 1:19 [Richmond, Va.] (2 Dec. 1809): 172. APS.

Fessenden, Thomas Green. "Physiognomy." *New England Farmer, and Horticultural Register* 3:36 [Boston] (1 April 1825): 288. APS.

———. *The Modern Philosopher, or, Terrible Tractoration!: in four cantos*. Philadelphia: Lorenzo Press of E. Bronson, 1806.

Fichtelberg, Joseph. *Critical Fictions: Sentiment and the American Market, 1780–1870*. Athens: University of Georgia Press, 2003.

Fiedler, Leslie. *Love and Death in the American Novel*. New York: Criterion, 1960.

Fielding, Henry. "An Essay on the Knowledge of the Characters of Men" (1743), in vol. 1, *Miscellanies*, 3 vols., from vol. 11 of *The Works of Henry Fielding*. New York: Charles Scribner's Sons, 1899.

Fisher, Philip. "Democratic Social Space: Whitman, Melville, and the Promise of American Transparency." *Representations* 24 (Fall 1988): 60–101.

Fiske, Nathan. *The Moral Monitor*. Worcester: I. Thomas, 1801.

Flavell, Kay. "Mapping Faces: National Physiognomies as Cultural Prediction." *Eighteenth-Century Life* 18 (1994–95): 8–22.

Fliegelman, Jay. *Declaring Independence: Jefferson, Natural Language, and the Culture of Performance*. Stanford: Stanford University Press, 1993.

Fluck, Winfried. "Novels of Transition: From Sentimental Novel to Domestic Novel." In

The Construction and Contestation of American Cultures and Identities in the Early National Period. Ed. Udo Hebel. Heidelberg, Germany: Carl Winter Universitätsverlag, 1999. 97–117.

———. "Reading Early American Fiction." In *A Companion to the Literatures of Colonial America.* Ed. Susan Castillo, and Ivy Schweitzer. Malden, Mass.: Blackwell, 2005. 566–86.

"The Following . . ." *New York Daily Gazette* 172 (16 July 1789): 686. EAN.

"The Following Animated Portrait of General Washington is just published by the masterly hand of the Marquis De Chastelleux . . ." *Daily Advertiser* [New York] 3:630 (2 March 1787): [2]. EAN.

"The Following Animated Portrait of General Washington is just published by the masterly hand of the Marquis De Chastelleux . . ." *Massachusetts Gazette* 6:313 (16 March 1787): [3]. EAN.

"The Following Little Narrative Savours so strongly of the romantic, that we should hesitate in believing it, had we not been told it by a Gentleman who witnessed part of the transaction." *Raleigh Register, and North-Carolina Gazette,* 941 [Raleigh, N.C.] (3 Oct. 1817): col B. 19C US NEWS.

"The following little Narrative savours so strongly of the romantic, that we should hesitate in believing it, had we not been told it by a Gentleman who witnessed part of the transaction (News) Raleigh Reg" *Daily National Intelligencer* 1482 (Washington, DC) (8 October 1817): col B. 19C US NEWS.

"The Following Portrait of General Washington . . ." *Newport Herald* 4:184 [Newport, R.I.] (2 Sept. 1790): [2]. EAN.

"The Folly of Statues." *Time Piece* [New York] (15 Nov. 1797): n. p.

Fortune, Brandon. "Charles Willson Peale's Portrait Gallery: Persuasion and the Plain Style." *Word and Image* 6:4 (1990): 308–24.

Foster, Hannah. *The Boarding School; or Lessons of a Preceptress to her Pupils: Consisting of Information, Instruction, and Advice, circulated to Improve the Manners, and Form the Character of Young Ladies[. . .]* Boston: I. Thomas & E. T. Andrews, 1798.

———. *The Coquette.* New York: Penguin, 1996.

Foucault, Michel. *Discipline and Punish: The Birth of the Prison.* Trans. Alan Sheridan. 1975. New York: Vintage, 1979.

[Fowler, Lorenzo]. "Phrenological Developments and Character of Stephen Burroughs." *American Phrenological Journal and Miscellany* 3:2 (1 Nov. 1840): 86–89. APS.

Franklin, Benjamin. *The Autobiography of Benjamin Franklin.* Ed. Kenneth Silverman. New York: Penguin, 1986.

———. *Autobiography of Benjamin Franklin.* Ed. John Bigelow. 4 vols. Illustrated by Joseph M. P. and Emily Price. 1868; Philadelphia: J. B. Lippincott, 1887.

Franklin, Wayne. *The New World of James Fenimore Cooper.* Chicago: University of Chicago Press, 1982.

Freeman, Joanne B. *Affairs of Honor: National Politics in the New Republic.* New Haven: Yale University Press, 2001.

Freneau, Philip. "The Picture Gallery." *Miscellaneous Works*. Ed. Lewis Leary. 1788. Delmar, N.Y.: Scholars' Facsimiles & Reprints, 1975.

Freund, Gisèle. *Photography and Society*. London: Gordon Fraser, 1980.

"From the Charleston Courier. Slander." *Eastern Argus* 2:69 (28 Dec. 1804): [4]. EAN.

"From the State of Penn. Original Anecdote." *Aurora General Advertiser* [Philadelphia] (27 Jan. 1824): col. E. 19C USNEWS.

Frost, Linda. "The Body Politic in Tabitha Tenney's *Female Quixotism*." *EAL* 32:2 (Sept. 1997): 113–34.

Fuseli, Henry. "Lecture IV: Invention." *Lectures on Painting by the Royal Academicians: Barry, Opie, and Fuseli*. Ed. Ralph N. Wornum. London: Henry Bohn, 1848.

Gardiner, W. H. [Review of *The Spy*] *North American Review* 15 (July 1822). In *Fenimore Cooper, The Critical Heritage*. Ed. George Dekker and John P. McWilliams. London: Routledge, 1973.

Gardner, Jared. *Master Plots: Race and the Founding of American Literature, 1787–1845*. Baltimore: Johns Hopkins University Press, 1998.

Gartman, David. "Culture as Class Symbolization or Mass Reification? A Critique of Bourdieu's *Distinction*." *American Journal of Sociology* 97:2 (Sept. 1991): 421–46.

Geary, Susan. "The Domestic Novel as a Commercial Commodity: Making a Best Seller in the 1850s." *Papers of the Bibliographic Society of America* 70 (1976): 365–93.

Gerdts, William. "Henry Inman: Genre Painter." *American Art Journal* (1977): 26–49.

Geryn. "Adventures of a Rambler . . . No. I." *American Monthly Magazine* 1:5 [Philadelphia] (May 1824): 426–34. APS.

Giles, Paul. *Virtual Americas: Transnational Fictions and the Transatlantic Imaginary*. Durham, N.C.: Duke University Press, 2002.

Gilmore, Michael T. "The Literature of the Revolutionary and Early National Periods." In *The Cambridge History of American Literature*, vol. 1. Ed. Sacvan Bercovitch. Cambridge: Cambridge University Press, 1994. 539–693.

———. "Eighteenth-Century Oppositional Ideology and Hugh Henry Brackenridge's *Modern Chivalry*." *Early American Literature* 13 (1978): 181–92.

———. "James Fenimore Cooper." in *The Cambridge History of American Literature*. Ed. Sacvan Bercovitch, vol. 1. Cambridge: Cambridge University Press, 1994. 676–693.

"The Gleaner: No. II." *Literary Magazine and American Register* 5:32 (May 1806): 379.

[Godwin, William]. "Article 3—No Title." *Analectic Magazine* 12 [Philadelphia] (Aug. 1818): 128. APS.

———. "Course of Study." *Weekly Visitor and Ladies' Museum* 5:16 [New York] (17 Aug. 1822): 245. APS.

Gombrich, E. H. "The Mask and The Face: The Perception of Physiognomic Likeness in Life and in Art." In *Art, Perception, and Reality*. Baltimore: Johns Hopkins University Press, 1972.

"The Gossip. No. XIII." *Boston Weekly Magazine* 1:13 (22 Jan. 1803): 53.

Gottesman, Rita S. *The Arts and Crafts in New York, 1777–99: Advertisements and News*

Items from New York City Newspapers. Vol. 81. New York: New-York Historical Society, 1954.

———. *The Arts and Crafts in New York, 1800–1804: Advertisements and News Items from New York City Newspapers.* Vol. 82. New York: New-York Historical Society, 1965.

Goudie, Sean. *Creole America: The West Indies and the Formation of Literature and Culture in the New Republic.* Philadelphia: University of Pennsylvania Press, 2006.

Gould, Philip. *Barbaric Traffic: Commerce and Antislavery in the Eighteenth-Century Atlantic World.* Cambridge, Mass.: Harvard University Press, 2003.

Gould, Stephen Jay. *The Mismeasure of Man.* New York: Norton, 1996.

Grabo, Norman. *The Coincidental Art of Charles Brockden Brown.* Chapel Hill: University of North Carolina Press, 1981.

Graham, John. "Lavater in England." *Journal of the History of Ideas* 22:4 (Oct. –Dec. 1961): 561–72.

———. "Character Description and Meaning in the Romantic Novel." *Studies in Romanticism* 5 (1966): 208–18.

———. *Lavater's Essays on Physiognomy: A Study in the History of Ideas.* Bern: Peter Lang, 1979.

Grasso, Christopher. *A Speaking Aristocracy: Transforming Public Discourse in Eighteenth-Century Connecticut.* Chapel Hill: University of North Carolina Press, 1999.

Grave, S. A. *The Scottish Philosophy of Common Sense.* Oxford: Clarendon Press, 1960.

Gray, Richard T. *About Face: Physiognomic Thought from Lavater to Auschwitz.* Detroit: Wayne State Press, 2004.

Greenspan, Ezra. "Pioneering American Authorship: James Fenimore Cooper in the 1820s." In *The Profession of Authorship: Essays in Honor of Matthew J. Bruccoli.* Ed. Richard Layman. Columbia: University of South Carolina Press, 1996. 106–120.

Griswold, Rufus. *The Prose Writers of America.* Philadelphia: Carey and Hart, 1847.

[Griswold, Rufus]. *International Magazine of Literature, Art, and Science* 3:1 (April 1851): 1.

[Grito]. "Spirit of Magazines, &c. On the Danger of confounding Moral with Personal Deformity." *Analectic Magazine* 5 [Philadelphia] (Jan. 1815): 60+. APS.

Grossman, James. *James Fenimore Cooper.* New York: W. Sloan Associates, 1949.

The Gubernatocial Collection, a Farce. As Acted at C------t-H------l. Which Point Out the Variety of Characters That Have Arisen in the Political Uproar, Since the Confusion of Distinctions. Together with Other Scenes for the Amusement of the Curious. Newport, R.I.: n. p., 1779.

Guillory, John. "Bourdieu's Refusal." *MLQ* 58:4 (Dec. 1997): 367–98.

Gulick, Sidney. *A Chesterfield Bibliography to 1800.* 2nd ed. Charlottesville: University Press of Virginia, 1979.

Gustafson, Sandra M. *Eloquence Is Power: Oratory and Performance in Early America.* Chapel Hill: University of North Carolina Press, 2000.

———. "Natty in the 1820s: Creole Subjects and Democratic Aesthetics in the Early Leatherstocking Tales." In *Creole Subjects* in the Colonial Americas, Empires, Texts, Identities. Ed. Ralph Bauer and José Mazzoti. Chapel Hill: University of North Carolina Press, 2008. 465–90.

Habermas, Jürgen. *The Structural Transformation of the Public Sphere.* Trans. Thomas Burger. 1962. Cambridge, Mass.: MIT Press, 1996.

Hackel, Heidi and Catherine E. Kelly, eds. *Reading Women: Literacy, Authorship, and Culture in the Atlantic World, 1500–1800.* Philadelphia: University of Pennsylvania Press, 2007.

Haltunnen, Karen. *Confidence Men and Painted Women: A Study of Middle-Class Culture in America, 1830–1870.* New Haven: Yale University Press, 1982.

The Hapless Orphan; or, Innocent victim of revenge. A novel, founded on incidents in real life. In a series of letters from Caroline Francis to Maria B———. . . . By an American lady. Boston: Belknap and Hall, 1793.

[Harlan, Richard]. "Art. I. Remarks on the Variety of Complexion and National Peculiarity of Feature. By Richard Harlan, M. D. Lecturer on Anatomy, Professor of Comparative Anatomy of the Philadelphia Museum." *American Medical Recorder* 5:4 [Philadelphia] (Oct. 1822): 591–605. APS.

Harris, Marc L. "What Politeness Demanded: Ethnic Omission in Franklin's *Autobiography.*" *Pennsylvania History* 61:3 (1994): 288–317.

Harris, Sharon. "Hannah Webster Foster's *The Coquette*: Critiquing Franklin's America." In *Redefining the Political Novel: American Women Writers, 1797–1901.* Ed. Sharon M. Harris. Knoxville: University of Tennessee Press, 1995. 1–22.

———. "Lost Boundaries: The Use of the Carnivalesque in Tabitha Tenney's *Female Quixotism.*" In *Speaking the Other Self: American Women Writers.* Ed. Jeanne Reesman. Athens: University of Georgia Press, 1997. 213–28.

Harris, Thaddeus. Entry for "Physiognomy." *The Minor Encyclopedia or Cabinet of General Knowledge.* Ed. Thaddeus Harris. 4 vols. Boston: West and Greenleaf, 1803. 4: 67–72.

Hartley, Lucy. *Physiognomy and the Meaning of Expression in Nineteenth-Century Culture.* Cambridge: Cambridge University Press, 2001.

"Harvey Birch and The Skinners." *Columbian Ladies' and Gentleman's Magazine* 7 (Jan. 1847): 30.

Hasting, Sarah Anderson. *Poems on different subjects . . .* Lancaster [Pa.]: William Dickson, 1808.

Hastings, George. "How Cooper Became a Novelist." *American Literature* 12:1 (1940): 20–51.

Hawthorne, Nathaniel. *The House of the Seven Gables.* Ed. Robert Levine. New York: W. W. Norton & Co., 2006.

Hemphill, C. Dallett. *Bowing to Necessities: A History of Manners in America, 1620–1860.* Oxford: Oxford University Press, 1999.

Hetherington, Hugh. *Melville's Reviewers: British and American, 1846–1891.* Chapel Hill: University of North Carolina Press, 1961.

Higgins, Brian. *Herman Melville: An Annotated Bibliography.* Boston: Twayne, 1979.

———. "Reading *Pierre.*" In *A Companion to Melville Studies.* Ed. John Bryant. New York: Greenwood Press, 1986. 211–39.

Higgins, Brian and Hershel Parker. "The Flawed Grandeur of Melville's *Pierre.*" In *New Perspectives on Melville.* Ed. Faith Pullin. Edinburgh: Edinburgh University Press, 1978. 162–96.

Higgins, Brian and Hershel Parker, eds. *Critical Essays on Herman Melville's Pierre; or The Ambiguities*. Boston: G. K. Hall, 1983.

———. *Herman Melville: The Contemporary Reviews*. Cambridge: Cambridge University Press, 1995.

Hillway, Tyrus. "Melville's Use of Two Pseudo-Sciences." *Modern Language Notes* 64:3 (1949): 145–50.

Hinds, Elizabeth. *Private Property: Charles Brockden Brown's Gendered Economics of Virtue*. Newark: University of Delaware Press, 1997.

"Hints Addressed to Both Sexes." *The Massachusetts Magazine* 5:4 (April 1793): 231. APS.

Hitchcock, Enos. *Memoirs of the Bloomsgrove Family*. 2 vols. Boston: Thomas & Andrews, 1790.

Hoffa, William R. "The Language of Rogues and Fools in Brackenridge's *Modern Chivalry*." *Studies in the Novel* 12 (1980): 289–300.

Homem, Rui Carvalho and Maria de Fátima Lambert, eds. *Writing and Seeing: Essays on Word and Image*. New York: Rodopi, 2006.

"Hon. Elias Boudinot." *Baltimore Patriot* 19:110 (11 May 1822): 2. EAN.

Hood, Graham. "Soul or Style? Questions about Early American Portraits." In *The Portrait in Eighteenth-Century America*. Ed. Ellen G. Miles. Newark: University of Delaware Press, 1993. 84–91.

Hopkinson, Francis. *The Miscellaneous Essays and Occasional Writings of Francis Hopkinson*. Vol. 2. Philadelphia: T. Dobson, 1792.

"Horrible Crime." *Ladies Port Folio* 1:22 [Boston] (27 May 1820): 170–71. APS.

"Hours of Leisure, Or Essays, In the Manner of Goldsmith." *Port Folio* 4:4 [Philadelphia] (25 July 1807): 56. APS.

House, Kay Seymour. *Cooper's Americans*. Columbus: Ohio State University Press, 1965.

Hoy, David Couzens. "Identifying Bodies and Bodily Identification. Critical Resistance: Foucault and Bourdieu." In *Perspectives on Embodiment: The Intersections of Nature and Culture*. Ed. Honi Fern Haber and Gail Weiss. New York: Routledge, 1999. 3–21.

Humboldt, Baron de. "General Considerations of the Extent and Physical Aspect of the Kingdom of New Spain, from Baron De Humboldt's Political Essay on the Kingdom of New Spain." In *The American Register, or, General Repository of History, Politics and Science*, vol. 7. Philadelphia: C. & A. Conrad, 1811. 278.

Humphrey, S. D. *American Handbook of the Daguerreotype*. 5th ed. New York: S. D. Humphrey, 1858.

Hunt, Margaret R. *The Middling Sort of People: Commerce, Gender, and the Family in England, 1680–1870*. Berkeley: University of California Press, 1996.

Ingrassia, Catherine. *Authorship, Commerce, and Gender in Early Eighteenth-Century England: A Culture of Paper Credit*. Cambridge: Cambridge University Press, 1998.

International Magazine of Literature, Art, and Science 3:1 (April 1851): 1.

"Introduction." *The United States Magazine* 1 [Philadelphia] (Jan. 1779): 10.

Iser, Wolfgang. *The Act of Reading: A Theory of Aesthetic Response*. Baltimore: Johns Hopkins University Press, 1978.

[J.] "Commentator, No. 3." *Philadelphia Repository and Weekly Register* 1:20 (28 March 1801): 4. APS.

Jackson, Emily. *Silhouettes: Notes and Dictionary*. New York: Charles Scribner and Sons, 1938.

"James F. Cooper." *American Magazine* 2 (Feb. 1836): 231.

Jay, Martin. *Downcast Eyes: The Denigration of Vision in Twentieth-Century French Thought*. Berkeley: University of California Press, 1993.

Jefferson, Thomas. Letter to John Adams. 28 October 1813. In *Thomas Jefferson: Writings*. New York: Library of America, 1984.

Jehlen, Myra. *American Incarnation: The Individual, the Nation, and the Continent*. Cambridge, Mass.: Harvard University Press, 1986.

Jones, Howard Mumford. "Prose and Pictures: James Fenimore Cooper." *Tulane Studies in English* 3 (1952): 133–54.

Judson, Barbara. "The Politics of Medusa: Shelley's Physiognomy of Revolution." *ELH* 68:1 (2001): 135–54.

Juengel, Scott. "Countenancing History: Mary Wollstonecraft, Samuel Stanhope Smith, and Enlightenment Racial Science." *ELH* 68:4 (2001): 897–927.

Juvenile Mirror and Teacher's Manual. New York: Smith and Forman, 1812.

Karcher, Carolyn. *Shadow over the Promised Land: Slavery, Race and Violence in Melville's America*. Baton Rouge: Louisiana State University Press, 1979.

Kasson, John F. *Rudeness and Civility: Manners in Nineteenth-Century Urban America*. New York: Hill and Wang, 1990.

Kelley, Mary. *Learning to Stand and Speak: Women, Education, and Public Life in America's Republic*. Chapel Hill: University of North Carolina Press, 2006.

———. "Crafting Subjectivities: Women, Reading, and Self-Imagining." In *Reading Women: Literacy, Authorship, and Culture in the Atlantic World, 1500–1800*. Ed. Heidi Brayman Hackel and Catherine E. Kelly. Philadelphia: University of Pennsylvania Press, 2008. 55–72.

Kelley, Wyn. *Melville's City: Literary and Urban Form in Nineteenth-Century New York*. New York: Cambridge University Press, 1996.

———. "*Pierre's* Domestic Ambiguities." In *The Cambridge Companion to Herman Melville*. Ed. Robert S. Levine. Cambridge: Cambridge University Press, 1998. 91–113.

Kelly, Catherine E. "Reading and the Problem of Accomplishment." In *Reading Women: Literacy, Authorship, and Culture in the Atlantic World, 1500–1800*. Ed. Heidi Brayman Hackel and Catherine E. Kelly. Philadelphia: University of Pennsylvania Press, 2008. 124–44.

Kennedy, Jennifer T. "Death Effects: Revisiting the Conceit of Franklin's *Memoir*." *EAL* 36:2 (2001): 201–34.

Kierner, Cynthia. *The Contrast: Manners, Morals, and Authority in the Early American Republic*. New York: New York University Press, 2007.

Klein, Lawrence. *Shaftesbury and the Culture of Politeness: Moral Discourse and Cultural Politics in Early Eighteenth-Century England*. Cambridge: Cambridge University Press, 1994.

———. "Politeness for Plebes: Consumption and Social Identity in Early Eighteenth-Century England." In *The Consumption of Culture, 1600–1800, Image, Object, Text*. Ed. Ann Bermingham and John Brewer. London: Routledge, 1995. 362–82.

Knott, Sarah. *Sensibility and the American Revolution*. Chapel Hill: University of North Carolina Press, 2009.

Knox, Katharine McCook. *The Sharples: Their Portraits of George Washington and His Contemporaries*. New York: Da Capo Press, 1972.

Korobkin, Laura. "'Can Your Volatile Daughter Ever Acquire Your Wisdom?' Luxury and False Ideals in *The Coquette*." *EAL* 41:1 (2006): 79–108.

Krause, Sidney. "*Ormond*: How Rapidly and How Well 'Composed, Arranged, and Delivered.'" *EAL* 13 (1979): 238–49.

Lady's Pocket Library. Philadelphia: M. Carey, 1792.

Lairesse, Gérard de. "Of Portraiture." In *The Art of Painting in All Its Branches*. Trans. John Frederick Fritsch. London: S. Vandebergh, 1778.

Lamoine, Georges. "Lord Chesterfield's Letters as Conduct-Books." In *The Crisis of Courtesy: Studies in the Conduct-Book in Britain, 1600–1900*. Ed. Jacques Carré. Leiden: Brill, 1994. 105–17.

Lang, Amy. *The Syntax of Class: Writing Inequality in Nineteenth-Century America*. Princeton, N.J.: Princeton University Press, 2003.

Langford, Paul. *Public Life and the Propertied Englishman, 1689–1798*. Oxford: Clarendon Press, 1991.

Lavater, Johann Caspar. *Essays on Physiognomy*. Trans. Henry Hunter. Engravings by Thomas Holloway. 3 vols. in 5 vols. London: John Murray et al., 1789–1798.

———. *Essai sur la physiognomie, destiné à faire connaitre l'homme et le faire aimer*. Trans. M. E. de La Fité, A. B. Caillard, et Henri Refner. 4 vols. The Hague, 1781.

———. "Of the Influence of Countenance on Countenance. [By Lavater.]" *New York Magazine or Literary Repository* n.s. 1.5 (May 1796): 251–52.

———. "Of the Influence of Countenance on Countenance. [By Lavater.]" *Literary Museum* 1 [Philadelphia] (April 1797): 200–2.

———. *The Pocket Lavater or, The Science of Physiognomy*. New York: Van Winkle & Riley, 1817.

"Lavater." *Lady's Monitor* [New York] 1:13 (14 Nov. 1801): 101–2. APS.

Laws of the State of New Jersey. New Brunswick, N. J.: Abraham Blauvelt, 1800.

Lawson-Peebles, Robert. "Property, Marriage, Women, and Fenimore Cooper's First Fictions." In *James Fenimore Cooper: New Literary and Historical Contexts*. Ed. W. M. Verhoeven. Amsterdam: Rodopi, 1993. 47–70.

Leander. "On Modern Novels." *Massachusetts Magazine* 3 (1791): 662–64.

Leitch, Vincent. *Theory Matters*. New York: Routledge, 2003.

Levine, Robert. "Villainy and the Fear of Conspiracy in Charles Brockden Brown's *Ormond*." *EAL* 15 (1980): 124–40.

Lewis, Jan. "The Republican Wife: Virtue and Seduction in the Early Republic." *William and Mary Quarterly* 44 (1987): 689–721.

Lewis, Paul. "Charles Brockden Brown and the Gendered Canon of Early American Fiction." *EAL* 31:2 (1996): 167–88.

Lipton, Leah. "William Dunlap, Samuel F. B. Morse, John Wesley Jarvis, and Chester Harding." *American Art Journal* 13:3 (1981): 34–50.

"Literary Article." *Salem Gazette* 44 (2 Nov. 1790): 1.

"Literary Intelligence. *The Pioneers.*" *Port Folio* 15 5th ser. (June 1823): 520.

"Literary Prospects of 1845." *American Whig Review* 1 (Feb. 1845): 146–51.

"Literature and Criticism." *Monthly Review and Literary Miscellany of the United States* [Charleston, S.C.] 1:1 (1806): 1–11.

Litvak, Joseph. *Strange Gourmets: Sophistication, Theory, and the Novel*. Durham, N.C.: Duke University Press, 1997.

"Living Literary Characters, No. IV. James Fenimore Cooper." *New Monthly Magazine* 31 (May 1831): 355–62.

"Living Pictures of American Notabilities, Literary and Scientific. No. VIII. Sketched by Motley Manners, Esq. J. Fenimore Cooper." *Holden's Dollar Magazine* 3:2 (Feb. 1849): 90.

Locke, John. *Some Thoughts Concerning Education* (1695). In Volume 9 of *The Works of John Locke*. 10 vols. London: Thomas Tegg, 1832. Reprinted in Scientia Verlag Aalen, 1963.

Lockridge, Kenneth. "Colonial Self-Fashioning: Paradoxes and Pathologies in the Construction of Genteel Identity in Eighteenth-Century America." In *Through a Glass Darkly: Reflections on Personal Identity in Early America*. Ed. Ronald Hoffman, Mechal Sobel, and Fredrika J. Teute. Chapel Hill: University of North Carolina Press, 1997. 274–342.

Loesberg, Jonathan. "Bourdieu and the Sociology of Aesthetics." *ELH* 60 (1993): 1033–56.

Looby, Christopher. *Voicing America: Language, Literary Form, and the Origins of the United States*. Chicago: University of Chicago Press, 1995.

Loshe, Lillian. *The Early American Novel*. New York: Columbia University Press, 1907.

Loughran, Trish. *The Republic in Print: Print Culture in the Age of U.S. Nation Building, 1770–1870*. New York: Columbia University Press, 2007.

Lovell, Margaretta. "Reading Eighteenth-Century American Family Portraits." *Winterthur Portfolio* 22:4 (1987): 243–64.

———. "Painters and Their Customers: Aspects of Art and Money in Eighteenth-Century America." In *Of Consuming Interests: The Style of Life in the Eighteenth Century*. Ed. Cary Carson, Ronald Hoffman, and Pete Alber. Charlottesville: University Press of Virginia, 1994. 284–305.

———. *Art in a Season of Revolution*. Philadelphia: University of Pennsylvania Press, 2005.

Lynch, Deidre. *The Economy of Character: Novels, Market Culture, and The Business of Inner Meaning*. Chicago: University of Chicago Press, 1998.

Lyon, John B. " 'The Science of Sciences': Replication and Reproduction in Lavater's Physiognomics." *Eighteenth-Century Studies* 40:2 (2007): 257–77.

M. "Physiognomy." *The Villager, A Literary Paper* 1:2 (April 1819): 20–21.

"The Man of the World." *New York Weekly Museum* 2:30 (27 Nov. 1813): n.p. APS.

Manvill, P. D. *Lucinda, or, The Mountain Mourner: being recent facts, in a series of letters, from Mrs. Manvill, in the state of New-York, to her sister in Pennsylvania*, 3rd ed., with additions. Ballston Spa [N.Y.]: J. Comstock, 1817. SABIN.

Marckwardt, Albert H. "The Chronology of the Bread and Cheese Club." *American Literature* 6 (1935): 389–99.

Marmontel, Jean-Francois. *Memoirs of Marmontel . . .* Philadelphia: Samuel Bradford, 1807.

Marsh, Philip, Ed. *The Prose of Philip Freneau*. New Brunswick, N.J.: Scarecrow Press, 1955.

———. *Freneau's Published Prose: A Bibliography*. Metuchen, N.J.: Scarecrow Press, 1970.

Marshall, David. *The Surprising Power of Sympathy*. Chicago: University of Chicago Press, 1988.

Marshall, Gordon M. "The Golden Age of Illustrated Biographies: Three Case Studies." *American Portrait Prints: Proceedings of the Tenth Annual American Print Conference* (1979): 29–83.

McCoubrey, John W. *American Art, 1700–1960*. Englewood Cliffs, N.J.: Prentice-Hall, 1965.

McGill, Meredith L. *American Literature and the Culture of Reprinting, 1834–1853*. Philadelphia: University of Pennsylvania Press, 2003.

McMaster, Juliet. *The Index of the Mind: Physiognomy in the Novel*. Lethbridge, Alberta: University of Lethbridge Press, 1990.

McWilliams, John. *Political Justice in a Republic: James Fenimore Cooper's America*. Berkeley: University of California Press, 1972.

———. *Hawthorne, Melville, and the American Character: A Looking Glass Business*. New York: Cambridge University Press, 1985.

Meijer, Miriam. *Race and Aesthetics in the Anthropology of Petrus Camper*. Amsterdam: Rodopi, 1999.

Meister, Jan C., Tom Kindt, and Wilhelm Schernus, eds. *Narratology Beyond Literary Criticism: Mediality and Disciplinarity*. New York: Walter de Gruyter, 2005.

"Melancholy Effects of Seduction." *Massachusetts Magazine* 7 (Nov. 1795): 467–73.

Melmoth, Courtney. [Samuel Pratt]. *The Pupil of Pleasure: A New Edition, Corrected and Improved*. Boston: John M'Dougall, 1780.

Melville, Herman. *Pierre*. New York: Penguin, 1996.

———. Letter to Nathaniel Hawthorne. 1 June 1851. In *Correspondence*. Ed. Lynn Horth. Evanston, Ill.: Northwestern University Press, 1993.

———. *The Letters of Herman Melville*. Ed. Merrell Davis and William Gilman. New Haven: Yale University Press, 1960.

———. *Journals. Vol. 15. The Writings of Herman Melville*. Ed. Howard C. Horsford and Lynn Horth. Evanston, Ill.: Northwestern University Press, 1989.

Memes, John S. *History of Sculpture, Painting, and Architecture*. Boston: Clapp and Broaders, 1834.

"Men of the World." *The Parlour Companion* 1:37 (13 Sept. 1817): 146–47.

Mercier, Louis-Sébastien. *The Night Cap . . .* Philadelphia: W. Spotswood, 1788.

Merish, Lori. *Sentimental Materialism: Gender, Commodity Culture, and Nineteenth-Century American Literature.* Durham: Duke University Press, 2000.

Middleton, Simon and Billy G. Smith. "Introduction." *Class Matters: Early North America and the Atlantic World.* Ed. Simon Middleton and Billy G. Smith. Philadelphia: University of Pennsylvania Press, 2008.

———. "Guest Editor's Introduction: Class Analysis in Early America and the Atlantic World: Foundations and Future." *Labor* 1:4 (Winter 2004): 7–15.

Milder, Robert. "Melville's Intentions in *Pierre.*" *Studies in the Novel* 6 (1974): 186–99.

Mihm, Stephen. *A Nation of Counterfeiters: Capitalists, Con Men, and the Making of the United States.* Cambridge, Mass.: Harvard University Press, 2007.

Miles, Ellen G. *Saint-Mémin and the Neo-Classical Profile Portrait in America.* Washington, D.C.: Smithsonian Institution Press, 1994.

———. "Saint-Mémin's Portraits of American Indians, 1804–1807." *American Art Journal* 20:4 (1988): 3–33.

———. "Fame and the Public Self in American Portraiture, 1725–1865." *A Brush with History: Painting from the National Portrait Gallery.* Washington, D.C.: National Portrait Gallery, 2001.

———. "'Memorials of Great and Good Men Who Were My Friends': Portraits in the Life of Oliver Wolcott, Jr." *Proceedings of The American Antiquarian Society* 107 Pt. 1 (1998): 105–59.

———. "1803—The Year of the Physiognotrace." In *Painting and Portrait Making in the American Northeast.* Ed. Peter Benes. Boston: Boston University Press, 1995. 118–38.

Miles, Ellen G., ed. *The Portrait in Eighteenth-Century America.* Newark: University of Delaware Press, 1993.

Miles, Robert. "'Tranced Griefs': Melville's *Pierre* and the Origins of the Gothic." *ELH* 66:1 (1999): 157–78.

Miller, Lillian. *In Pursuit of Fame: Rembrandt Peale, 1778–1860.* Washington, D.C.: National Portrait Gallery, 1992.

Miller, Perry and Thomas Johnson, eds. *The Puritans.* New York: Harper, 1938.

Miller, Samuel. *A Brief Retrospect of the Eighteenth Century.* New York: T. and J. Swords, 1803.

"Miscellanies in Prose and Verse. By Mrs. Chapone." *Pennsylvania Magazine* 1 (June 1775): 276.

"Miscellanist." *Herald of Freedom* 2:33 [Boston] (7 July 1789): [129]. NEWS.

"Miscellany." *Mirrour* 4:202 [Concord, N.H.] (6 Sept. 1796): [4]. EAN.

"Miscellany." *Vermont Gazette* 8:16 (13 Sept. 1790): [1]. EAN.

"Miscellany. For the Mirror of Taste. On Novel and Novel Reading." *Mirror of Taste and Dramatic Censor* 3:2 (Feb. 1811): 86–94. APS.

"Miscellany. Portrait of Burr." *Port Folio* 3:20 [Philadelphia] (16 May 1807): 314. APS.

"Miscellany. Slander." *Farmer's Cabinet* 2:45 (11 Sept. 1804): [1]. EAN.

Mitchell, W. J. T. *Picture Theory*. Chicago: University of Chicago Press, 1993.

———. *Iconology: Image, Text, Ideology*. Chicago: University of Chicago Press, 1986.

———. *What Do Pictures Want?* Chicago: University of Chicago Press, 2005.

[Musaeus]. "Musaeus's Physiognomical Journal; Chapter IV. St. Pancras's Day. A Dialogue." *Literary Mirror* 1:8 [Portsmouth] 9 (April 1808): 29–30. APS.

Moi, Toril. "The Challenge of the Particular Case: Bourdieu's Sociology of Culture and Literary Criticism." *MLQ* 58:4 (1997): 497–508.

Moore, Richard S. *That Cunning Alphabet: Melville's Aesthetics of Nature*. Amsterdam: Rodopi, 1982.

Mulford, Carla, ed. Introduction to *William Hill Brown. The Power of Sympathy. Hannah Webster Foster. The Coquette*. New York: Penguin, 1996.

Murray, Henry A. Introduction to the Hendricks House edition of *Pierre*. New York: Farrar Straus, 1949.

Murray, Judith Sargent. *The Story of Margaretta* in *Selected Writings of Judith Sargent Murray*. Ed. Sharon Harris. New York: Oxford University Press, 1995.

Nance, William L. "Satiric Elements in Brackenridge's *Modern Chivalry*." *Texas Studies in Language and Literature* 9 (1967): 381–89.

"Narrative of Mrs. Dholson, a Widow Lady, as related by herself. J F." *New York Magazine, or Literary Repository* (Nov. 1797): 600. APS.

"Nationality in Literature." *Literary World* 5:127 (7 July 1849): 11–12.

"Nationality in Literature." *North American Review* (July 1849). Reprinted in *Literary World* 5:127 (7 July 1849): 11–12.

Nelson, Carl. "A Just Reading of Charles Brockden Brown's *Ormond*." *EAL* 8 (1973): 163–78.

Nelson, Dana. *The Word in Black and White: Reading Race in American Literature 1638–1863*. Oxford: Oxford University Press, 1993.

———. *National Manhood: Capitalist Citizenship and the Imagined Fraternity of White Men*. Durham, N.C.: Duke University Press, 1998.

———. "Cooper's Leatherstocking Conversations: Identity, Friendship, and Democracy in the New Nation." In *A Historical Guide to James Fenimore Cooper*. Ed. Leland Person. Oxford: Oxford University Press, 2007. 123–54.

Nevius, Blake. *Cooper's Landscapes: An Essay on the Picturesque Vision*. Berkeley: University of California Press, 1976.

Newlin, Claude. *The Life and Writings of Hugh Henry Brackenridge*. 1932. Mamaroneck, N.Y.: Paul P. Appel, 1971.

Newman, Simon P. "Theorizing Class in Glasgow and the Atlantic World." In *Class Matters: Early North America and the Atlantic World*. Ed. Simon Middleton and Billy G. Smith. Philadelphia: University of Pennsylvania Press, 2008. 16–34.

Newton, Sarah Emily. "Wise and Foolish Virgins: 'Usable Fiction' and the Early American Conduct Tradition." *EAL* 25 (1990): 139–67.

Nixon, Nicola. "Compromising Politics and Herman Melville's *Pierre*." *American Literature* 69 (1997): 719–41.

Nobles, Greg. "Class." In *A Companion to Colonial America*. Ed. Daniel Vickers. Oxford: Blackwell, 2003. 259–86.

"New Office of Initiation for All Youths of the Superior Class. *Lord* Chesterfield's *Creed.*" *New Haven Gazette and Connecticut Magazine* 1:42 (30 Nov. 1786): 327–28.

"New York, August 14." *American Herald* 5:252 [Boston] (21 Aug. 1786): [3]. EAN.

"New York, March 2." *New York Packet* Iss. 676 (2 March 1787): [2]. EAN.

"No Title." *The Carlisle Gazette, and the Western Repository of Knowledge* 5:231 (6 Jan. 1790): [4]. EAN.

"Noble Authors." *United States Magazine and Democratic Review* 12 (May 1843): 479–84.

"Novel-Reading A Cause of Female Depravity." *Athenaeum; or Spirit of English Magazine* 1:10 [Boston] (15 Aug. 1817): 718–19.

"The Novelist, No. 1. On Novel Reading." *Minerviad; Devoted to Literature and Amusement, For the Ladies* 1:1 [Boston] (30 March 1822): 5.

"Novels." *The New Star* 1:1 (11 April 1797): 3.

[Observator]. "The Old Soldier." *The Balance and State Journal* 2:24 [Albany] (23 March 1810): 2. APS.

"Of General Washington." *American Recorder* 2:100 [Charlestown, Mass.] (16 March 1787): [4]. EAN.

"Of Physiognomy; Or, the Similitude between the Person and the Mind." *South Carolina Weekly Museum and Complete Magazine of Entertainment and Intelligence* 1 (13 May 1797): 590–91. APS.

"Old Nick; A Satirical Story. Chap. XVI." *Philadelphia Repository and Weekly Register* 2:10 (16 Jan. 1802): 73. APS.

"Old Times." *Carolina Observer* 353 (Fayetteville, N.C.) (4 March 1824): col. B. 19C US-NEWS.

"On Chesterfield's Letters." *Massachusetts Magazine* 1:2 [Boston] (Feb. 1789): 119. APS

"On the Moral Tendency of Novel Reading." *Minerva* [New York] 2:28 (18 Oct. 1823): 223.

"On Novel-Reading." *Minerva* [New York] 2:30 (1 Nov. 1823): 239.

"On Novels." *Weekly Visitor, or Ladies' Miscellany* 1:15 (15 Jan. 1803): 116.

"On the Qualifications Necessary to Success in Life." *Saturday Magazine: Being in Great Part a Compilation From the British Reviews, Magazines, and Scientific Journals* 1:20 [Philadelphia] (17 Nov. 1821): 470–73.

"Opinions Upon Novel Reading, No. I." *Minerviad: Devoted to Literature & Amusement, For the Ladies* 1:6 [Boston] (1 June 1822): 45.

Orians, G. Harrison. "Censure of Fiction in American Romances and Magazines 1789–1810." *PMLA* 52 (1937): 195–214.

"Original Anecdote." *Pensacola Gazette and West Florida Advertiser* 1 [Tallahassee, Fla.] (13 March 1824): col. A. 19C USNEWS.

"Original Letters from Paris; Addressed by Rembrandt Peale to C. W. Peale, and Rubens Peale." *Port Folio* 4:3 [Philadelphia] (Sept. 1810): 275–79. APS.

Otter, Samuel. *Melville's Anatomies*. Berkeley: University of California Press, 1999.

"Our Portrait Gallery." *Holden's Magazine* 7 (May 1851): 209.

Parker, Hershel. *Herman Melville: A Biography, Volume 1, 1819–1851.* Baltimore: Johns Hopkins University Press, 1996.

———. *Herman Melville: A Biography, Volume 2, 1851–1891.* Baltimore: Johns Hopkins University Press, 2002.

Parker, Hershel, and Leon Howard. "Historical Note." In *Pierre.* Evanston, Ill.: Northwestern University Press and Newberry Library, 1971. 365–410.

Parrish, Susan Scott. *American Curiosity: Cultures of Natural History in the Colonial British Atlantic World.* Chapel Hill: University of North Carolina Press, 2006.

Patterson, Mark. "Representation in Brackenridge's Modern Chivalry." *Texas Studies in Literature and Language* 28:2 (1986): 121–39.

Peale, Charles Willson. *Guide to the Philadelphia Museum.* Philadelphia: At the Museum Press, 1805.

———. *The Philadelphia Museum, or Register of Natural History and the Arts.* Philadelphia: Museum Press, 1824.

———. *The Selected Papers of Charles Willson Peale and His Family.* Ed. Lillian B. Miller. 5 vols. New Haven: Yale University Press, 1983.

Peck, H. Daniel. *A World by Itself: The Pastoral Moment in Cooper's Fiction.* New Haven: Yale University Press, 1977.

Penry, Tara. "Sentimental and Romantic Masculinities in *Moby-Dick* and *Pierre.*" In *Sentimental Men: Masculinity and the Politics of Affect in American Culture.* Ed. Glenn Hendler. Berkeley: University of California Press, 1999. 227–43.

Percival, Melissa. *The Appearance of Character: Physiognomy and Facial Expression in Eighteenth-Century France.* Leeds: W. S. Maney for the Modern Humanities Research Association, 1999.

Percival, Melissa and Graeme Tytler, eds. *Physiognomy in Profile: Lavater's Impact on European Culture.* Newark: University of Delaware Press, 2005.

Pestana, Carla and Sharon Salinger, eds. *Inequality in Early America.* Hanover, N.H.: University Press of New England, 1999.

Petter, Henry. *The Early American Novel.* Columbus: Ohio State University Press, 1971.

[Philalethes]. "Letter 2. On The Practice of Reading Novels and Romances." *United States Magazine; or General Repository of Useful Instruction . . .* 1:1 (May 1794): 80. APS.

———. "Letter 4. On The Practice of Reading Novels and Romances." *United States Magazine; or General Repository of Useful Instruction . . .* 1 (July 1794): 242. APS.

[Philo]. "To the Baltimorean." *Maryland Journal* 12:68 (26 Aug. 1785): 2. EAN.

"Physiognomical Anecdotes. From Lavater." *Weekly Visitor or Ladies' Miscellany* 2:60 (7 Jan. 1804): 61. APS.

"The Physiognomical Fragments of M. Lavater; translated by Tho. Holcroft." *Virginia Chronicle* [Norfolk, Va.] 169 (17 Nov. 1792): [4]. EAN.

"Physiognomy." *Pennsylvania Herald and General Advertiser* 5:62 (25 Aug. 1787): [4]. EAN.

"Physiognomy." *Philadelphia Minerva* 2:87 (1 Oct. 1796): n. p.

"Physiognomy." *Weekly Museum* 9:14 [New York] (24 Sept. 1796): [2].

"Physiognomy." *Salem Gazette* 16:1133 (2 July 1802): [3]. EAN.

"Physiognomy." *Kenebac Gazette* 2:90 [Augusta, Maine] (2 Aug. 1802): [3]. EAN.

"Physiognomy." *New England Galaxy & Masonic Magazine* [Boston] 7 no. 357 (18 Aug. 1824): n. p. APS.

"Physiognomy." *American Phrenological Journal* 13:1 (Jan. 1851): 7.

"Physiognomy of Murderers." *Republican Star* 25:19 [Easton, Md.] (23 Dec. 1823): [3]. EAN.

Pochman, Henry A. *German Culture in America: Philosophical and Literary Influences: 1600–1900*. Madison: University of Wisconsin Press, 1957.

Pocock, J. G. A. *Virtue, Commerce, and History: Essays on Political Thought and History, Chiefly in the Eighteenth Century*. Cambridge: Cambridge University Press, 1985.

———. *The Machiavellian Moment: Florentine Thought and the Atlantic Republican Tradition*. Princeton, N.J.: Princeton University Press, 1972.

Pointon, Marcia. *Hanging The Head: Portraiture and Social Formation in Eighteenth-Century Art and Culture*. New Haven: Yale University Press, 1993.

Porte, Joel. *The Romance in America: Cooper, Poe, Hawthorne, Melville, James*. Middletown: Wesleyan University Press, 1969.

Porter, Martin. *Windows of the Soul: European Physiognomy, 1470–1780*. Oxford: Oxford University Press, 2005.

"Portrait of General Washington, By the Marquis Chastellux." *Independent Chronicle* [Boston] 32:1984 (27 March 1800): [1]. NEWS.

Post-Lauria, Sheila. *Correspondent Colorings: Melville in the Marketplace*. Amherst: University of Massachusetts Press, 1996.

"Preface." *The United States Magazine* 1 [Philadelphia] (Jan. 1779): n.p.

Pressman, Richard S. "Class Positioning and Shays' Rebellion: Resolving the Contradictions of *The Contrast*." *EAL* 21 (1986): 87–101.

"Protestantism in the Society Islands." *United States Catholic Magazine and Monthly Review* [Baltimore] 7 (January 1848): 1–10.

Pudaloff, Ross J. "Cooper's Genres and American Problems." *ELH* 50:4 (1983): 711–27.

Pullen, Charles. "Lord Chesterfield and Eighteenth-Century Appearance and Reality." *Studies in English Literature, 1500–1900* 8 (1968): 501–15.

Ramsay, David. *The History of South-Carolina, from its first settlement in 1670, to the year 1808 . . .* Volume 2. Charleston, 1809.

"The Reading of Novels." *Weekly Visitor or Ladies' Miscellany* 2:94 (21 July 1804): 332.

Reaves, Wendy Wick. *George Washington, an American Icon*. Charlottesville: University Press of Virginia, 1982.

Redfield, James. *Outlines of a new system of physiognomy: illustrated by numerous engravings, indicating the location of the signs of the different mental faculties*. New York: J. S. Redfield, 1849.

———. *Comparative Physiognomy or Resemblances Between Men and Animals*. Clinton Hall, N.Y.: Redfield, 1852.

Reilly, Elizabeth Carroll, and David D. Hall. "Customers and The Market for Books." In *A*

History of the Book in America. Vol. 1. The Colonial Book in the Atlantic World. Ed. Hugh Armory and David D. Hall. Cambridge: Cambridge University Press, 2000. 387–99.

———. "Modalities of Reading." In *A History of the Book in America. Vol. 1. The Colonial Book in the Atlantic World*. Ed. Hugh Armory and David D. Hall. Cambridge: Cambridge University Press, 2000. 404–10.

"Remarks on Chesterfield's Letters." *American Museum* (Feb. 1791): 89–91.

"Remarks on Physiognomy." *Philadelphia Repository and Weekly Register* 2:21 (3 April 1802): 166.

"Remarks on *The Pioneers*." *Newcastle Magazine* 3 (Jan. 1824): 35–37.

Renker, Elizabeth. *Strike Through the Mask*. Baltimore: Johns Hopkins University Press, 1996.

Review of *The Moral for Authors*. *Literary World* 4:122 (2 June 1849): 475.

Review of *The Physiognomist; A Novel; by the Author of the Bachelor and the Married Man*. *Analectic Magazine* 12 [Philadelphia] (Nov. 1818): 409. APS.

Review of *Pierre*. Boston *Evening Traveller* (17 Aug. 1852).

Review of *Pierre*. *Congregational Journal* [Concord, N.H.] (25 Aug. 1852).

Review of *Pierre*. New York *Herald* (18 Sept. 1852).

Review of *The Pioneers*. *Port Folio* 15 5th ser. (March 1823): 230–48.

Review of *The Pioneers*. *The Album* 3 (May 1823): 155–78.

Review of *Precaution*. *New York Literary Journal* 4 (Nov. 1820): 38–41.

Review of *Precaution*. *Godey's Lady's Book* 19 (Aug. 1839): 96.

Review of Richard Brown's *An Essay on the Truth of Physiognomy, and Its Application to Medicine*. *Philadelphia Medical Museum* 4:4 (1807): ciii–cix. APS.

Review of *The Spy*. *Port Folio* 13 5th ser. (Feb. 1822): 90–101.

Review of *The Ways of the Hour*. *North American Review* 71 (July 1850): 120–35.

Review of *White-Jacket*. *Holden's Dollar Magazine* 5:5 (May 1850): 314–16.

Reynolds, David. *Beneath the American Renaissance*. New York: Knopf, 1988.

Reynolds, Joshua. "Discourse Four." *Discourses on Art*. 1771. New York: Collier Books, 1961.

Rice, Grantland. *Transformation of Authorship in America*. Chicago: University of Chicago Press, 1997.

Richards, Jeffrey. *Drama, Theatre, and Identity in the American New Republic*. Cambridge: Cambridge University Press, 2005.

Rigal, Laura. *The American Manufactory: Art, Labor, and the World of Things in the Early Republic*. Princeton, N.J.: Princeton University Press, 1998.

Rinehart, Lucy. "A Nation's Noble Spectacle: Royall Tyler's *The Contrast* as Metatheatrical Commentary." *American Drama* 3:2 (1994): 29–52.

Ringe, Donald. *Charles Brockden Brown*. Rev. ed. 1966. Boston: Twayne, 1991.

———. "James Fenimore Cooper and Thomas Cole: An Analogous Technique." *American Literature* 30 (1958): 26–43.

———. *The Pictorial Mode: Space and Time in the Art of Bryant, Irving, and Cooper*. Lexington: University Press of Kentucky, 1971.

Rivers, Christopher. *Face Value*. Madison: University of Wisconsin Press, 1993.

Roberts, William. *Too high a pitch may be given to the mind in early life. Story of Eugenio and Amelia: or, the vicissitudes of life. Extracted from that Celebrated Work the "Looker-on," by the Reverend William Roberts, A.M.F.R.S. Fellow of Corpus Christi College, Oxford.* 1st ed. Worcester, Mass.: Isaiah Thomas, 1798.

Robertson, Andrew. *The Language of Democracy: Political Rhetoric in the United States and Britain, 1790–1900.* Ithaca, N.Y.: Cornell University Press, 1995.

Robertson-Lorant, Laurie. *Melville: A Biography.* New York: Clarkson Potter, 1996.

Robillard, Douglas. "Melville's Reading in the Visual Arts." In *Savage Eye: Melville and the Visual Arts.* Ed. Christopher Sten. Kent, Ohio: Kent State University Press, 1991. 40–55.

Rockman, Seth. "The Contours of Class in the Early Republic City." *Labor: Studies in Working- Class History of the Americas* 1:4 (Winter 2004): 91–107.

———. *Scraping By: Wage Labor, Slavery, and Survival in Early Baltimore.* Baltimore: Johns Hopkins University Press, 2009.

Rodgers, Paul C. "Brown's *Ormond*: The Fruits of Improvisation." *American Quarterly* 26 (1974): 4–22.

Roediger, David. *The Wages of Whiteness: Race and the Making of the American Working Class.* London: Verso, 1991.

Rogin, Michael. *Subversive Genealogy: The Politics and Art of Herman Melville.* New York: Knopf, 1983.

Rosenfeld, Richard. *American Aurora: A Democratic Republic Returns.* New York: St. Martin's, 1997.

Ross, Marlon. "Pleasuring Identity, or the Delicious Politics of Belonging." *New Literary History* 31:4 (2000): 827–50.

Rosswurm, Steven. *Arms, Country, and Class: The Philadelphia Militia and the "Lower Sort" During the American Revolution.* New Brunswick, N.J.: Rutgers University Press, 1987.

Rothfield, Lawrence. *Vital Signs: Medical Realism in Nineteenth-Century Fiction.* Princeton, N.J.: Princeton University Press, 1992.

Rowe, John Carlos. *At Emerson's Tomb.* New York: Columbia University Press, 1997.

Rowson, Susanna. *Charlotte Temple.* Philadelphia: D. Humphreys for M. Carey, 1794.

———. *The Inquisitor; or, Invisible Rambler.* Philadelphia: William Gibbons, 1793.

———. *Mentoria; Or The Young Lady's Friend.* Philadelphia: Robert Campbell, 1794.

———. *The Fille De Chambre, A Novel . . .* Philadelphia: H. & P. Rice, 1794.

"Royal Authors." *United States Magazine and Democratic Review* 12 (April 1843): 392–400.

Rozbicki, Michael. *The Complete Colonial Gentleman: Cultural Legitimacy in Plantation America.* Charlottesville: University Press of Virginia, 1998.

Rush, Benjamin. "The Influence of Physical Causes Upon the Moral Faculty" (1786). In *The Selected Writings of Benjamin Rush.* Ed. Dagobert Runes. New York: Philosophical Library, 1947.

Russo, James R. "The Tangled Web of Deception and Imposture in Charles Brockden Brown's *Ormond.*" *EAL* 14 (1979): 205–27.

Rust, Marion. *Susanna Rowson and the Problem of the Sentimental*. Chapel Hill: University of North Carolina Press, 2008.

Ruttenberg, Nancy. *Democratic Personality: Popular Voice and the Trials of American Authorship*. Stanford: Stanford University Press, 1999.

St. George, Robert Blair. *Conversing by Signs: Poetics of Implication in Colonial New England Culture*. Chapel Hill: University of North Carolina Press, 1998.

Samuels, Shirley. "The Family, the State, and the Novel in the Early Republic." *American Quarterly* 38 (1986): 381–95.

———. *Romances of the Republic: Women, the Family, and Violence in the Literature of Early America*. New York: Oxford University Press, 1996.

Sanchez-Eppler, Karen. *Touching Liberty: Abolition, Feminism, and The Politics of the Body*. Berkeley: University of California Press, 1993.

Sans Souci, Alias Free and Easy: Or An Evening's Peep into a Polite Circle. An Intire New Entertainment. In Three Acts. Boston: Warden and Russell, 1785. Proquest Lion American Drama.

Sartre, Jean Paul. "The Look/*Le Regard*." *Being and Nothingness* (1943). Trans. Hazel E. Barnes. New York: Philosophical Library, 1970. 252–303.

Schieck, William. "The Problem of Origination in Brown's *Ormond*." In *Critical Essays on Charles Brockden Brown*. Ed. Bernard Rosenthal. Boston: Hall, 1981. 126–41.

Schwarzschild, Edward. "From the Physiognotrace to the Kinematoscope: Visual Technology and the Preservation of the Peale Family." *Yale Journal of Criticism* 12:1 (1999): 57–71.

Schweitzer, Ivy. *Politics and Affiliation in Early American Literature*. Chapel Hill: University of North Carolina Press, 2006.

Scudder, Harold. "What Mr. Cooper Read to His Wife." *Sewanee Review* 36 (April–June 1928): 177–79.

Sealts, Merton. *Melville's Reading*. Madison: University of Wisconsin Press, 1966.

"Seduction. A Tale Founded in Fact." *Weekly Visitor, or Ladies' Miscellany* 1:14 (8 Jan. 1803): 105–6.

"Seduction: A Tale Founded on Fact." *Weekly Visitor, or Ladies' Miscellany* 1:15 (15 Jan. 1803): 113–14.

"Seduction: A Tale Founded on Fact. (Concluded from p. 114)." *Weekly Visitor, or Ladies' Miscellany* 1:16 (22 Jan. 1803): 121–22.

Seelye, John D. *Melville: The Ironic Diagram*. Evanston, Ill.: Northwestern University Press, 1970.

Sekula, Allan. "The Body and the Archive." *October* (1986): 3–63.

Sennett, Richard. *The Fall of Public Man: On the Social Psychology of Capitalism*. New York: Vintage, 1974.

Shaffer, Jason. *Performing Patriotism: National Identity in the Colonial and Revolutionary American Theater*. Philadelphia: University of Pennsylvania Press, 2007.

Shields, David S. *Civil Tongues and Polite Letters in North America*. Chapel Hill: University of North Carolina Press, 1997.

Shookman, Ellis, Ed. *The Faces of Physiognomy: Interdisciplinary Approaches to Johann Caspar Lavater*. Columbia, S.C.: Camden House, 1993.

Shortland, Michael. "The Power of a Thousand Eyes: Johann Caspar Lavater's Science of Physiognomical Perception." *Criticism* 28:4 (1986): 379–408.

Shurr, William H. "'Now Gods, Stand Up, for Bastards': Reinterpreting Benjamin Franklin's *Autobiography*." *American Literature* 64:3 (1992): 435–51.

Siebert, Donald. "Royall Tyler's 'Bold Example': *The Contrast* and the English Comedy of Manners." *EAL* 13 (1978): 3–11.

Silverman, Gillian. "Textual Sentimentalism: Incest and Authorship in Melville's *Pierre*." *American Literature* 74:2 (2002): 345–72.

Simpson, Mark. *Trafficking Subjects: The Politics of Mobility in Nineteenth-Century America*. Minneapolis: University of Minnesota Press, 2005.

"Sketch of Lavater." *Lady's Magazine and Musical Repository* 1 [New York] (May 1801): 290.

"Sketches of the Presidential Candidates." *Collections, Historical and Miscellaneous, and Monthly Literary Journal* 3 [Concord] (Aug 1824): 247. APS.

Slauter, Eric. *The State as a Work of Art: The Cultural Origins of The Constitution*. Chicago: University of Chicago Press, 2009.

Smail, John. *The Origins of Middle-Class Culture: Halifax, Yorkshire, 1660–1780*. Ithaca: Cornell University Press, 1994.

Smith, Richard Dean. *Melville's Science: "Devilish Tantalization of the Gods."* New York: Garland, 1993.

Smith, Samuel Stanhope. *An Essay on the Causes of the Variety of Complexion and Figure in the Human Species: to which are added, animadversions on certain remarks made . . .* 2nd ed., enl. and improved. New Brunswick, N.J.: J. Simpson, 1810.

———. *An Essay on the Causes of the Variety of Complexion and Figure in the Human Species*. Ed. Winthrop Jordan. Cambridge, Mass.: Belknap, 1965.

Smith-Rosenberg, Carroll. "Black Gothic: The Shadowy Origins of the American Bourgeoisie." In *Possible Pasts: Becoming Colonial in Early America*. Ed. Robert B. St. George. Ithaca, N.Y.: Cornell University Press, 2000. 243–69.

———. "Domesticating Virtue: Coquettes and Revolutionaries in Young America." In *Literature and the Body: Essays on Populations and Persons*. Ed. Elaine Scarry. Baltimore: Johns Hopkins University Press, 1988. 160–84.

———. "Subject Female: Authorizing an Identity." *ALH* 5 (1993): 481–511.

Smyth, Heather. "Imperfect Disclosures: Cross-Dressing and Containment in Charles Brockden Brown's *Ormond*." In *Sex and Sexuality in Early America*. Ed. Merril D. Smith. New York: New York University Press, 1998. 240–61.

Spanos, William V. *Herman Melville and the American Calling: The Fiction After Moby Dick, 1851–1857*. Albany: State University of New York Press, 2008.

Spengemann, William C. Introduction to *Pierre*. New York: Penguin, 1996.

Spurzheim, J. G. *Phrenology, In Connexion with the Study of Physiognomy. Part 1. Characters with 34 plates*. London: Treuttel, Wurtz, and Richter, 1826.

———. *Phrenology, In Connexion with the Study of Physiognomy*. Intro. Nahum Capen. Boston: Marsh, Capen, and Lyon, 1833.

Stack, George J., and Robert W. Plant. "The Phenomenon of the 'The Look.'" *Philosophy and Phenomenological Research* 42:3 (1982): 359–73.

Staiti, Paul. "Character and Class: The Portraits of John Singleton Copley." In *Reading American Art*. Ed. Marianne Doezma and Elizabeth Milroy. New Haven: Yale University Press, 1998. 12–37.

Stafford, Barbara. *Body Criticism: Imagining the Unseen in Enlightenment Art and Medicine*. Cambridge: MIT Press, 1991.

Stanford, John. *The Christian's Pocket Library*. Vol. 1. New York: T. & J. Swords, 1796. Evans.

Starke, Catherine. *Black Portraiture in American Fiction*. New York: Basic Books, 1971.

Steinberg, David. "Facing Painting and Painting Faces Before Lavater." In *Painting and Portrait Making in the American Northeast*. Ed. Peter Benes. Boston: Boston University Press, 1995. 201–17.

Sten, Christopher. "Melville and the Visual Arts: An Overview." In *Savage Eye: Melville and the Visual Arts*. Ed. Christopher Sten. Kent, Ohio: Kent State University Press, 1991. 1–39.

Stern, Julia. *The Plight of Feeling: Sympathy and Dissent in the Early American Novel*. Chicago: University of Chicago Press, 1997.

Stoehr, Taylor. *Hawthorne's Mad Scientists: Pseudoscience and Social Science in Nineteenth Century Life and Letters*. Hamden: Archon Books, 1978.

Stowe, Harriet Beecher. *Uncle Tom's Cabin Or, Life Among the Lowly*. New York: Penguin, 1986.

Sundquist, Eric. *Home As Found: Authority and Genealogy in Nineteenth-Century American Literature*. Baltimore: Johns Hopkins University Press, 1979.

Sweet, John Wood. *Bodies Politic: Negotiating Race in the American North, 1730–1830*. Baltimore: Johns Hopkins University Press, 2003.

"Symptoms of Self Importance." *Evening Fire-Side; or, Literary Miscellany* 1:4 [Philadelphia] (5 Jan. 1805): 30. APS.

Taggart, John. "Mere Illustrations: Maurice Sendak and Melville." *Arizona-Quarterly* 56:2 (2000): 111–56.

Tawil, Ezra. *The Making of Racial Sentiment: Slavery and the Birth of the Frontier Romance*. New York: Cambridge University Press, 2006.

Taylor, Isaac. *Advice to the Teens, or Practical Helps Towards the Formation of One's Own Character*. Boston: Wells & Lilly, 1820.

Tennenhouse, Leonard. "Libertine America." *Differences* 11:3 (1999–2000): 1–27.

———. *The Importance of Feeling English: American Literature and the British Diaspora, 1750–1850*. Princeton, N.J.: Princeton University Press, 2007.

Tenney, Tabitha. *Female Quixotism*. Oxford: Oxford University Press, 1992.

Thomas, Brook. "The Writer's Procreative Urge in *Pierre*: Fictional Freedom or Convoluted Incest?" *Studies in the Novel* 11 (Winter 1979): 416–30.

Thoughtless, Betsy. "Amusing." *Boston Weekly Magazine* 1:23 (2 April 1803): 94.

Tochlin, Neal. *Mourning, Gender, and Creativity in the Art of Herman Melville*. New Haven: Yale University Press, 1988.

Tompkins, Jane. *Sensational Designs: The Cultural Work of American Fiction, 1790–1860*. New York: Oxford University Press, 1985.

Toner, Jennifer D. "'The Accustomed Signs of the Family: Rereading Genealogy in Melville's *Pierre*." *American Literature* 70 (1998): 237–63.

"The Tendency of Novels: Pro and Con." *Merrimack Magazine and Ladies' Literary Cabinet* 1:31 (15 March 1806): 122.

"To the Printer . . ." *Freeman's Journal* 6: 304 [Philadelphia] (14 Feb. 1787): [3]. EAN.

Traister, Bryce. "Libertinism and Authorship in America's Early Republic." *American Literature* 72:1 (2000): 1–30.

Truepenny, Jonathan. "To Peter Sketch." *Providence Gazette* 40:2051 (23 April 1803): [2]. EAN.

Tyler, Royall. *The Contrast.* In *Early American Drama.* Ed. Jeffrey Richards. New York: Penguin, 1997.

Tytler, Graeme. *Physiognomy and the European Novel.* Princeton, N.J.: Princeton University Press, 1982.

———. "Lavater and Physiognomy in English Fiction 1790–1832." *Eighteenth-Century Fiction* 7:3 (1995): 293–310.

———. "'Faith in the Hand of Nature': Physiognomy in Sir Walter Scott's Fiction." *Studies in Scottish Literature* 33–34 (2004): 223–46.

"The Ubiquitarian, No. XV." *Weekly Magazine of Original Essays . . .* 2:17 (26 May 1798): 110–12.

Ulpian. "For the New Hampshire Journal . . ." *New Hampshire Journal* [Walpole, N.H.] 1:43 (31 Jan. 1794), [1].

Verheyen, Egon. "'The Most Exact Representation of the Original': Remarks on Portraits of George Washington by Gilbert Stuart and Rembrandt Peale." *Studies in the History of Art* 20 (1989): 127–39.

Verhoeven, W. M. "Displacing the Discontinuous: Or, Labyrinths of Reason: Fictional Design and Eighteenth-Century Thought in Charles Brockden Brown's *Ormond*." In *Rewriting the Dream: Reflections on the Changing American Literary Canon.* Ed. W. M. Verhoeven. Amsterdam: Rodopi, 1992. 202–29.

———. "Neutralizing the Land: The Myth of Authority and The Authority of Myth in Fenimore Cooper's *The Spy*." In *James Fenimore Cooper: New Historical and Literary Contexts.* Ed. W. M. Verhoeven. Amsterdam: Rodopi, 1993. 71–88.

"The Visitant. No IV. On Politeness." *American Museum* 5:2 (Sept. 1788): 218–20.

Von Tromp, Christian. "Physiognomy." *Minerva; Or Literary, Entertaining, And Scientific Journal* [Philadelphia] 1 n.s. no. 2 (17 April 1824): 28–30.

Wagner. Peter. "Introduction: Ekphrasis, Iconotexts, and Intermediality—The State(s) of the Art(s)." In *Icons—Texts—Iconotexts: Essays on Ekphrasis and Intermediality.* Ed. Peter Wagner. Berlin: Walter de Gruyter, 1996. 1–40.

Wahrman, Dror. *The Making of The Modern Self: Identity and Culture in Eighteenth-Century England.* New Haven: Yale University Press, 2004.

Wald, Priscilla. "Hearing Narrative Voices in Melville's *Pierre*." *Boundary 2* 17:1 (1990): 100–32.

Waldstreicher, David. "'Fallen Under My Observation': Vision and Virtue in *The Coquette*." *EAL* 27:3 (1992): 204–18.

Wallace, James D. "Cultivating an Audience: From *Precaution* to *The Spy*." in *James Fenimore Cooper: New Critical Essays*. Ed. Robert Clark. London: Vision, 1985. 38–54.

———. *Early Cooper and His Audience*. New York: Columbia University Press, 1986.

Wallace, Robert K. "Melville's Prints: The Reese Collection." *Harvard Library Bulletin* n.s. 3 (Oct. 1993): 6–42.

———. *Melville's Prints: The Melville Chaplin Collection*. Cambridge, Mass.: Harvard University Library, 2000.

Warner, Michael. *The Letters of the Republic: Publication and the Public Sphere in Eighteenth-Century America*. Cambridge, Mass.: Harvard University Press, 1990.

———. "The Mass Public and the Mass Subject." In *Habermas and the Public Sphere*. Ed. Craig Calhoun. Cambridge, Mass.: MIT Press, 1997. 377–401.

———. "What's Colonial About Colonial America?" In *Possible Pasts: Becoming Colonial in Early America*. Ed. Robert B. St. George. Ithaca, N.Y.: Cornell University Press, 2000. 49–70.

Warren, Caroline M. *The Gamesters; or Ruins of Innocence. An Original Novel Founded in Truth*. Boston: Thomas and Andrews, 1805.

Waterman, Bryan. *The Republic of Intellect: The Friendly Club of New York City and the Making of American Literature*. Baltimore: Johns Hopkins University Press, 2007.

Watt, Ian. *The Rise of the Novel: Studies in Defoe, Richardson, and Fielding*. Berkeley: University of California Press, 1974.

Watts, Steven. *The Republic Reborn: War and the Making of Liberal America, 1790–1820*. Baltimore: Johns Hopkins University Press, 1987.

———. *The Romance of Real Life*. Baltimore: Johns Hopkins University Press, 1994.

Weaver, Raymond. *Herman Melville: Mariner and Mystic*. New York: George H. Doran, 1921.

Webster, Noah. *The Prompter; or A Commentary on Common Sayings and Subjects . . .* Hartford, Conn.: Hudson & Goodwin, 1791.

Weems, Mason. *The Life of George Washington*. Philadelphia: Mathew Carey, 1810.

Weil, Dorothy. *In Defense of Women: Susanna Rowson (1762–1824)*. University Park: Pennsylvania State University Press, 1976.

Weschler, Judith. "Lavater, Stereotype, and Prejudice." In *The Faces of Physiognomy*. Ed. Ellis Shookman. Columbia, S.C.: Camden House, 1993. 104–26.

———. *A Human Comedy: Physiognomy and Caricature in Nineteenth-Century Paris*. Chicago: University of Chicago Press, 1982.

"What Is Talked About." *Literary World* 5:137 (15 Sept. 1849): 231–32.

Wheeler, Roxann. *The Complexion of Race: Categories of Difference in Eighteenth-Century British Culture*. Philadelphia: University of Pennsylvania Press, 2000.

———. "Racial Legacies: The Speaking Countenance and the Character Sketch in the Novel." In *A Companion to the Eighteenth-Century English Novel and Culture*. Ed. Paula R. Backscheider and Catherine Ingrassia. Malden, Mass.: Blackwell, 2005. 419–40.

Williams, Daniel E. "In Defense of Self: Author and Authority in the *Memoirs of Stephen Burroughs*." *EAL* 25:3 (1990): 96–122.

Williams, Susan L. *Confounding Images: Photography and Portraiture in Antebellum American Fiction*. Philadelphia: University of Pennsylvania Press, 1997.

Williamson, Joel. *A New People: Miscegenation and Mulattoes in the United States*. Baton Rouge: Louisiana State University Press, 1995.

Wood, Gordon. *The Radicalism of the American Revolution*. New York: Vintage Books, 1991.

———. *The Americanization of Benjamin Franklin*. New York: Penguin, 2004.

———. "Interests and Disinterestedness in the Making of the Constitution." In *Beyond Confederation: Origins of the Constitution and American National Identity*. Ed. Richard Beeman, Stephen Botein, and Edward C. Carter II. Chapel Hill: University of North Carolina Press, 1987. 69–109.

Wood, Sarah F. *Quixotic Fictions of the USA, 1792–1815*. Oxford: Oxford University Press, 2006.

Wright, Esmond. *Franklin of Philadelphia*. Cambridge, Mass.: Harvard University Press, 1986.

Wright, Frances. *Views of Society and Manners in America: in a series of letters from that Country to a friend in England, during the years 1818, 1819, and 1820*. New-York, 1821.

Y. "Physiognomy and Craniology." *New Monthly Magazine and Literary Journal* 3:14 (1822): 121–25.

Yanella, Donald. "Writing the 'Other' Way: Melville, the Duyckinck Crowd, and Literature for the Masses." In *A Companion to Melville Studies*. Ed. John Bryant. New York: Greenwood Press, 1986. 63–84.

Young, Philip. *The Private Melville*. University Park: Pennsylvania State University Press, 1993.

Zabin, Serena. *Dangerous Economies: Status and Commerce in Imperial New York*. Philadelphia: University of Pennsylvania Press, 2009.

Zakim, Michael. *Ready-Made Democracy: A History of Men's Dress in the American Republic, 1760–1860*. Chicago: University of Chicago Press, 2003.

Zelle, Carsten. "Soul Semiology: On Lavater's Physiognomic Principles." In *The Faces of Physiognomy*. Ed. Ellis Shookman. Columbia, S.C.: Camden House, 1993. 40–64.

Ziff, Larzer. *Writing in the New Nation: Prose, Print, and Politics in the Early United States*. New Haven: Yale University Press, 1991.

[Zophyrus]. "Physiognomy." *Companion and Weekly Miscellany* [Baltimore] 2:19 (8 March 1806): 146–48. APS.

———. "Physiognomy. No V." *Companion and Weekly Miscellany* [Baltimore] 2:36 (5 July 1806): 283–84. APS.

Zuckerman, Michael. "Tocqueville, Turner, and Turds: Four Stories of Manners in Early America." *Journal of American History* 85:1 (1998): 13–42.

Index

Page numbers in italics indicate illustrations.

Acknowledgments

THIS BOOK IS the culmination of years of intellectual exchange with teachers, colleagues, students, friends, and family whose written and verbal contributions, I hope, can be felt throughout these pages. Among my teachers and colleagues, my greatest thanks go to Sharon Cameron and Larry Ziff, who nurtured this project at its inception and invested countless hours in my work. Walter Benn Michaels, Michael Fried, and Michael Moon deserve special praise for providing important feedback on the book in its earliest stages. Jerry Christensen, Frances Ferguson, Allen Grossman, John Guillory, Ronald Paulson, Robert Reid-Pharr and Mark Strand helped make Johns Hopkins an exceptionally rigorous intellectual environment, and Scott Black, Erica Burleigh, Abigail Cheever, Theo Davis, Dan Denecke, Frances Dickey, Karen Fang, Andy Franta, Anne Frey, Amy Hungerford, Oren Izenberg, Jennifer Karyshyn, Jack Kerkering, Ruth Mack, Tim Mackin, Stacy Margolis, Steve Newman, and Leah Pettway helped me to survive it. Before arriving in Baltimore, I was incredibly fortunate to have studied with Charles Altieri, Norman Bryson, LeRoy Searle, and Ross Posnock at the University of Washington.

My colleagues in the English Department at Boston University—particularly Eliza Richards, Jack Matthews, and Laura Korobkin—offered invaluable criticism, advice, and friendship as the book was coming into shape. I would like to thank them as well as Bill Carroll, Bonnie Costello, Jill Lepore, Chris Martin, Susan Mizruchi, Erin Murphy, Anita Patterson, John Paul Riquelme, Jim Siemon, Matthew Smith, Andy Stauffer, and James Winn. Since joining the Department of English at Purdue University, I have benefitted from the kindness, encouragement, and guidance of my colleagues Wendy Flory, Bob Lamb, and especially Ryan Schneider. I am grateful to them as well as to Dorrie Armstrong, Kris Bross, Susan Curtis, Bill Mullen, Bich Nguyen, Porter Shreve, and Irwin Weiser. For their helpful suggestions and incisive criticism on various aspects of this book, I am indebted to Tom Augst, Chris Castiglia, Ann Fabian, Sean Goudie, Philip Gould, Cathy Kelly, Shirley Samuels, Ivy

Schweitzer, David Shields, and Michael Zuckerman. A number of people have been valuable interlocutors over the years, including Wendy Bellion, Sarah Blackwood, Dave Broustis, Martin Brückner, Steve Bullock, Cari Carpenter, Jenny Davidson, Nina Dayton, Marcy Dinius, Carolyn Eastman, Mary Esteve, Karsten Fitz, James Green, Robert Gross, Peter Jaros, Jane Kamensky, Caroline Levander, Cindy Lobel, Tilar Mazzeo, Martha McNamara, Ellen Miles, Simon Newman, Sam Otter, Susan Scott Parrish, Jen Putzi, Jim Sidbury, Manisha Sinha, Eric Slauter, Bryan Waterman, Roxann Wheeler, and Wendy Woloson.

This book would have been unimaginable without the incredible staffs and collections of the American Antiquarian Society, the Library Company of Philadelphia, the Massachusetts Historical Society, the Winterthur Library and Museum, and the Special Collections of the Sheridan Libraries at Johns Hopkins University. Georgia Barnhill, Gretchen Buggelen, Joanne Chaison, Ellen Dunlap, James N. Green, John Hench, Marie Lamoureux, Caroline Sloat, and Conrad E. Wright were indispensable resources as I conducted research for the book. A number of institutions provided financial support for this project at crucial points of its development, including long-term fellowships from The Johns Hopkins University, the Boston University Humanities Foundation, Purdue University and the Purdue University Research Foundation, and the National Endowment for the Humanities and the American Antiquarian Society. I would like to thank the Fulbright Program of the United States Department of State and the Philippine-American Education Foundation for giving me the opportunity to lecture at the University of the Philippines, where the book's arguments were presented to and improved by a remarkable set of graduate students and colleagues.

At the University of Pennsylvania Press, I would like to thank Bob Lockhart, who carefully guided this project through the editorial process, and Noreen O'Connor-Abel and Eileen Wolfberg who diligently prepared the manuscript for publication. I am grateful to Cathy Kelly and the other anonymous reader at the University of Pennsylvania Press as well for their thoughtful suggestions as I brought this book into its final form.

Earlier versions of sections of Chapters 2, 3, and 4 appeared as, respectively: "Breeding and Reading: Chesterfieldian Civility in the Early Republic" in *A Companion to American Fiction, 1780–1865*, ed. Shirley Samuels (Oxford: Blackwell, 2004), 158–68; "'The Vanity of Physiognomy': Dissimulation and Discernment in Charles Brockden Brown's *Ormond*," *Amerikastudien/American Studies* 50:3 (2005): 485–50; and "The Face of the Public," *Early*

American Literature 39:3 (2004): 413–65. I would like to thank Blackwell, Udo Hebel, and the University of North Carolina Press for permission to reprint material from these publications.

Finally, I would like to thank my parents, Gail and Jerry Lukasik, and my sister, Laurie, for their seemingly inexhaustible support over the years. The last and most important acknowledgment must go to Charlyne Fabi and my daughters, Ainsley and Quincy, whose love, laughter, and understanding made this book possible. To them, the author owes everything.